The FLASH

BLOOD WILL RUN

Dan DiDio Senior VP-Executive Editor   Joey Cavalieri Editor-original series   Bob Joy Editor-collected edition   Robbin Brosterman Senior Art Director   Paul Levitz President & Publisher   Georg Brewer VP-Design & DC Direct Creative   Richard Bruning Senior VP-Creative Director   Patrick Caldon Executive VP-Finance & Operations   Chris Caramalis VP-Finance   John Cunningham VP-Marketing   Terri Cunningham VP-Managing Editor   Alison Gill VP-Manufacturing   David Hyde VP-Publicity   Hank Kanalz VP-General Manager, WildStorm   Jim Lee Editorial Director-WildStorm   Paula Lowitt Senior VP-Business & Legal Affairs   MaryEllen McLaughlin VP-Advertising & Custom Publishing   John Nee Senior VP-Business Development   Gregory Noveck Senior VP-Creative Affairs   Sue Pohja VP-Book Trade Sales   Steve Rotterdam Senior VP-Sales & Marketing   Cheryl Rubin Senior VP-Brand Management   Jeff Trojan VP-Business Development, DC Direct   Bob Wayne VP-Sales

Cover art by Brian Bolland

THE FLASH: BLOOD WILL RUN

DC Comics, 1700 Broadway, New York, NY 10019
A Warner Bros. Entertainment Company
Printed in Canada. First Printing.
ISBN: 978-1-4012-1647-4

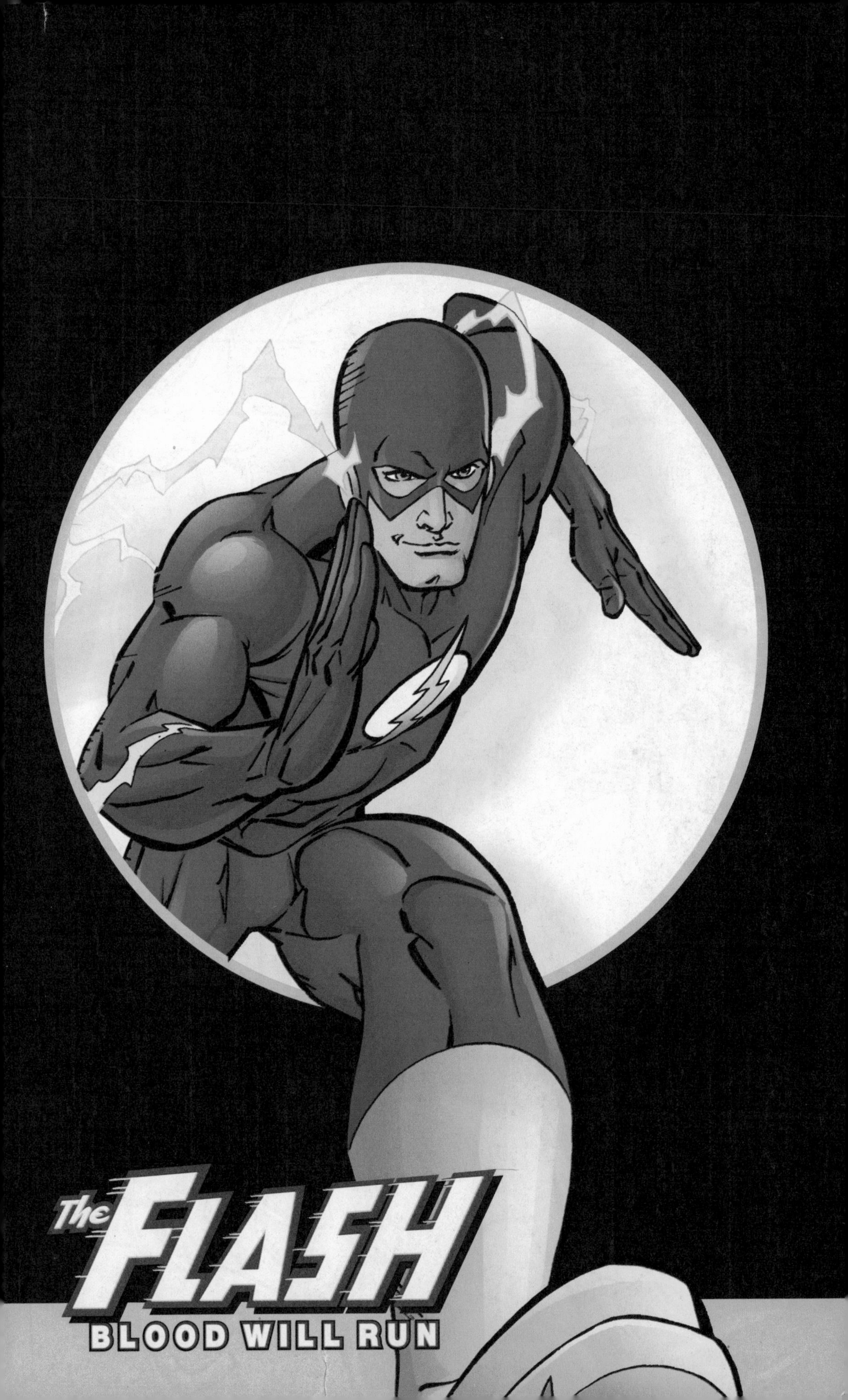
The FLASH
BLOOD WILL RUN

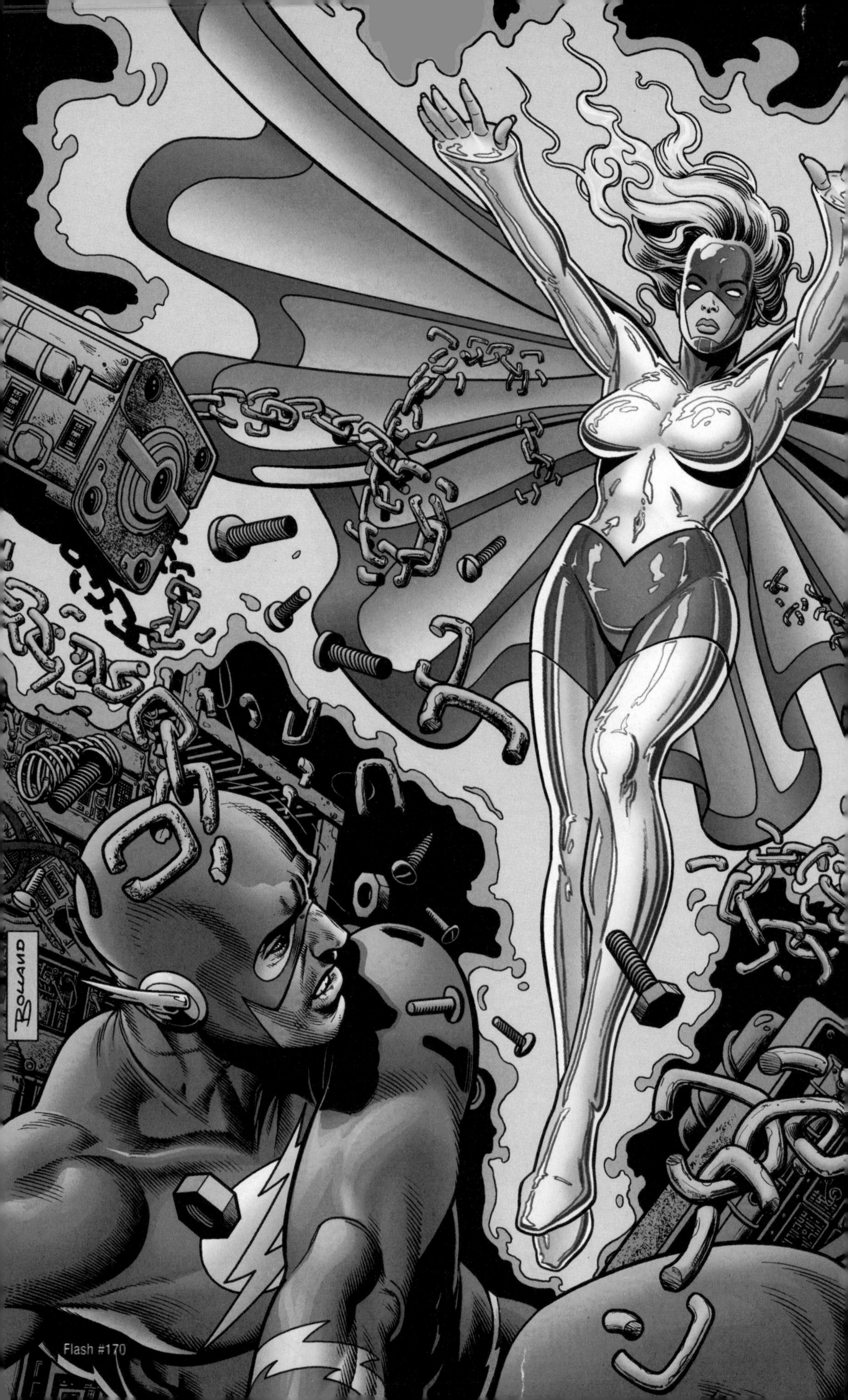
BOLLAND

Flash #170

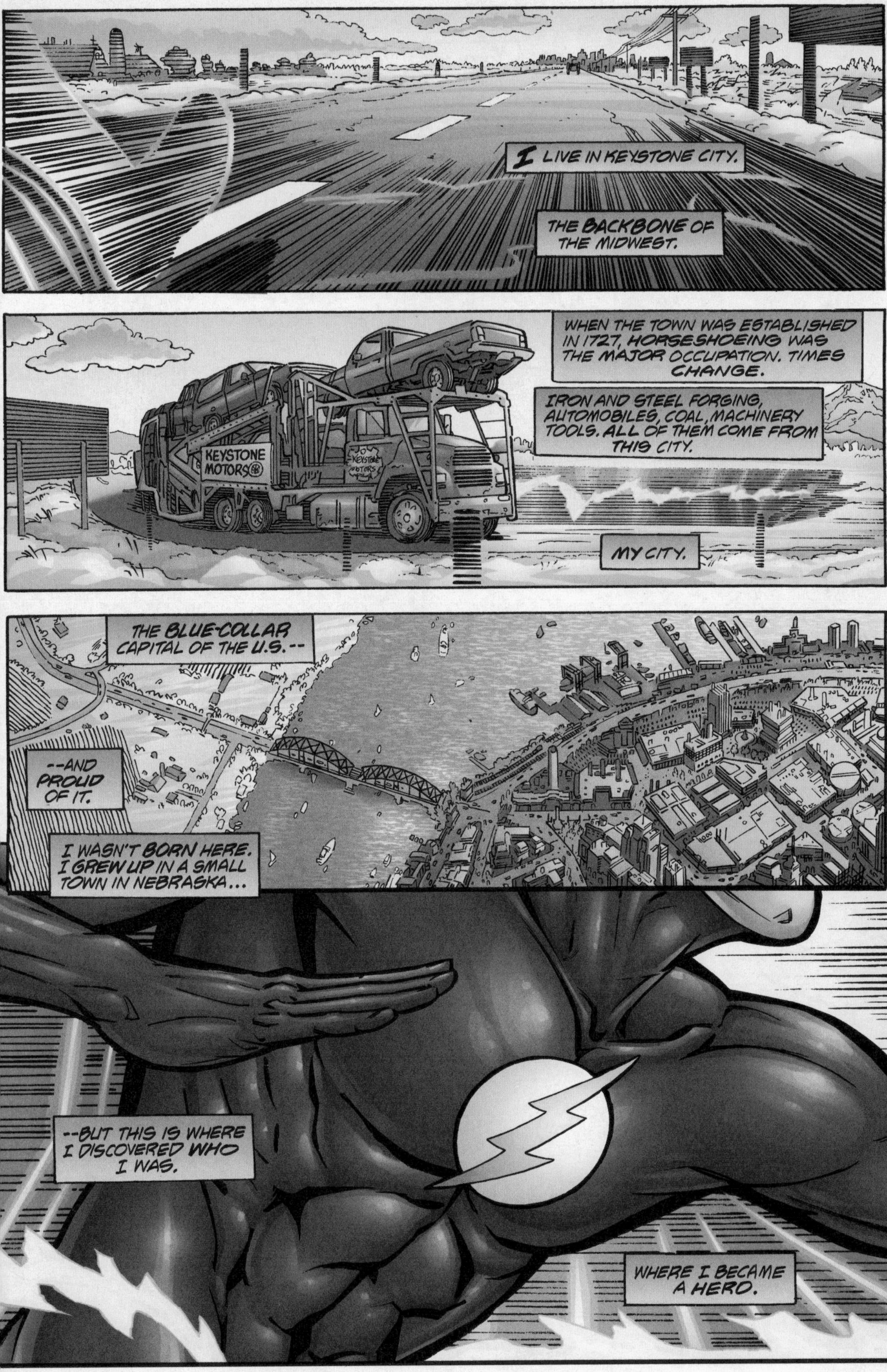
I LIVE IN KEYSTONE CITY.
THE BACKBONE OF THE MIDWEST.
WHEN THE TOWN WAS ESTABLISHED IN 1727, HORSESHOEING WAS THE MAJOR OCCUPATION. TIMES CHANGE.
IRON AND STEEL FORGING, AUTOMOBILES, COAL, MACHINERY TOOLS. ALL OF THEM COME FROM THIS CITY.
KEYSTONE MOTORS
MY CITY.
THE BLUE-COLLAR CAPITAL OF THE U.S.--
--AND PROUD OF IT.
I WASN'T BORN HERE. I GREW UP IN A SMALL TOWN IN NEBRASKA...
--BUT THIS IS WHERE I DISCOVERED WHO I WAS.
WHERE I BECAME A HERO.

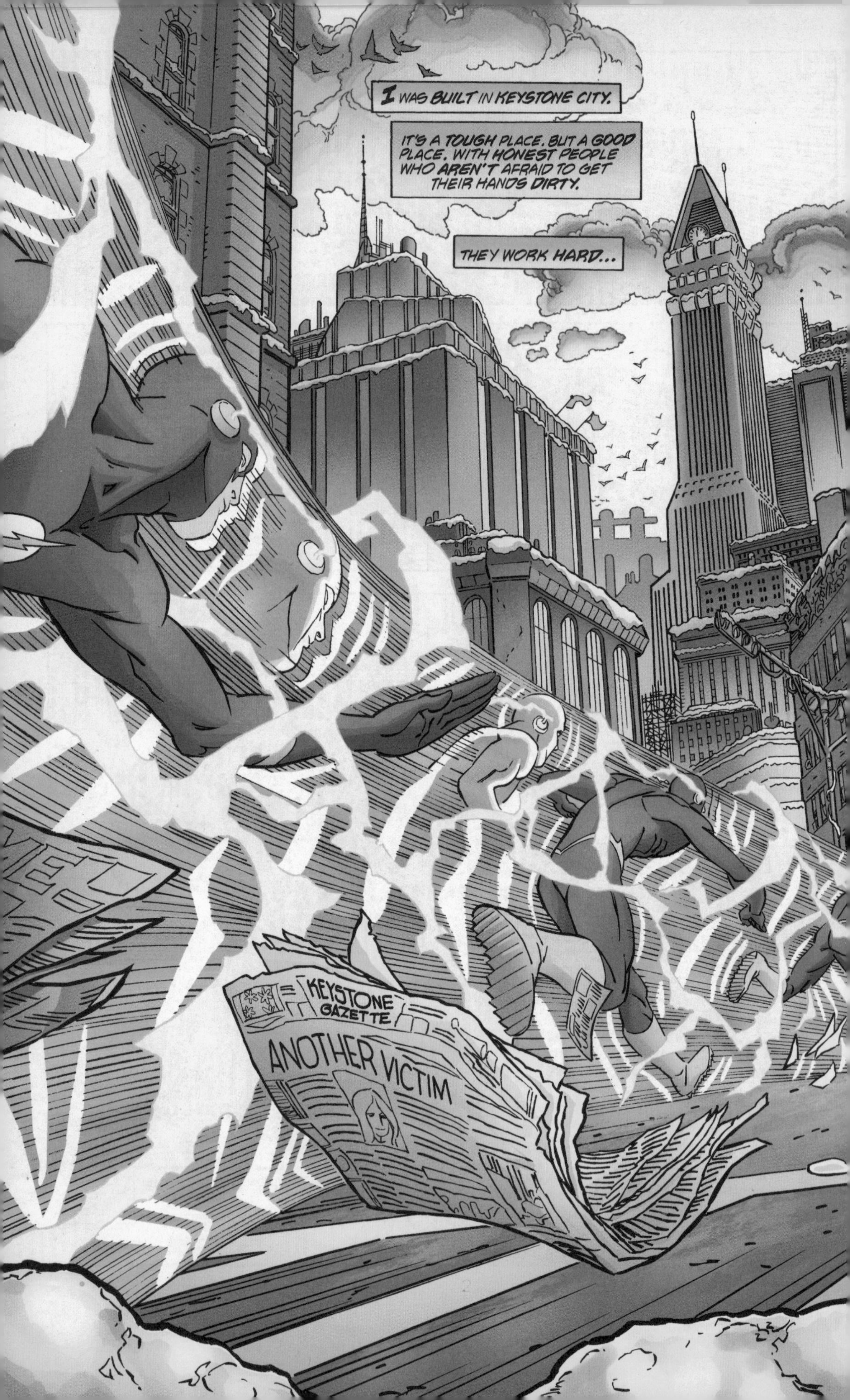
I WAS BUILT IN KEYSTONE CITY.
IT'S A TOUGH PLACE. BUT A GOOD PLACE. WITH HONEST PEOPLE WHO AREN'T AFRAID TO GET THEIR HANDS DIRTY.
THEY WORK HARD...
KEYSTONE GAZETTE
ANOTHER VICTIM

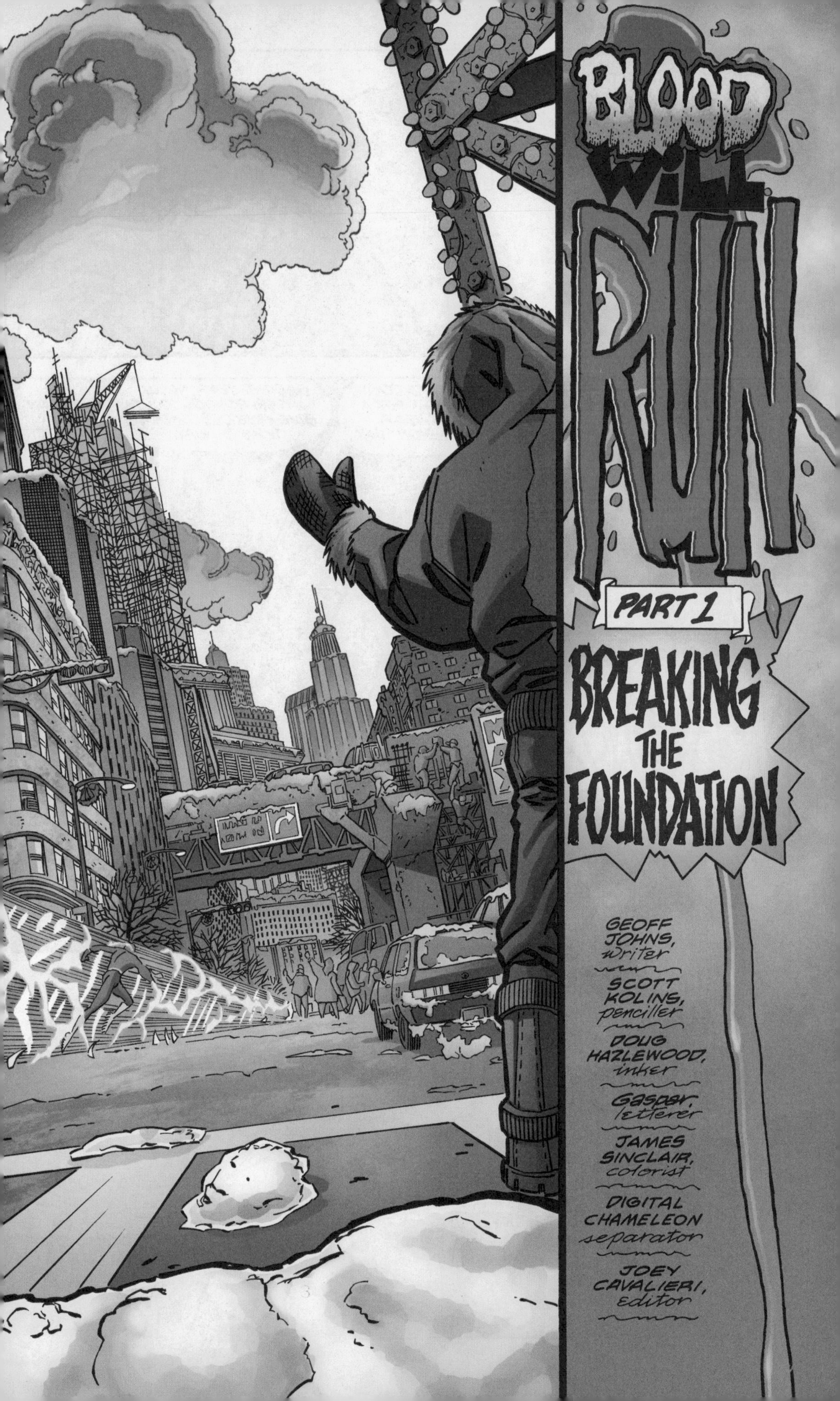
BLOOD WILL RUN
PART 1
BREAKING THE FOUNDATION
GEOFF JOHNS, writer
SCOTT KOLINS, penciller
DOUG HAZLEWOOD, inker
Gaspar, letterer
JAMES SINCLAIR, colorist
DIGITAL CHAMELEON separator
JOEY CAVALIERI, editor

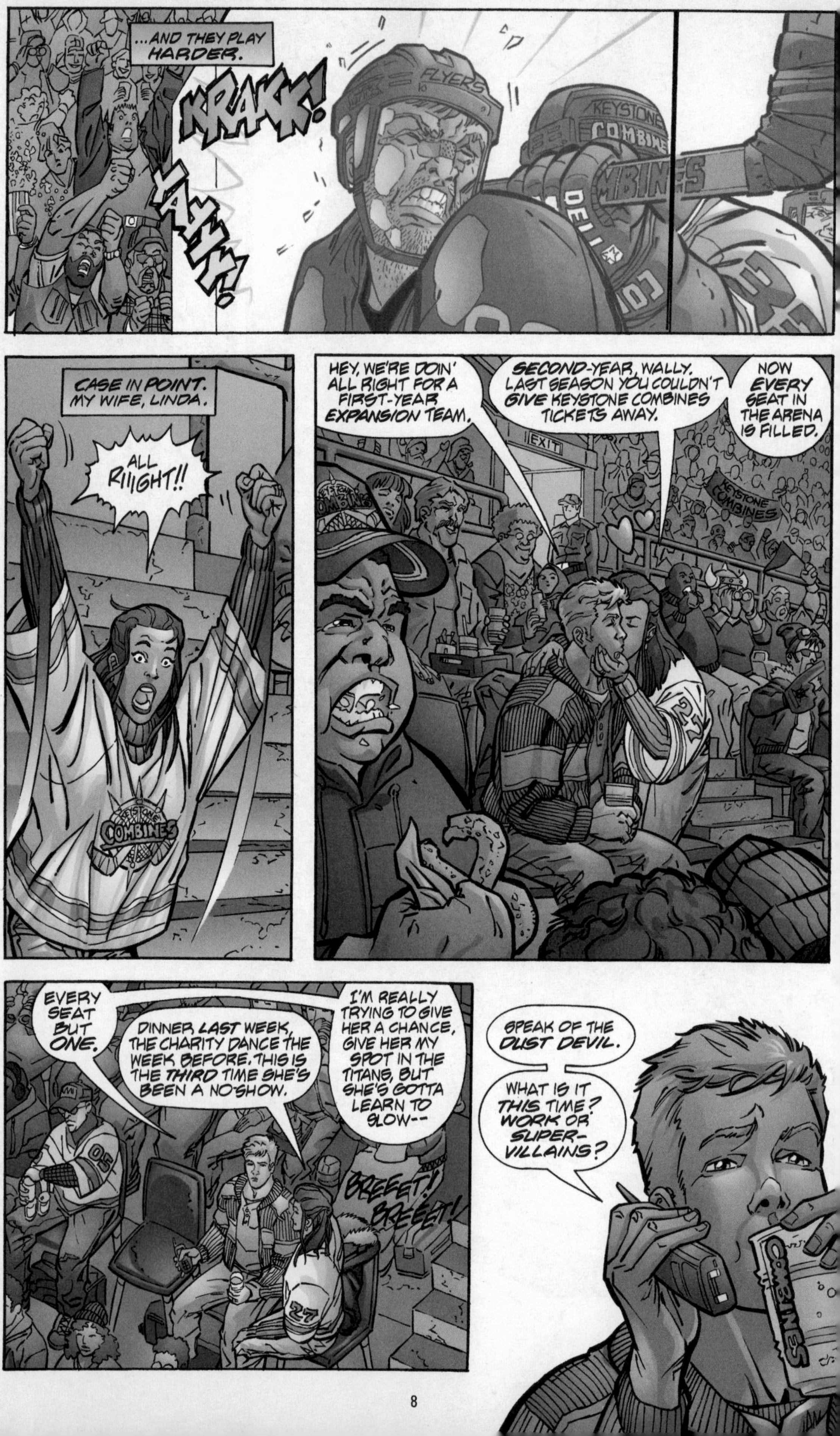

...AND THEY PLAY HARDER.
KRAKK!
YAHNK!
FLYERS
KEYSTONE COMBINES
CASE IN POINT. MY WIFE, LINDA.
ALL RIIIGHT!!
HEY, WE'RE DOIN' ALL RIGHT FOR A FIRST-YEAR EXPANSION TEAM.
SECOND-YEAR, WALLY. LAST SEASON YOU COULDN'T GIVE KEYSTONE COMBINES TICKETS AWAY.
NOW EVERY SEAT IN THE ARENA IS FILLED.
EXIT
KEYSTONE COMBINES
EVERY SEAT BUT ONE.
DINNER LAST WEEK, THE CHARITY DANCE THE WEEK BEFORE. THIS IS THE THIRD TIME SHE'S BEEN A NO-SHOW.
I'M REALLY TRYING TO GIVE HER A CHANCE, GIVE HER MY SPOT IN THE TITANS, BUT SHE'S GOTTA LEARN TO SLOW--
BREEET! BREEET!
SPEAK OF THE DUST DEVIL.
WHAT IS IT THIS TIME? WORK OR SUPER-VILLAINS?
COMBINES

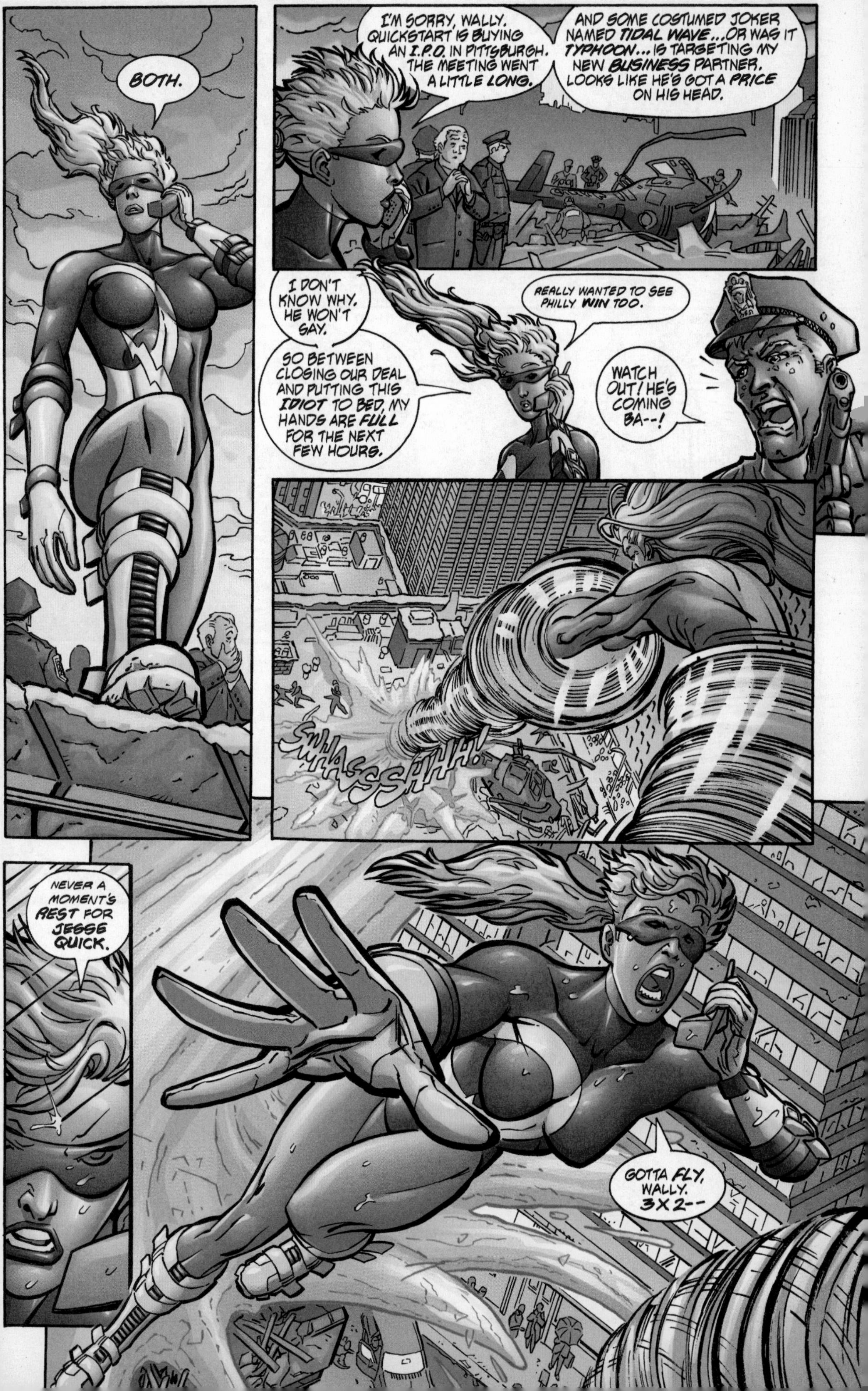
BOTH.
I'M SORRY, WALLY. QUICKSTART IS BUYING AN I.P.O. IN PITTSBURGH. THE MEETING WENT A LITTLE LONG.
AND SOME COSTUMED JOKER NAMED TIDAL WAVE...OR WAS IT TYPHOON...IS TARGETING MY NEW BUSINESS PARTNER. LOOKS LIKE HE'S GOT A PRICE ON HIS HEAD.
I DON'T KNOW WHY. HE WON'T SAY.
SO BETWEEN CLOSING OUR DEAL AND PUTTING THIS IDIOT TO BED, MY HANDS ARE FULL FOR THE NEXT FEW HOURS.
REALLY WANTED TO SEE PHILLY WIN TOO.
WATCH OUT! HE'S COMING BA--!
SWHASSSHHH!
NEVER A MOMENT'S REST FOR JESSE QUICK.
GOTTA FLY, WALLY. 3 X 2--

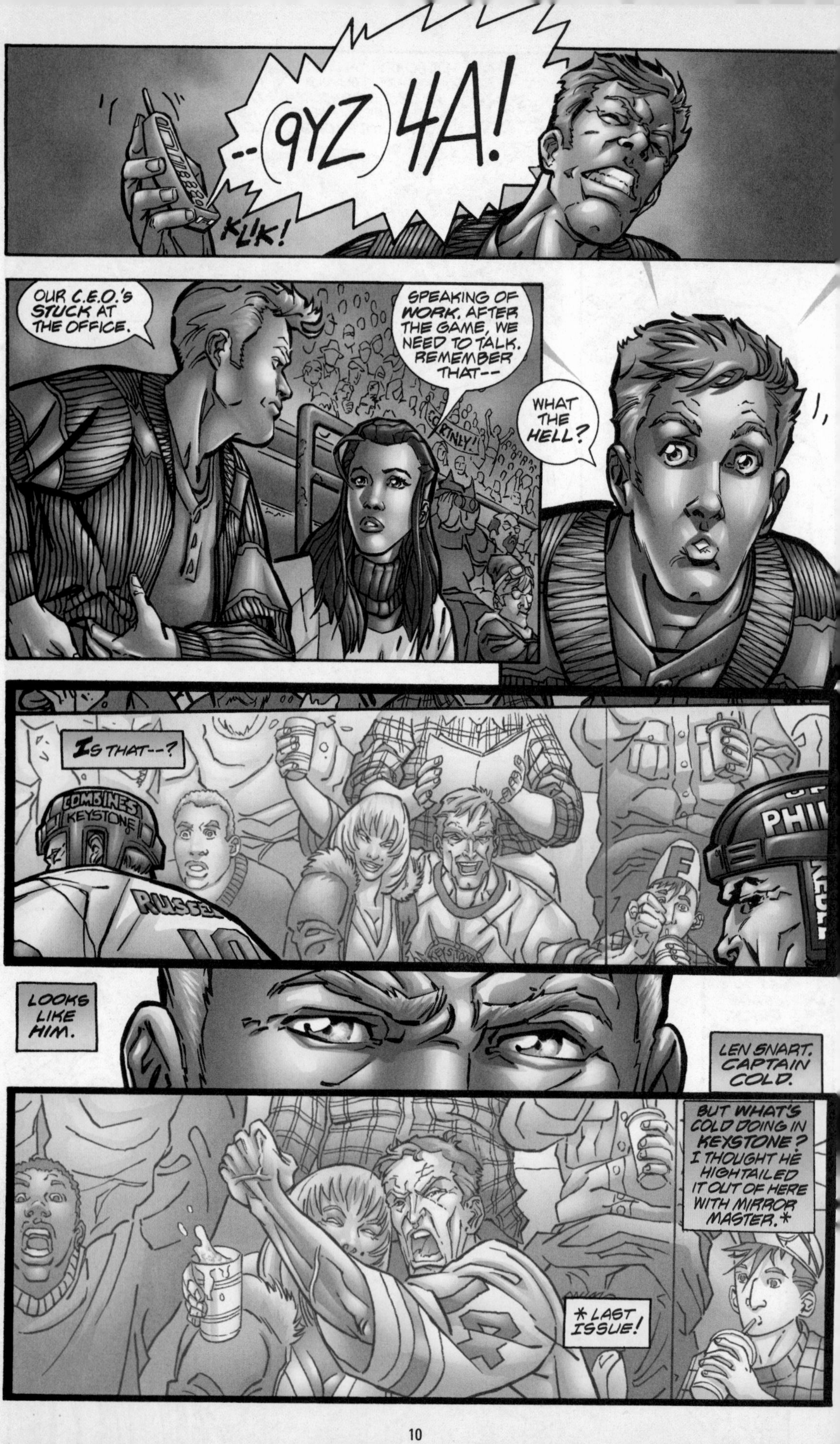
--(9YZ)4A!
KL!K!
OUR C.E.O.'s STUCK AT THE OFFICE.
SPEAKING OF WORK. AFTER THE GAME, WE NEED TO TALK. REMEMBER THAT--
WHAT THE HELL?
IS THAT--?
KEYSTONE
RUSSEL
PHIL
LOOKS LIKE HIM.
LEN SNART. CAPTAIN COLD.
BUT WHAT'S COLD DOING IN KEYSTONE? I THOUGHT HE HIGHTAILED IT OUT OF HERE WITH MIRROR MASTER.*
*LAST ISSUE!

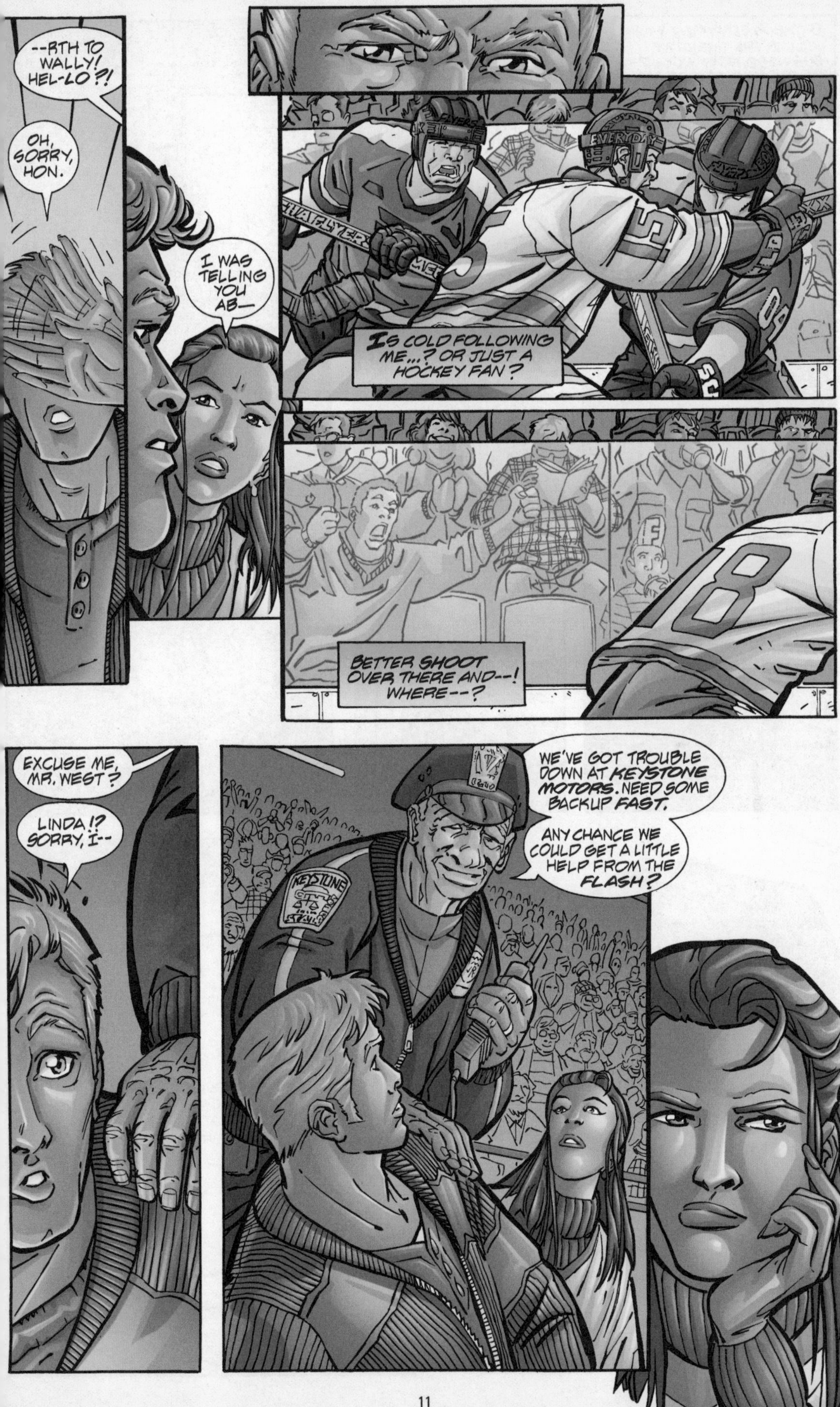
--RTH TO WALLY! HEL-LO?!
OH, SORRY, HON.
I WAS TELLING YOU AB—
IS COLD FOLLOWING ME...? OR JUST A HOCKEY FAN?
BETTER SHOOT OVER THERE AND--! WHERE--?
EXCUSE ME, MR. WEST?
LINDA!? SORRY, I--
WE'VE GOT TROUBLE DOWN AT KEYSTONE MOTORS. NEED SOME BACKUP FAST.
ANY CHANCE WE COULD GET A LITTLE HELP FROM THE FLASH?

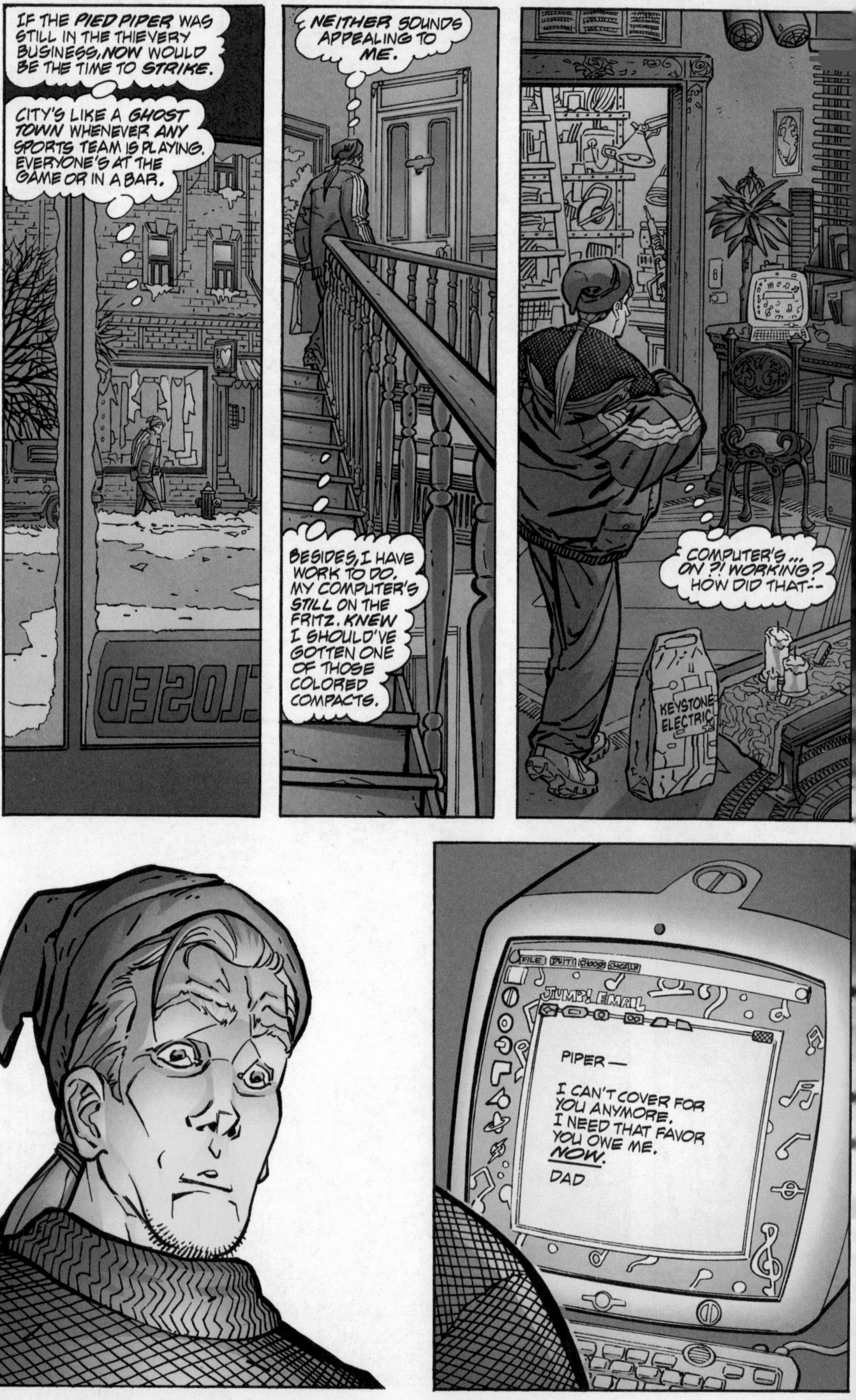
IF THE PIED PIPER WAS STILL IN THE THIEVERY BUSINESS, NOW WOULD BE THE TIME TO STRIKE.
CITY'S LIKE A GHOST TOWN WHENEVER ANY SPORTS TEAM IS PLAYING. EVERYONE'S AT THE GAME OR IN A BAR.
CLOSED
NEITHER SOUNDS APPEALING TO ME.
BESIDES, I HAVE WORK TO DO. MY COMPUTER'S STILL ON THE FRITZ. KNEW I SHOULD'VE GOTTEN ONE OF THOSE COLORED COMPACTS.
COMPUTER'S... ON ?! WORKING? HOW DID THAT--
KEYSTONE ELECTRIC
FILE
JUMP! EMAIL
PIPER —
I CAN'T COVER FOR YOU ANYMORE. I NEED THAT FAVOR YOU OWE ME. NOW.
DAD

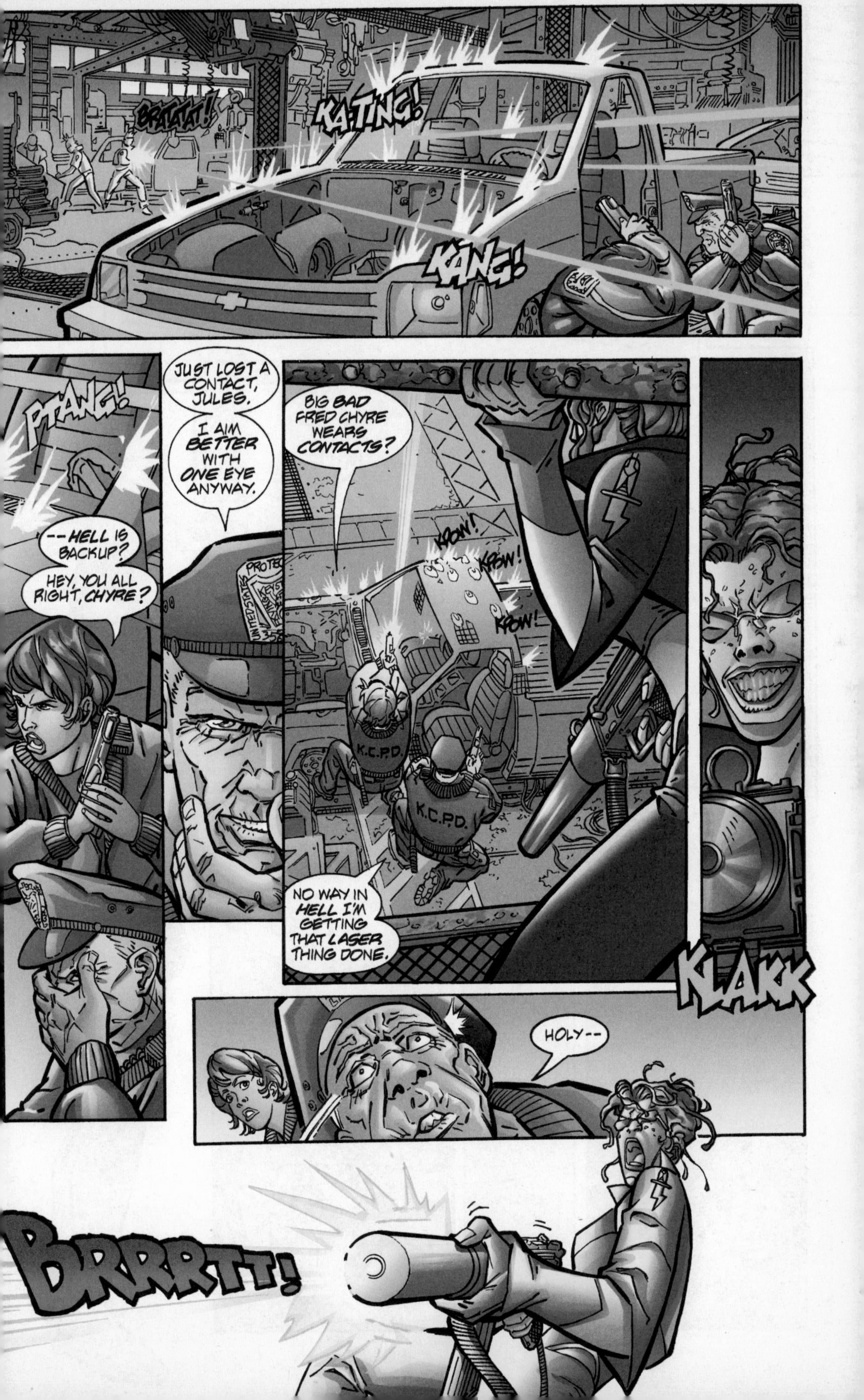
BRATATAT!
KA-TING!
KANG!
PTANG!
JUST LOST A CONTACT, JULES.
I AIM BETTER WITH ONE EYE ANYWAY.
BIG BAD FRED CHYRE WEARS CONTACTS?
--HELL IS BACKUP?
HEY, YOU ALL RIGHT, CHYRE?
KPOW!
KPOW!
KPOW!
K.C.P.D.
K.C.P.D.
NO WAY IN HELL I'M GETTING THAT LASER THING DONE.
KLAKK
HOLY--
BRRRTTT!

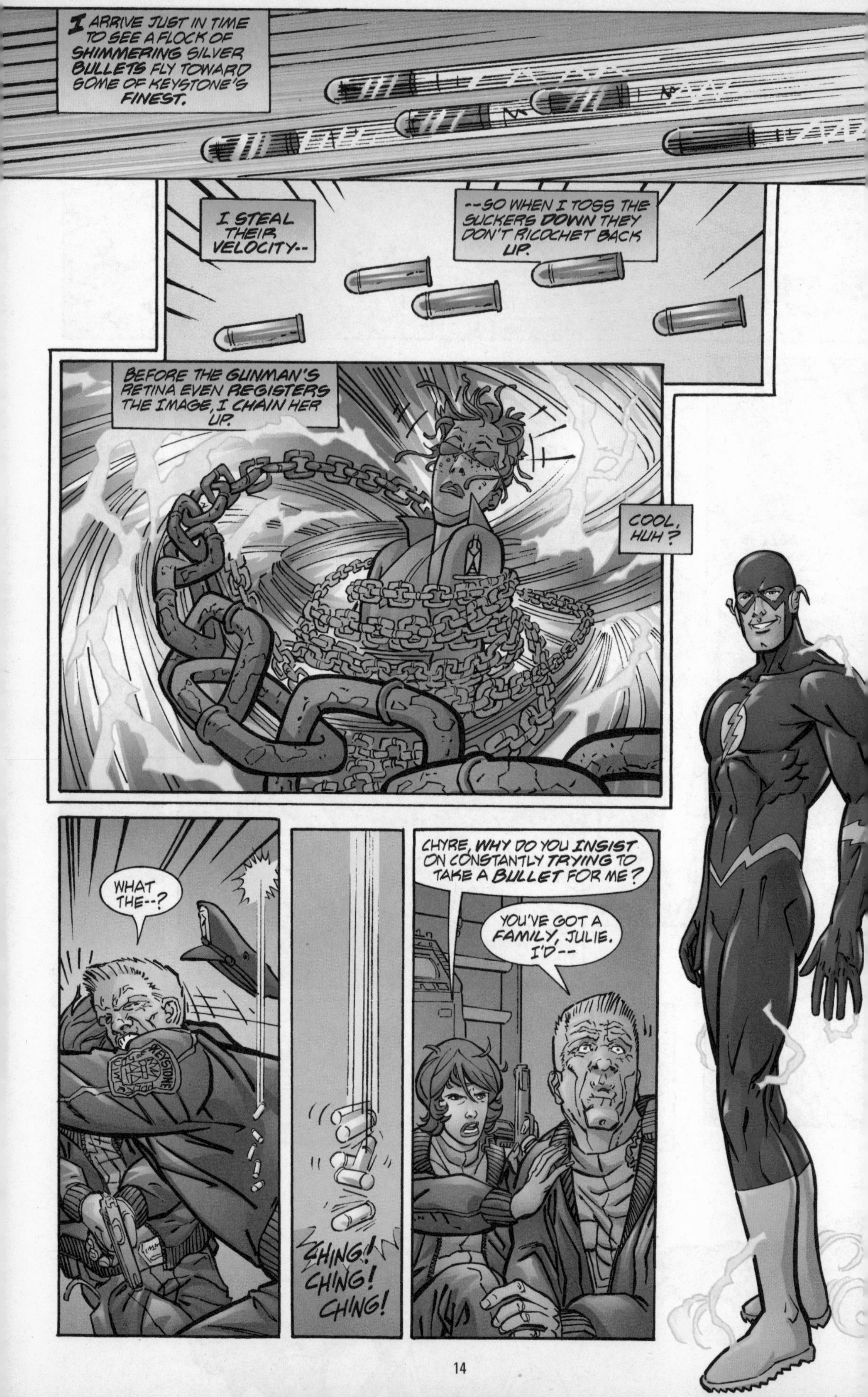

I ARRIVE JUST IN TIME TO SEE A FLOCK OF SHIMMERING SILVER BULLETS FLY TOWARD SOME OF KEYSTONE'S FINEST.
I STEAL THEIR VELOCITY--
--SO WHEN I TOSS THE SUCKERS DOWN THEY DON'T RICOCHET BACK UP.
BEFORE THE GUNMAN'S RETINA EVEN REGISTERS THE IMAGE, I CHAIN HER UP.
COOL, HUH?
WHAT THE--?
CHING! CHING! CHING!
CHYRE, WHY DO YOU INSIST ON CONSTANTLY TRYING TO TAKE A BULLET FOR ME?
YOU'VE GOT A FAMILY, JULIE. I'D--

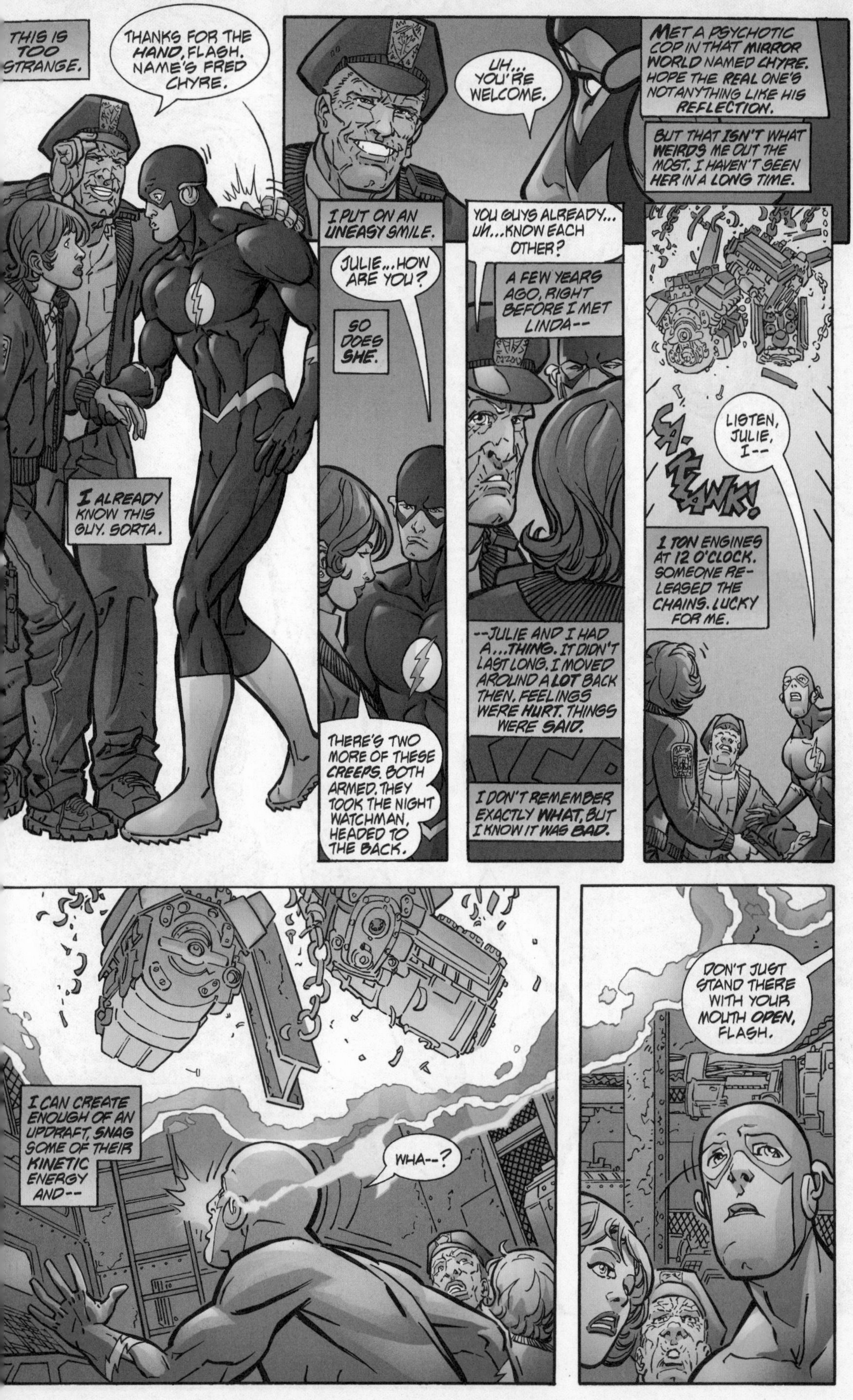
THIS IS TOO STRANGE.
THANKS FOR THE HAND, FLASH. NAME'S FRED CHYRE.
I ALREADY KNOW THIS GUY. SORTA.
UH... YOU'RE WELCOME.
MET A PSYCHOTIC COP IN THAT MIRROR WORLD NAMED CHYRE. HOPE THE REAL ONE'S NOT ANYTHING LIKE HIS REFLECTION.
BUT THAT ISN'T WHAT WEIRDS ME OUT THE MOST. I HAVEN'T SEEN HER IN A LONG TIME.
I PUT ON AN UNEASY SMILE.
JULIE... HOW ARE YOU?
SO DOES SHE.
THERE'S TWO MORE OF THESE CREEPS. BOTH ARMED. THEY TOOK THE NIGHT WATCHMAN, HEADED TO THE BACK.
YOU GUYS ALREADY... UH... KNOW EACH OTHER?
A FEW YEARS AGO, RIGHT BEFORE I MET LINDA--
--JULIE AND I HAD A... THING. IT DIDN'T LAST LONG. I MOVED AROUND A LOT BACK THEN. FEELINGS WERE HURT. THINGS WERE SAID.
I DON'T REMEMBER EXACTLY WHAT, BUT I KNOW IT WAS BAD.
CA-KLANK!
LISTEN, JULIE, I--
1 TON ENGINES AT 12 O'CLOCK. SOMEONE RELEASED THE CHAINS. LUCKY FOR ME.
I CAN CREATE ENOUGH OF AN UPDRAFT, SNAG SOME OF THEIR KINETIC ENERGY AND--
WHA--?
DON'T JUST STAND THERE WITH YOUR MOUTH OPEN, FLASH.

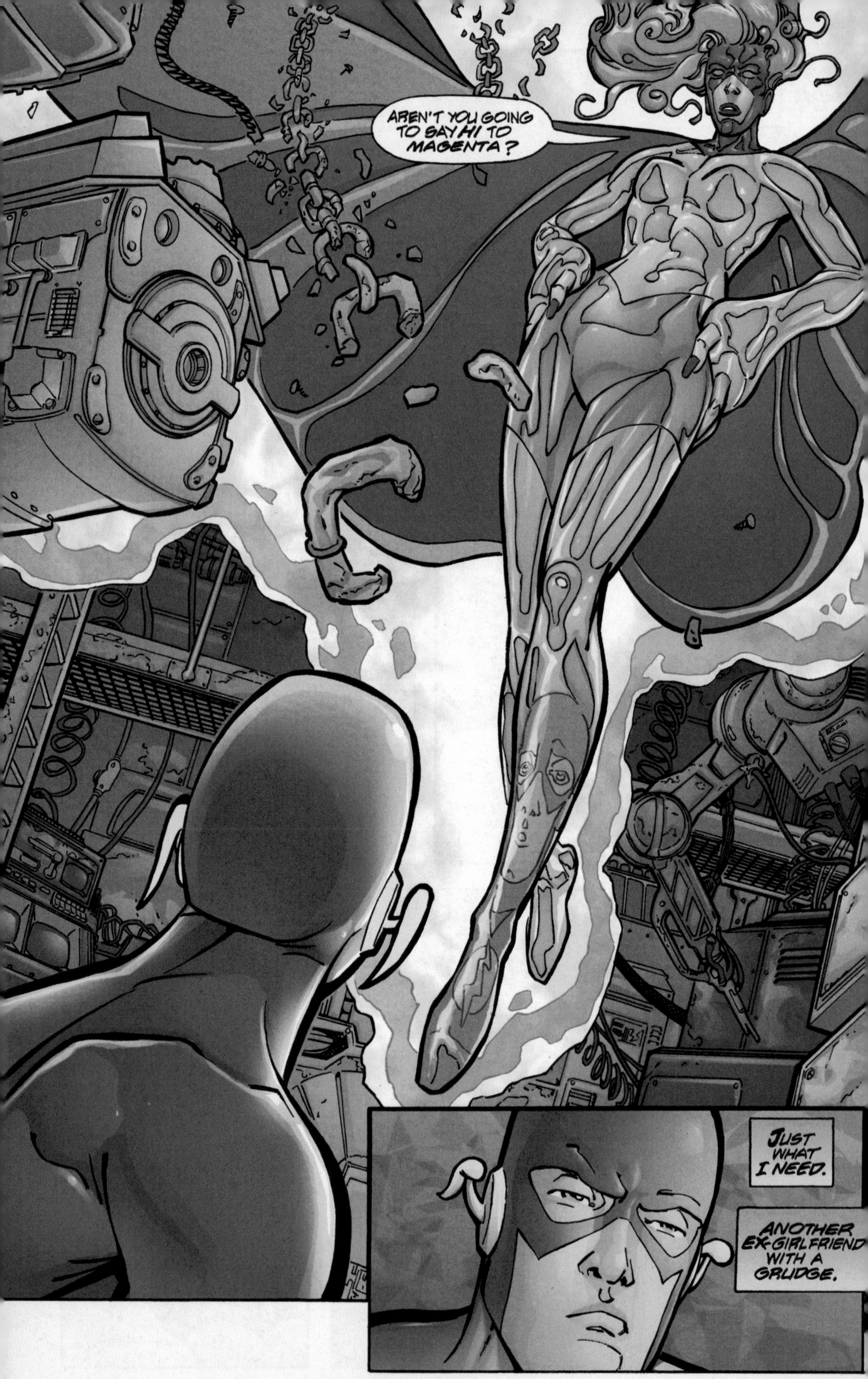

AREN'T YOU GOING TO SAY HI TO MAGENTA?
JUST WHAT I NEED.
ANOTHER EX-GIRLFRIEND WITH A GRUDGE.

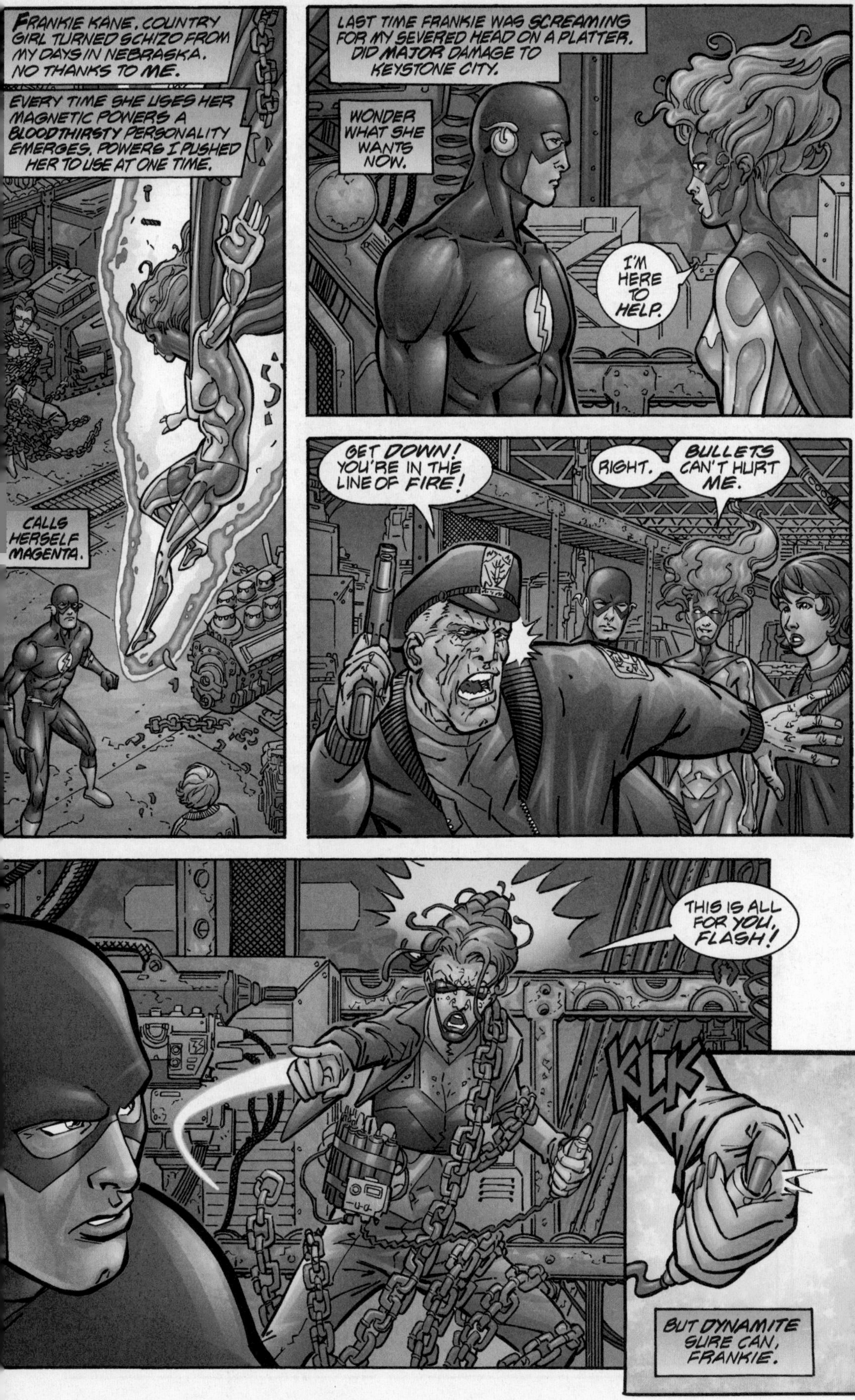
FRANKIE KANE. COUNTRY GIRL TURNED SCHIZO FROM MY DAYS IN NEBRASKA. NO THANKS TO ME.
EVERY TIME SHE USES HER MAGNETIC POWERS A BLOODTHIRSTY PERSONALITY EMERGES. POWERS I PUSHED HER TO USE AT ONE TIME.
CALLS HERSELF MAGENTA.
LAST TIME FRANKIE WAS SCREAMING FOR MY SEVERED HEAD ON A PLATTER. DID MAJOR DAMAGE TO KEYSTONE CITY.
WONDER WHAT SHE WANTS NOW.
I'M HERE TO HELP.
GET DOWN! YOU'RE IN THE LINE OF FIRE!
BULLETS CAN'T HURT ME.
RIGHT.
THIS IS ALL FOR YOU, FLASH!
KLIK
BUT DYNAMITE SURE CAN, FRANKIE.

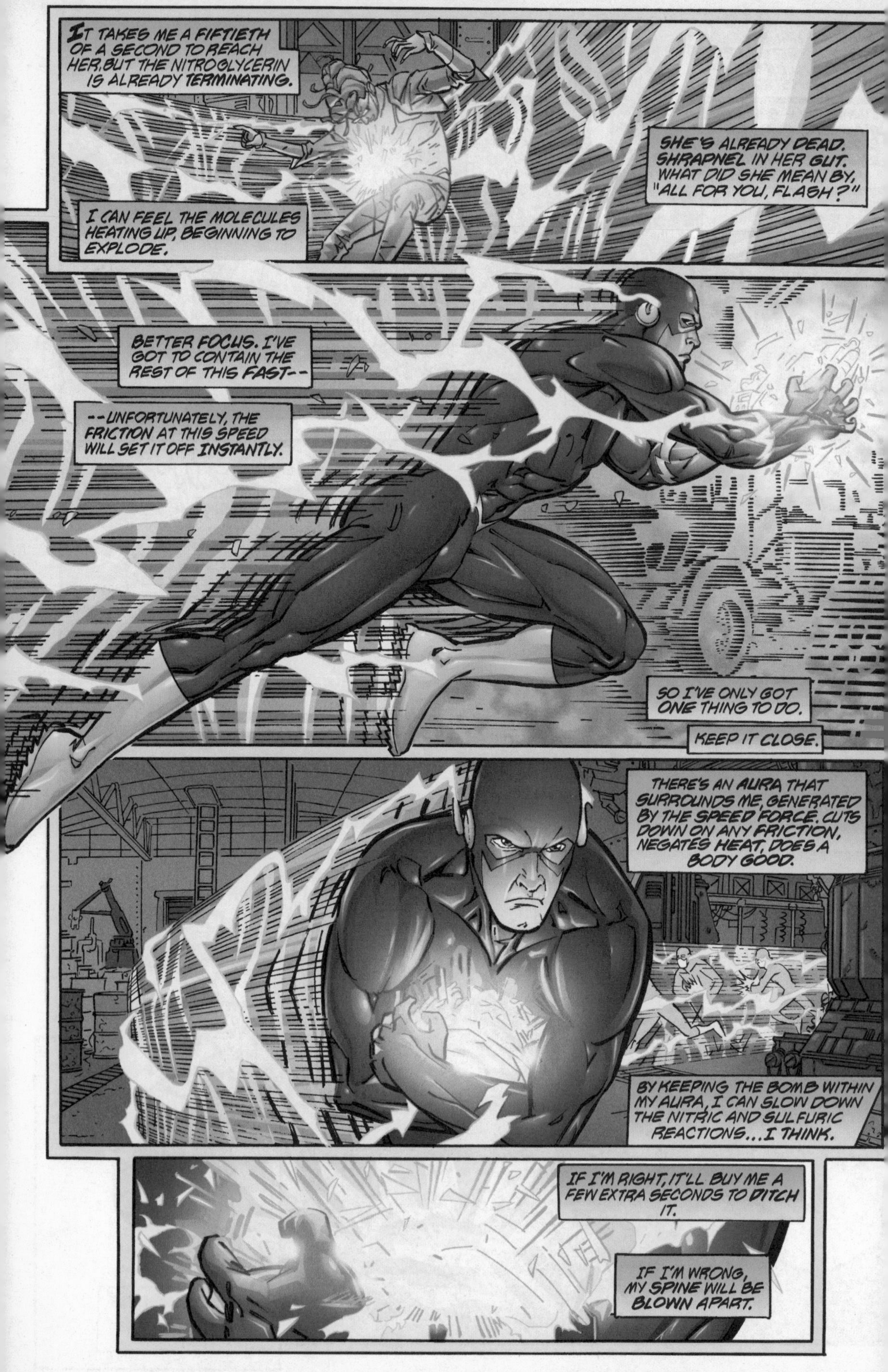
IT TAKES ME A FIFTIETH OF A SECOND TO REACH HER, BUT THE NITROGLYCERIN IS ALREADY TERMINATING.
SHE'S ALREADY DEAD. SHRAPNEL IN HER GUT. WHAT DID SHE MEAN BY, "ALL FOR YOU, FLASH?"
I CAN FEEL THE MOLECULES HEATING UP, BEGINNING TO EXPLODE.
BETTER FOCUS. I'VE GOT TO CONTAIN THE REST OF THIS FAST--
--UNFORTUNATELY, THE FRICTION AT THIS SPEED WILL SET IT OFF INSTANTLY.
SO I'VE ONLY GOT ONE THING TO DO.
KEEP IT CLOSE.
THERE'S AN AURA THAT SURROUNDS ME, GENERATED BY THE SPEED FORCE. CUTS DOWN ON ANY FRICTION, NEGATES HEAT, DOES A BODY GOOD.
BY KEEPING THE BOMB WITHIN MY AURA, I CAN SLOW DOWN THE NITRIC AND SULFURIC REACTIONS...I THINK.
IF I'M RIGHT, IT'LL BUY ME A FEW EXTRA SECONDS TO DITCH IT.
IF I'M WRONG, MY SPINE WILL BE BLOWN APART.

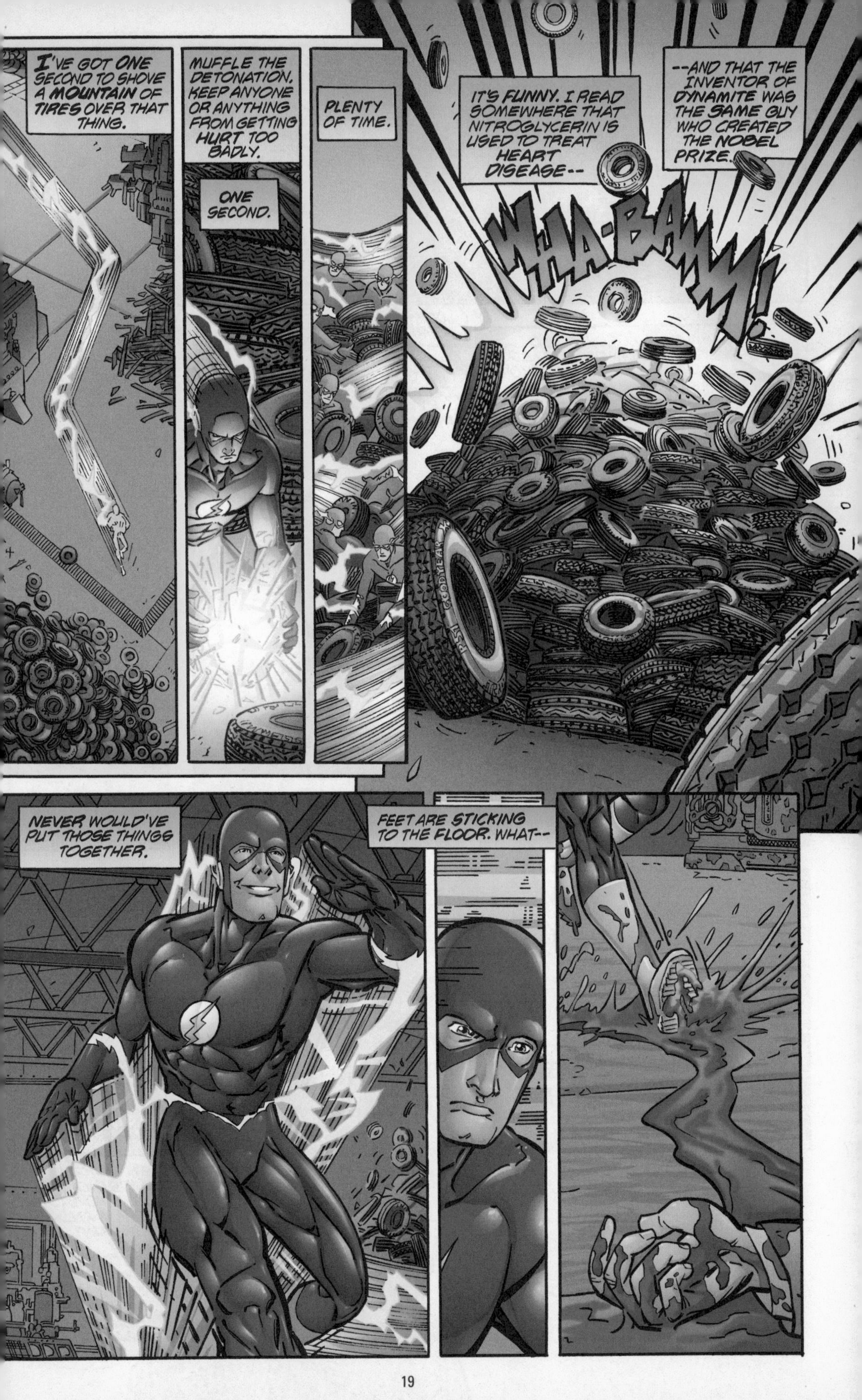
I'VE GOT ONE SECOND TO SHOVE A MOUNTAIN OF TIRES OVER THAT THING.
MUFFLE THE DETONATION. KEEP ANYONE OR ANYTHING FROM GETTING HURT TOO BADLY.
ONE SECOND.
PLENTY OF TIME.
IT'S FUNNY. I READ SOMEWHERE THAT NITROGLYCERIN IS USED TO TREAT HEART DISEASE--
--AND THAT THE INVENTOR OF DYNAMITE WAS THE SAME GUY WHO CREATED THE NOBEL PRIZE.
WHA-BAMM!
NEVER WOULD'VE PUT THOSE THINGS TOGETHER.
FEET ARE STICKING TO THE FLOOR. WHAT--

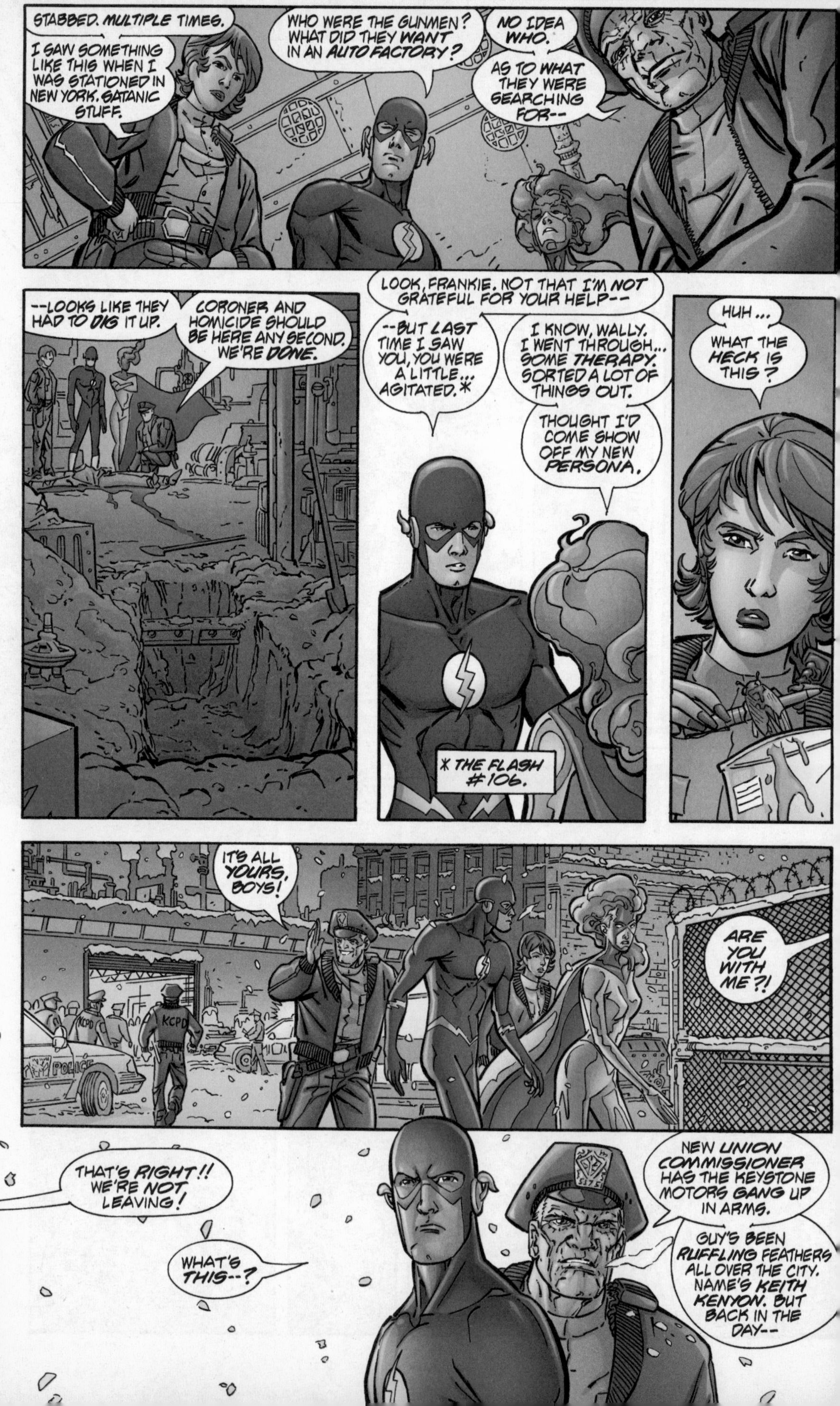

STABBED. MULTIPLE TIMES.
I SAW SOMETHING LIKE THIS WHEN I WAS STATIONED IN NEW YORK. SATANIC STUFF.
WHO WERE THE GUNMEN? WHAT DID THEY WANT IN AN AUTO FACTORY?
NO IDEA WHO.
AS TO WHAT THEY WERE SEARCHING FOR--
--LOOKS LIKE THEY HAD TO DIG IT UP.
CORONER AND HOMICIDE SHOULD BE HERE ANY SECOND. WE'RE DONE.
LOOK, FRANKIE. NOT THAT I'M NOT GRATEFUL FOR YOUR HELP--
--BUT LAST TIME I SAW YOU, YOU WERE A LITTLE... AGITATED.*
I KNOW, WALLY. I WENT THROUGH... SOME THERAPY. SORTED A LOT OF THINGS OUT.
THOUGHT I'D COME SHOW OFF MY NEW PERSONA.
* THE FLASH #106.
HUH...
WHAT THE HECK IS THIS?
IT'S ALL YOURS, BOYS!
ARE YOU WITH ME?!
KCPD
POLICE
THAT'S RIGHT!! WE'RE NOT LEAVING!
WHAT'S THIS--?
NEW UNION COMMISSIONER HAS THE KEYSTONE MOTORS GANG UP IN ARMS.
GUY'S BEEN RUFFLING FEATHERS ALL OVER THE CITY. NAME'S KEITH KENYON. BUT BACK IN THE DAY--

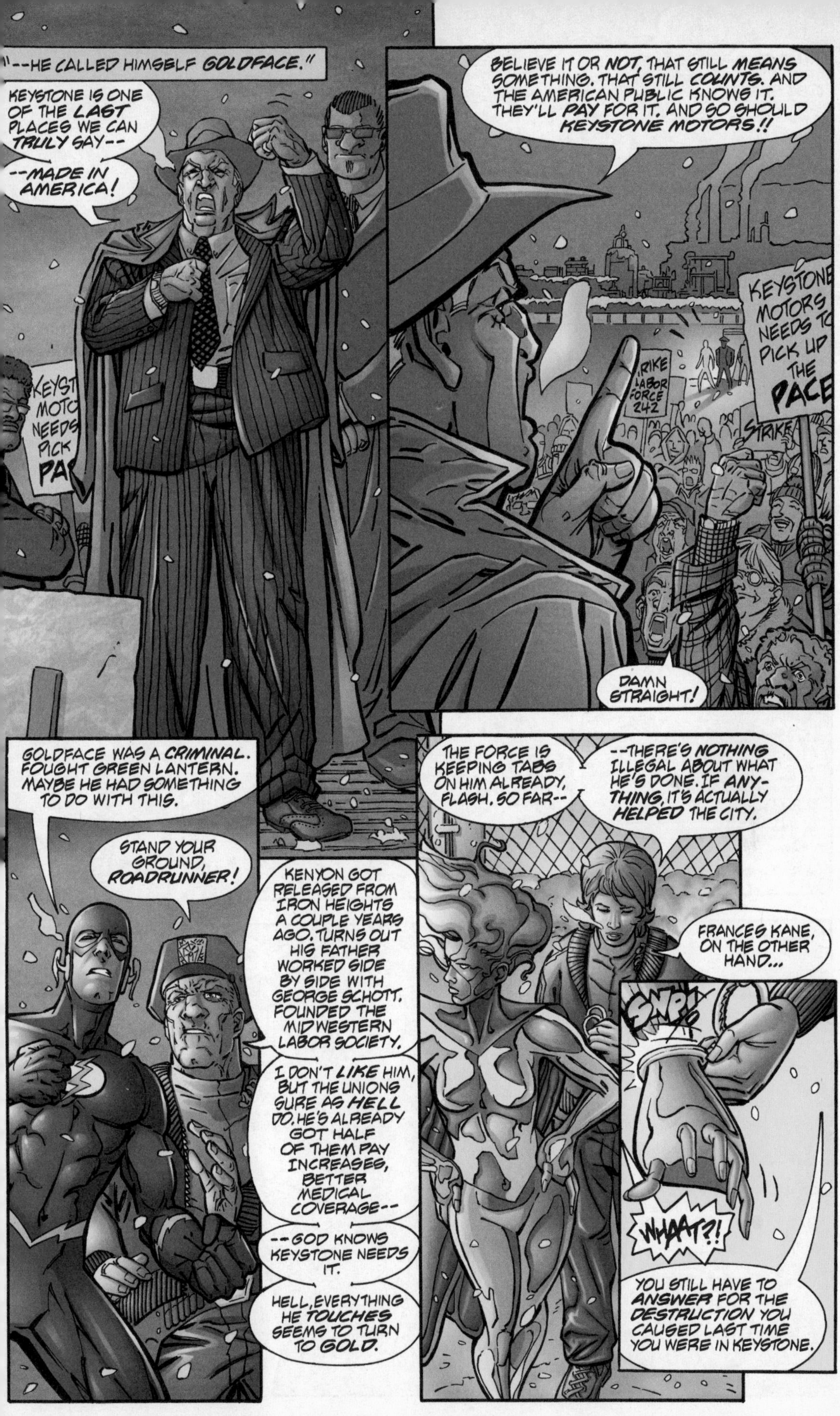
"--HE CALLED HIMSELF GOLDFACE."
KEYSTONE IS ONE OF THE LAST PLACES WE CAN TRULY SAY--
--MADE IN AMERICA!
BELIEVE IT OR NOT, THAT STILL MEANS SOMETHING. THAT STILL COUNTS. AND THE AMERICAN PUBLIC KNOWS IT. THEY'LL PAY FOR IT. AND SO SHOULD KEYSTONE MOTORS!!
KEYSTONE MOTORS NEEDS TO PICK UP THE PACE
STRIKE LABOR FORCE 242
STRIKE
DAMN STRAIGHT!
GOLDFACE WAS A CRIMINAL. FOUGHT GREEN LANTERN. MAYBE HE HAD SOMETHING TO DO WITH THIS.
STAND YOUR GROUND, ROADRUNNER!
KENYON GOT RELEASED FROM IRON HEIGHTS A COUPLE YEARS AGO. TURNS OUT HIS FATHER WORKED SIDE BY SIDE WITH GEORGE SCHOTT. FOUNDED THE MIDWESTERN LABOR SOCIETY.
I DON'T LIKE HIM, BUT THE UNIONS SURE AS HELL DO. HE'S ALREADY GOT HALF OF THEM PAY INCREASES, BETTER MEDICAL COVERAGE--
--GOD KNOWS KEYSTONE NEEDS IT.
HELL, EVERYTHING HE TOUCHES SEEMS TO TURN TO GOLD.
THE FORCE IS KEEPING TABS ON HIM ALREADY, FLASH. SO FAR--
--THERE'S NOTHING ILLEGAL ABOUT WHAT HE'S DONE. IF ANYTHING, IT'S ACTUALLY HELPED THE CITY.
FRANCES KANE, ON THE OTHER HAND...
SNP!
WHAAT?!
YOU STILL HAVE TO ANSWER FOR THE DESTRUCTION YOU CAUSED LAST TIME YOU WERE IN KEYSTONE.

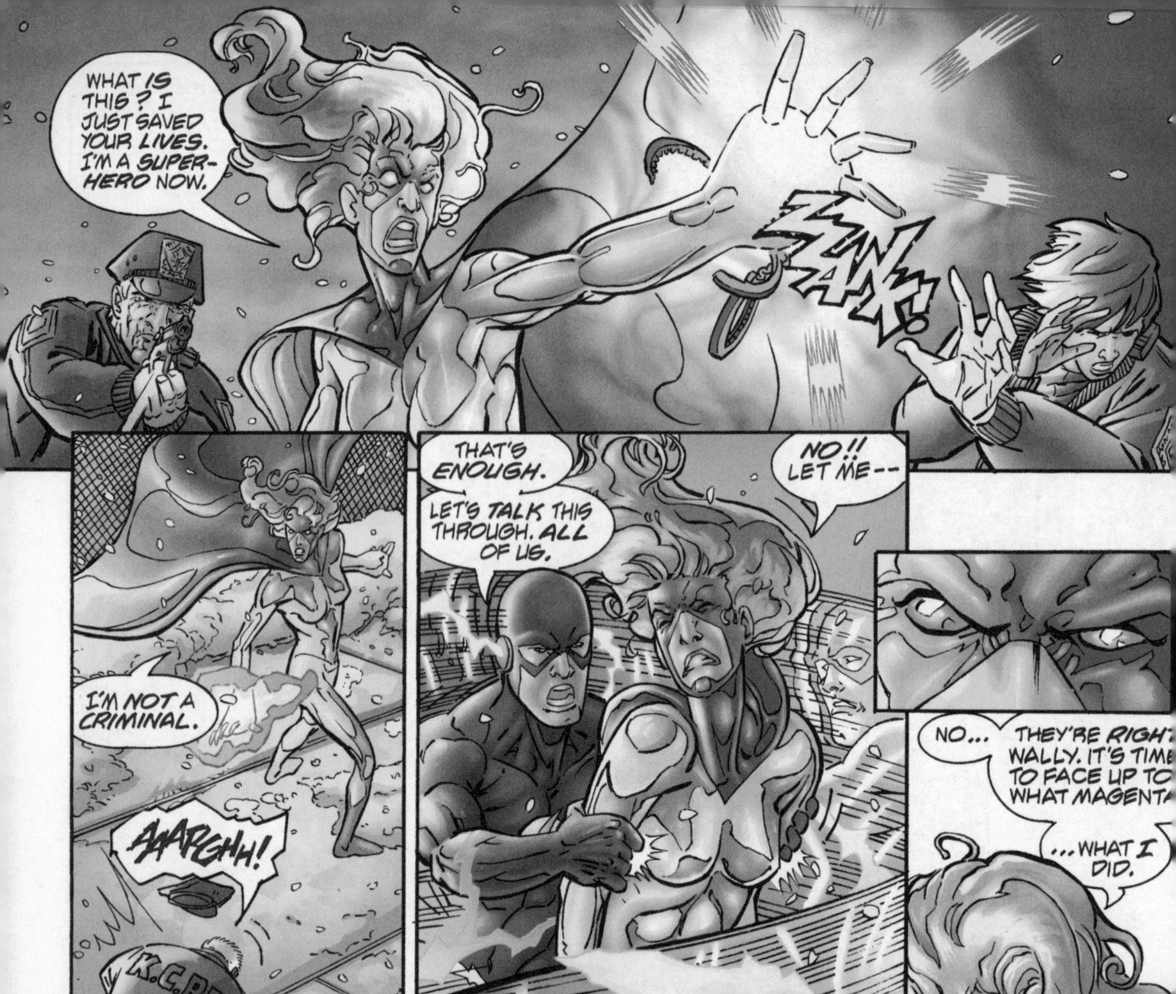
WHAT IS THIS? I JUST SAVED YOUR LIVES. I'M A SUPER-HERO NOW.
ZZAK ZAK!
I'M NOT A CRIMINAL.
AAARGHH!
K.C.P.D.
THAT'S ENOUGH.
LET'S TALK THIS THROUGH. ALL OF US.
NO!! LET ME--
NO...
THEY'RE RIGHT WALLY. IT'S TIME TO FACE UP TO WHAT MAGENTA
...WHAT I DID.
CHYRE?
THE WITCH--AHHH--RIPPED MY FILLINGS OUT.
SORRY.
KEYSTONE

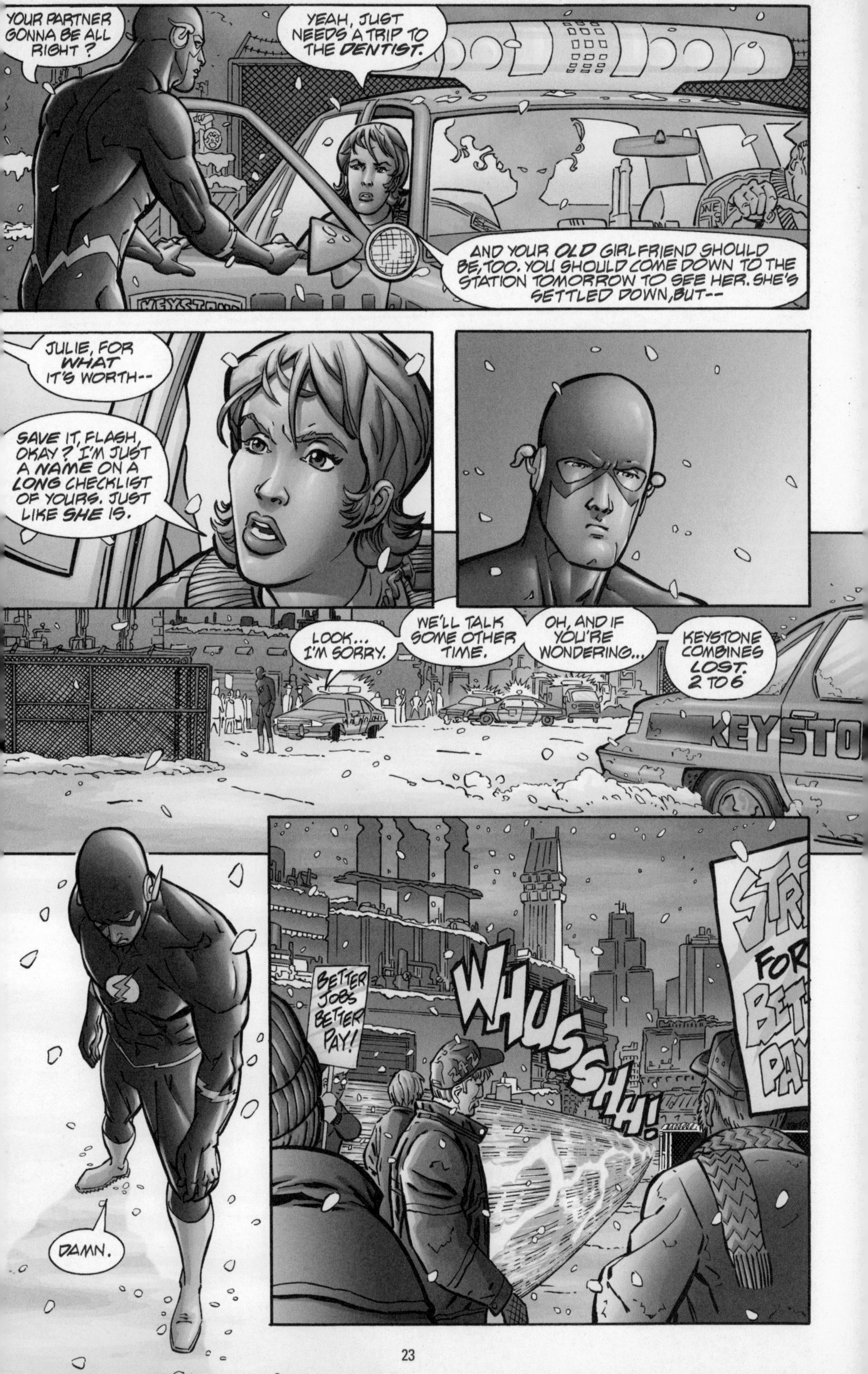

YOUR PARTNER GONNA BE ALL RIGHT?
YEAH, JUST NEEDS A TRIP TO THE DENTIST.
AND YOUR OLD GIRLFRIEND SHOULD BE, TOO. YOU SHOULD COME DOWN TO THE STATION TOMORROW TO SEE HER. SHE'S SETTLED DOWN, BUT--
JULIE, FOR WHAT IT'S WORTH--
SAVE IT, FLASH, OKAY? I'M JUST A NAME ON A LONG CHECKLIST OF YOURS. JUST LIKE SHE IS.
LOOK... I'M SORRY.
WE'LL TALK SOME OTHER TIME.
OH, AND IF YOU'RE WONDERING...
KEYSTONE COMBINES LOST. 2 TO 6
KEYSTO
DAMN.
BETTER JOBS BETTER PAY!
WHUSSHH!

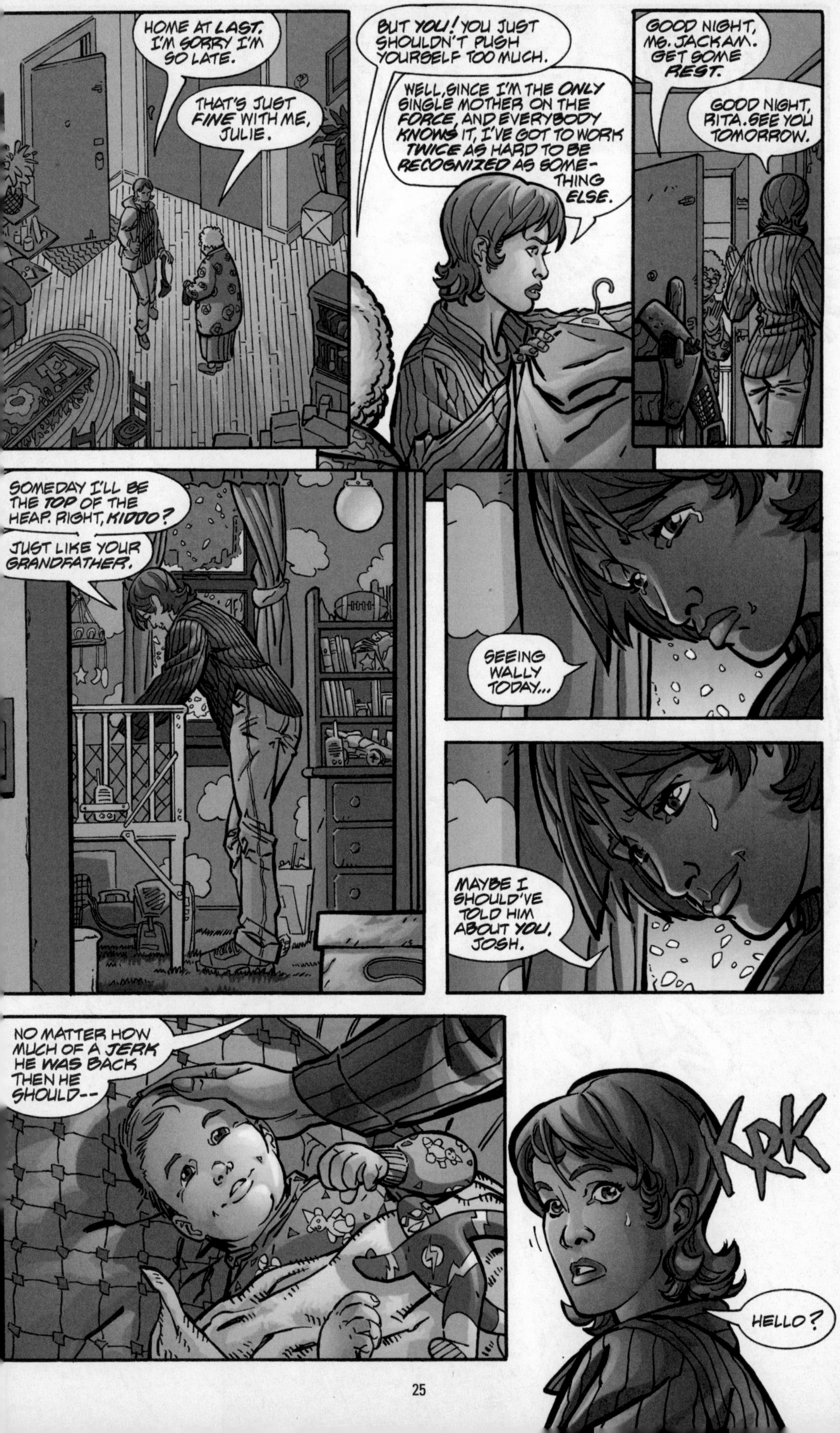
HOME AT LAST. I'M SORRY I'M SO LATE.
THAT'S JUST FINE WITH ME, JULIE.
BUT YOU! YOU JUST SHOULDN'T PUSH YOURSELF TOO MUCH.
WELL, SINCE I'M THE ONLY SINGLE MOTHER ON THE FORCE, AND EVERYBODY KNOWS IT, I'VE GOT TO WORK TWICE AS HARD TO BE RECOGNIZED AS SOMETHING ELSE.
GOOD NIGHT, MS. JACKAM. GET SOME REST.
GOOD NIGHT, RITA. SEE YOU TOMORROW.
SOMEDAY I'LL BE THE TOP OF THE HEAP. RIGHT, KIDDO?
JUST LIKE YOUR GRANDFATHER.
SEEING WALLY TODAY...
MAYBE I SHOULD'VE TOLD HIM ABOUT YOU, JOSH.
NO MATTER HOW MUCH OF A JERK HE WAS BACK THEN HE SHOULD--
KRK
HELLO?

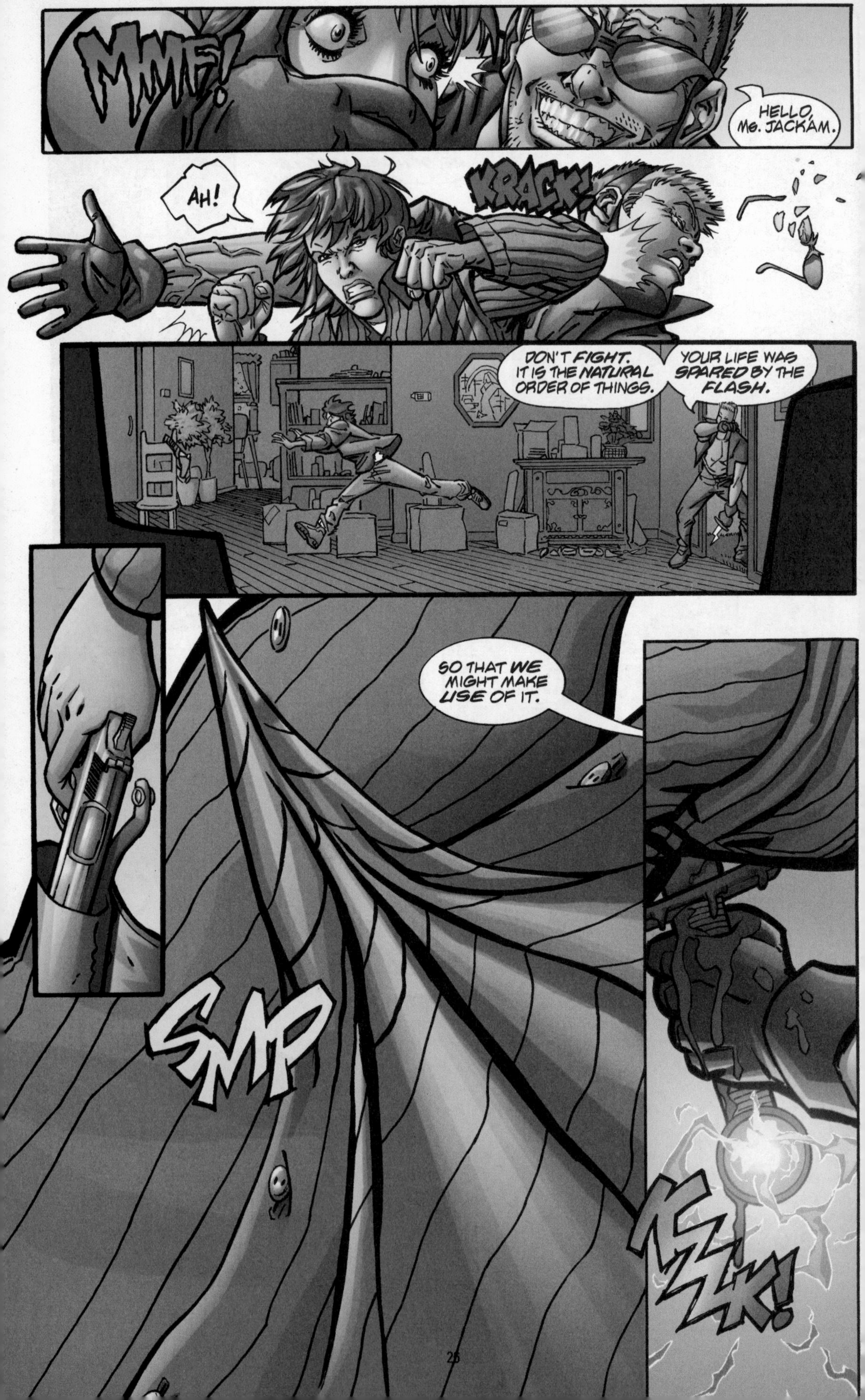
MMF!
HELLO, Ms. JACKAM.
AH!
KRACK!
DON'T FIGHT. IT IS THE NATURAL ORDER OF THINGS.
YOUR LIFE WAS SPARED BY THE FLASH.
SO THAT WE MIGHT MAKE USE OF IT.
SNAP
KZZK!

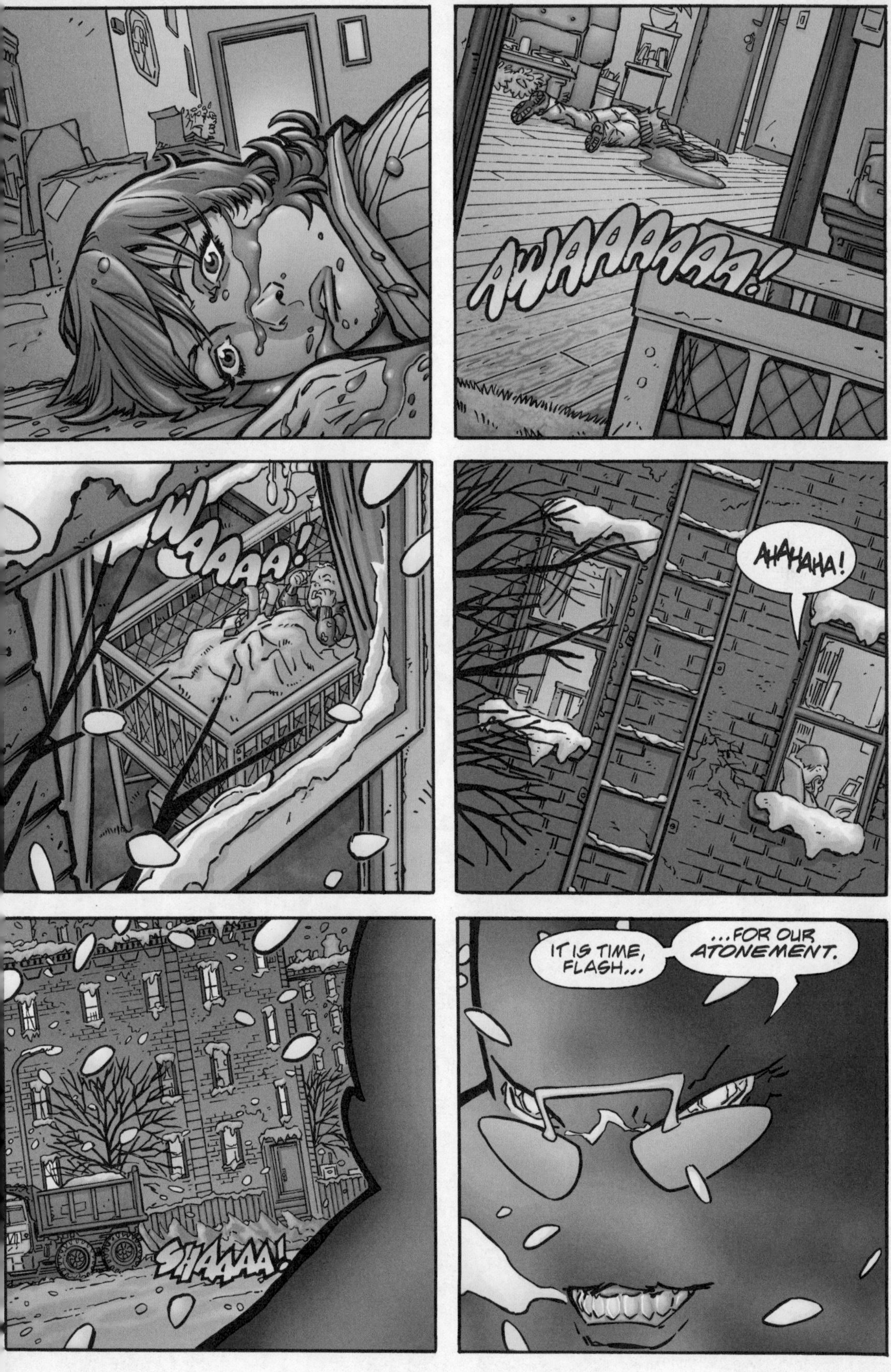
AWAAAAAAA!
WAAAA!
AHAHAHA!
SHAAAA!
IT IS TIME, FLASH...
...FOR OUR ATONEMENT.

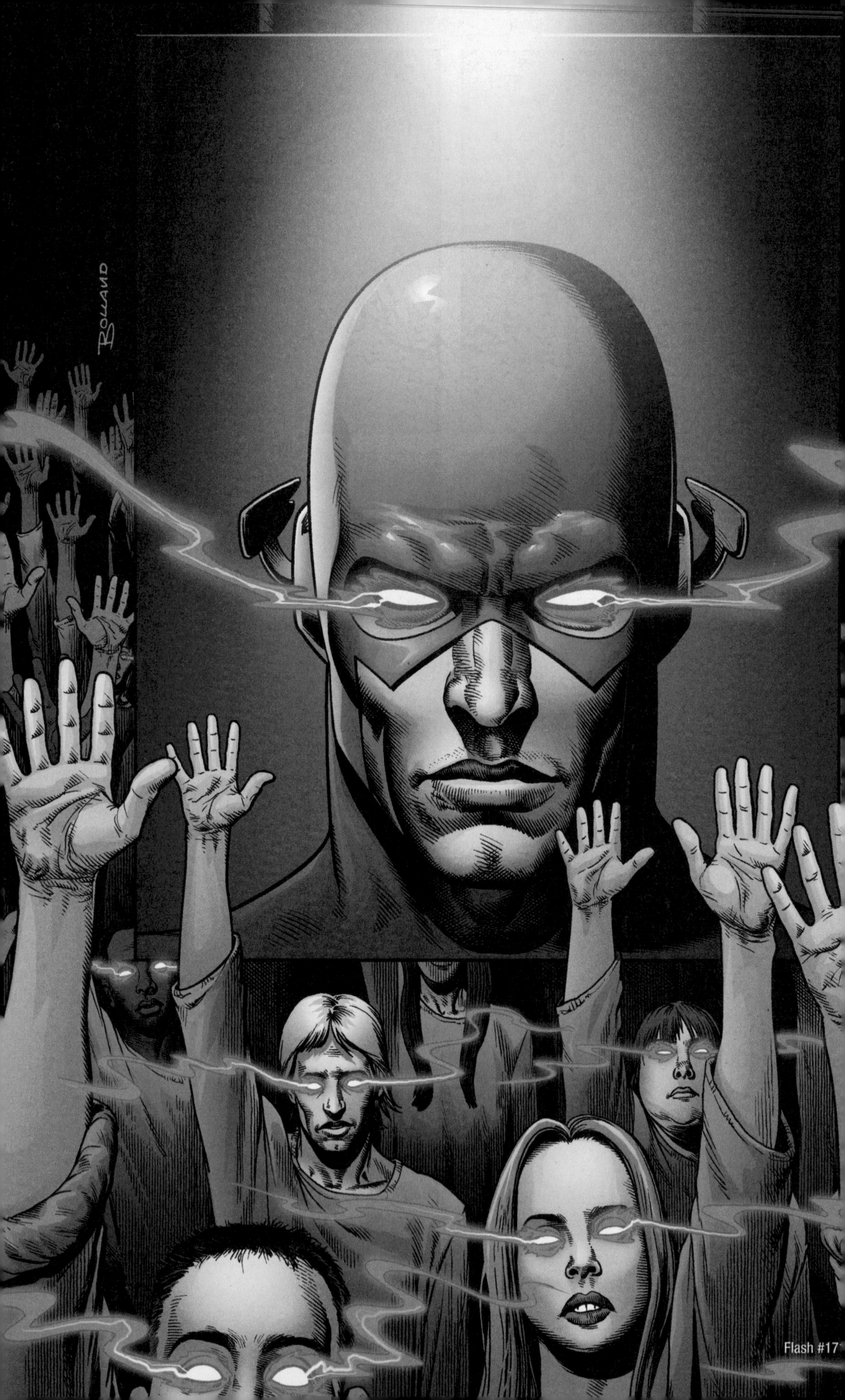
BOLLAND
Flash #17

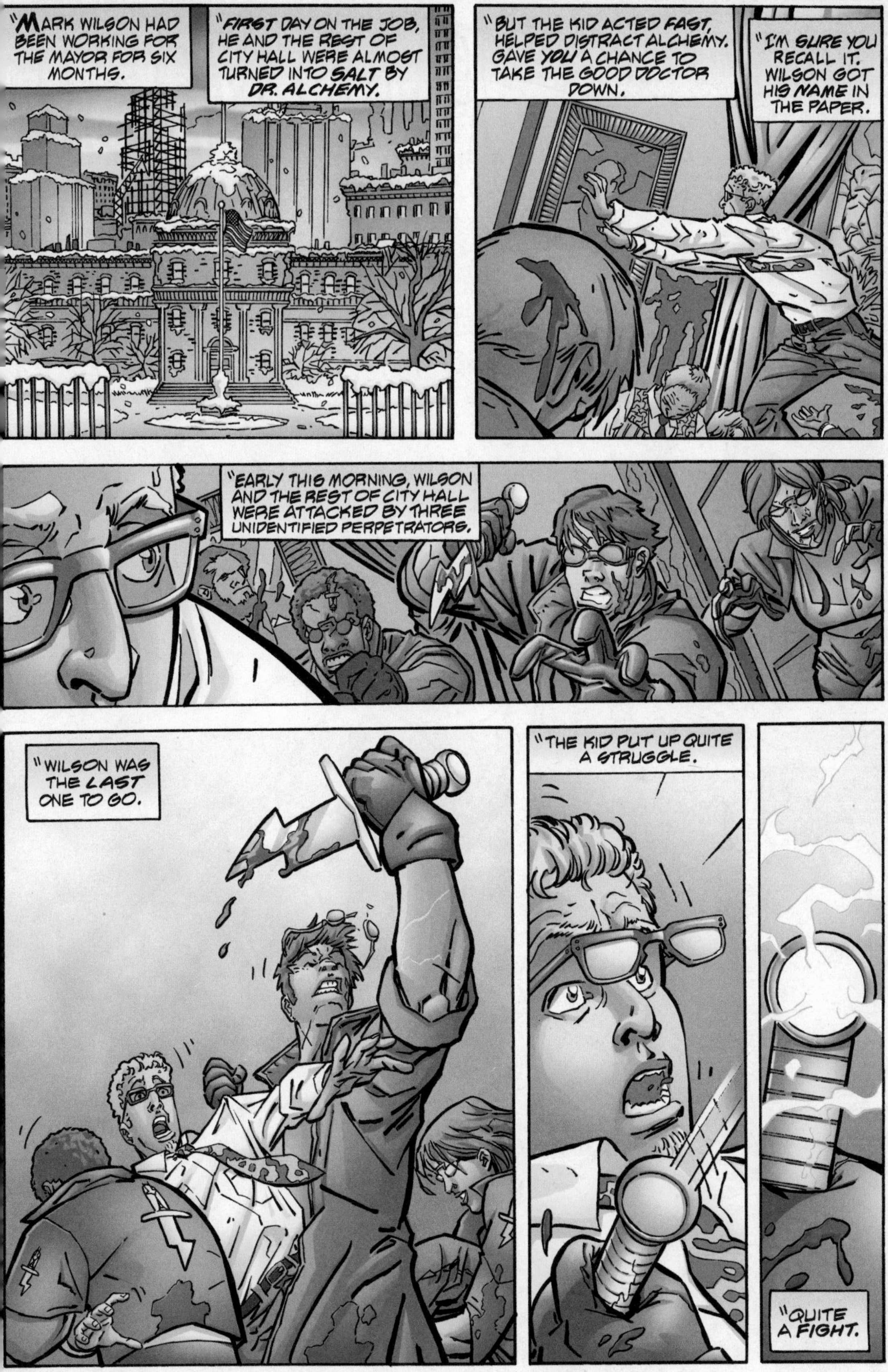
"MARK WILSON HAD BEEN WORKING FOR THE MAYOR FOR SIX MONTHS.
"FIRST DAY ON THE JOB, HE AND THE REST OF CITY HALL WERE ALMOST TURNED INTO SALT BY DR. ALCHEMY.
"BUT THE KID ACTED FAST, HELPED DISTRACT ALCHEMY. GAVE YOU A CHANCE TO TAKE THE GOOD DOCTOR DOWN.
"I'M SURE YOU RECALL IT. WILSON GOT HIS NAME IN THE PAPER.
"EARLY THIS MORNING, WILSON AND THE REST OF CITY HALL WERE ATTACKED BY THREE UNIDENTIFIED PERPETRATORS.
"WILSON WAS THE LAST ONE TO GO.
"THE KID PUT UP QUITE A STRUGGLE.
"QUITE A FIGHT.

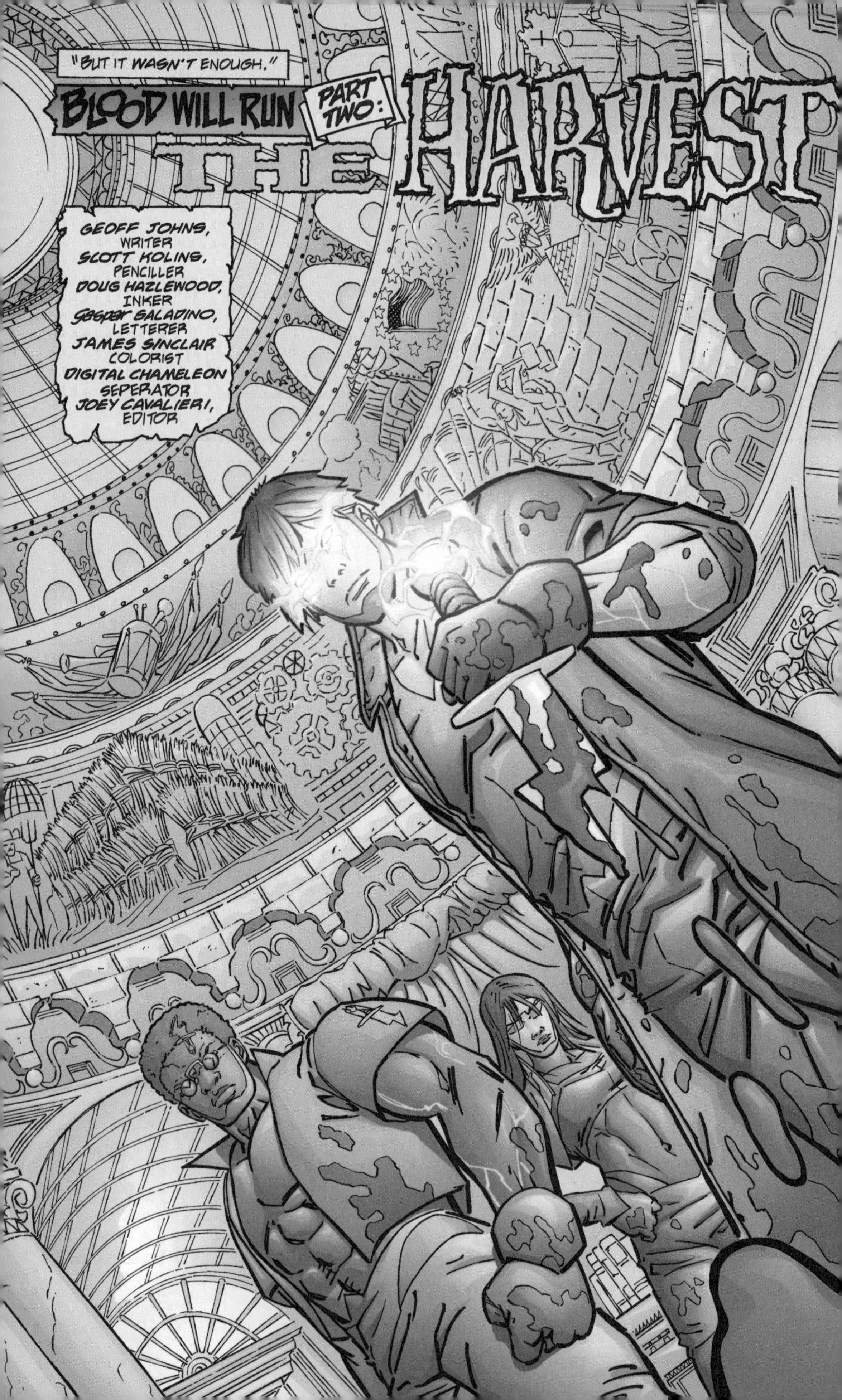
"BUT IT WASN'T ENOUGH."
BLOOD WILL RUN
PART TWO:
THE HARVEST
GEOFF JOHNS, WRITER
SCOTT KOLINS, PENCILLER
DOUG HAZLEWOOD, INKER
GASPAR SALADINO, LETTERER
JAMES SINCLAIR COLORIST
DIGITAL CHAMELEON SEPERATOR
JOEY CAVALIERI, EDITOR

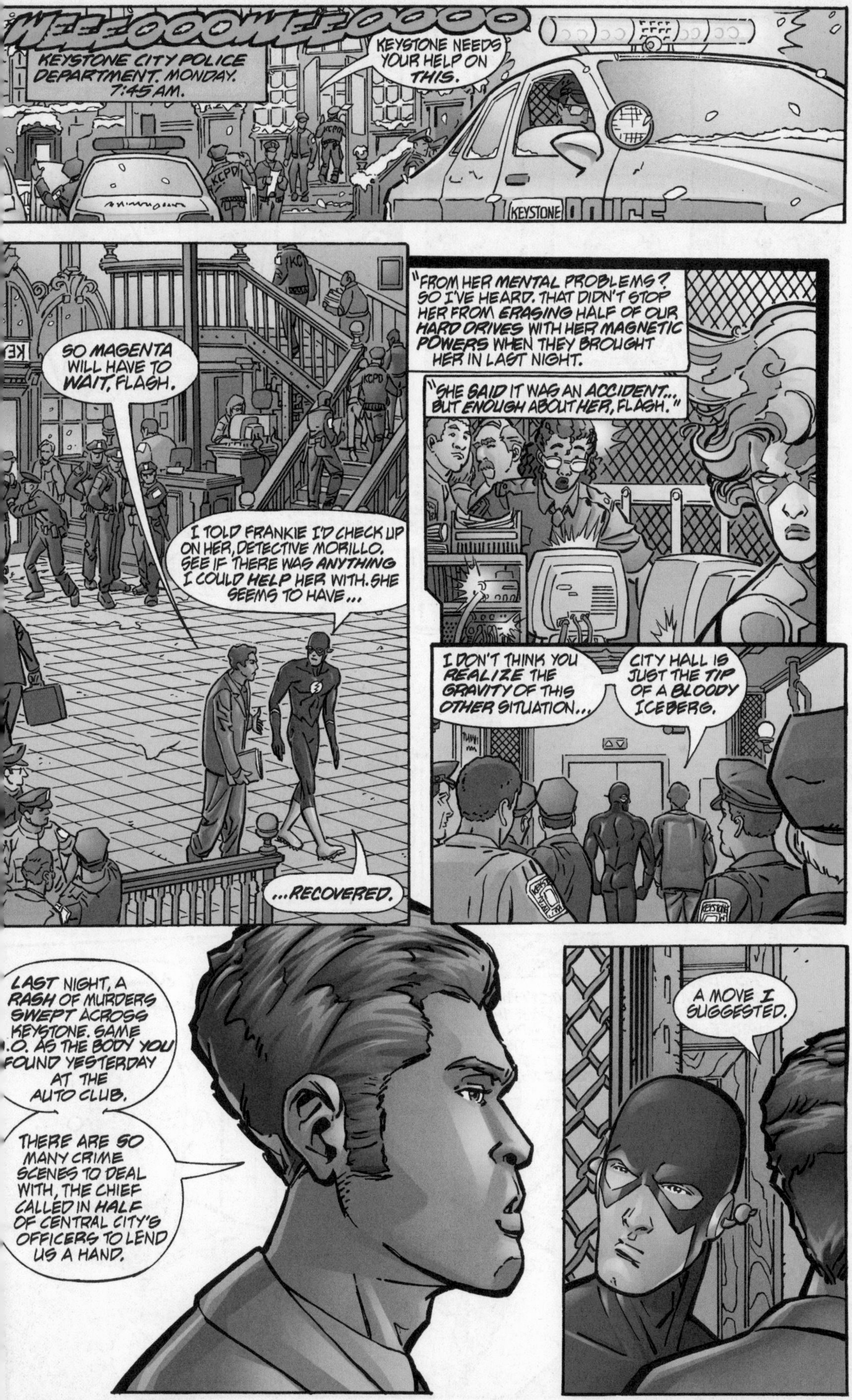
WEEEOOOWEEEOOOO
KEYSTONE CITY POLICE DEPARTMENT. MONDAY. 7:45 AM.
KEYSTONE NEEDS YOUR HELP ON THIS.
KEYSTONE POLICE
SO MAGENTA WILL HAVE TO WAIT, FLASH.
I TOLD FRANKIE I'D CHECK UP ON HER, DETECTIVE MORILLO. SEE IF THERE WAS ANYTHING I COULD HELP HER WITH. SHE SEEMS TO HAVE...
...RECOVERED.
"FROM HER MENTAL PROBLEMS? SO I'VE HEARD. THAT DIDN'T STOP HER FROM ERASING HALF OF OUR HARD DRIVES WITH HER MAGNETIC POWERS WHEN THEY BROUGHT HER IN LAST NIGHT.
"SHE SAID IT WAS AN ACCIDENT... BUT ENOUGH ABOUT HER, FLASH."
I DON'T THINK YOU REALIZE THE GRAVITY OF THIS OTHER SITUATION...
CITY HALL IS JUST THE TIP OF A BLOODY ICEBERG.
LAST NIGHT, A RASH OF MURDERS SWEPT ACROSS KEYSTONE. SAME M.O. AS THE BODY YOU FOUND YESTERDAY AT THE AUTO CLUB.
THERE ARE SO MANY CRIME SCENES TO DEAL WITH, THE CHIEF CALLED IN HALF OF CENTRAL CITY'S OFFICERS TO LEND US A HAND.
A MOVE I SUGGESTED.

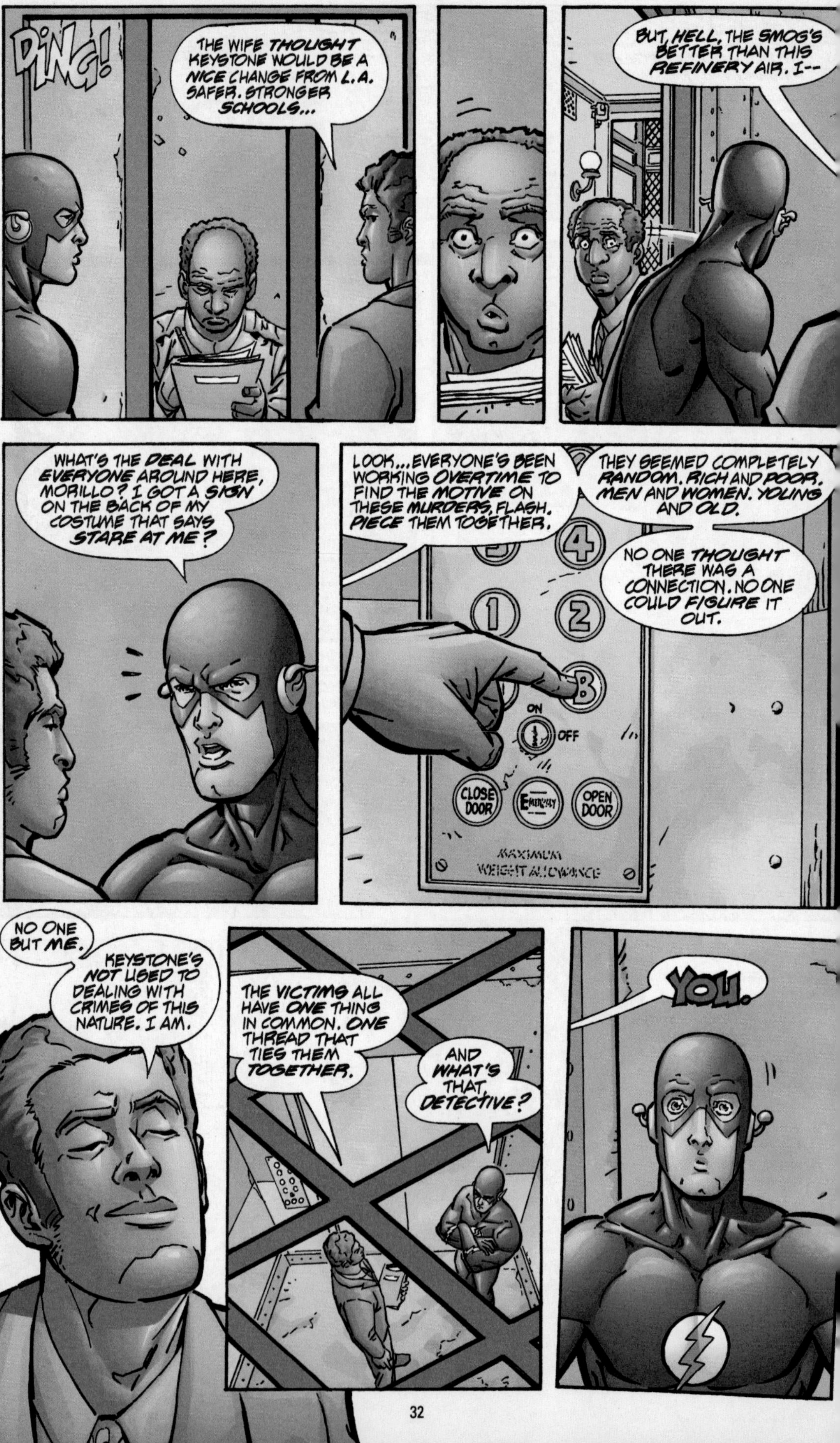

DING!
THE WIFE THOUGHT KEYSTONE WOULD BE A NICE CHANGE FROM L.A. SAFER. STRONGER SCHOOLS...
BUT, HELL, THE SMOG'S BETTER THAN THIS REFINERY AIR. I--
WHAT'S THE DEAL WITH EVERYONE AROUND HERE, MORILLO? I GOT A SIGN ON THE BACK OF MY COSTUME THAT SAYS STARE AT ME?
LOOK...EVERYONE'S BEEN WORKING OVERTIME TO FIND THE MOTIVE ON THESE MURDERS, FLASH. PIECE THEM TOGETHER.
THEY SEEMED COMPLETELY RANDOM. RICH AND POOR. MEN AND WOMEN. YOUNG AND OLD.
NO ONE THOUGHT THERE WAS A CONNECTION. NO ONE COULD FIGURE IT OUT.
4
1
2
B
ON
OFF
CLOSE DOOR
OPEN DOOR
MAXIMUM WEIGHT ALLOWANCE
NO ONE BUT ME.
KEYSTONE'S NOT USED TO DEALING WITH CRIMES OF THIS NATURE. I AM.
THE VICTIMS ALL HAVE ONE THING IN COMMON. ONE THREAD THAT TIES THEM TOGETHER.
AND WHAT'S THAT, DETECTIVE?
YOU.

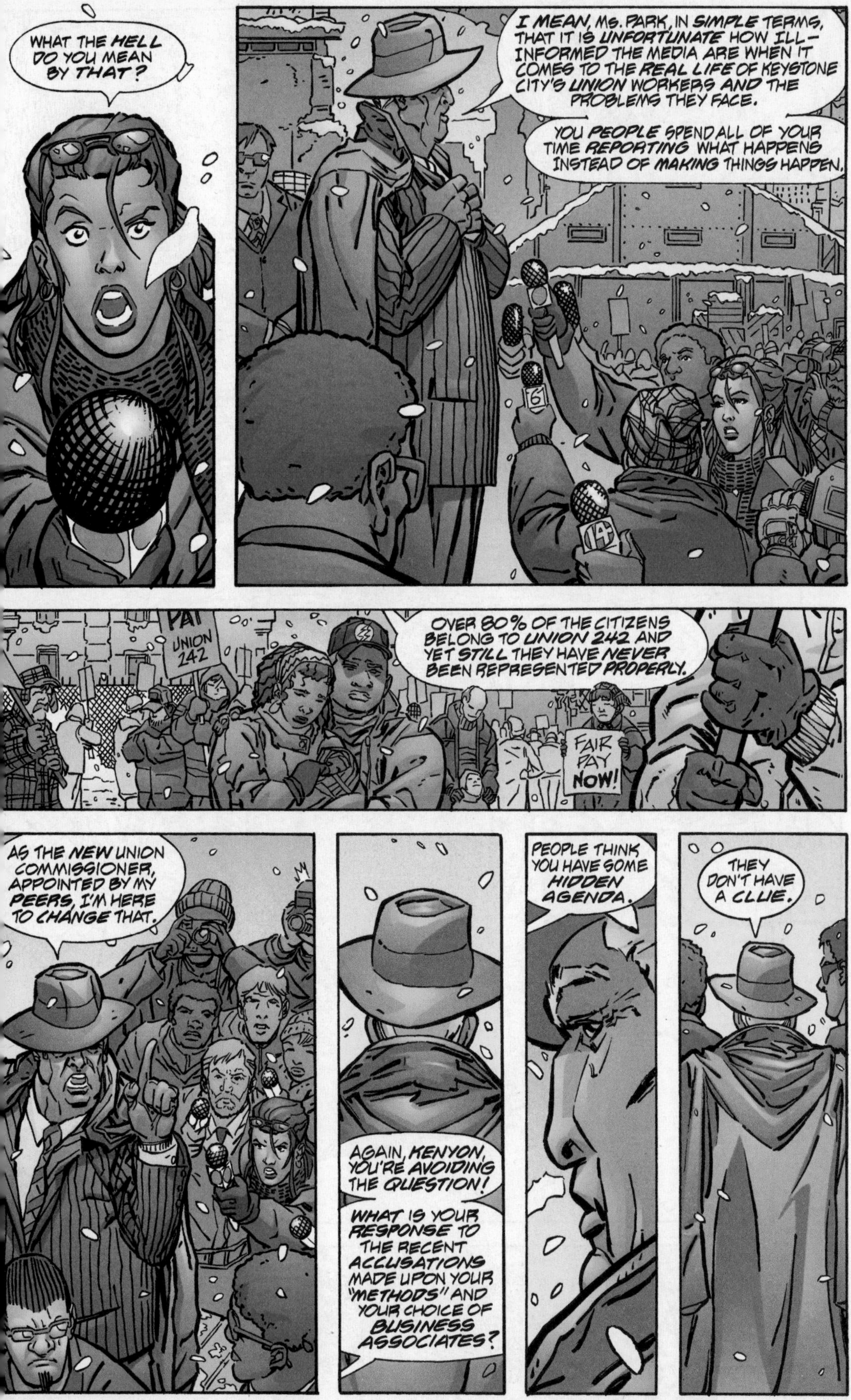
WHAT THE HELL DO YOU MEAN BY THAT?
I MEAN, Ms. PARK, IN SIMPLE TERMS, THAT IT IS UNFORTUNATE HOW ILL-INFORMED THE MEDIA ARE WHEN IT COMES TO THE REAL LIFE OF KEYSTONE CITY'S UNION WORKERS AND THE PROBLEMS THEY FACE.
YOU PEOPLE SPEND ALL OF YOUR TIME REPORTING WHAT HAPPENS INSTEAD OF MAKING THINGS HAPPEN.
61
14
PAY
UNION 242
OVER 80% OF THE CITIZENS BELONG TO UNION 242 AND YET STILL THEY HAVE NEVER BEEN REPRESENTED PROPERLY.
FAIR PAY NOW!
AS THE NEW UNION COMMISSIONER, APPOINTED BY MY PEERS, I'M HERE TO CHANGE THAT.
AGAIN, KENYON, YOU'RE AVOIDING THE QUESTION!
WHAT IS YOUR RESPONSE TO THE RECENT ACCUSATIONS MADE UPON YOUR "METHODS" AND YOUR CHOICE OF BUSINESS ASSOCIATES?
PEOPLE THINK YOU HAVE SOME HIDDEN AGENDA.
THEY DON'T HAVE A CLUE.

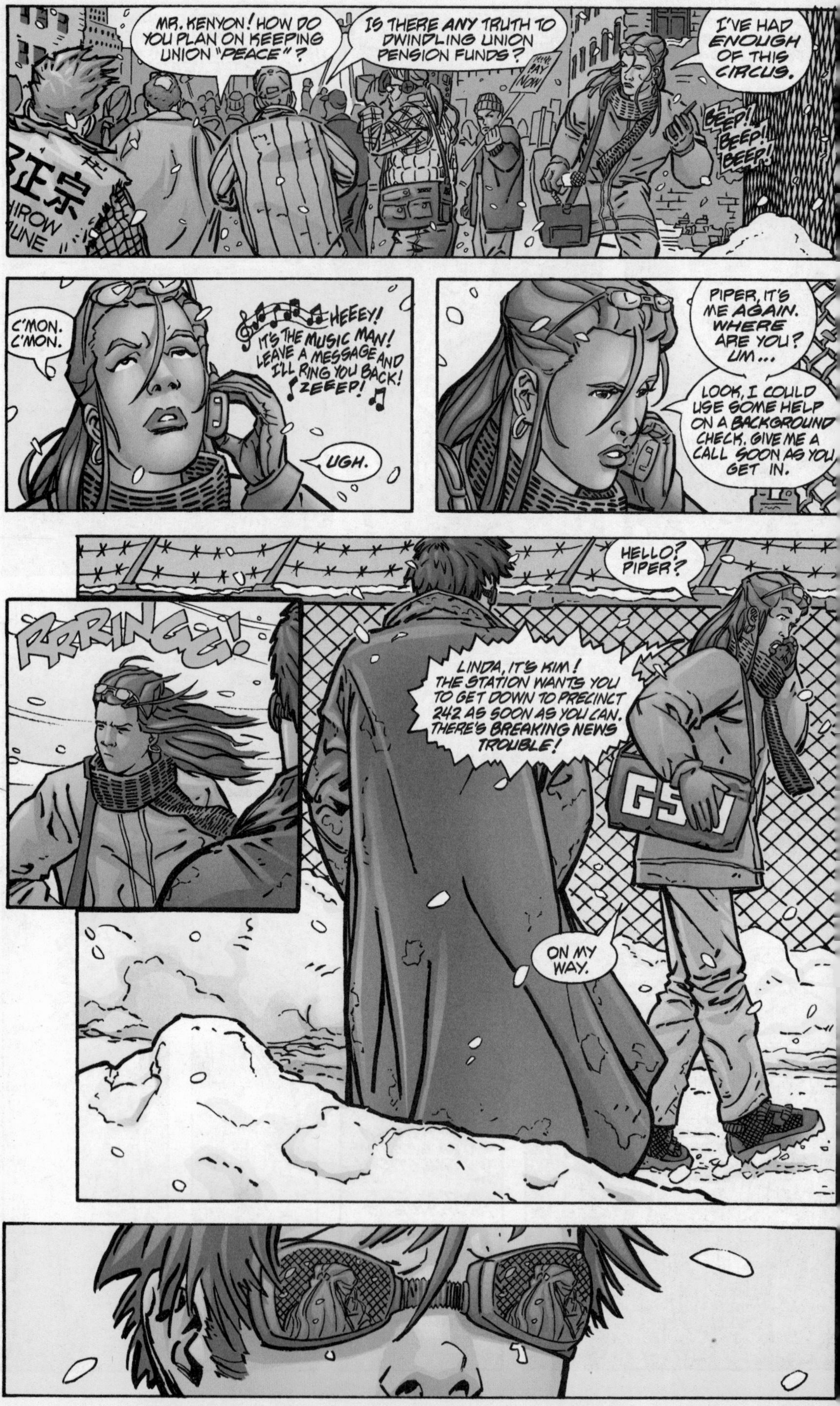

MR. KENYON! HOW DO YOU PLAN ON KEEPING UNION "PEACE"?
IS THERE ANY TRUTH TO DWINDLING UNION PENSION FUNDS?
PAY NOW
I'VE HAD ENOUGH OF THIS CIRCUS.
BEEP! BEEP! BEEP!
C'MON. C'MON.
HEEEY! IT'S THE MUSIC MAN! LEAVE A MESSAGE AND I'LL RING YOU BACK! ZEEEP!
UGH.
PIPER, IT'S ME AGAIN. WHERE ARE YOU? UM...
LOOK, I COULD USE SOME HELP ON A BACKGROUND CHECK. GIVE ME A CALL SOON AS YOU GET IN.
HELLO? PIPER?
RRRINGG!
LINDA, IT'S KIM! THE STATION WANTS YOU TO GET DOWN TO PRECINCT 242 AS SOON AS YOU CAN. THERE'S BREAKING NEWS TROUBLE!
GSN
ON MY WAY.

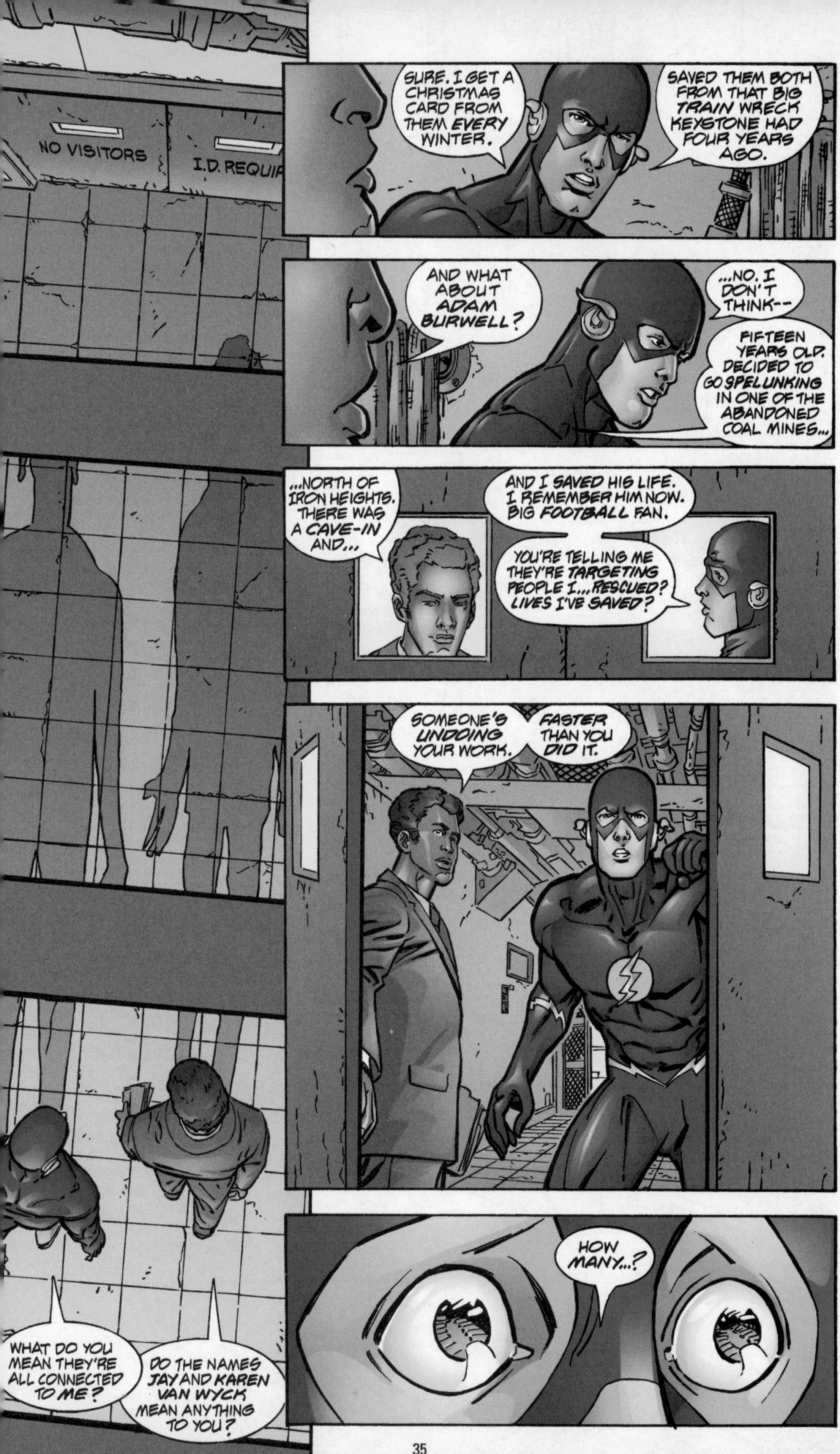
NO VISITORS
I.D. REQUIR
SURE. I GET A CHRISTMAS CARD FROM THEM EVERY WINTER.
SAVED THEM BOTH FROM THAT BIG TRAIN WRECK KEYSTONE HAD FOUR YEARS AGO.
AND WHAT ABOUT ADAM BURWELL?
...NO. I DON'T THINK--
FIFTEEN YEARS OLD. DECIDED TO GO SPELUNKING IN ONE OF THE ABANDONED COAL MINES...
...NORTH OF IRON HEIGHTS. THERE WAS A CAVE-IN AND...
AND I SAVED HIS LIFE. I REMEMBER HIM NOW. BIG FOOTBALL FAN.
YOU'RE TELLING ME THEY'RE TARGETING PEOPLE I... RESCUED? LIVES I'VE SAVED?
SOMEONE'S UNDOING YOUR WORK.
FASTER THAN YOU DID IT.
HOW MANY...?
WHAT DO YOU MEAN THEY'RE ALL CONNECTED TO ME?
DO THE NAMES JAY AND KAREN VAN WYCK MEAN ANYTHING TO YOU?

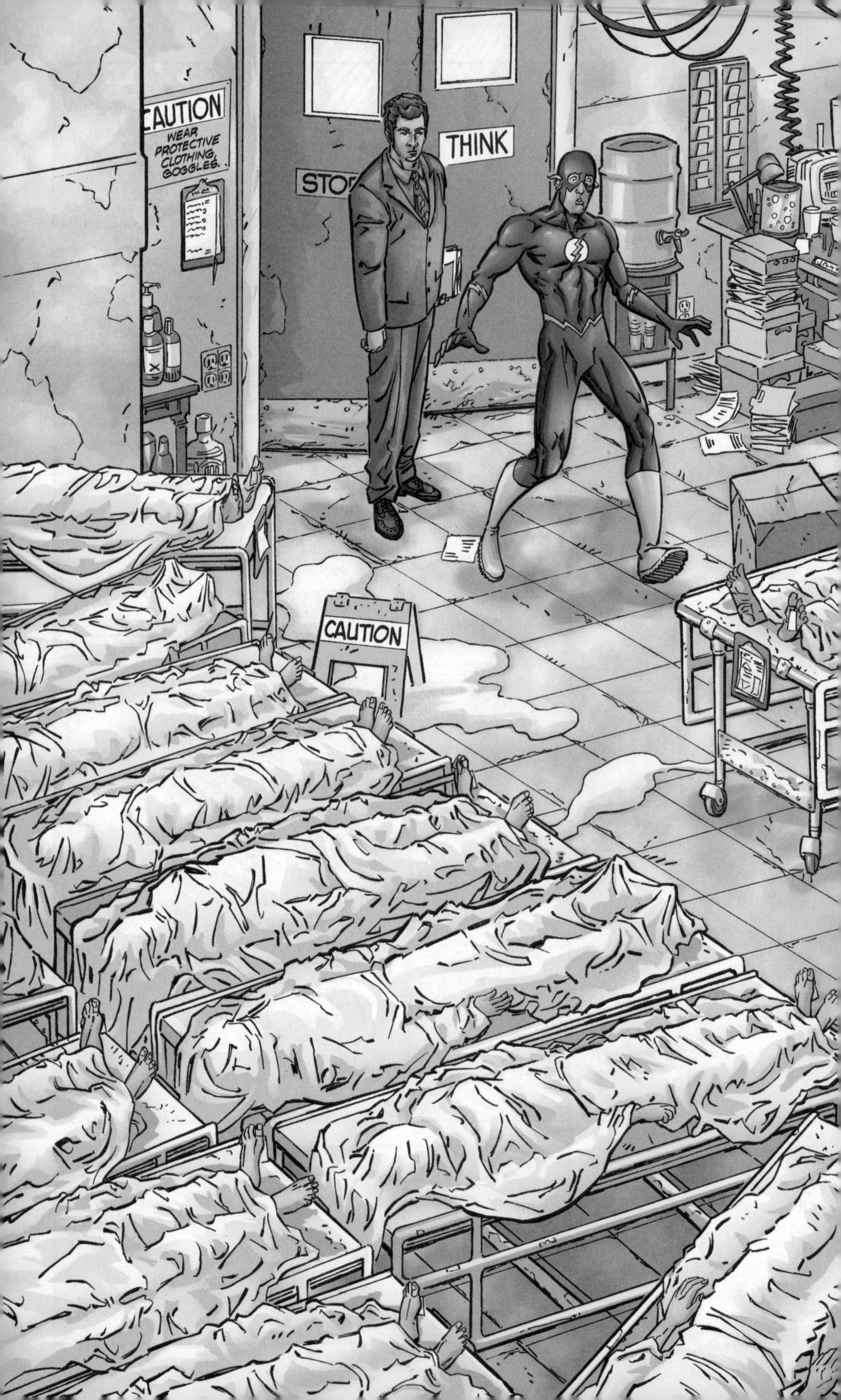
CAUTION
WEAR PROTECTIVE CLOTHING, GOGGLES.
THINK
CAUTION

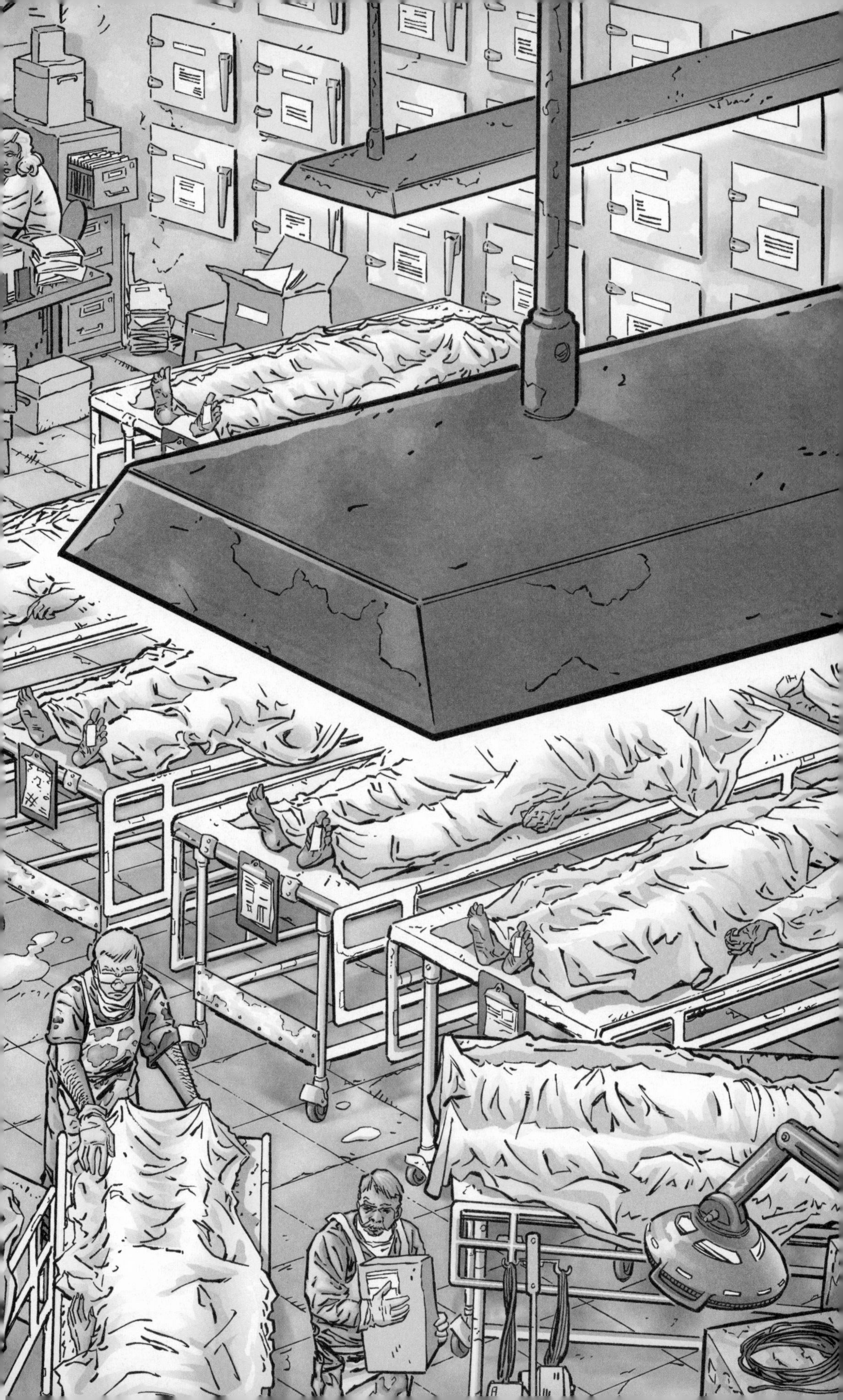

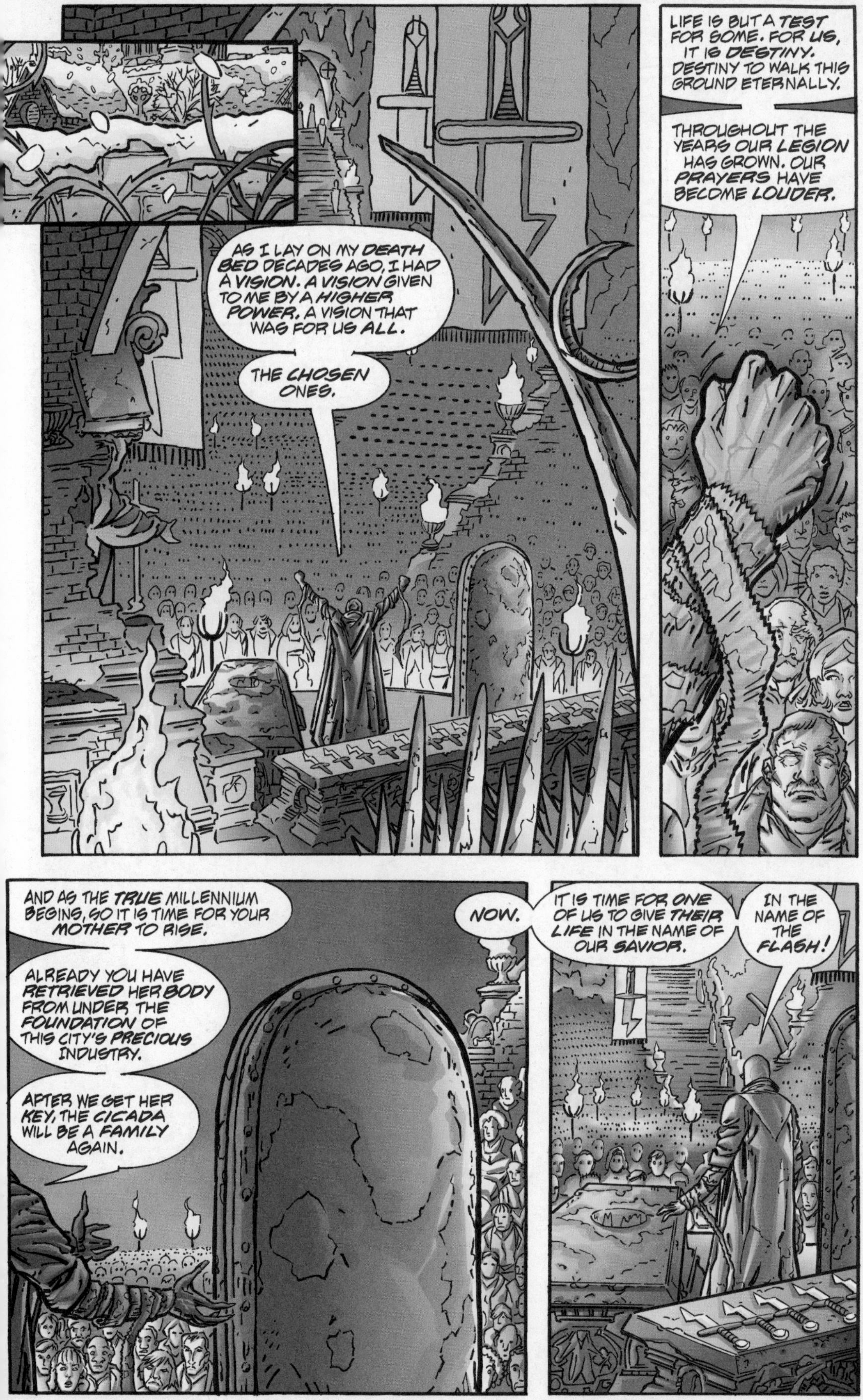

AS I LAY ON MY DEATH BED DECADES AGO, I HAD A VISION. A VISION GIVEN TO ME BY A HIGHER POWER. A VISION THAT WAS FOR US ALL.
THE CHOSEN ONES.
LIFE IS BUT A TEST FOR SOME. FOR US, IT IS DESTINY. DESTINY TO WALK THIS GROUND ETERNALLY.
THROUGHOUT THE YEARS OUR LEGION HAS GROWN. OUR PRAYERS HAVE BECOME LOUDER.
AND AS THE TRUE MILLENNIUM BEGINS, SO IT IS TIME FOR YOUR MOTHER TO RISE.
ALREADY YOU HAVE RETRIEVED HER BODY FROM UNDER THE FOUNDATION OF THIS CITY'S PRECIOUS INDUSTRY.
AFTER WE GET HER KEY, THE CICADA WILL BE A FAMILY AGAIN.
NOW.
IT IS TIME FOR ONE OF US TO GIVE THEIR LIFE IN THE NAME OF OUR SAVIOR.
IN THE NAME OF THE FLASH!

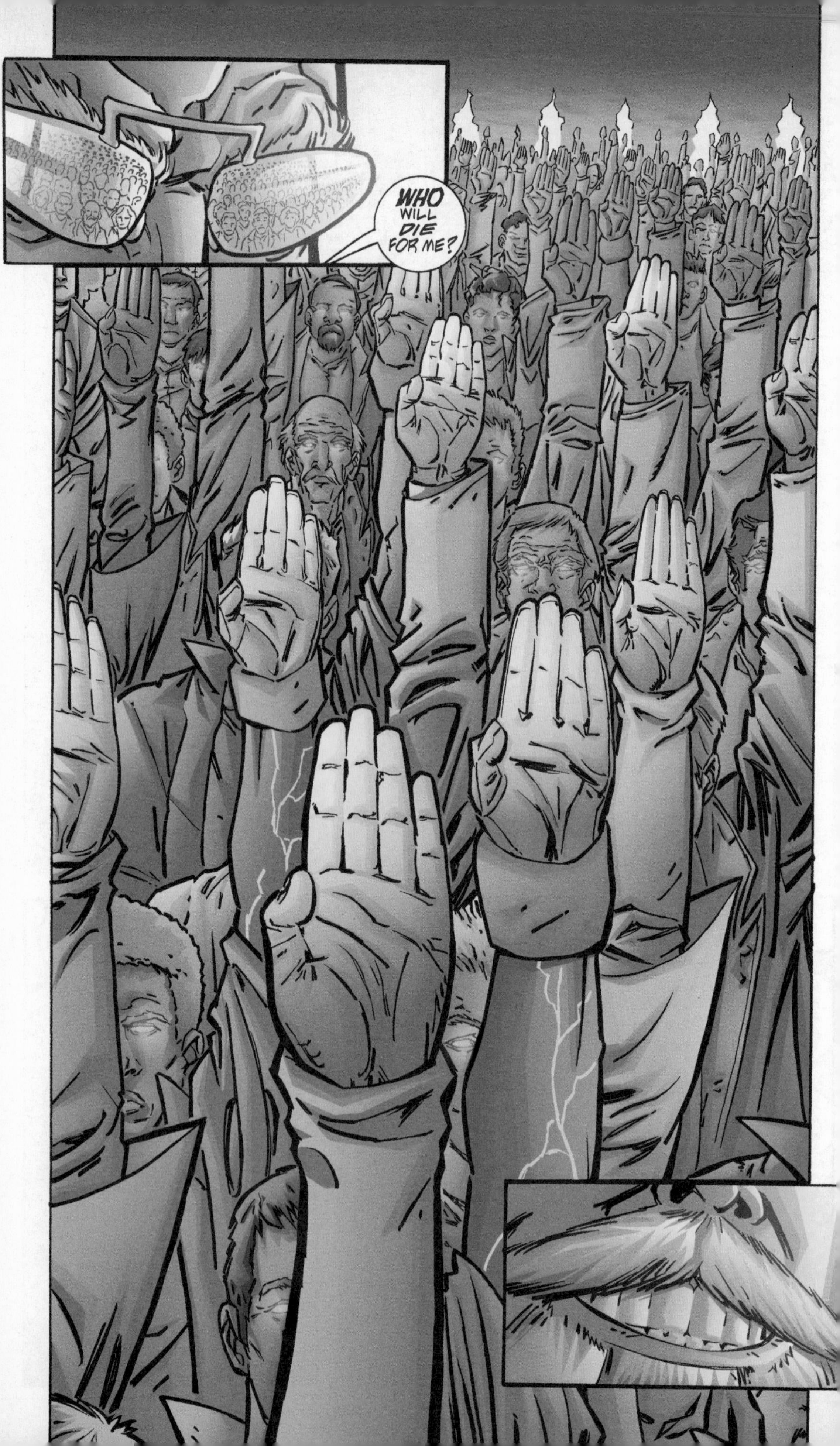
WHO WILL DIE FOR ME?

IT TAKES ME TEN MINUTES TO CONVINCE DETECTIVE MORILLO TO LET ME HELP THE PRECINCT OUT BY COLLECTING EVIDENCE AT THE CRIME SCENES.

MOSTLY, I THINK, BECAUSE IT WASN'T HIS IDEA.

I READ THE HANDBOOK ON FORENSIC SCIENCE IN ABOUT TEN SECONDS. I HAVE TO READ IT THREE TIMES MORE TO GET IT TO REGISTER.

IT'S LIKE CRAMMING FOR THOSE SCHOOL EXAMS. I LEARN IT QUICK, AND FORGET IT QUICKER. BUT IT SHOULD GET ME THROUGH THIS LIST. OVER 100 PEOPLE...

NO ONE ELSE IS GOING TO DIE EVEN IF I HAVE TO--

OH, NO.

NO.

Anne Conson
254 Knickerbocker Dr.
West Nyack, Keystone

Officer Julie Jackam 909 8th street,
Apartment 110, Downtown Keystone.

Howard Hoganith, 238th street
Downtown Keystone

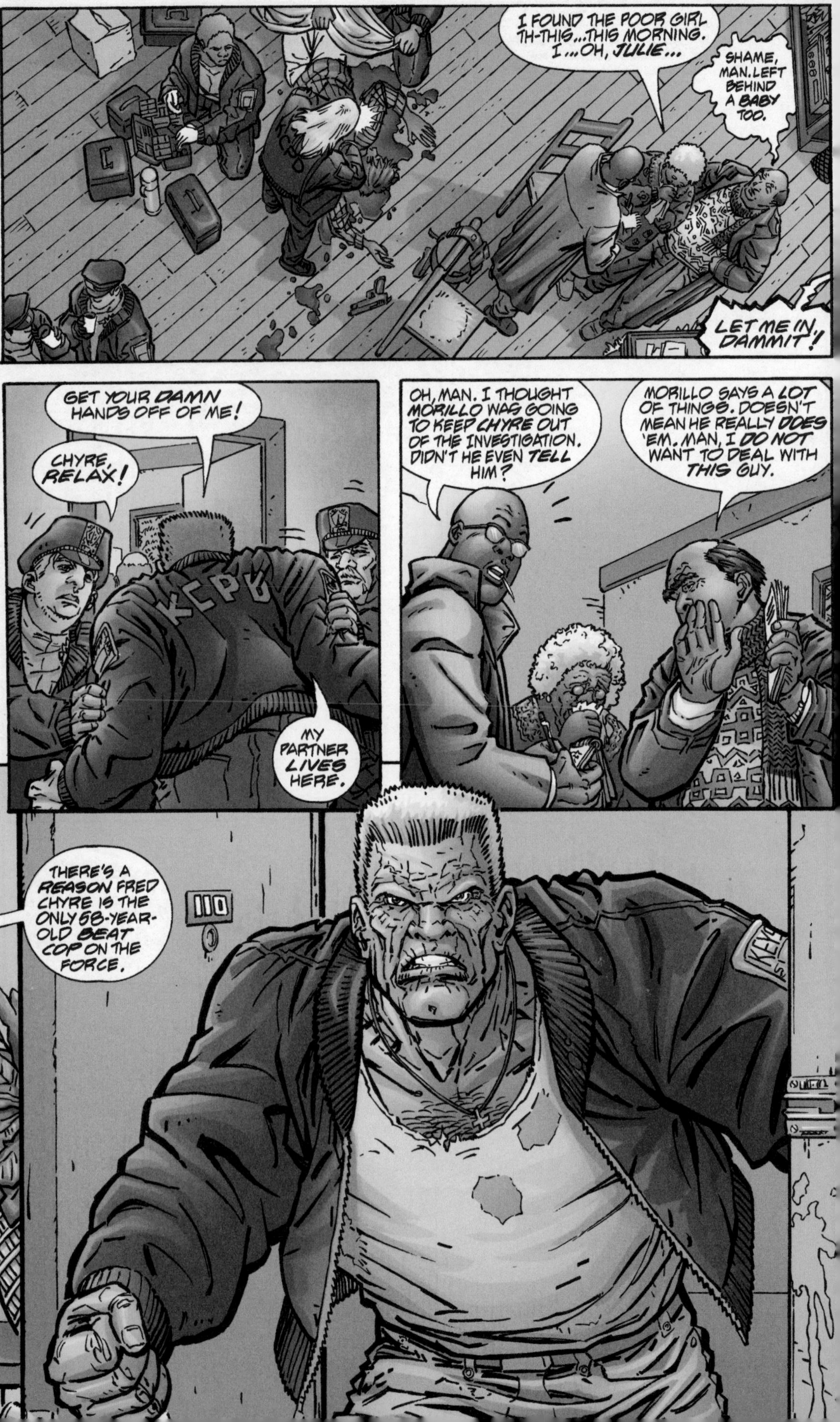

I FOUND THE POOR GIRL TH-THIS...THIS MORNING. I...OH, JULIE...
SHAME, MAN. LEFT BEHIND A BABY TOO.
LET ME IN, DAMMIT!
GET YOUR DAMN HANDS OFF OF ME!
CHYRE, RELAX!
KCPD
MY PARTNER LIVES HERE.
OH, MAN. I THOUGHT MORILLO WAS GOING TO KEEP CHYRE OUT OF THE INVESTIGATION. DIDN'T HE EVEN TELL HIM?
MORILLO SAYS A LOT OF THINGS. DOESN'T MEAN HE REALLY DOES 'EM. MAN, I DO NOT WANT TO DEAL WITH THIS GUY.
THERE'S A REASON FRED CHYRE IS THE ONLY 58-YEAR-OLD BEAT COP ON THE FORCE.
110

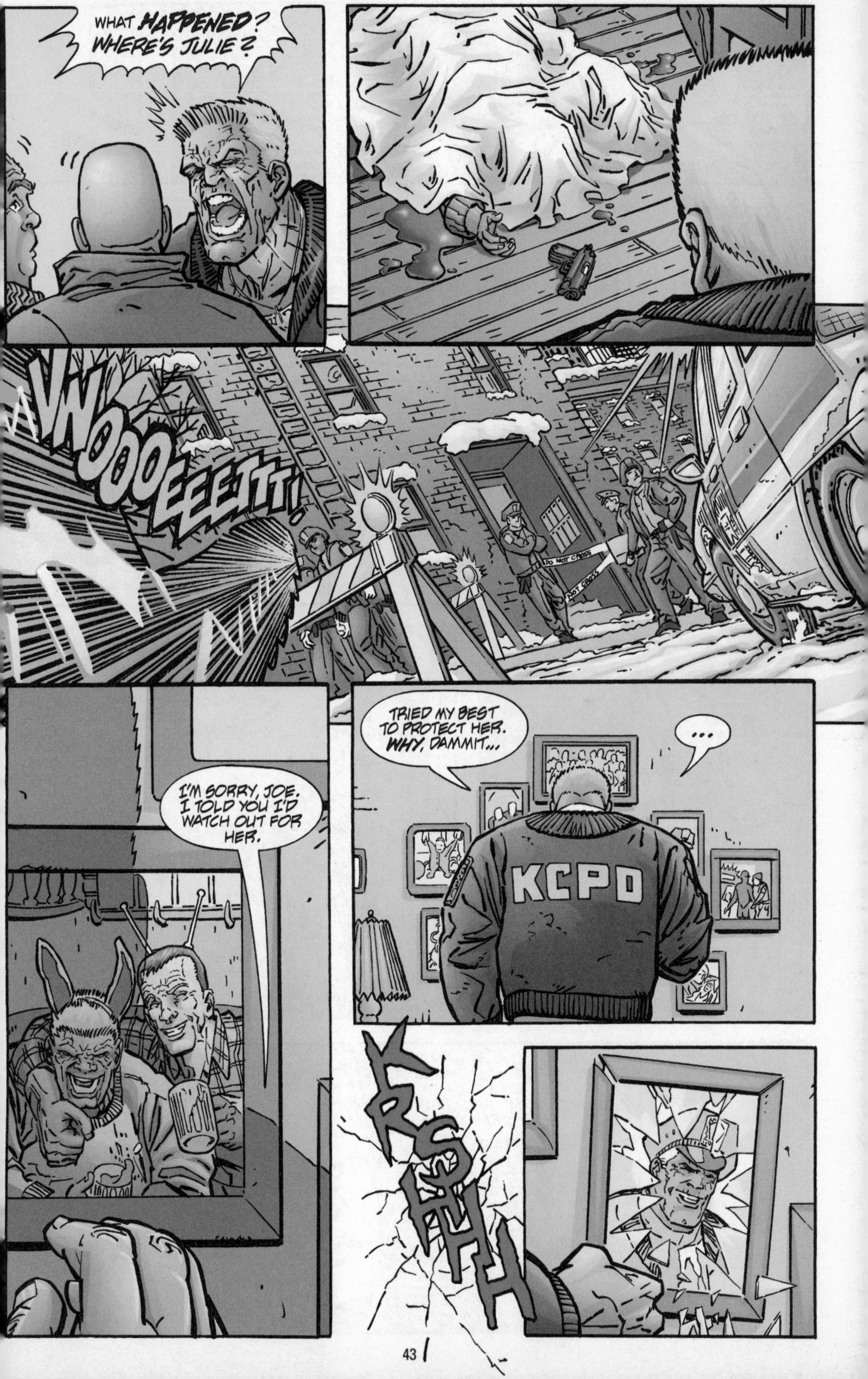

WHAT HAPPENED? WHERE'S JULIE?
VWOOOEEEITTT!
DO NOT CROSS
TRIED MY BEST TO PROTECT HER. WHY, DAMMIT...
...
I'M SORRY, JOE. I TOLD YOU I'D WATCH OUT FOR HER.
KCPD
KRSHHH

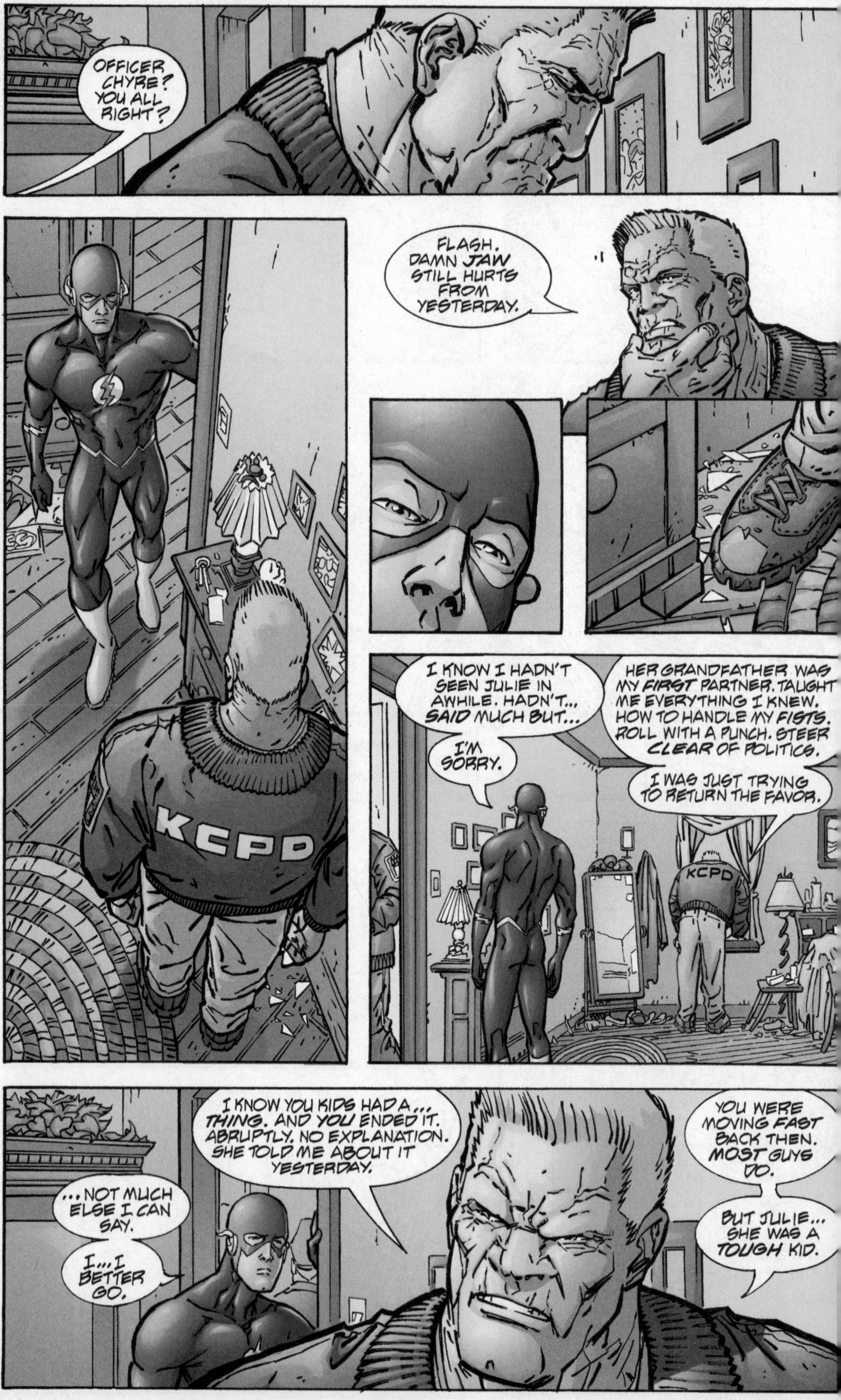
OFFICER CHYRE? YOU ALL RIGHT?
FLASH. DAMN JAW STILL HURTS FROM YESTERDAY.
I KNOW I HADN'T SEEN JULIE IN AWHILE. HADN'T... SAID MUCH BUT...
I'M SORRY.
HER GRANDFATHER WAS MY FIRST PARTNER. TAUGHT ME EVERYTHING I KNEW. HOW TO HANDLE MY FISTS. ROLL WITH A PUNCH. STEER CLEAR OF POLITICS.
I WAS JUST TRYING TO RETURN THE FAVOR.
KCPD
...NOT MUCH ELSE I CAN SAY.
I... I BETTER GO.
I KNOW YOU KIDS HAD A... THING. AND YOU ENDED IT. ABRUPTLY. NO EXPLANATION. SHE TOLD ME ABOUT IT YESTERDAY.
YOU WERE MOVING FAST BACK THEN. MOST GUYS DO.
BUT JULIE... SHE WAS A TOUGH KID.

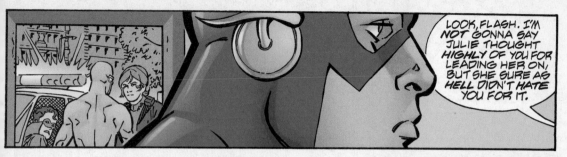

LOOK, FLASH. I'M *NOT* GONNA SAY JULIE THOUGHT *HIGHLY* OF YOU FOR LEADING HER ON, BUT SHE SURE AS HELL DIDN'T *HATE* YOU FOR IT.

IF IT'S *ONE* THING I'VE LEARNED IT'S YA GOTTA BE *UPFRONT* WITH WOMEN. JUST LIKE YOU WANT THEM TO BE *UPFRONT* WITH YOU.

YOU CAN'T *HIDE* YOUR FEELINGS.

THANKS. THERE'S SOMEONE I'VE GOT TO TALK TO.

AND THEN I *PROMISE* YOU. I'M GOING TO *FIND* WHO DID THIS--

--AND WE'LL *NAIL* THEM.

CHYRE!

YOU KNOW HOW WE CAN CONTACT THE *FATHER?* THERE'S NO RECORD ON FILE.

ZILCH!

WAAAWA!

GOT... NO IDEA.

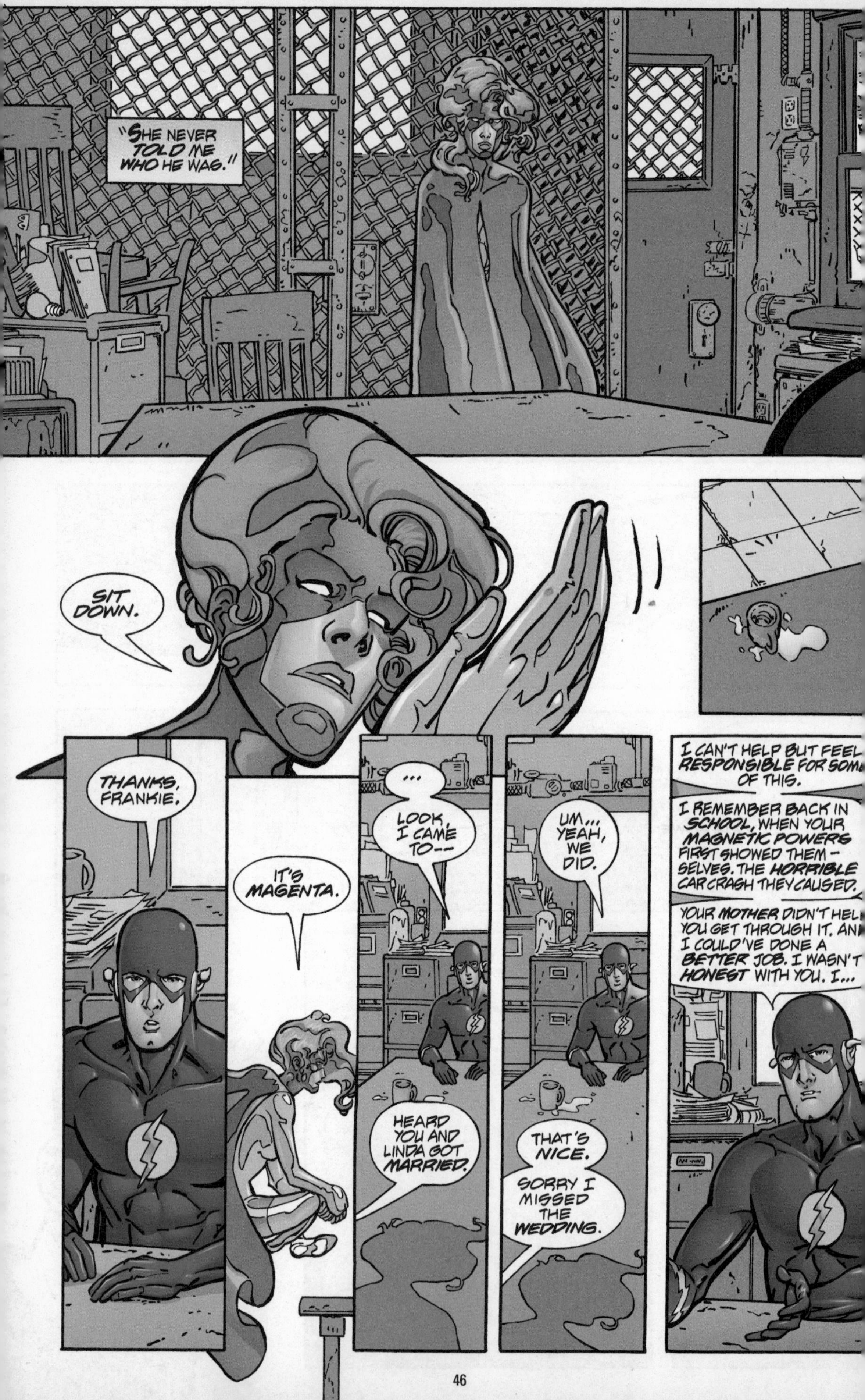
"SHE NEVER TOLD ME WHO HE WAS."
SIT DOWN.
THANKS, FRANKIE.
IT'S MAGENTA.
...
LOOK, I CAME TO--
HEARD YOU AND LINDA GOT MARRIED.
UM... YEAH, WE DID.
THAT'S NICE.
SORRY I MISSED THE WEDDING.
I CAN'T HELP BUT FEEL RESPONSIBLE FOR SOM OF THIS.
I REMEMBER BACK IN SCHOOL, WHEN YOUR MAGNETIC POWERS FIRST SHOWED THEM-SELVES. THE HORRIBLE CAR CRASH THEY CAUSED.
YOUR MOTHER DIDN'T HEL YOU GET THROUGH IT. AN I COULD'VE DONE A BETTER JOB. I WASN'T HONEST WITH YOU. I...

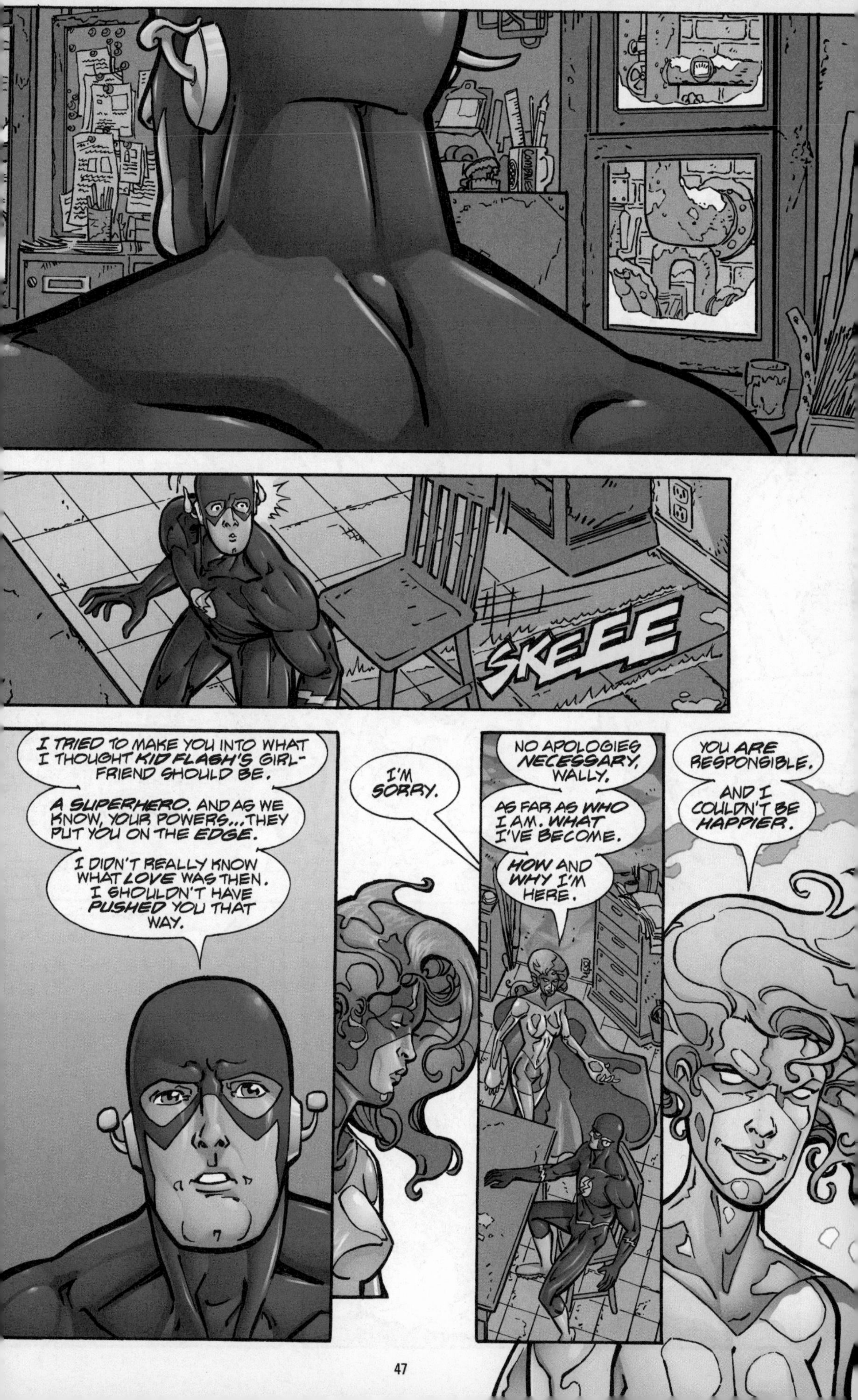
SKEEE
I TRIED TO MAKE YOU INTO WHAT I THOUGHT KID FLASH'S GIRL-FRIEND SHOULD BE.
A SUPERHERO. AND AS WE KNOW, YOUR POWERS... THEY PUT YOU ON THE EDGE.
I DIDN'T REALLY KNOW WHAT LOVE WAS THEN. I SHOULDN'T HAVE PUSHED YOU THAT WAY.
I'M SORRY.
NO APOLOGIES NECESSARY, WALLY.
AS FAR AS WHO I AM. WHAT I'VE BECOME.
HOW AND WHY I'M HERE.
YOU ARE RESPONSIBLE.
AND I COULDN'T BE HAPPIER.

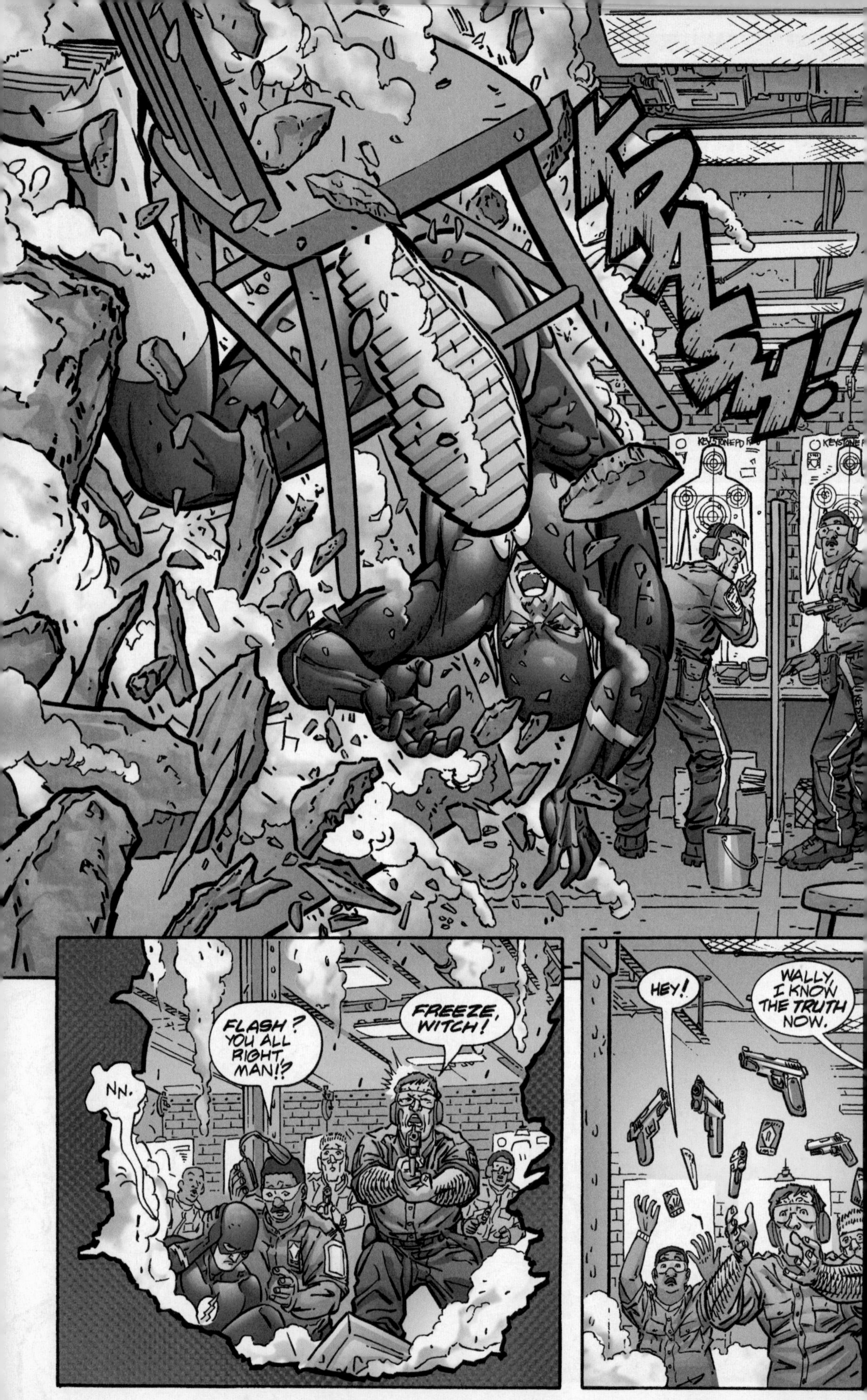
KRASH!
KEYSTONE PD
FLASH? YOU ALL RIGHT, MAN!?
FREEZE, WITCH!
NN.
HEY!
WALLY, I KNOW THE TRUTH NOW.

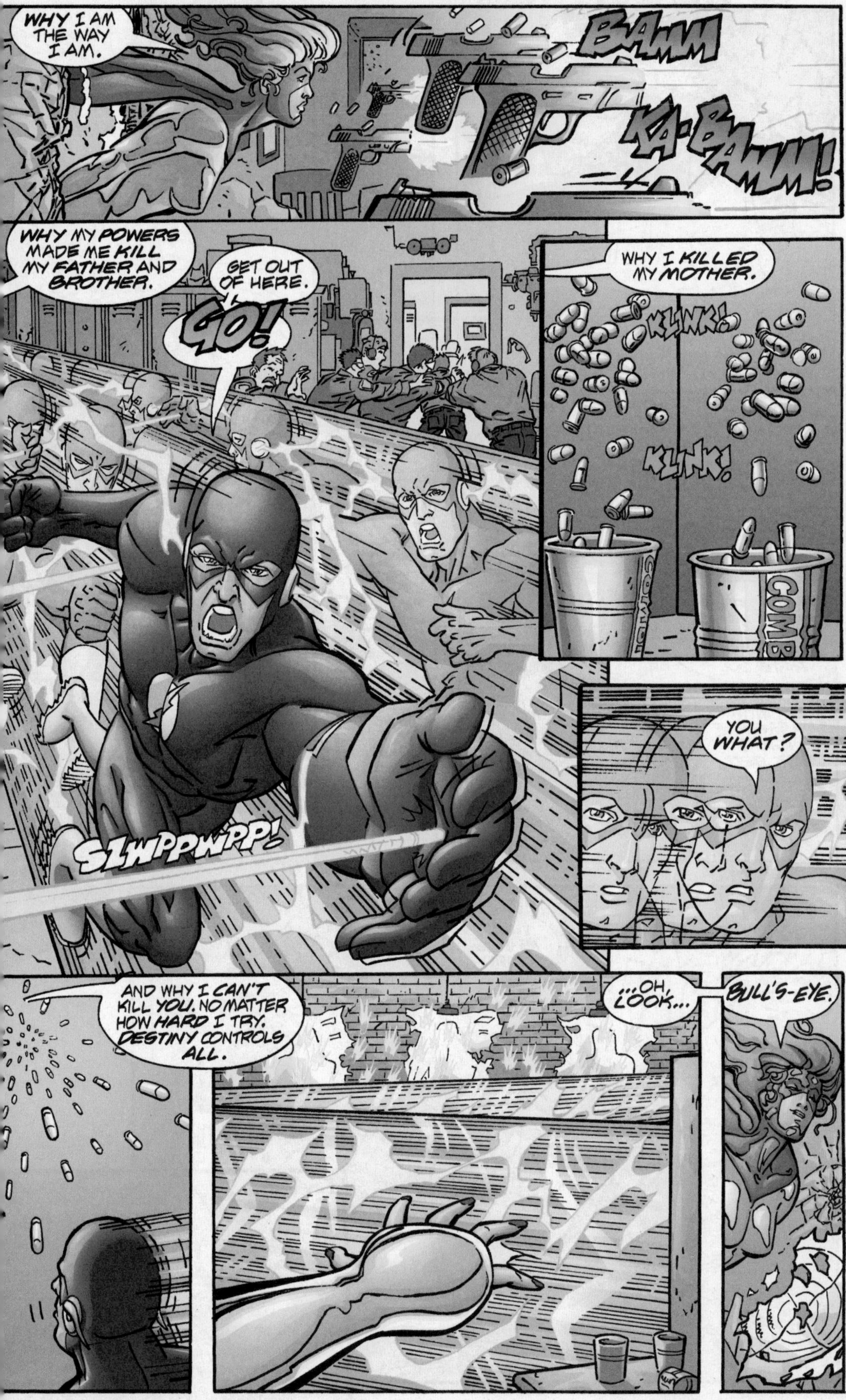

WHY I AM THE WAY I AM.
BAMM
KA-BAMM!
WHY MY POWERS MADE ME KILL MY FATHER AND BROTHER.
GET OUT OF HERE.
GO!
WHY I KILLED MY MOTHER.
KLINK!
KLINK!
SIWPPWPP!
YOU WHAT?
AND WHY I CAN'T KILL YOU. NO MATTER HOW HARD I TRY. DESTINY CONTROLS ALL.
...OH, LOOK...
BULL'S-EYE.

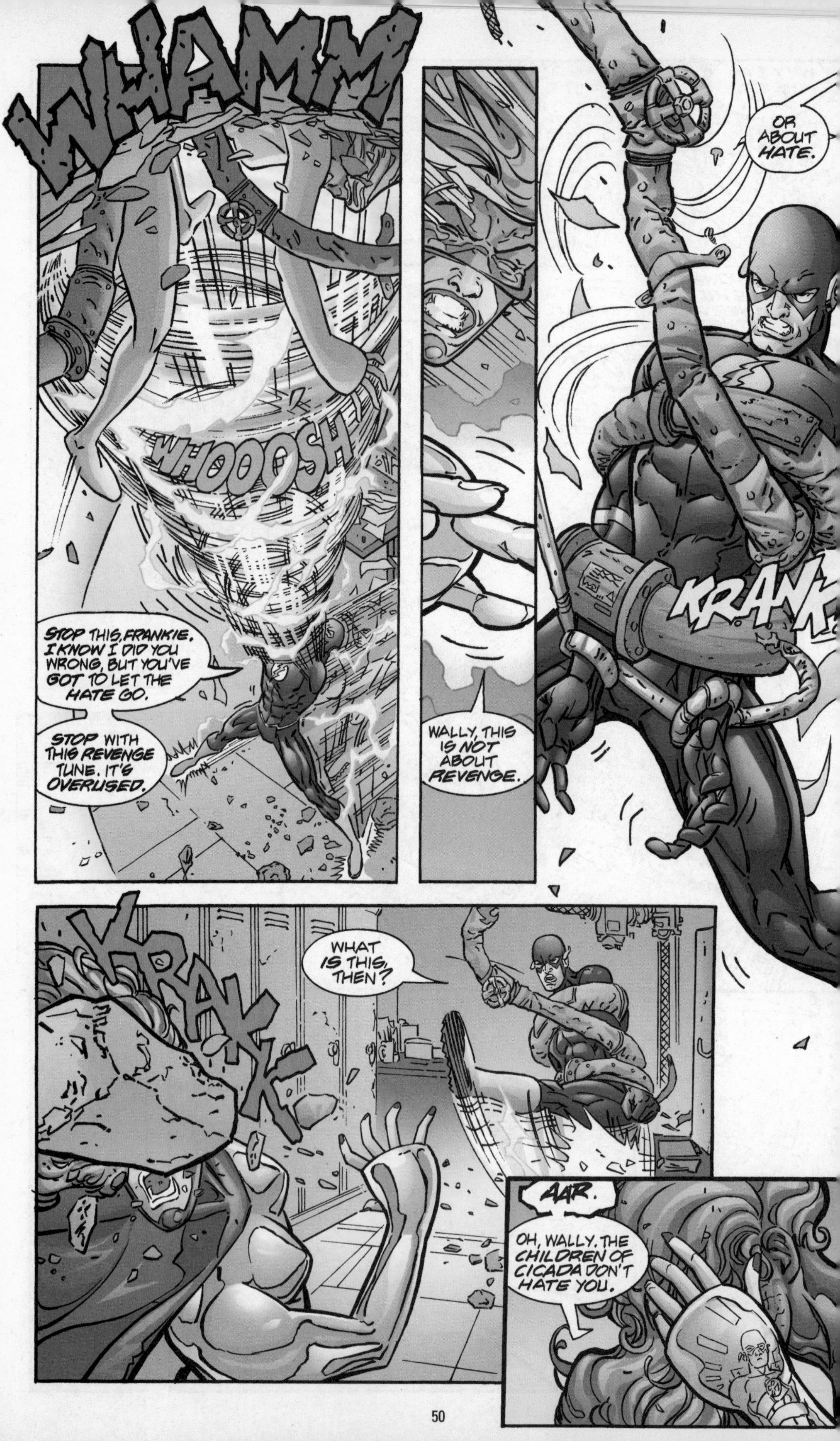

WHAMM
WHOOOSH
STOP THIS, FRANKIE. I KNOW I DID YOU WRONG, BUT YOU'VE GOT TO LET THE HATE GO.
STOP WITH THIS REVENGE TUNE. IT'S OVERUSED.
WALLY, THIS IS NOT ABOUT REVENGE.
OR ABOUT HATE.
KRANK
KRAKK
WHAT IS THIS, THEN?
AAR.
OH, WALLY. THE CHILDREN OF CICADA DON'T HATE YOU.

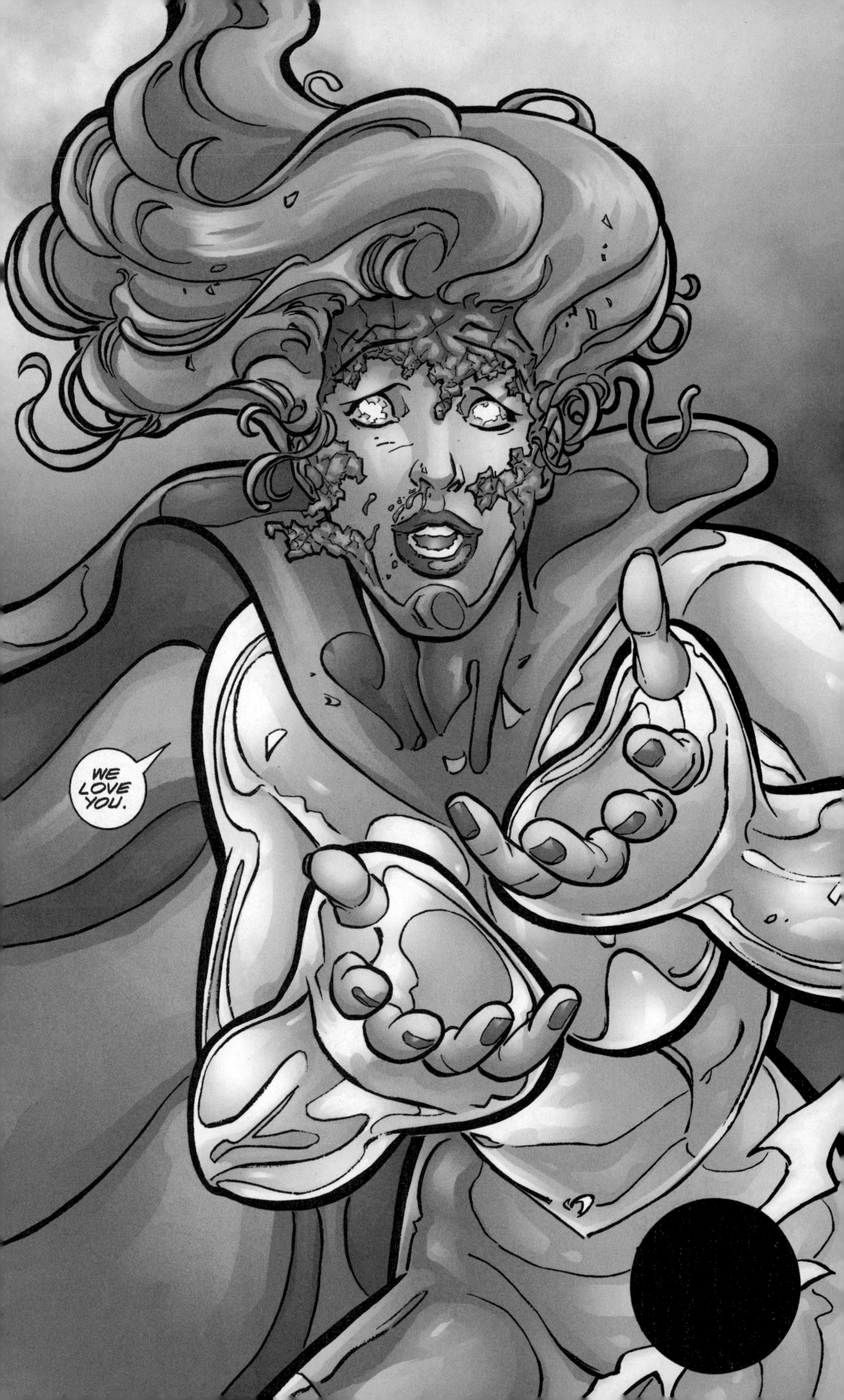
WE LOVE YOU.

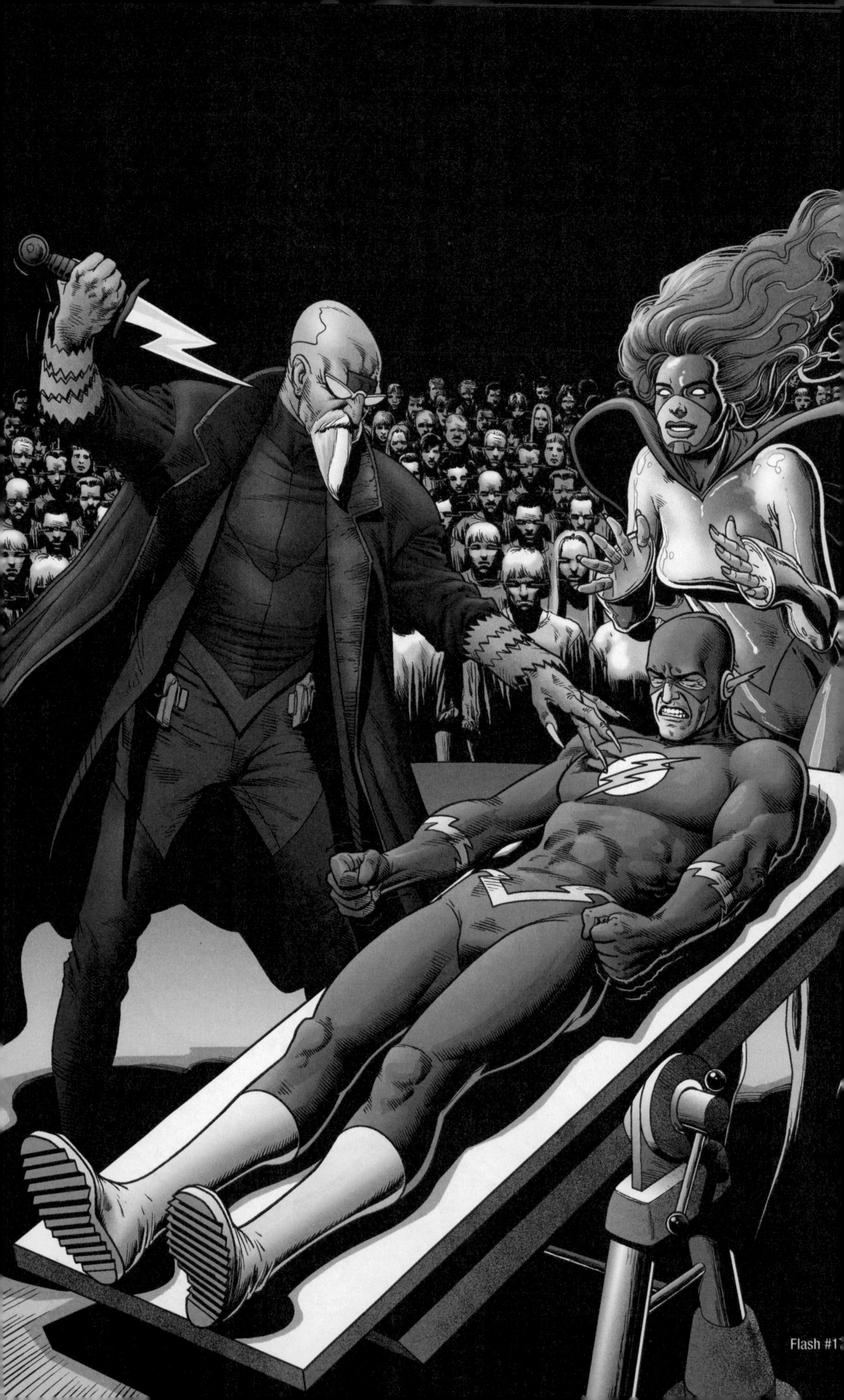

Flash #11

YEAH, FLASH IS HERE. JUST WENT TO TALK TO SOMEONE IN LOCK-UP.

NO, ALL WE'VE REALLY GOT IS SOME KIND OF DEAD *BUG*. NO BIG LEADS YE--

FLASH JUST BROUGHT IN EVIDENCE FROM OVER 100 CRIME SCENES, WE HAVEN'T HAD TIME TO GO--

DETECTIVE JARED MORILLO

NO, HONEY... LOOK, *YOU* WERE THE ONE THAT WANTED TO GET OUT OF *L.A.*, COME TO THE MIDWE--

YOU GREW UP *HERE*, IT WAS DIFFERENT BACK THEN, *I* KNOW BUT YOU--

DETECTIVE JARED MOR...

HONEY, HOLD ON A SEC.

KAM RRRWWWGG

AMATEURS.

NO, HONEY, I WASN'T TALKING TO YOU. I--

NO, I SWEAR.

HEY, MORILLO!

I'M ON THE *PHONE.* WHAT THE *HELL* DO *YOU* WANT?

53

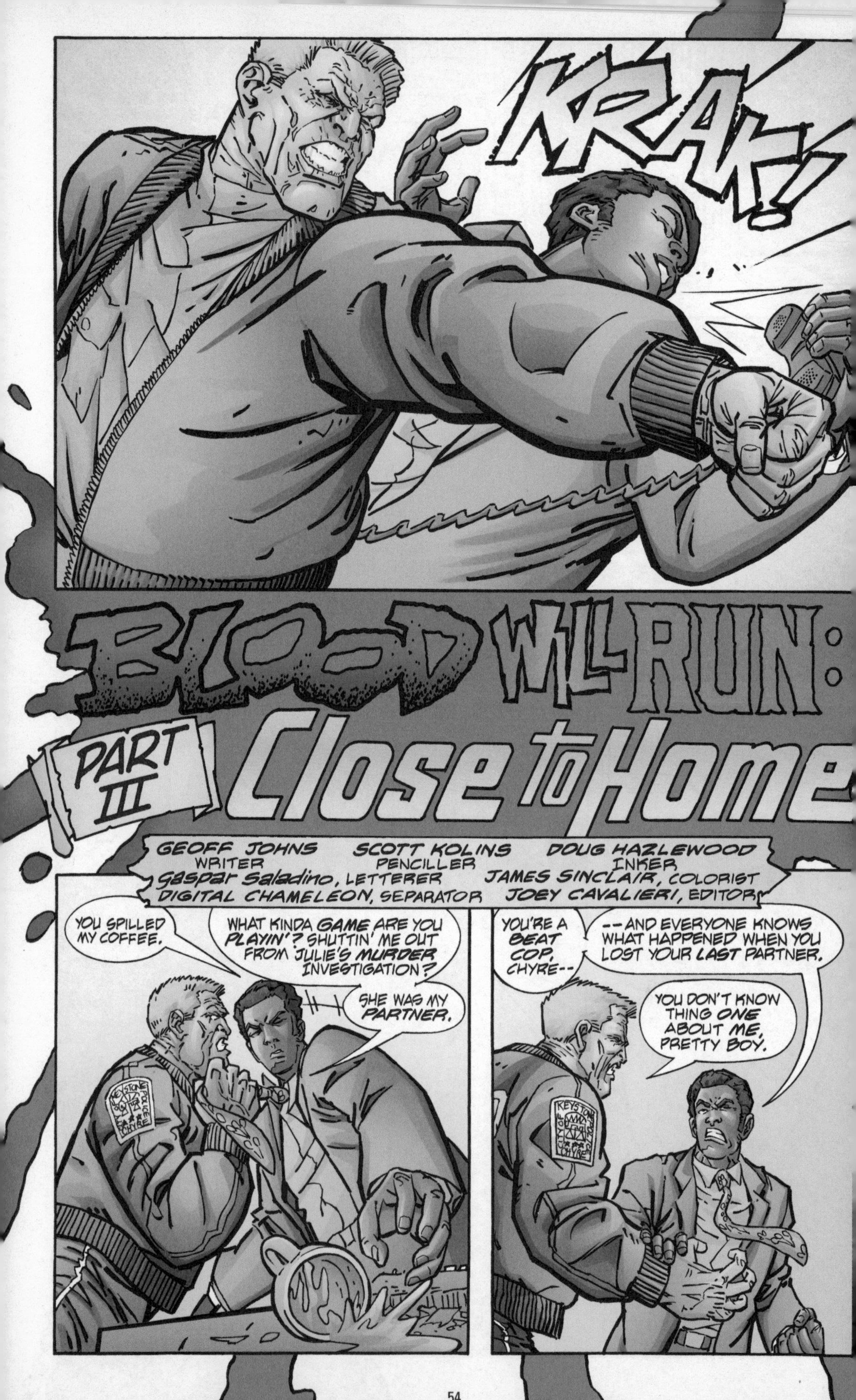
KRAK!
BLOOD WILL RUN:
PART III
Close to Home
GEOFF JOHNS WRITER
SCOTT KOLINS PENCILLER
DOUG HAZLEWOOD INKER
Gaspar Saladino, LETTERER
JAMES SINCLAIR, COLORIST
DIGITAL CHAMELEON, SEPARATOR
JOEY CAVALIERI, EDITOR
YOU SPILLED MY COFFEE.
WHAT KINDA GAME ARE YOU PLAYIN'? SHUTTIN' ME OUT FROM JULIE'S MURDER INVESTIGATION?
SHE WAS MY PARTNER.
YOU'RE A BEAT COP, CHYRE--
--AND EVERYONE KNOWS WHAT HAPPENED WHEN YOU LOST YOUR LAST PARTNER.
YOU DON'T KNOW THING ONE ABOUT ME, PRETTY BOY.

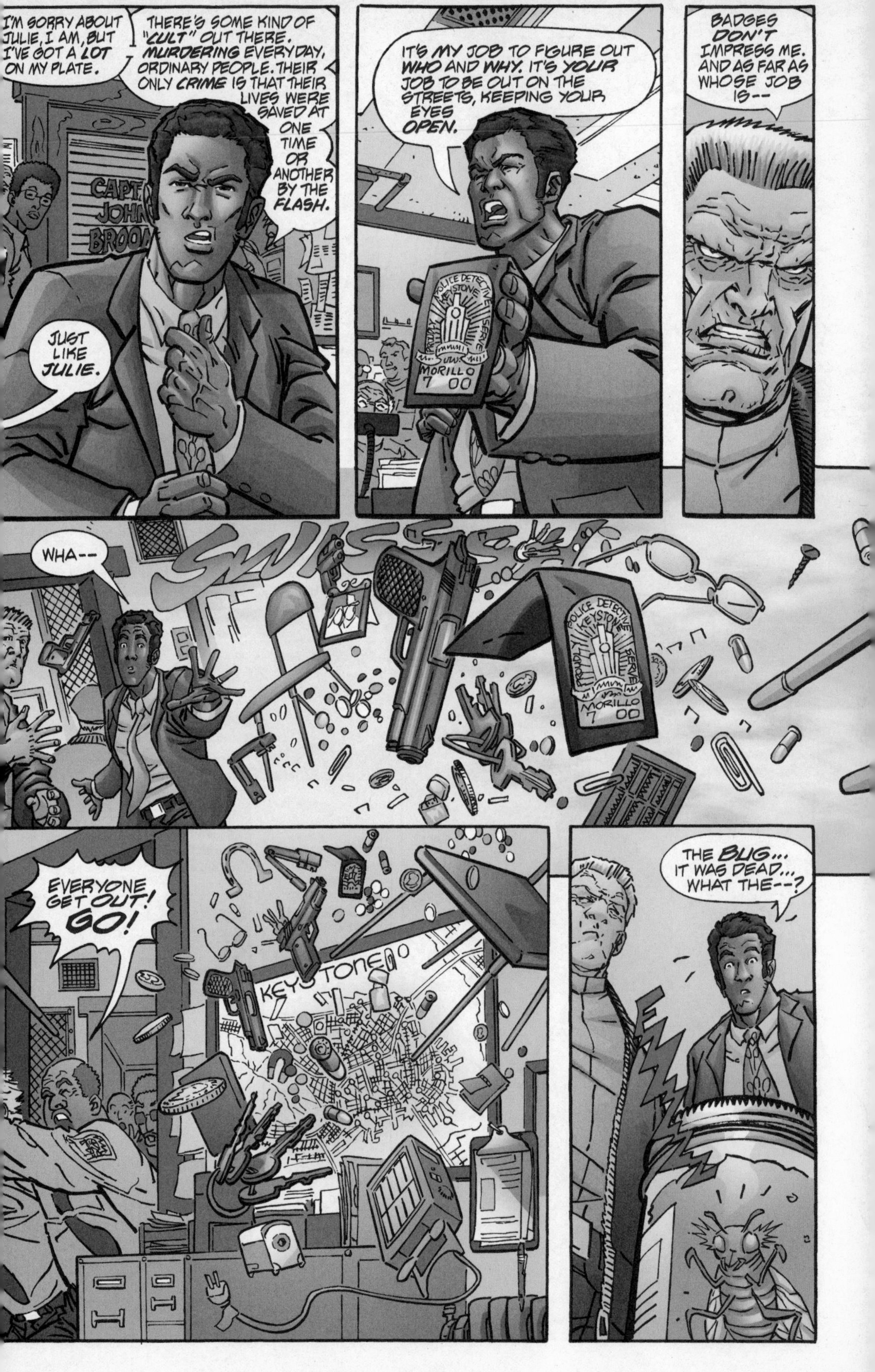

I'M SORRY ABOUT JULIE, I AM, BUT I'VE GOT A LOT ON MY PLATE.
THERE'S SOME KIND OF "CULT" OUT THERE. MURDERING EVERYDAY, ORDINARY PEOPLE. THEIR ONLY CRIME IS THAT THEIR LIVES WERE SAVED AT ONE TIME OR ANOTHER BY THE FLASH.
CAPT. JOHN BROOM
JUST LIKE JULIE.
IT'S MY JOB TO FIGURE OUT WHO AND WHY. IT'S YOUR JOB TO BE OUT ON THE STREETS, KEEPING YOUR EYES OPEN.
POLICE DETECTIVE KEYSTONE PROUDLY SERVE MORILLO 7 00
BADGES DON'T IMPRESS ME. AND AS FAR AS WHOSE JOB IS--
WHA--
SWISSS
POLICE DETECTIVE KEYSTONE PROUDLY SERVE MORILLO 7 00
EVERYONE GET OUT! GO!
KEYSTONE
THE BUG... IT WAS DEAD... WHAT THE--?

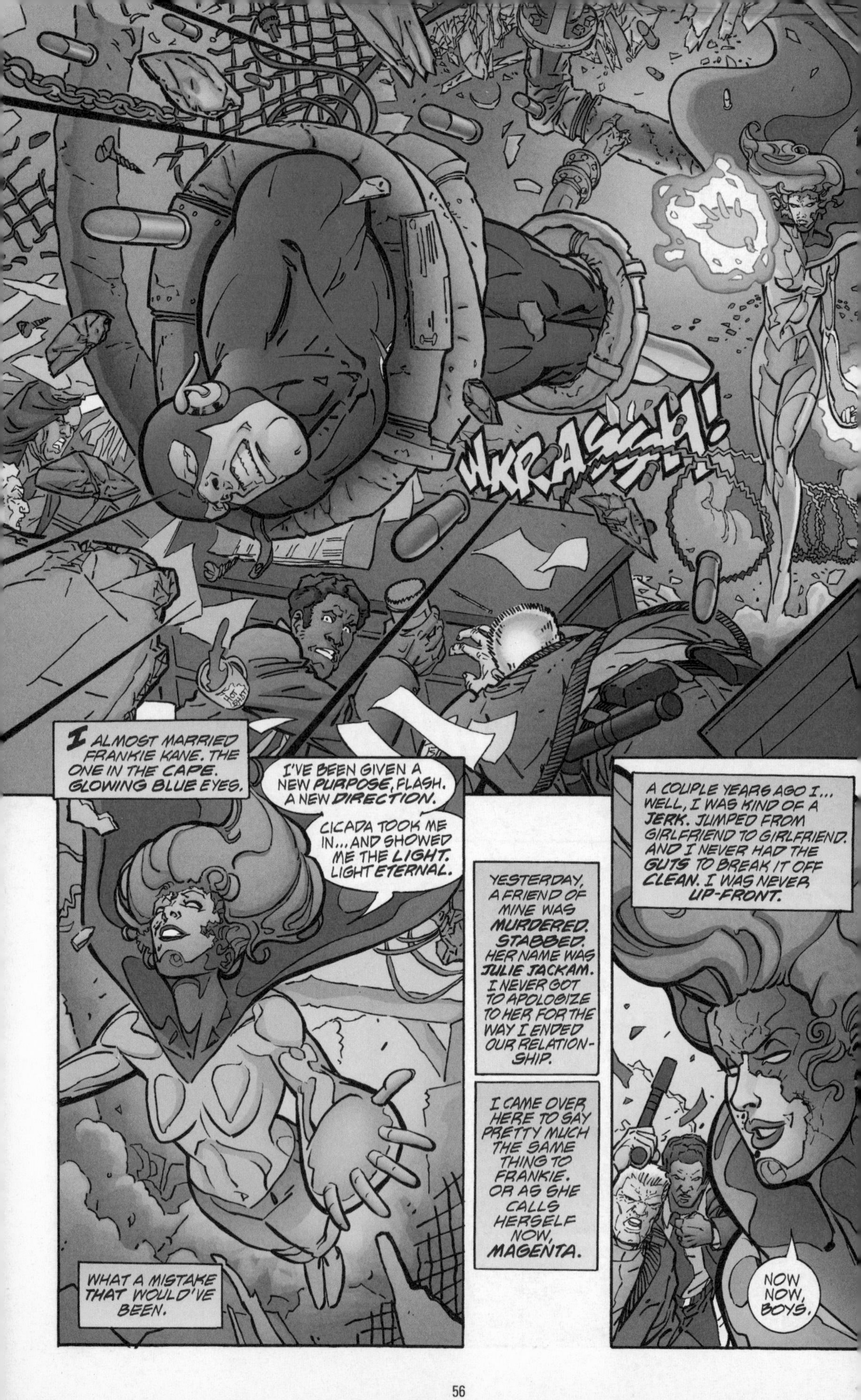

WKRASSH!
I ALMOST MARRIED FRANKIE KANE. THE ONE IN THE CAPE. GLOWING BLUE EYES.
I'VE BEEN GIVEN A NEW PURPOSE, FLASH. A NEW DIRECTION.
CICADA TOOK ME IN... AND SHOWED ME THE LIGHT. LIGHT ETERNAL.
WHAT A MISTAKE THAT WOULD'VE BEEN.
YESTERDAY, A FRIEND OF MINE WAS MURDERED. STABBED. HER NAME WAS JULIE JACKAM. I NEVER GOT TO APOLOGIZE TO HER FOR THE WAY I ENDED OUR RELATION-SHIP.
I CAME OVER HERE TO SAY PRETTY MUCH THE SAME THING TO FRANKIE. OR AS SHE CALLS HERSELF NOW, MAGENTA.
A COUPLE YEARS AGO I... WELL, I WAS KIND OF A JERK. JUMPED FROM GIRLFRIEND TO GIRLFRIEND. AND I NEVER HAD THE GUTS TO BREAK IT OFF CLEAN. I WAS NEVER UP-FRONT.
NOW NOW, BOYS.

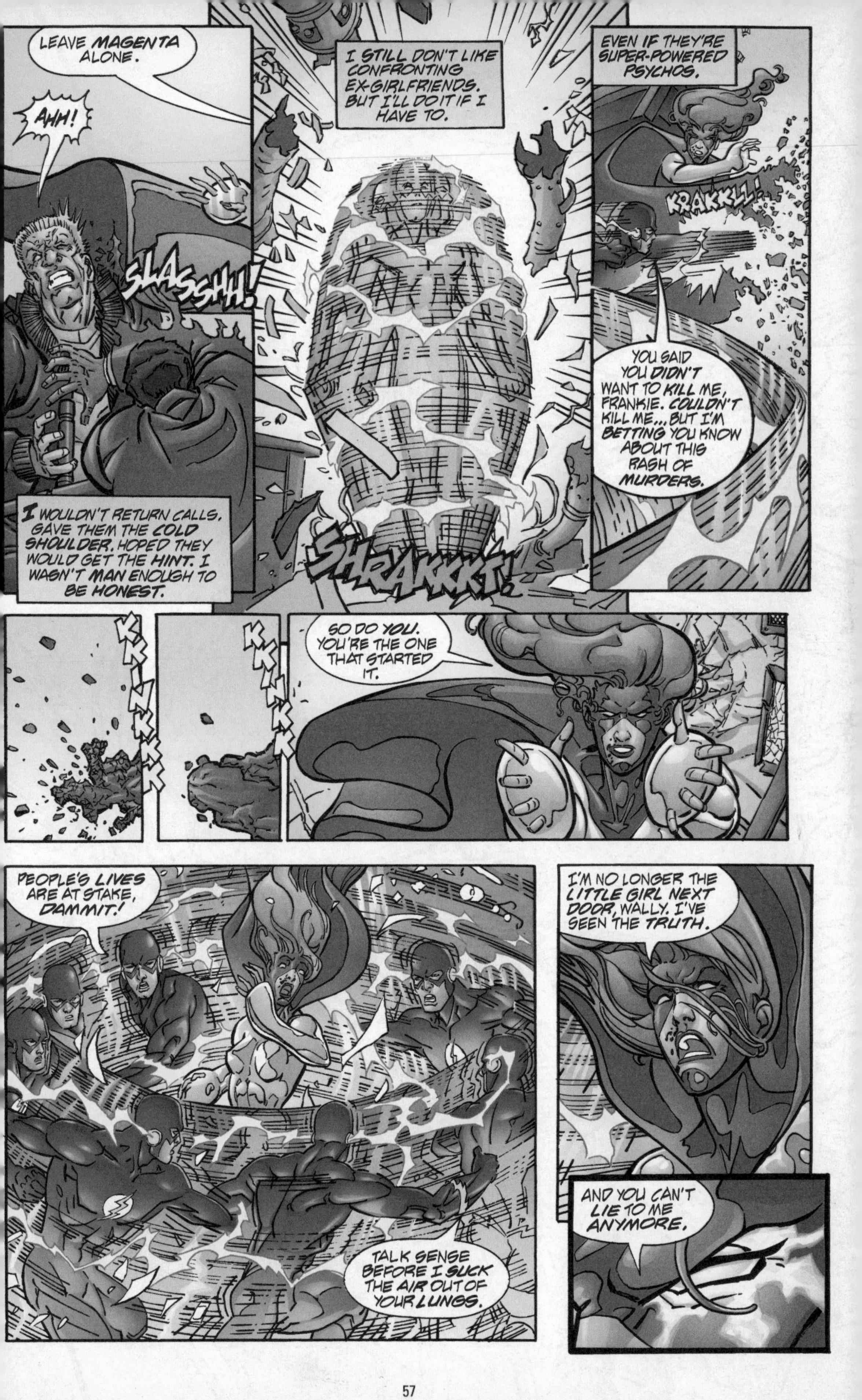

LEAVE MAGENTA ALONE.
AHH!
SLASSHH!
I STILL DON'T LIKE CONFRONTING EX-GIRLFRIENDS. BUT I'LL DO IT IF I HAVE TO.
EVEN IF THEY'RE SUPER-POWERED PSYCHOS.
KRAKKLL!
I WOULDN'T RETURN CALLS, GAVE THEM THE COLD SHOULDER. HOPED THEY WOULD GET THE HINT. I WASN'T MAN ENOUGH TO BE HONEST.
SHRAKKKT!
YOU SAID YOU DIDN'T WANT TO KILL ME, FRANKIE. COULDN'T KILL ME... BUT I'M BETTING YOU KNOW ABOUT THIS RASH OF MURDERS.
KKRINKKK
KKRINKK
SO DO YOU. YOU'RE THE ONE THAT STARTED IT.
PEOPLE'S LIVES ARE AT STAKE, DAMMIT!
TALK SENSE BEFORE I SUCK THE AIR OUT OF YOUR LUNGS.
I'M NO LONGER THE LITTLE GIRL NEXT DOOR, WALLY. I'VE SEEN THE TRUTH.
AND YOU CAN'T LIE TO ME ANYMORE.

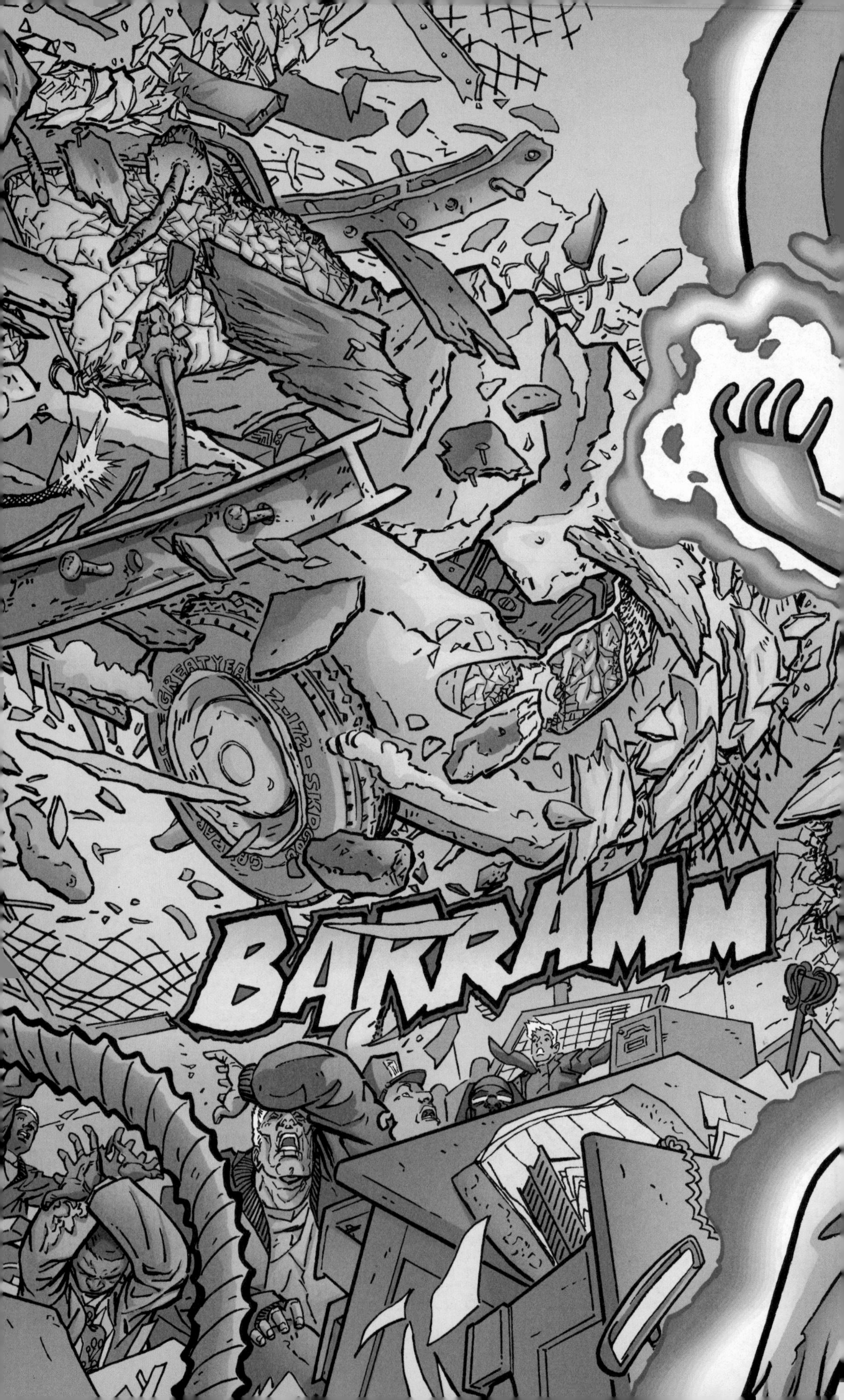
BARRAMM

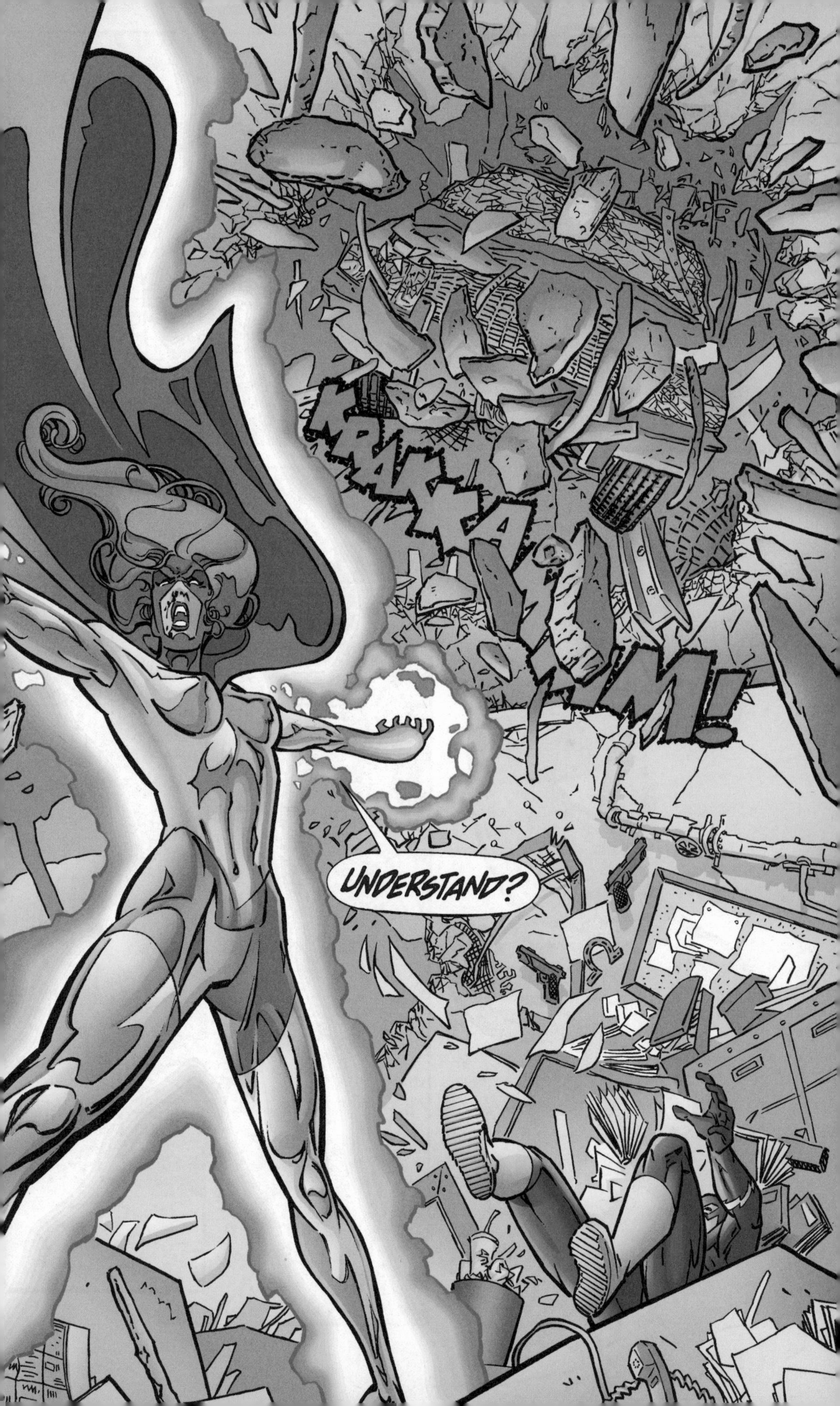
KRAKKA-BLAM!
UNDERSTAND?

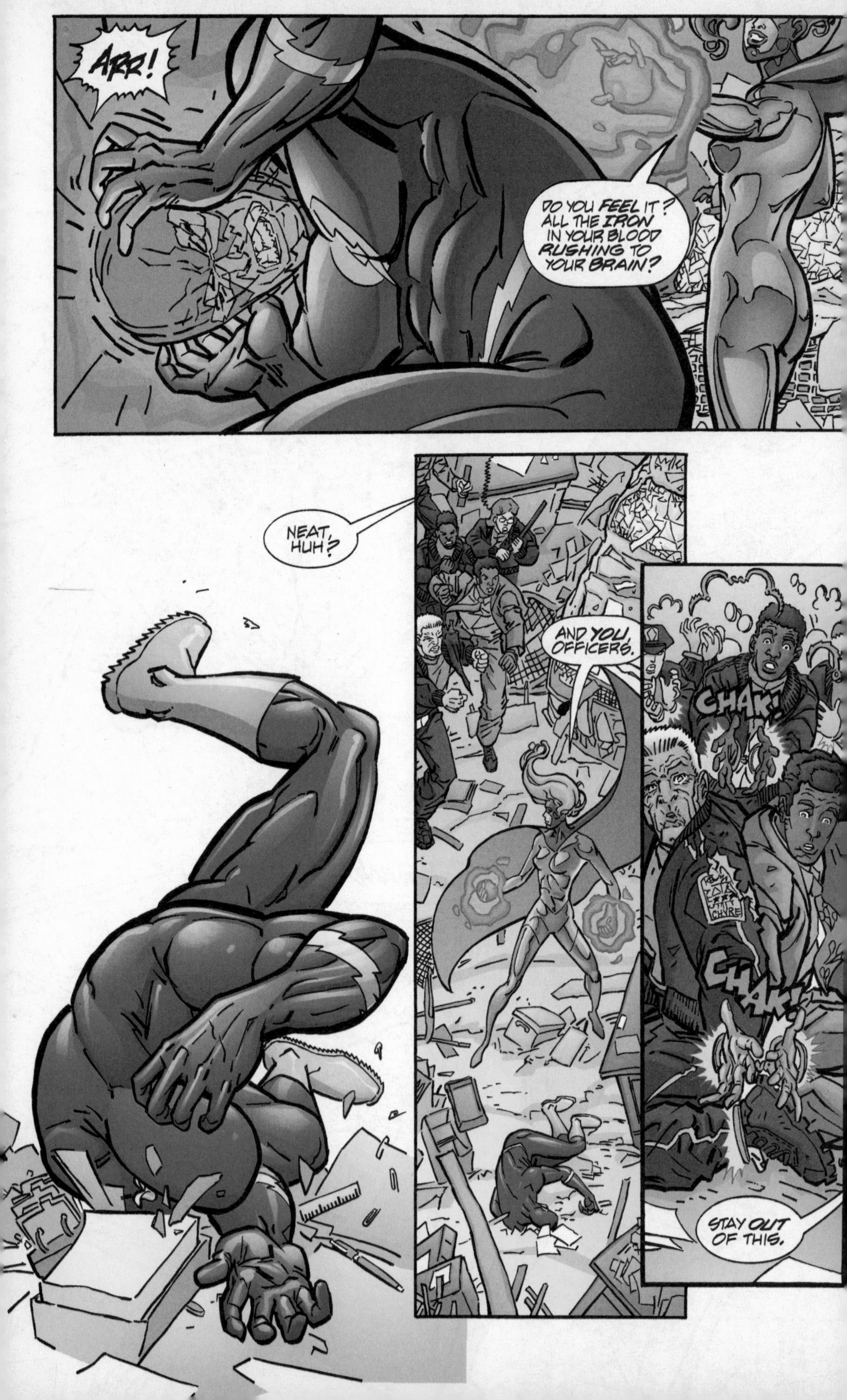
ARR!
DO YOU FEEL IT? ALL THE IRON IN YOUR BLOOD RUSHING TO YOUR BRAIN?
NEAT, HUH?
AND YOU, OFFICERS,
CHAK!
CHAK!
STAY OUT OF THIS.

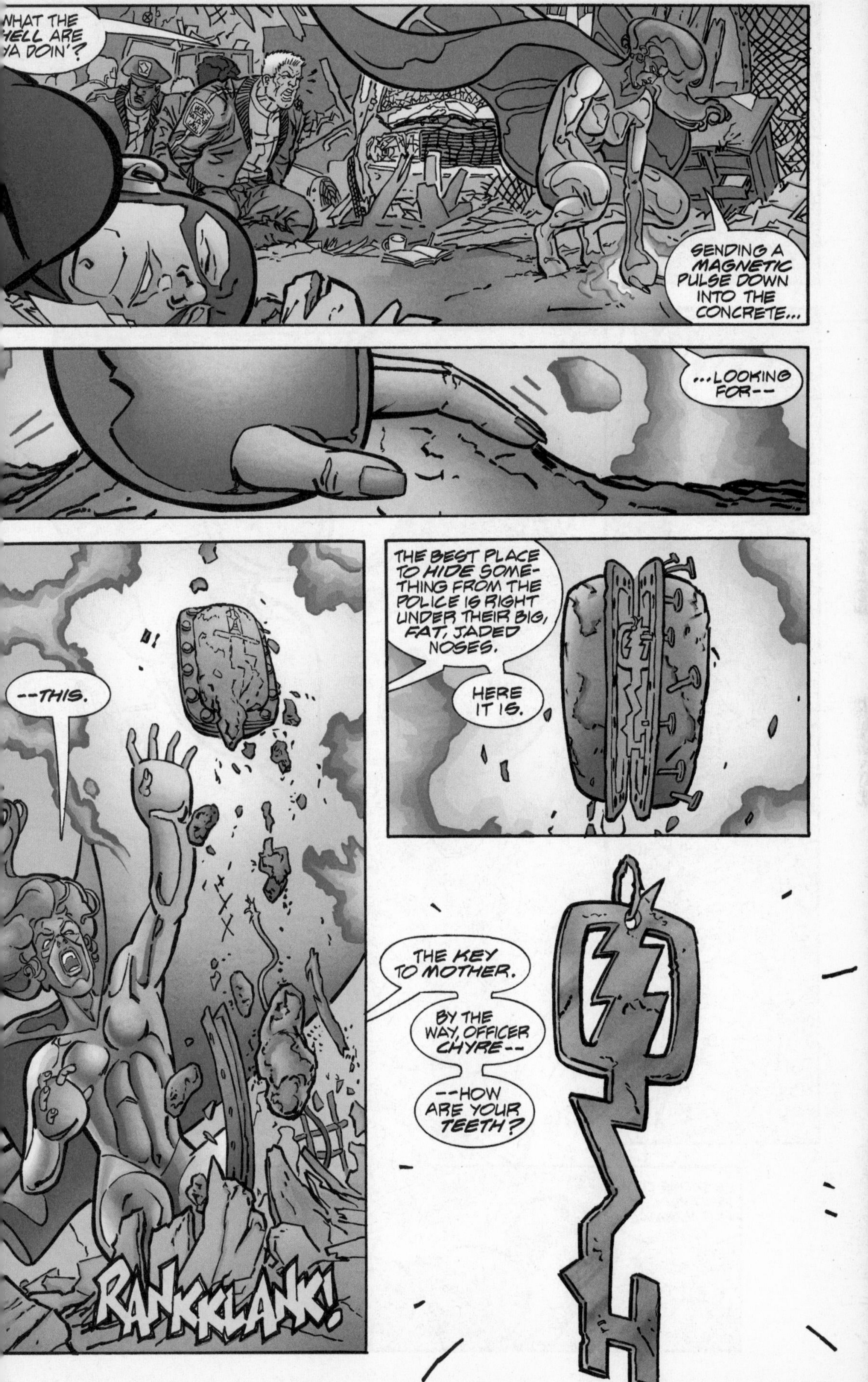
WHAT THE HELL ARE YA DOIN'?
SENDING A MAGNETIC PULSE DOWN INTO THE CONCRETE...
...LOOKING FOR--
--THIS.
THE BEST PLACE TO HIDE SOMETHING FROM THE POLICE IS RIGHT UNDER THEIR BIG, FAT, JADED NOSES.
HERE IT IS.
THE KEY TO MOTHER.
BY THE WAY, OFFICER CHYRE--
--HOW ARE YOUR TEETH?
RANKKLANK!

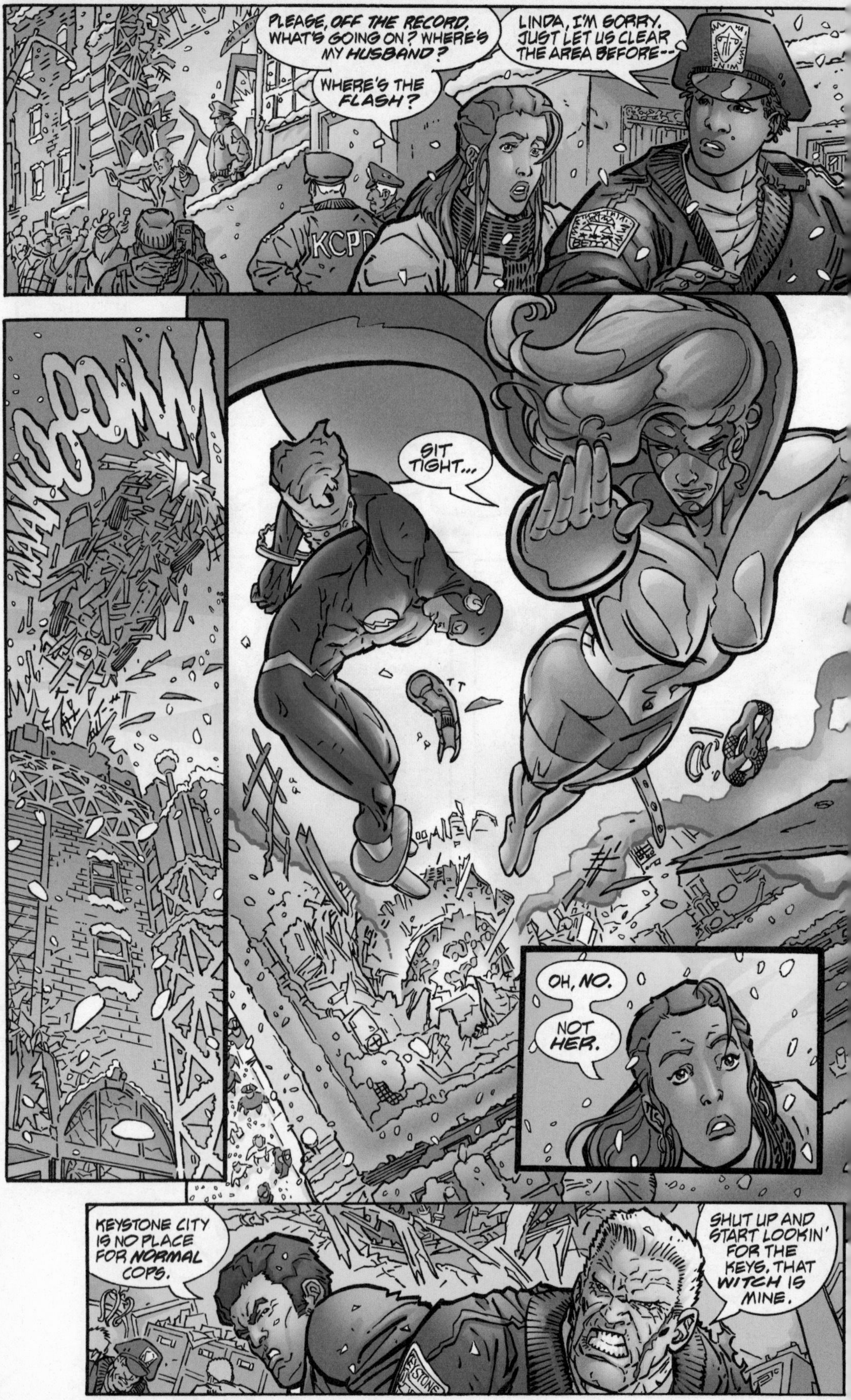
PLEASE, OFF THE RECORD. WHAT'S GOING ON? WHERE'S MY HUSBAND?
WHERE'S THE FLASH?
LINDA, I'M SORRY. JUST LET US CLEAR THE AREA BEFORE--
KCPD
WHAAKOOOM
SIT TIGHT...
OH, NO.
NOT HER.
KEYSTONE CITY IS NO PLACE FOR NORMAL COPS.
SHUT UP AND START LOOKIN' FOR THE KEYS. THAT WITCH IS MINE.

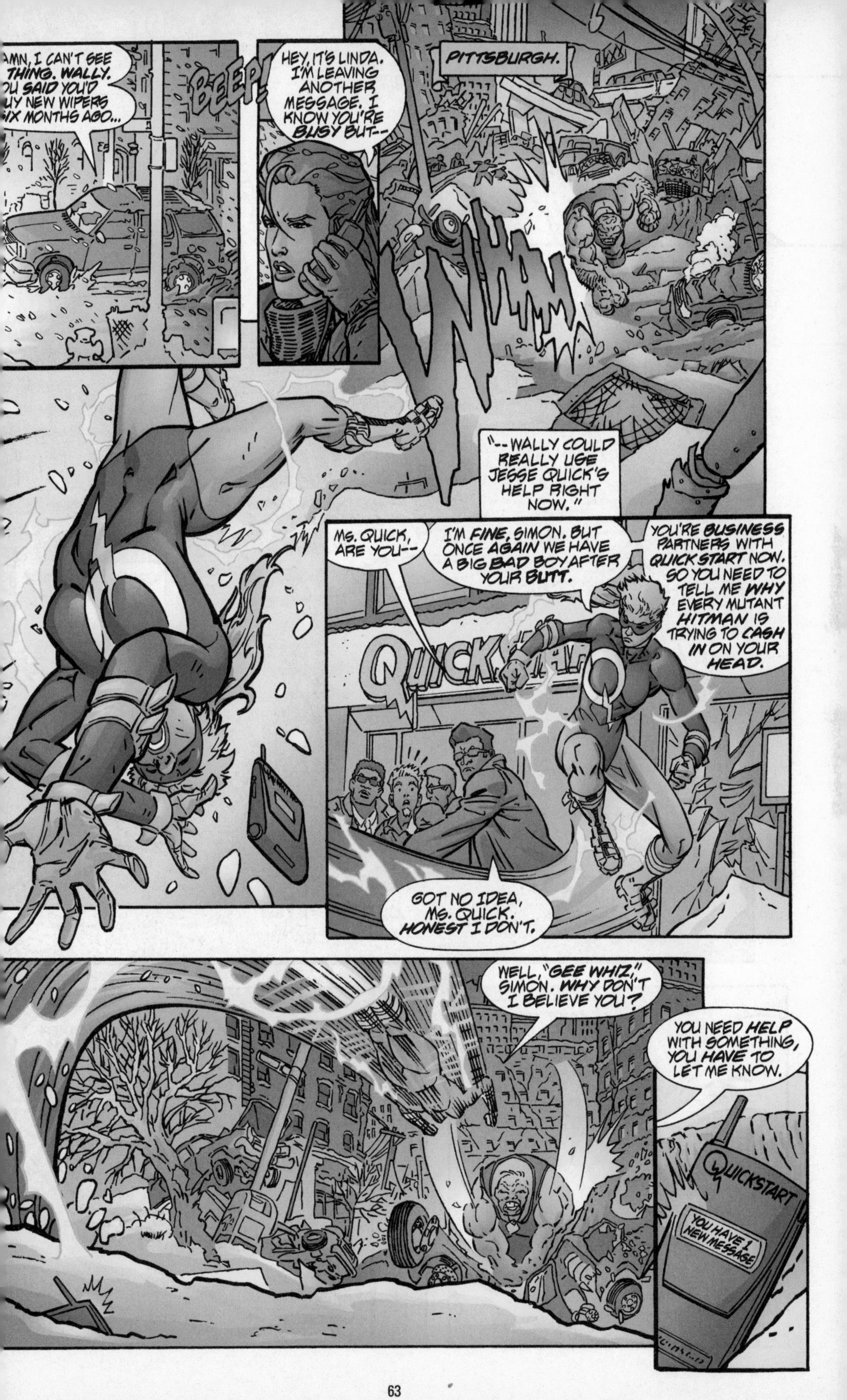
AMN, I CAN'T SEE
THING. WALLY.
OU SAID YOU'D
UY NEW WIPERS
SIX MONTHS AGO...
BEEP!
HEY, IT'S LINDA. I'M LEAVING ANOTHER MESSAGE. I KNOW YOU'RE BUSY BUT--
PITTSBURGH.
WHAM
"--WALLY COULD REALLY USE JESSE QUICK'S HELP RIGHT NOW."
Ms. QUICK, ARE YOU--
I'M FINE, SIMON. BUT ONCE AGAIN WE HAVE A BIG BAD BOY AFTER YOUR BUTT.
YOU'RE BUSINESS PARTNERS WITH QUICK START NOW. SO YOU NEED TO TELL ME WHY EVERY MUTANT HITMAN IS TRYING TO CASH IN ON YOUR HEAD.
QUICK
GOT NO IDEA, Ms. QUICK. HONEST I DON'T.
WELL, "GEE WHIZ," SIMON. WHY DON'T I BELIEVE YOU?
YOU NEED HELP WITH SOMETHING, YOU HAVE TO LET ME KNOW.
QUICKSTART
YOU HAVE 1 NEW MESSAGE

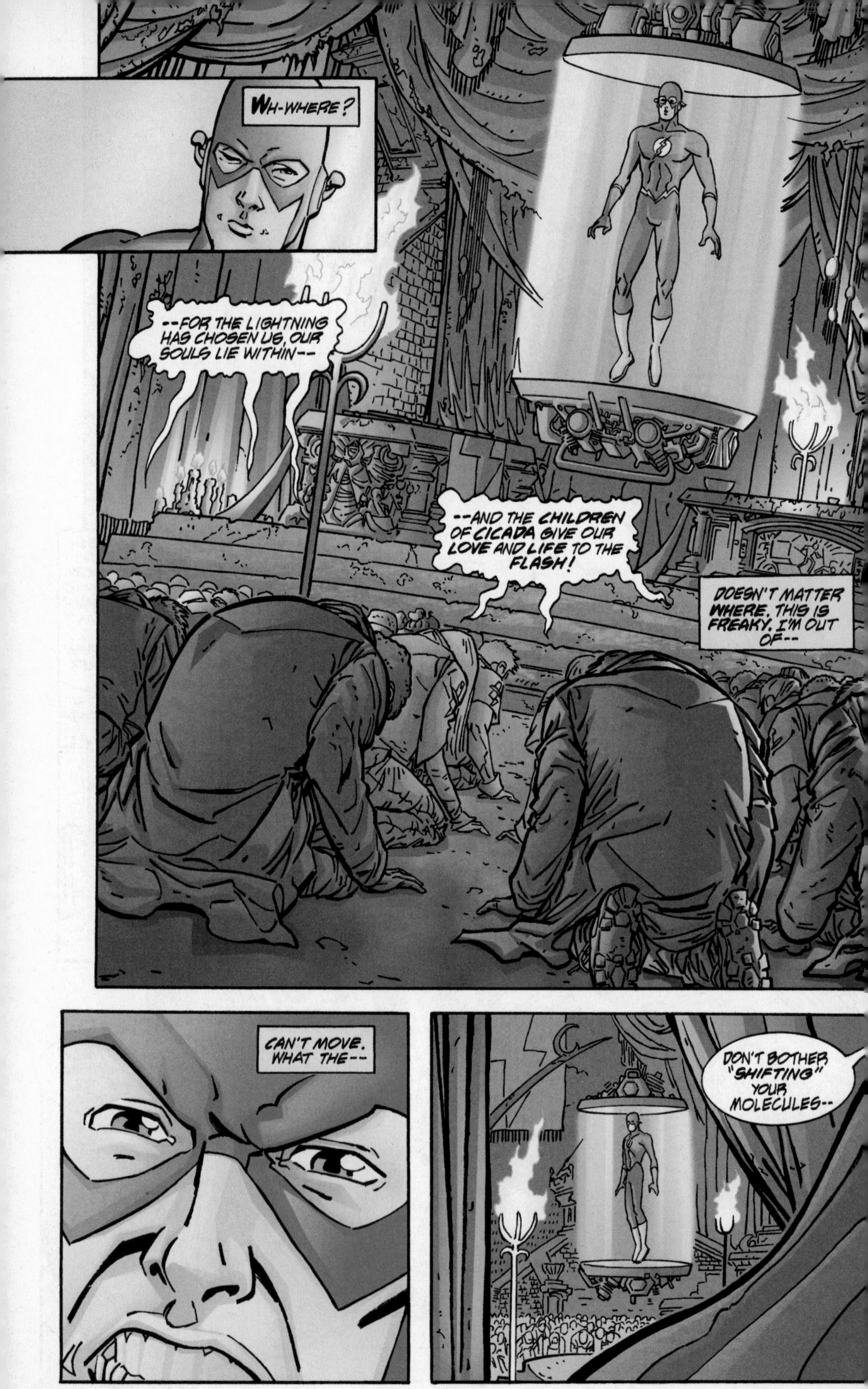

WH-WHERE?
--FOR THE LIGHTNING HAS CHOSEN US, OUR SOULS LIE WITHIN--
--AND THE CHILDREN OF CICADA GIVE OUR LOVE AND LIFE TO THE FLASH!
DOESN'T MATTER WHERE. THIS IS FREAKY. I'M OUT OF--
CAN'T MOVE. WHAT THE--
DON'T BOTHER "SHIFTING" YOUR MOLECULES--

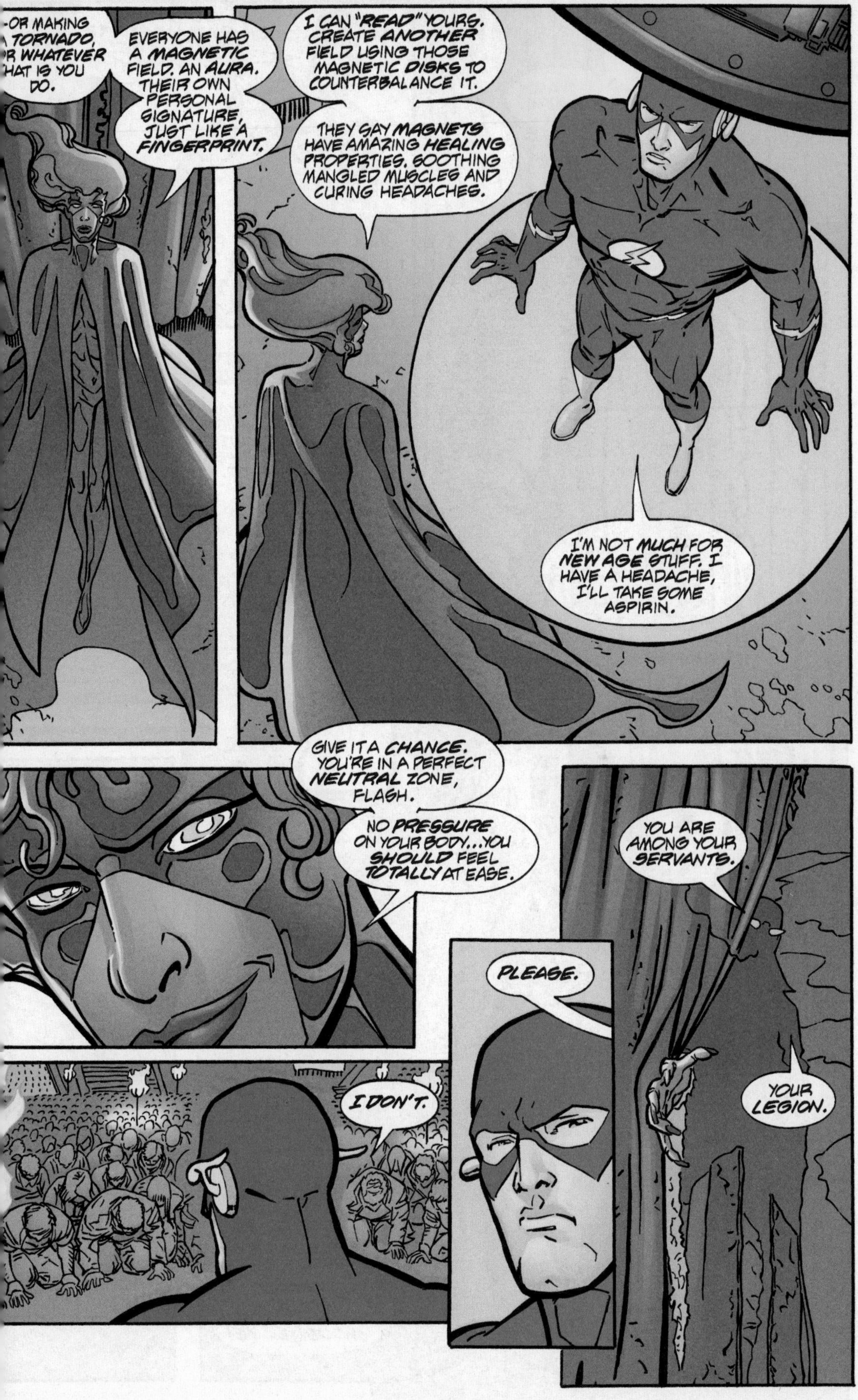
-OR MAKING A TORNADO, OR WHATEVER THAT IS YOU DO.
EVERYONE HAS A MAGNETIC FIELD. AN AURA. THEIR OWN PERSONAL SIGNATURE, JUST LIKE A FINGERPRINT.
I CAN "READ" YOURS. CREATE ANOTHER FIELD USING THOSE MAGNETIC DISKS TO COUNTERBALANCE IT.
THEY SAY MAGNETS HAVE AMAZING HEALING PROPERTIES. SOOTHING MANGLED MUSCLES AND CURING HEADACHES.
I'M NOT MUCH FOR NEW AGE STUFF. I HAVE A HEADACHE, I'LL TAKE SOME ASPIRIN.
GIVE IT A CHANCE. YOU'RE IN A PERFECT NEUTRAL ZONE, FLASH.
NO PRESSURE ON YOUR BODY...YOU SHOULD FEEL TOTALLY AT EASE.
YOU ARE AMONG YOUR SERVANTS.
PLEASE.
I DON'T.
YOUR LEGION.

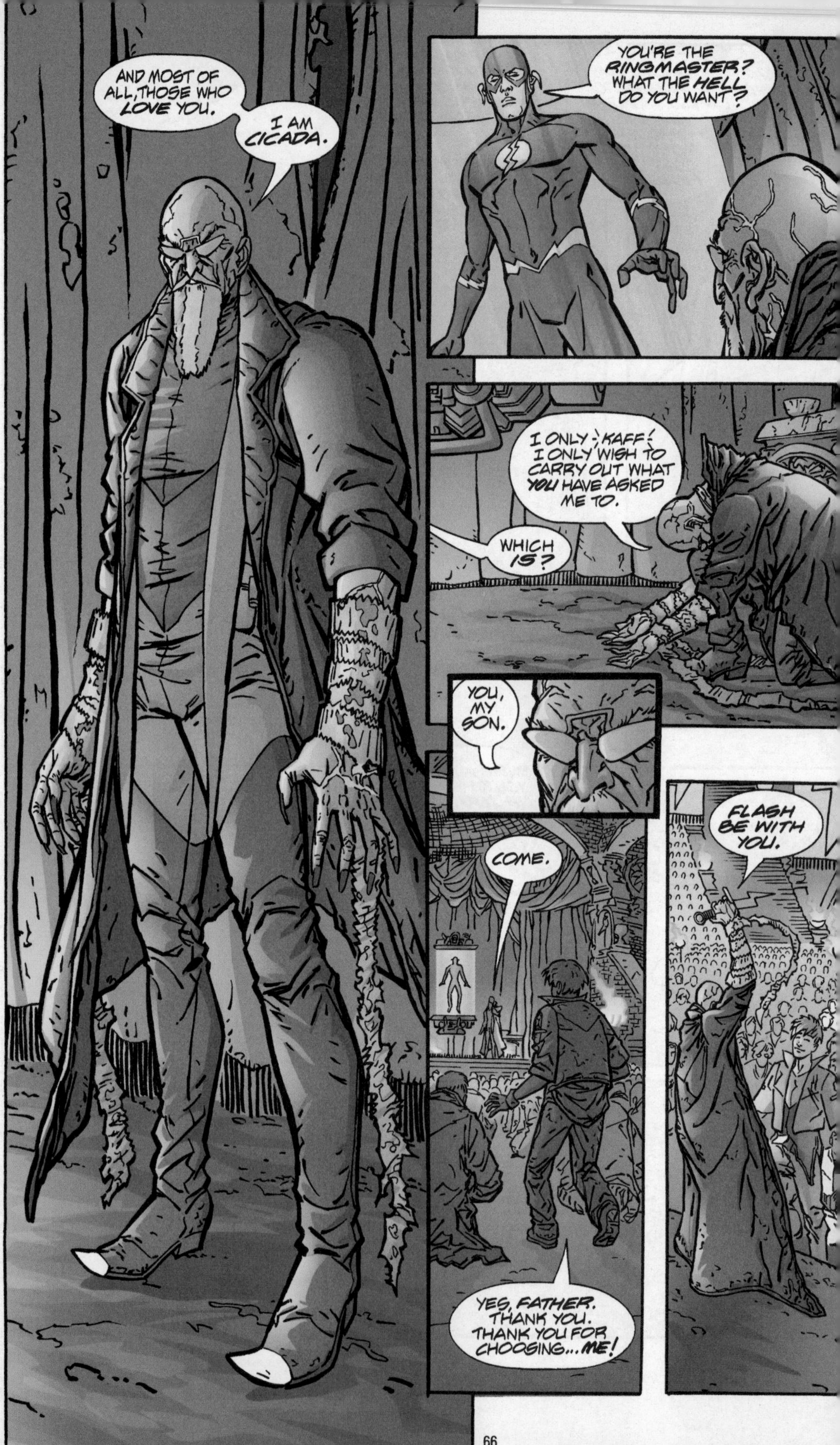
AND MOST OF ALL, THOSE WHO LOVE YOU.
I AM CICADA.
YOU'RE THE RINGMASTER? WHAT THE HELL DO YOU WANT?
I ONLY -KAFF! I ONLY WISH TO CARRY OUT WHAT YOU HAVE ASKED ME TO.
WHICH IS?
YOU, MY SON.
COME.
YES, FATHER. THANK YOU. THANK YOU FOR CHOOSING... ME!
FLASH BE WITH YOU.

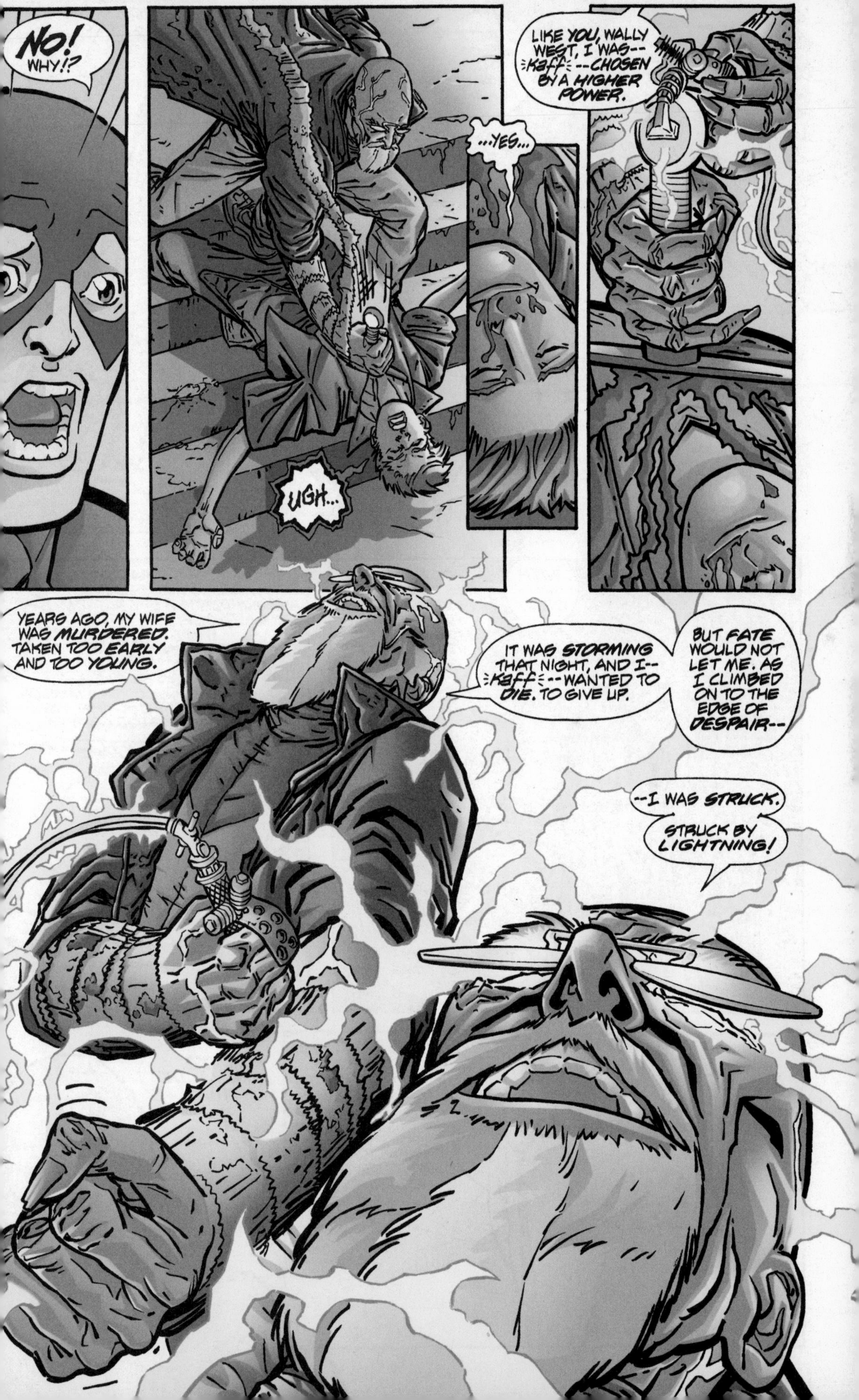

NO! WHY!?
UGH...
...YES...
LIKE YOU, WALLY WEST, I WAS-- *Kaff* --CHOSEN BY A HIGHER POWER.
YEARS AGO, MY WIFE WAS MURDERED. TAKEN TOO EARLY AND TOO YOUNG.
IT WAS STORMING THAT NIGHT, AND I-- *Kaff* --WANTED TO DIE. TO GIVE UP.
BUT FATE WOULD NOT LET ME. AS I CLIMBED ON TO THE EDGE OF DESPAIR--
--I WAS STRUCK. STRUCK BY LIGHTNING!

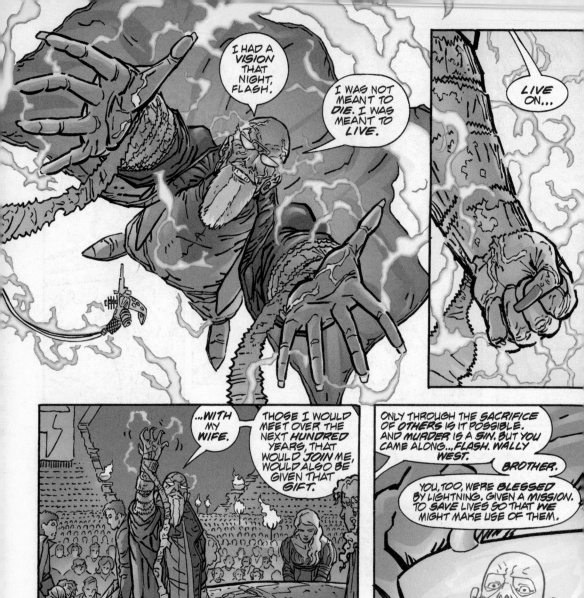

I HAD A VISION THAT NIGHT, FLASH.

I WAS NOT MEANT TO *DIE.* I WAS MEANT TO *LIVE.*

LIVE ON...

...WITH MY *WIFE.*

THOSE I WOULD MEET OVER THE NEXT *HUNDRED* YEARS, THAT WOULD *JOIN* ME, WOULD ALSO BE GIVEN THAT *GIFT.*

BUT *IMMORTALITY* DOES NOT COME *CHEAP.*

ONLY THROUGH THE *SACRIFICE* OF OTHERS IS IT POSSIBLE. AND *MURDER* IS A SIN. BUT YOU CAME ALONG...FLASH. WALLY WEST.

BROTHER.

YOU, TOO, WERE *BLESSED* BY LIGHTNING. GIVEN A MISSION. TO SAVE LIVES SO THAT *WE* MIGHT MAKE USE OF THEM.

YOU'RE TELLING ME YOU THINK I SAVE PEOPLE... SAVE THEIR LIVES SO *YOU* CAN TAKE THEM?

WHAT KIND OF *SICK, TWISTED* BRAIN IS IN THAT *NASTY SKULL* OF YOURS?

MODESTY. WE *VALUE* THAT.

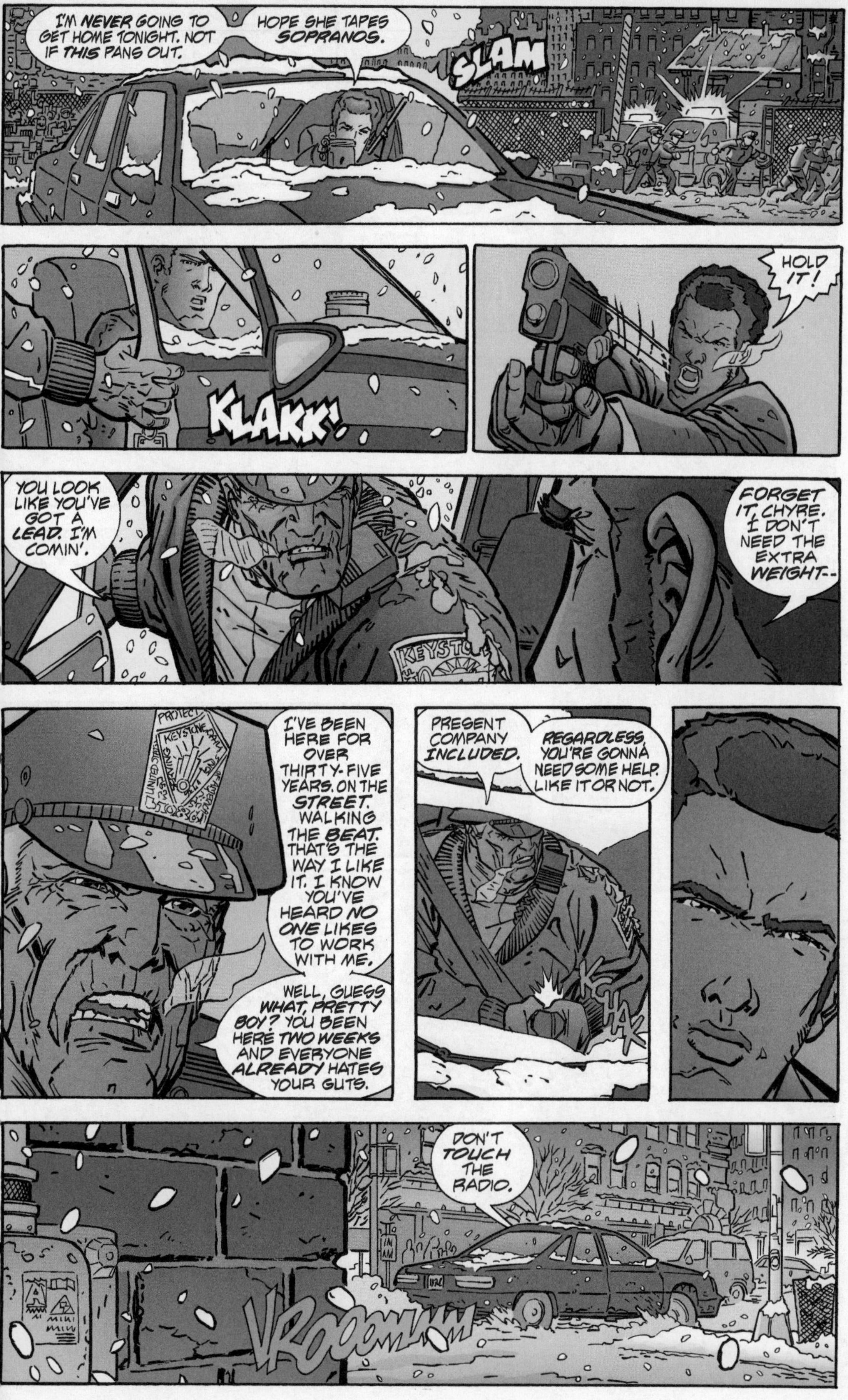

I'M NEVER GOING TO GET HOME TONIGHT. NOT IF THIS PANS OUT.
HOPE SHE TAPES SOPRANOS.
SLAM
KLAKK!
HOLD IT!
YOU LOOK LIKE YOU'VE GOT A LEAD. I'M COMIN'.
FORGET IT, CHYRE. I DON'T NEED THE EXTRA WEIGHT--
I'VE BEEN HERE FOR OVER THIRTY-FIVE YEARS. ON THE STREET. WALKING THE BEAT. THAT'S THE WAY I LIKE IT. I KNOW YOU'VE HEARD NO ONE LIKES TO WORK WITH ME.
WELL, GUESS WHAT, PRETTY BOY? YOU BEEN HERE TWO WEEKS AND EVERYONE ALREADY HATES YOUR GUTS.
PRESENT COMPANY INCLUDED.
REGARDLESS, YOU'RE GONNA NEED SOME HELP. LIKE IT OR NOT.
DON'T TOUCH THE RADIO.
VROOOMMM

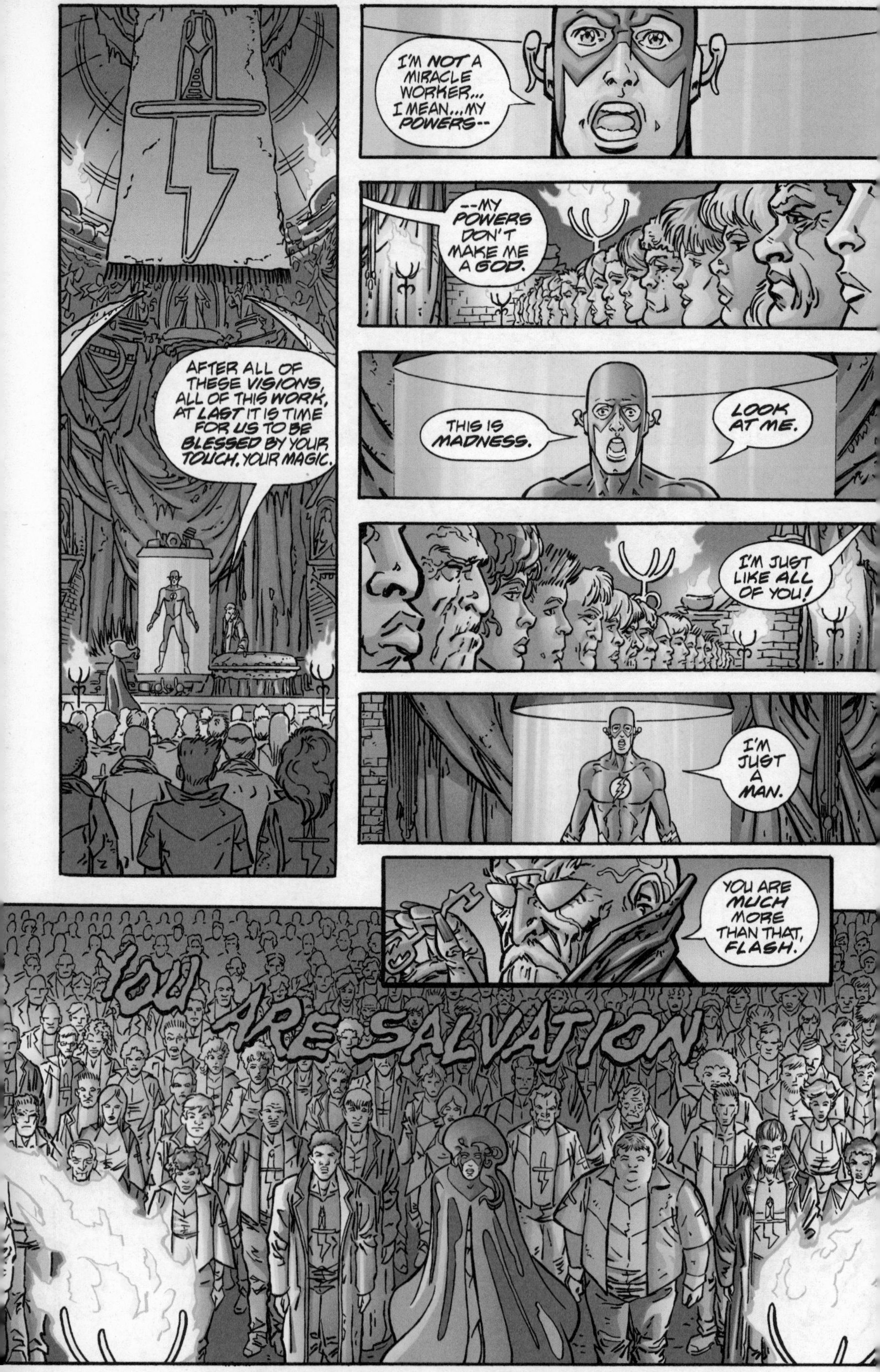
AFTER ALL OF THESE VISIONS, ALL OF THIS WORK, AT LAST IT IS TIME FOR US TO BE BLESSED BY YOUR TOUCH. YOUR MAGIC.
I'M NOT A MIRACLE WORKER... I MEAN... MY POWERS--
--MY POWERS DON'T MAKE ME A GOD.
THIS IS MADNESS.
LOOK AT ME.
I'M JUST LIKE ALL OF YOU!
I'M JUST A MAN.
YOU ARE MUCH MORE THAN THAT, FLASH.
YOU ARE SALVATION

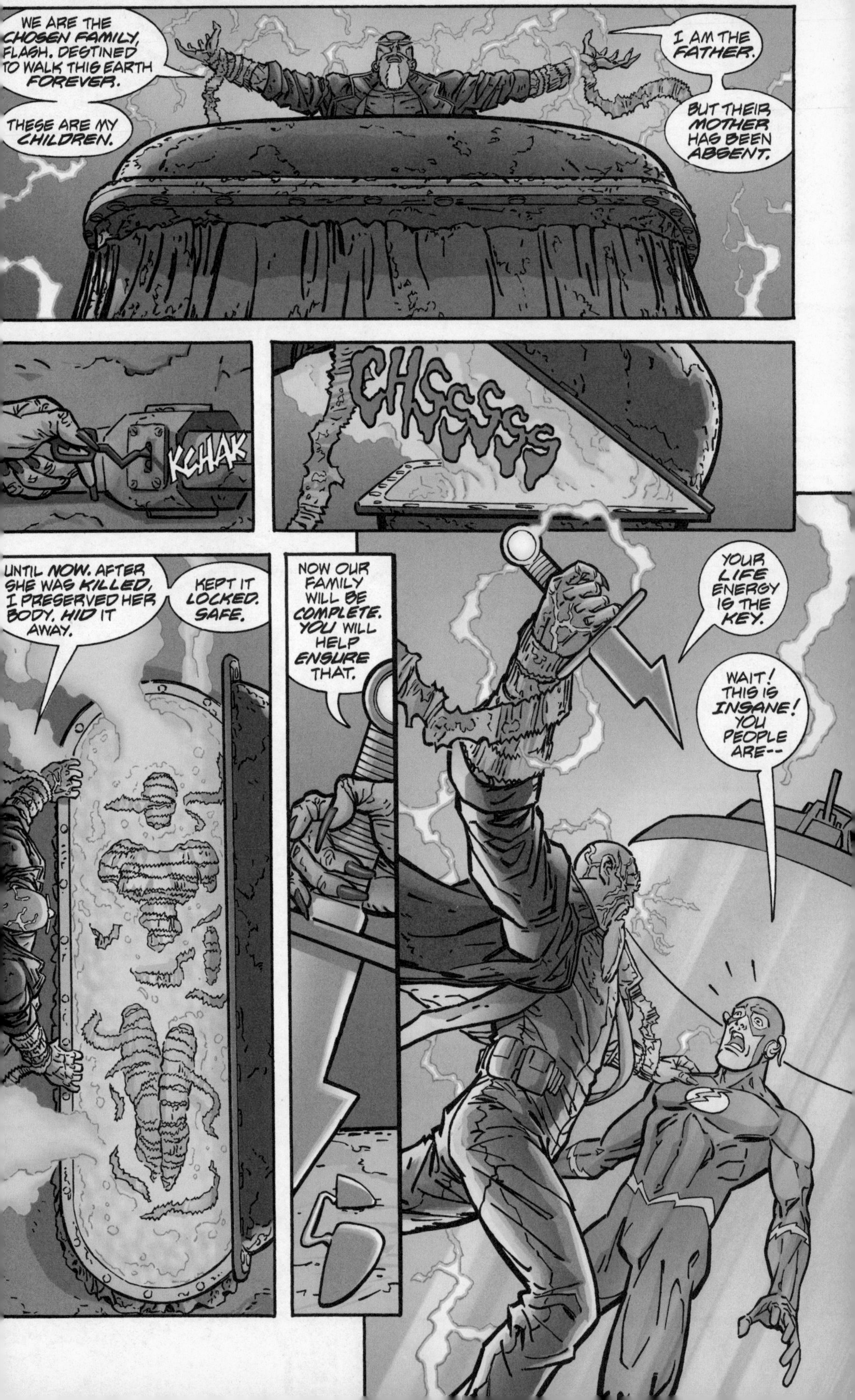

WE ARE THE CHOSEN FAMILY, FLASH. DESTINED TO WALK THIS EARTH FOREVER.
THESE ARE MY CHILDREN.
I AM THE FATHER.
BUT THEIR MOTHER HAS BEEN ABSENT.
KCHAK
CHSSSSS
UNTIL NOW. AFTER SHE WAS KILLED, I PRESERVED HER BODY. HID IT AWAY.
KEPT IT LOCKED. SAFE.
NOW OUR FAMILY WILL BE COMPLETE. YOU WILL HELP ENSURE THAT.
YOUR LIFE ENERGY IS THE KEY.
WAIT! THIS IS INSANE! YOU PEOPLE ARE--

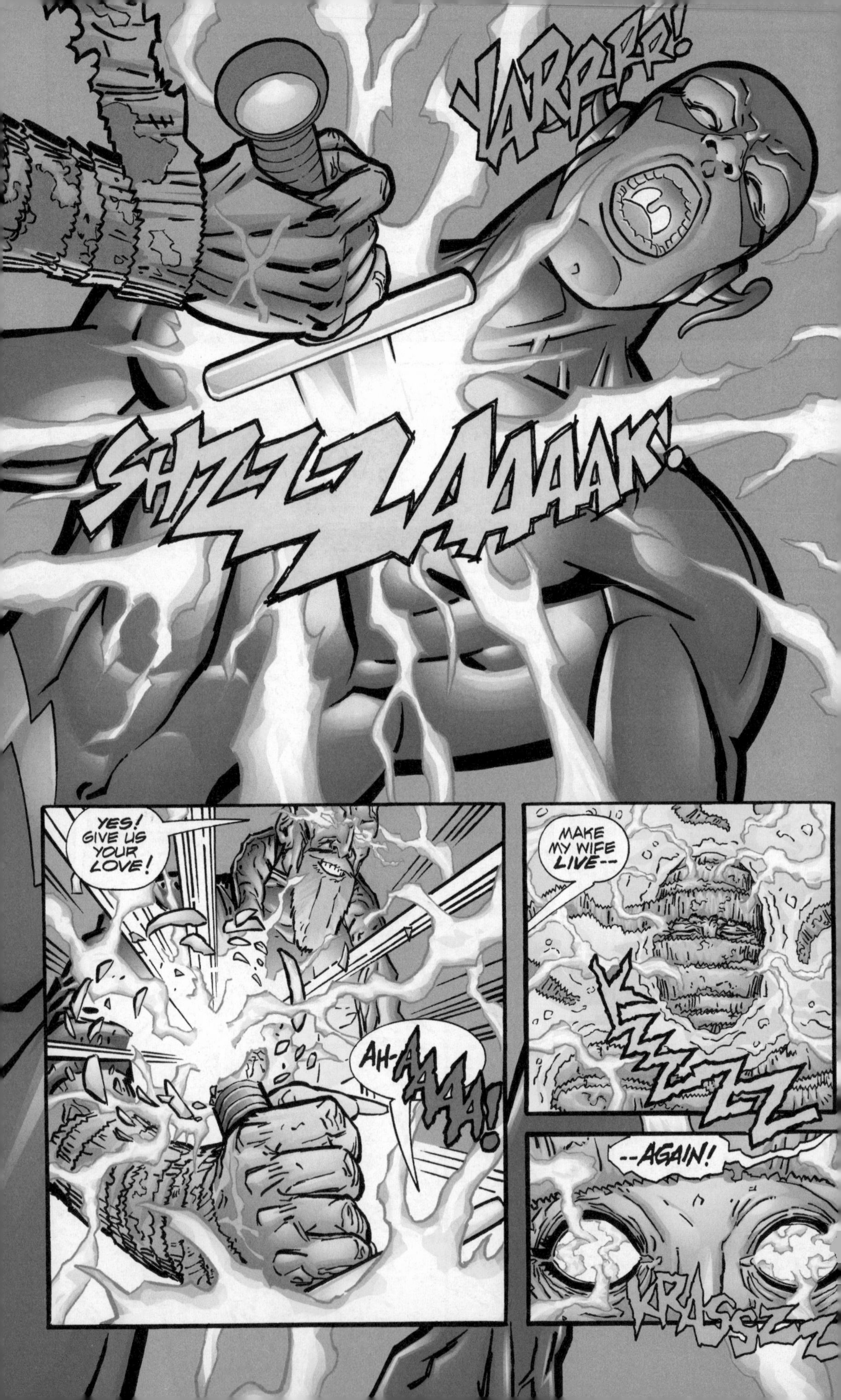

YARRRR!
SHZZZAAAAK!
YES! GIVE US YOUR LOVE!
AH-AAAA!
MAKE MY WIFE LIVE--
KZZZZZ
--AGAIN!
KRASSZZ

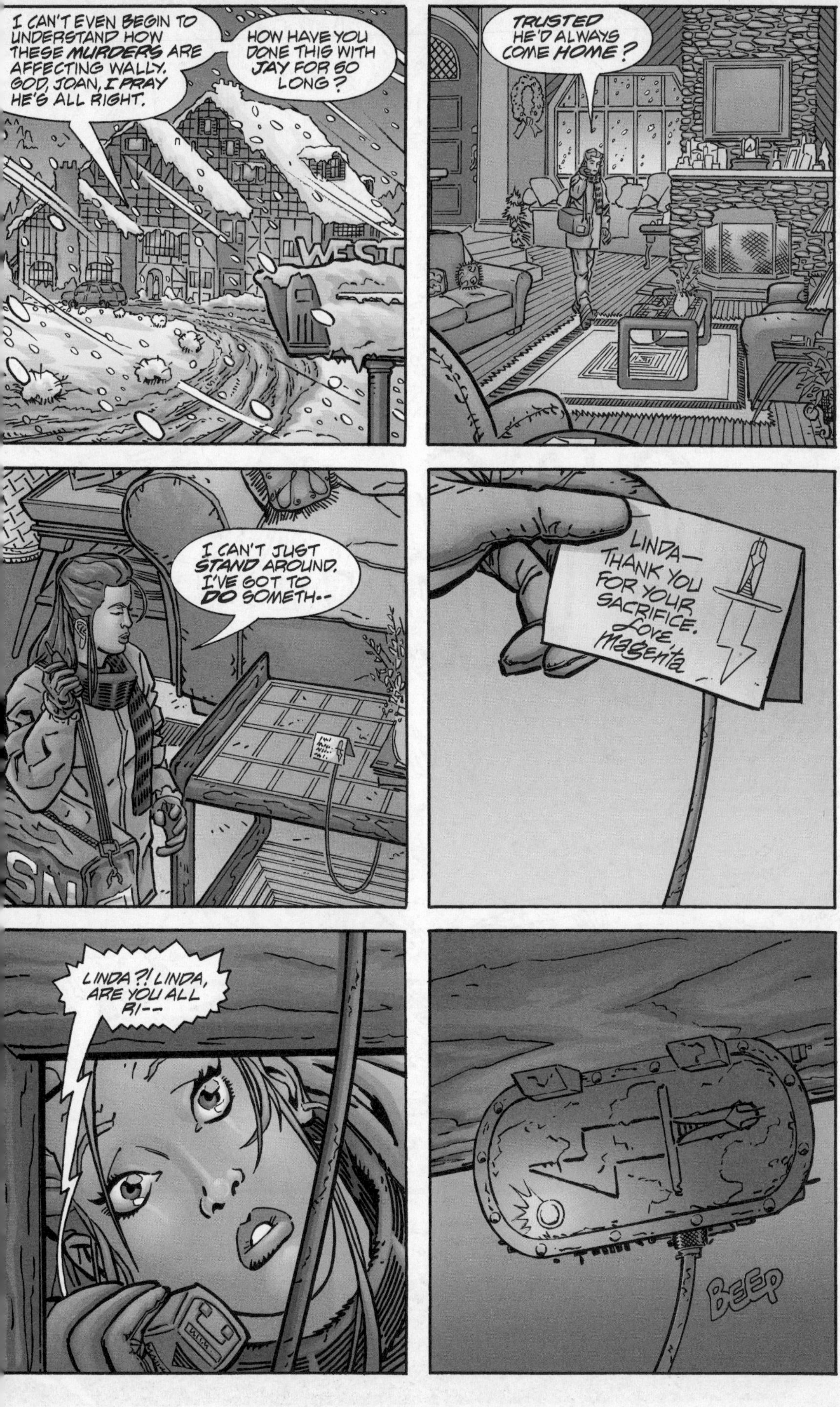
I CAN'T EVEN BEGIN TO UNDERSTAND HOW THESE MURDERS ARE AFFECTING WALLY. GOD, JOAN, I PRAY HE'S ALL RIGHT.
HOW HAVE YOU DONE THIS WITH JAY FOR SO LONG?
WEST
TRUSTED HE'D ALWAYS COME HOME?
I CAN'T JUST STAND AROUND. I'VE GOT TO DO SOMETH--
LINDA— THANK YOU FOR YOUR SACRIFICE. Love, Magenta
LINDA?! LINDA, ARE YOU ALL RI--
BEEP

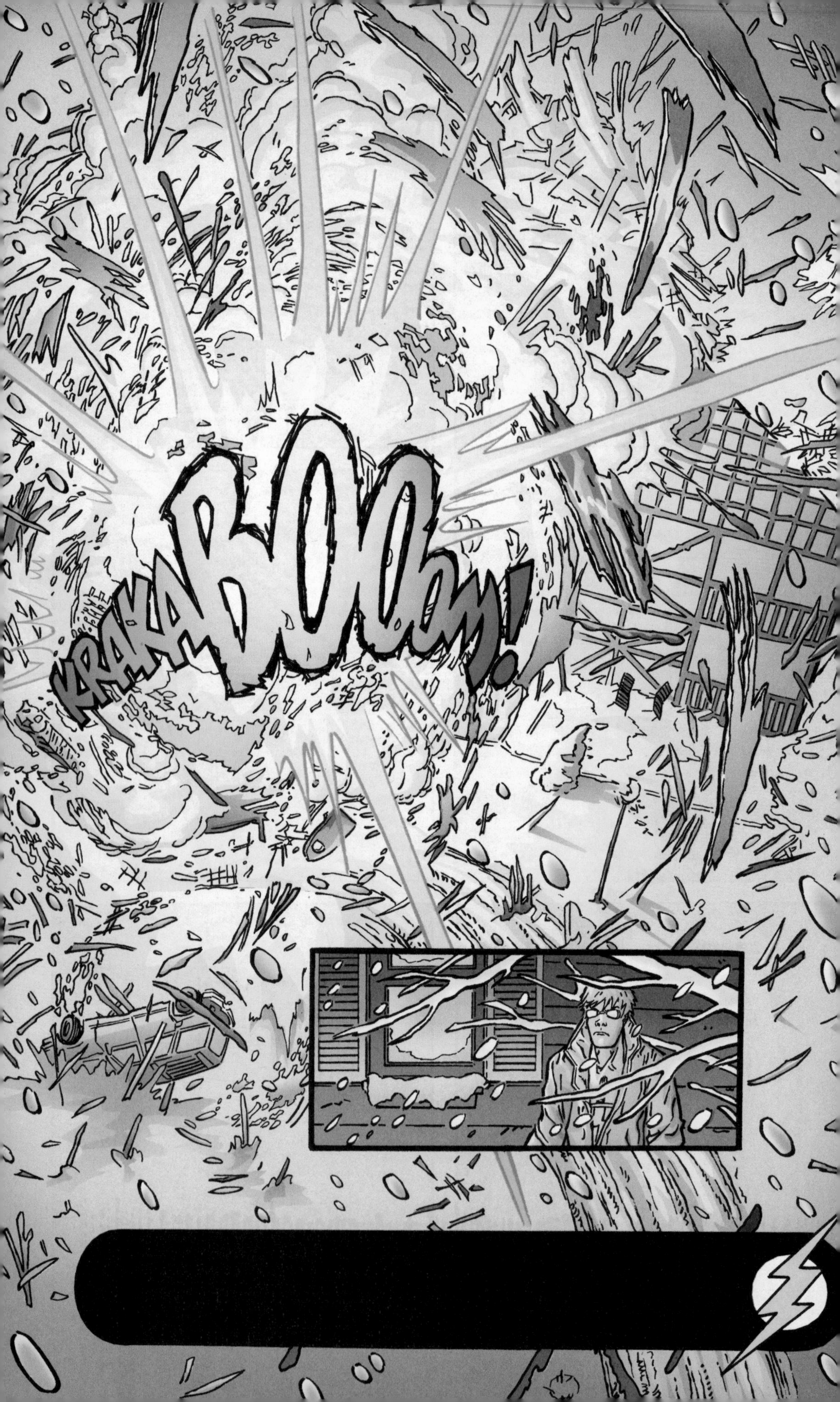
KRAKABOOOM!

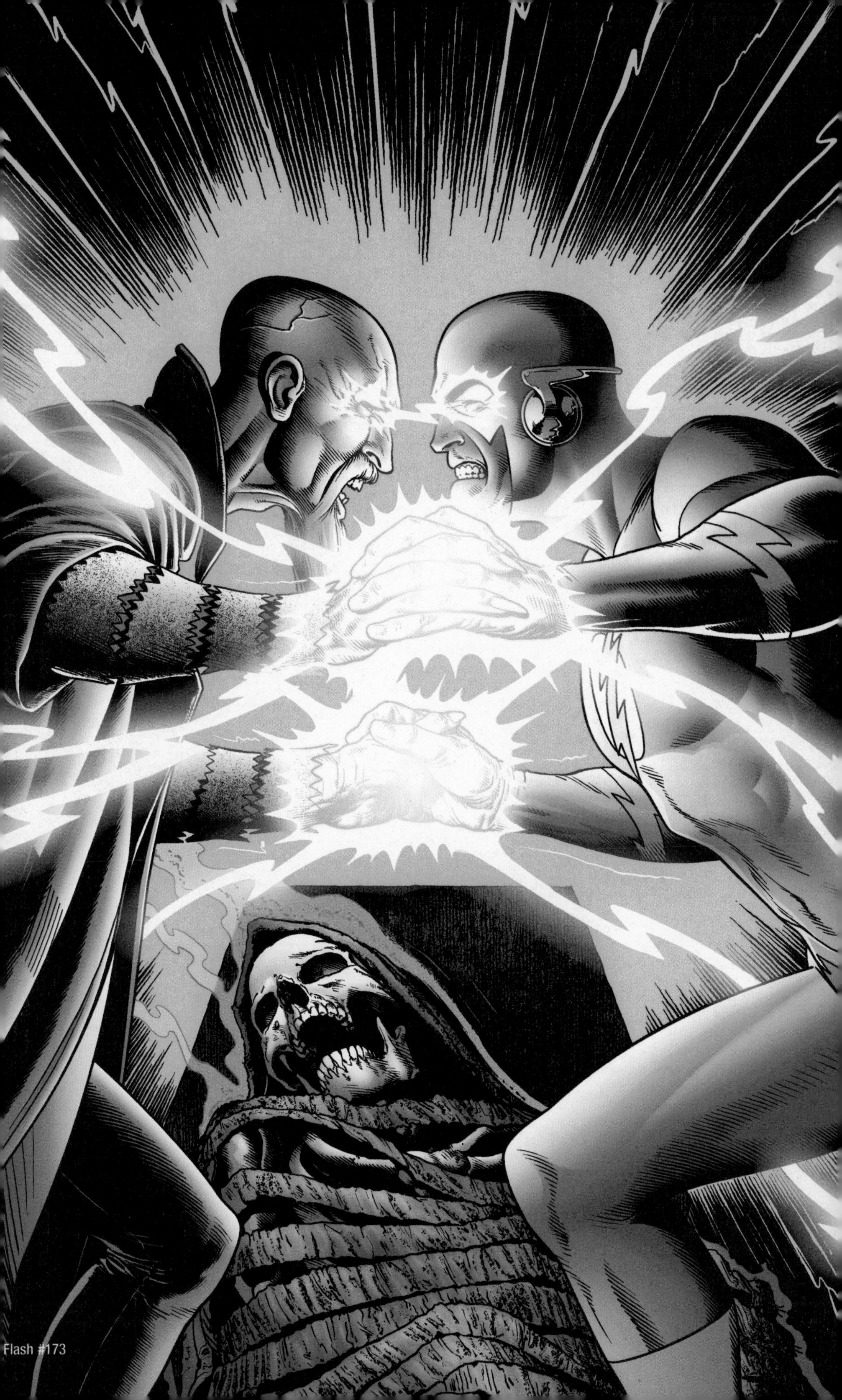

Flash #173

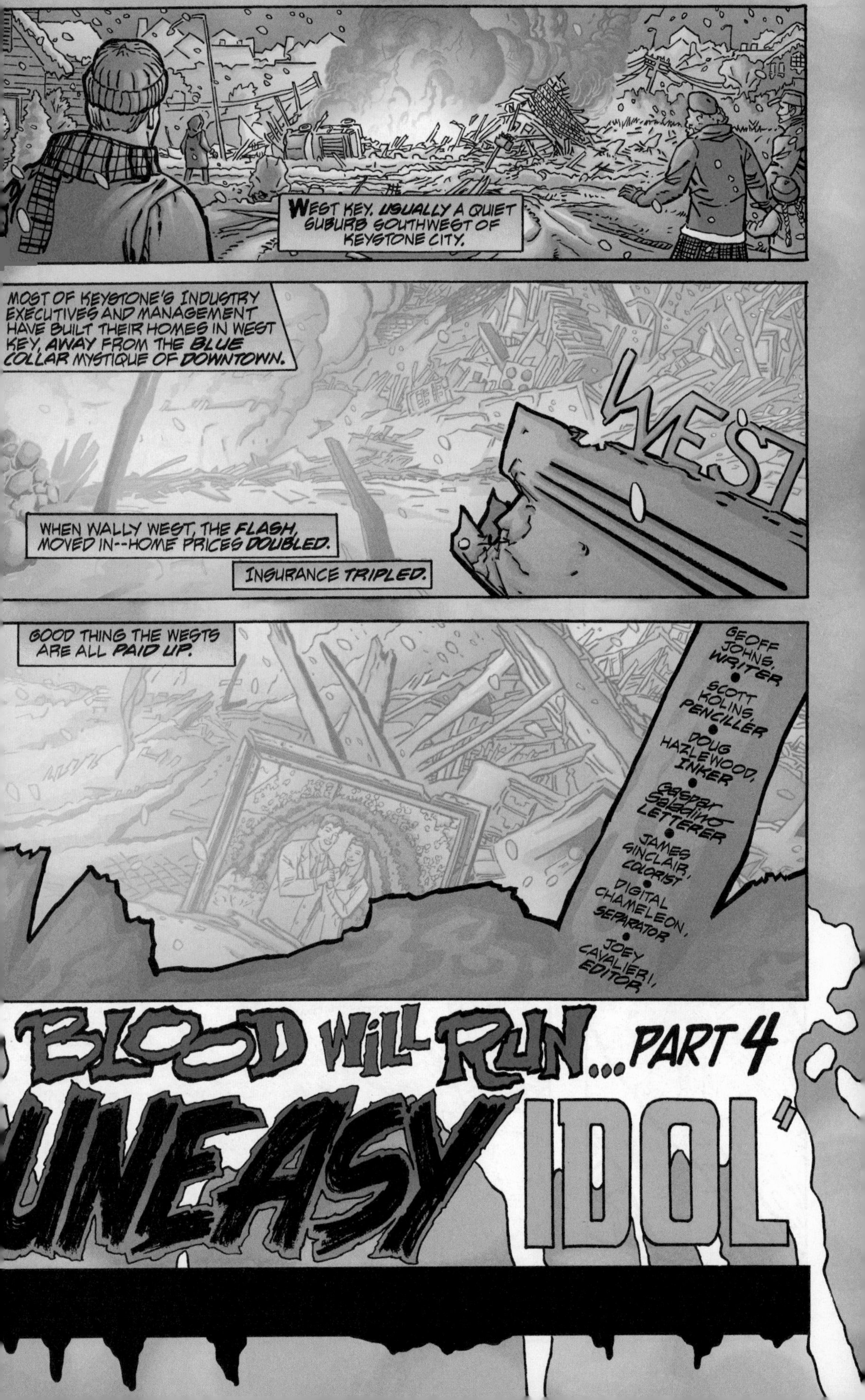
WEST KEY. USUALLY A QUIET SUBURB SOUTHWEST OF KEYSTONE CITY.
MOST OF KEYSTONE'S INDUSTRY EXECUTIVES AND MANAGEMENT HAVE BUILT THEIR HOMES IN WEST KEY, AWAY FROM THE BLUE COLLAR MYSTIQUE OF DOWNTOWN.
WEST
WHEN WALLY WEST, THE FLASH, MOVED IN--HOME PRICES DOUBLED.
INSURANCE TRIPLED.
GOOD THING THE WESTS ARE ALL PAID UP.
GEOFF JOHNS, WRITER • SCOTT KOLINS, PENCILLER • DOUG HAZLEWOOD, INKER • Gaspar Saladino LETTERER • JAMES SINCLAIR, COLORIST • DIGITAL CHAMELEON, SEPARATOR • JOEY CAVALIERI, EDITOR
BLOOD WILL RUN... PART 4
"UNEASY IDOL"

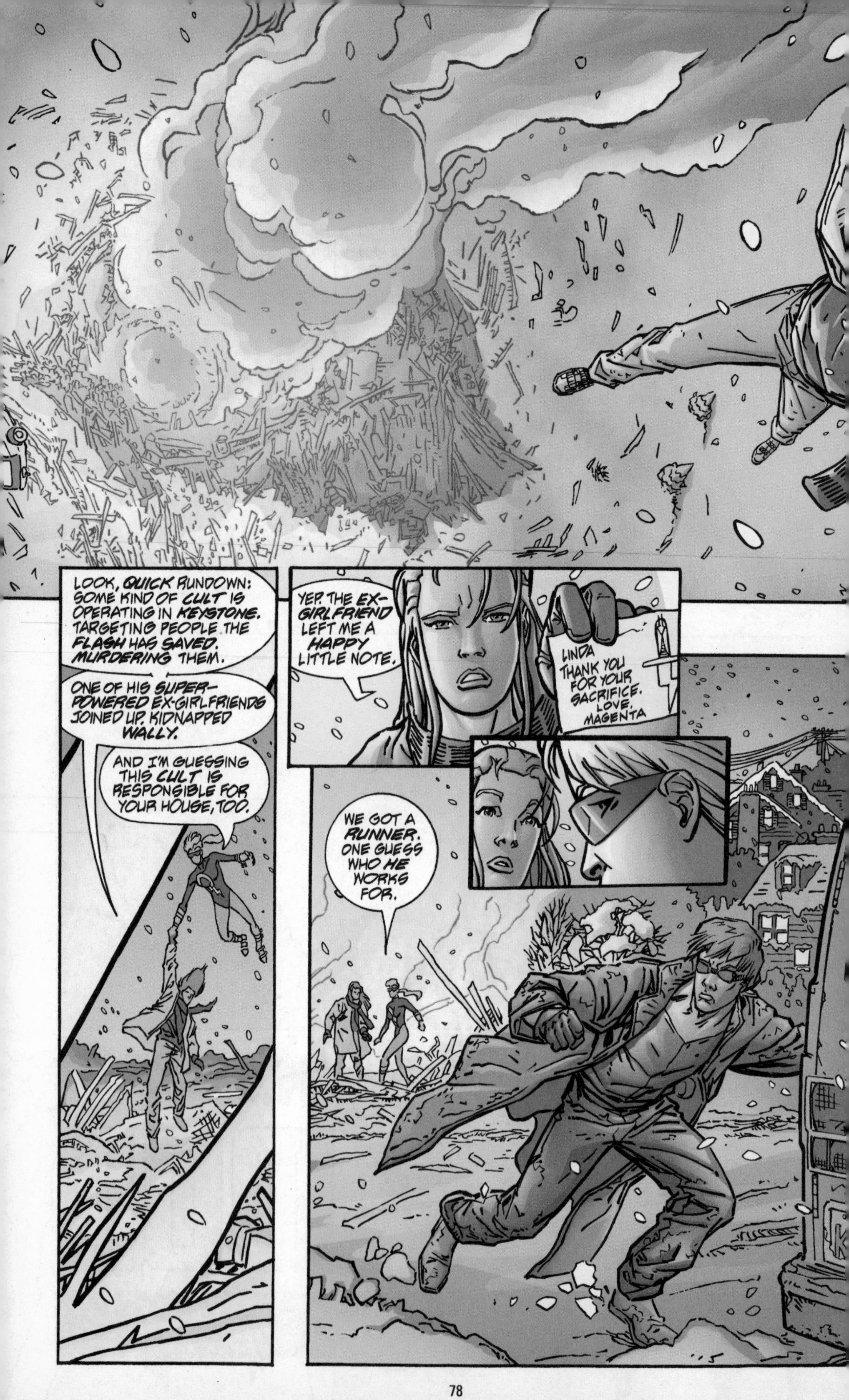
LOOK, QUICK RUNDOWN: SOME KIND OF CULT IS OPERATING IN KEYSTONE. TARGETING PEOPLE THE FLASH HAS SAVED. MURDERING THEM.
ONE OF HIS SUPER-POWERED EX-GIRLFRIENDS JOINED UP, KIDNAPPED WALLY.
AND I'M GUESSING THIS CULT IS RESPONSIBLE FOR YOUR HOUSE, TOO.
YEP. THE EX-GIRLFRIEND LEFT ME A HAPPY LITTLE NOTE.
LINDA THANK YOU FOR YOUR SACRIFICE. LOVE, MAGENTA
WE GOT A RUNNER. ONE GUESS WHO HE WORKS FOR.

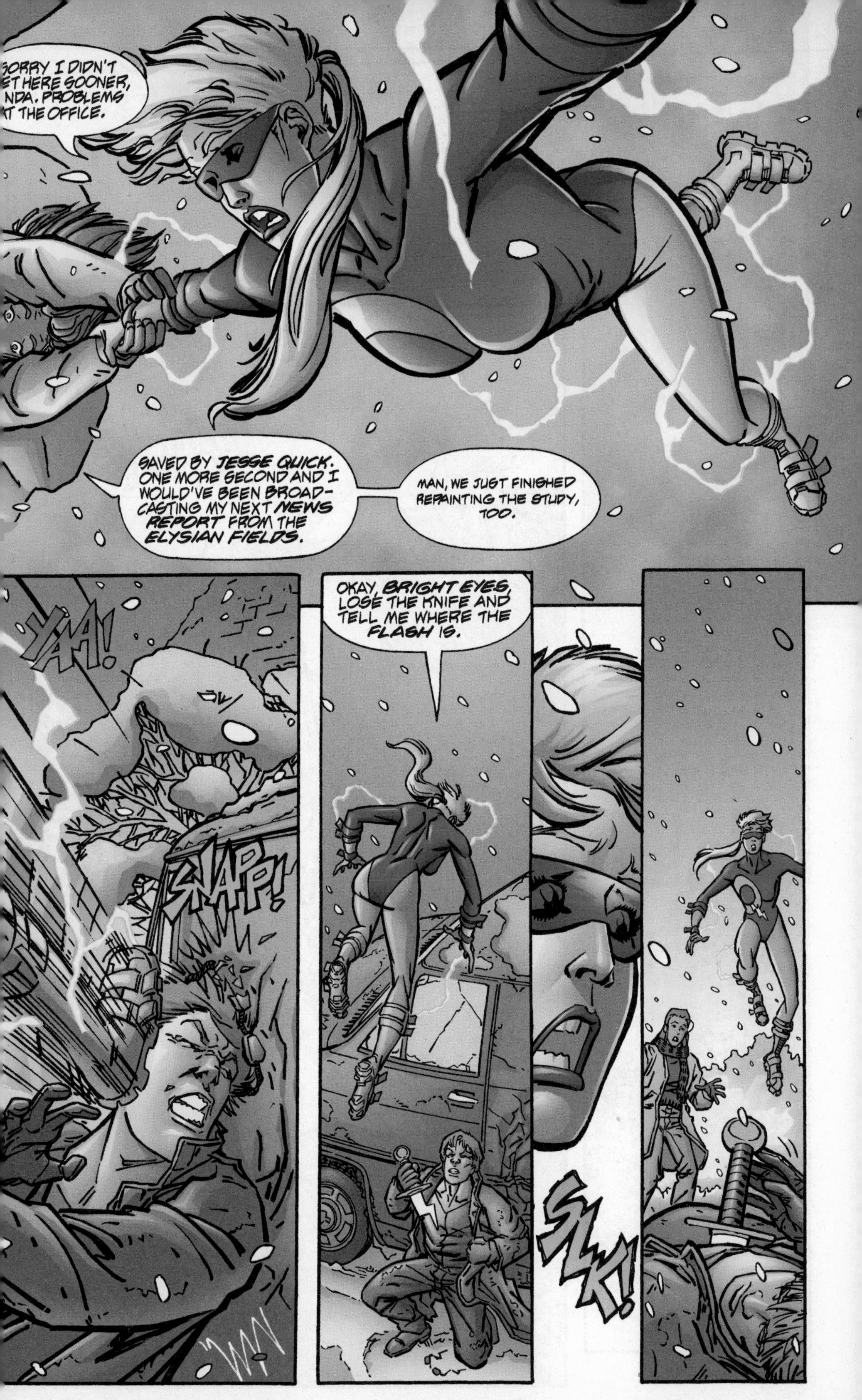

SORRY I DIDN'T GET HERE SOONER, LINDA. PROBLEMS AT THE OFFICE.
SAVED BY JESSE QUICK. ONE MORE SECOND AND I WOULD'VE BEEN BROAD-CASTING MY NEXT NEWS REPORT FROM THE ELYSIAN FIELDS.
MAN, WE JUST FINISHED REPAINTING THE STUDY, TOO.
YAA!
SNAPP!
OKAY, BRIGHT EYES, LOSE THE KNIFE AND TELL ME WHERE THE FLASH IS.
SNKT!

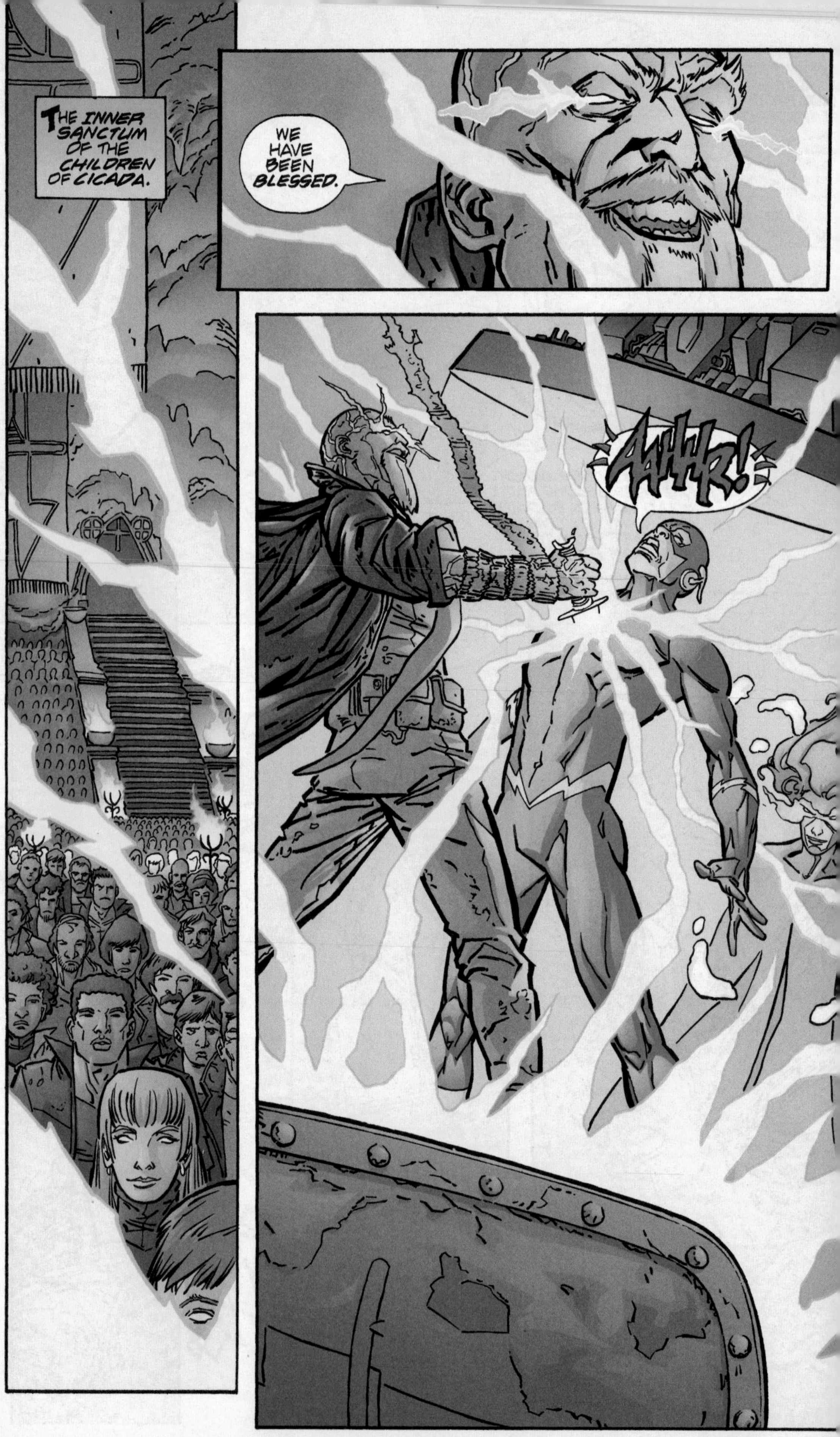
THE INNER SANCTUM OF THE CHILDREN OF CICADA.
WE HAVE BEEN BLESSED.
AAHHR!

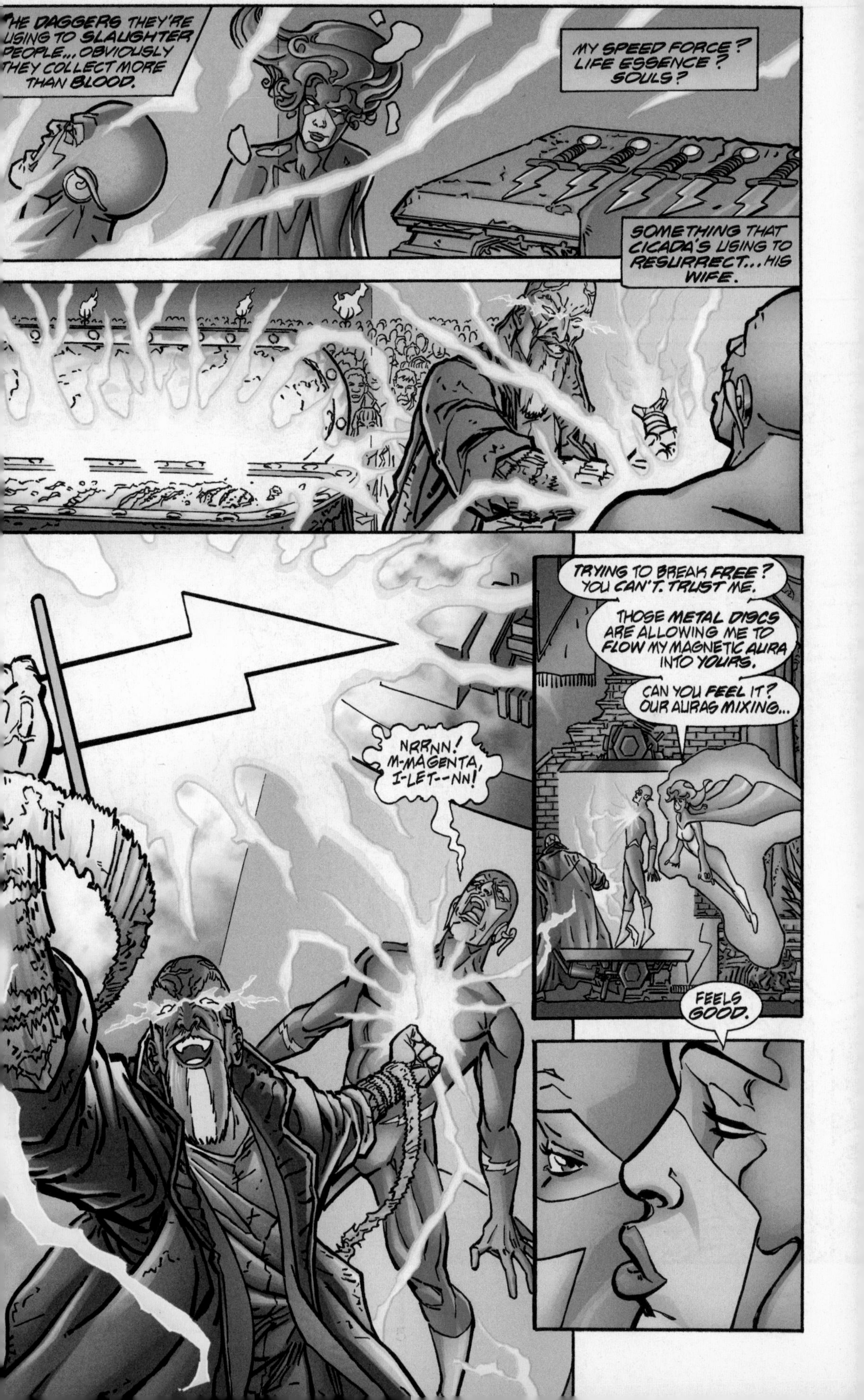

THE DAGGERS THEY'RE USING TO SLAUGHTER PEOPLE... OBVIOUSLY THEY COLLECT MORE THAN BLOOD.
MY SPEED FORCE? LIFE ESSENCE? SOULS?
SOMETHING THAT CICADA'S USING TO RESURRECT... HIS WIFE.
TRYING TO BREAK FREE? YOU CAN'T. TRUST ME.
THOSE METAL DISCS ARE ALLOWING ME TO FLOW MY MAGNETIC AURA INTO YOURS.
CAN YOU FEEL IT? OUR AURAS MIXING...
NRRNN! M-MAGENTA, I-LET--NN!
FEELS GOOD.

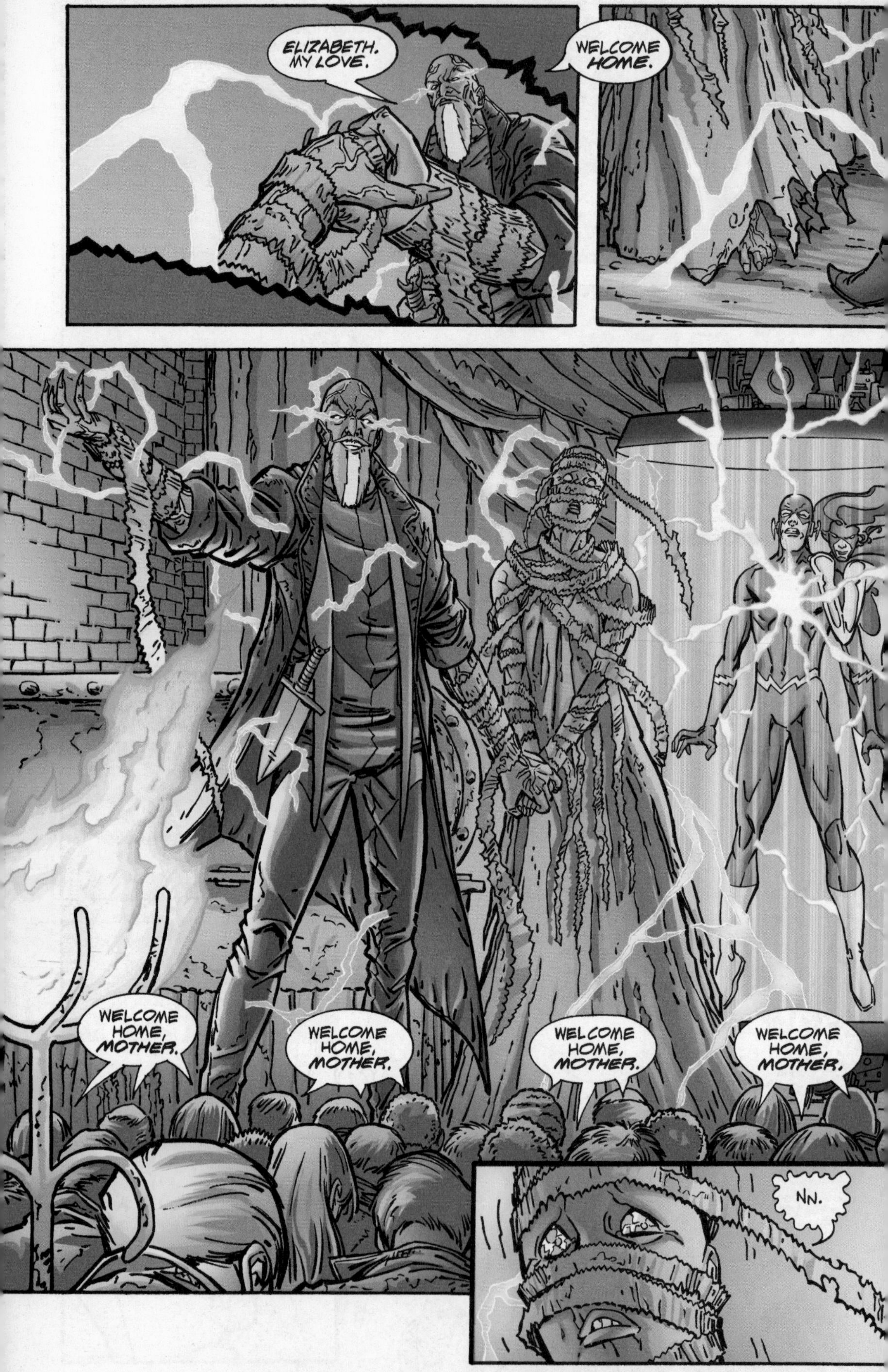
ELIZABETH. MY LOVE.
WELCOME HOME.
WELCOME HOME, MOTHER.
WELCOME HOME, MOTHER.
WELCOME HOME, MOTHER.
WELCOME HOME, MOTHER.
NN.

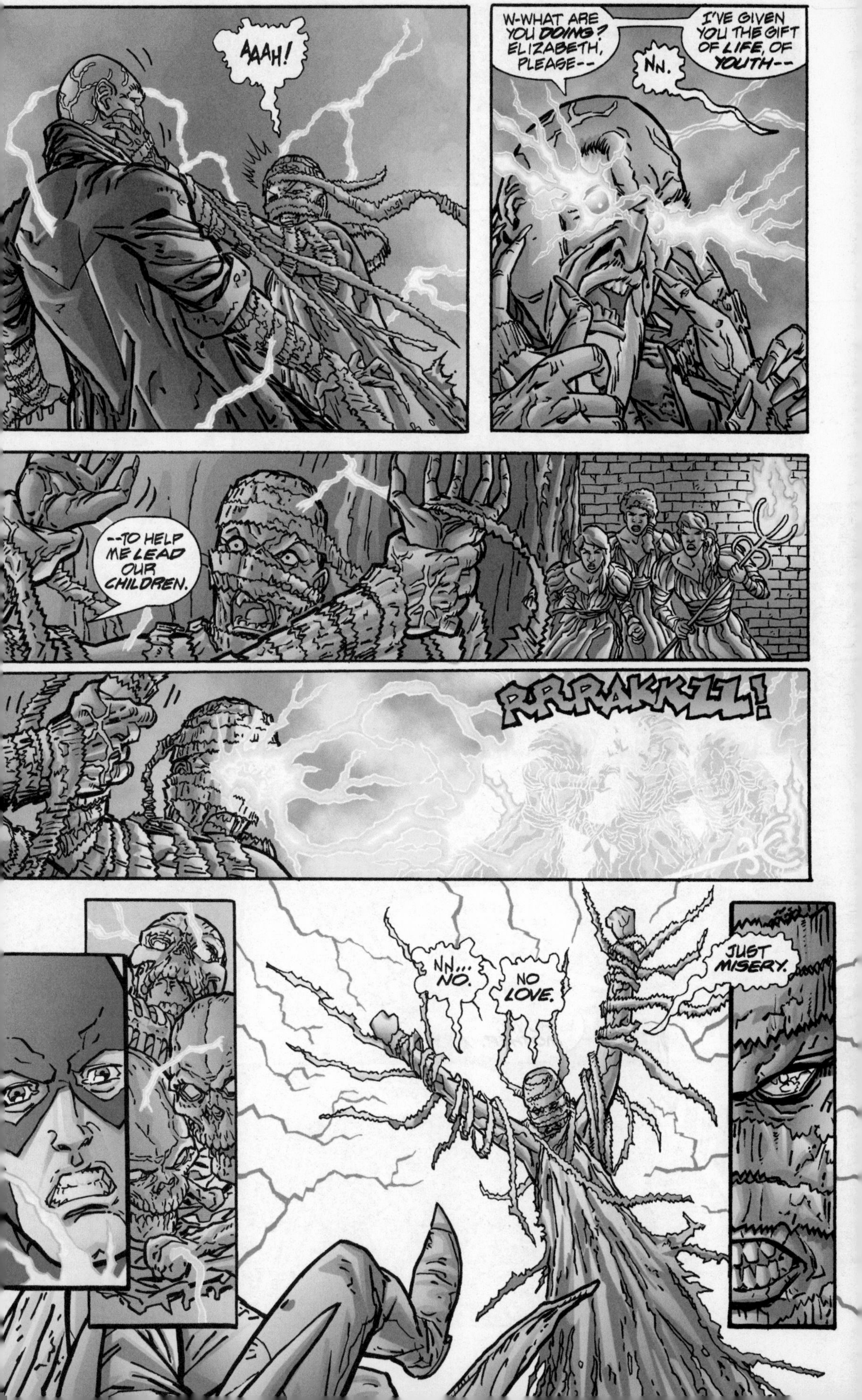
AAAH!
W-WHAT ARE YOU DOING? ELIZABETH, PLEASE--
NN.
I'VE GIVEN YOU THE GIFT OF LIFE, OF YOUTH--
--TO HELP ME LEAD OUR CHILDREN.
RRRAKKLL!
NN... NO.
NO LOVE.
JUST MISERY.

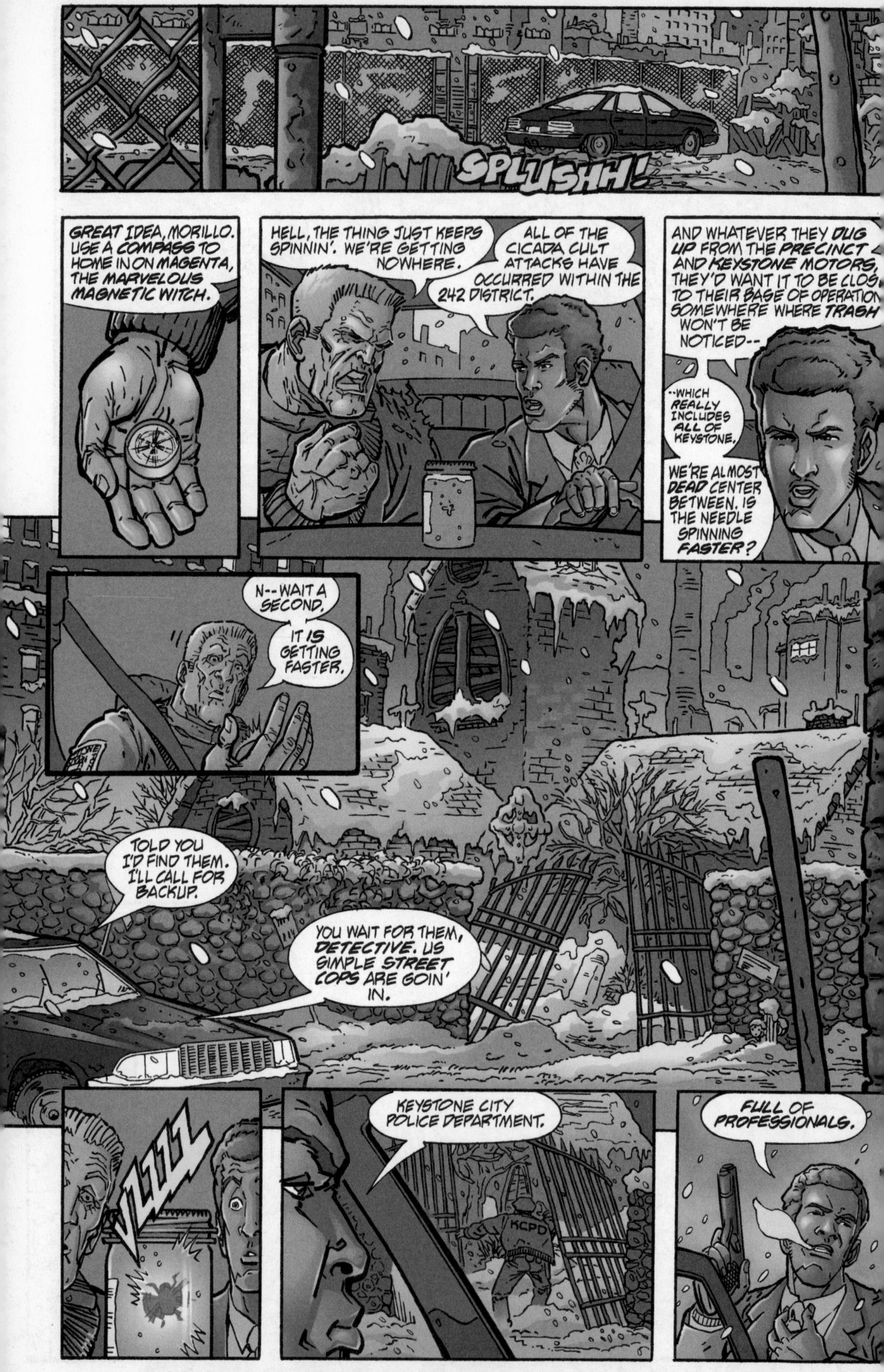
SPLUSHH!
GREAT IDEA, MORILLO. USE A COMPASS TO HOME IN ON MAGENTA, THE MARVELOUS MAGNETIC WITCH.
HELL, THE THING JUST KEEPS SPINNIN'. WE'RE GETTING NOWHERE.
ALL OF THE CICADA CULT ATTACKS HAVE OCCURRED WITHIN THE 242 DISTRICT.
AND WHATEVER THEY DUG UP FROM THE PRECINCT AND KEYSTONE MOTORS, THEY'D WANT IT TO BE CLOS TO THEIR BASE OF OPERATION SOMEWHERE WHERE TRASH WON'T BE NOTICED--
--WHICH REALLY INCLUDES ALL OF KEYSTONE.
WE'RE ALMOST DEAD CENTER BETWEEN. IS THE NEEDLE SPINNING FASTER?
N--WAIT A SECOND.
IT IS GETTING FASTER.
TOLD YOU I'D FIND THEM. I'LL CALL FOR BACKUP.
YOU WAIT FOR THEM, DETECTIVE. US SIMPLE STREET COPS ARE GOIN' IN.
VZZZZ
KEYSTONE CITY POLICE DEPARTMENT.
KCPD
FULL OF PROFESSIONALS.

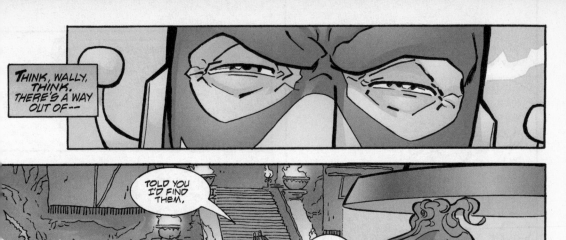

THINK, WALLY, THINK. THERE'S A WAY OUT OF--

TOLD YOU I'D FIND THEM.

I HEARD YOU THE *FIRST* TIME.

OH GREAT. THE *IVY LEAGUE* DETECTIVE AND THE OVER-THE-HILL *BEAT COP*.

A LOT OF HELP THEY'LL GIVE ME. LIKE MIXING GASOLINE AND FIRE.

MIXING.

M-MAGENTA.

HUSH, DARL--

Y-YOU WANT TO SHARE AURAS?

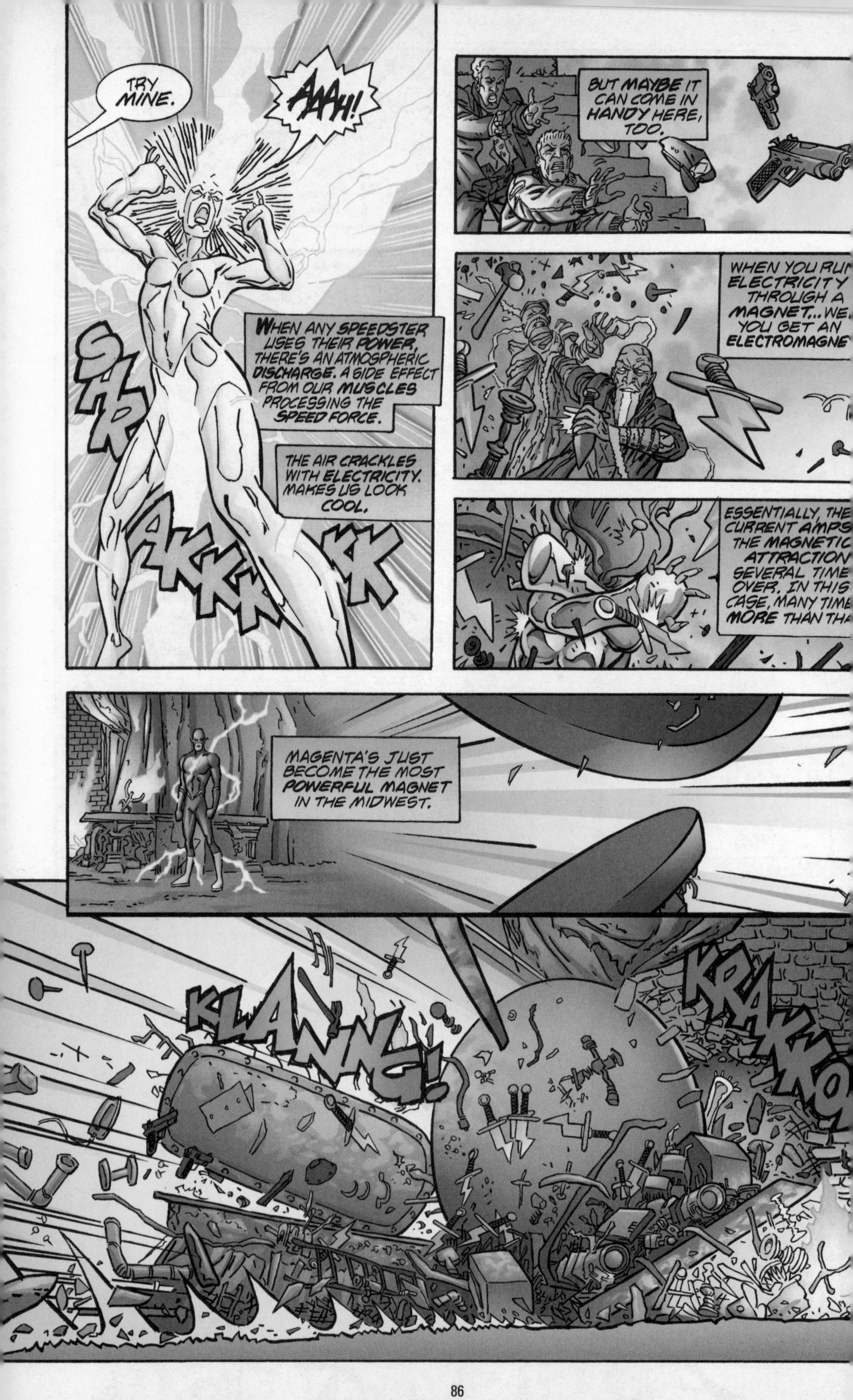
TRY MINE.
AAAH!
WHEN ANY SPEEDSTER USES THEIR POWER, THERE'S AN ATMOSPHERIC DISCHARGE. A SIDE EFFECT FROM OUR MUSCLES PROCESSING THE SPEED FORCE.
SHR
THE AIR CRACKLES WITH ELECTRICITY. MAKES US LOOK COOL.
AKKKKK
BUT MAYBE IT CAN COME IN HANDY HERE, TOO.
WHEN YOU RUN ELECTRICITY THROUGH A MAGNET... WE YOU GET AN ELECTROMAGNE
ESSENTIALLY, THE CURRENT AMPS THE MAGNETIC ATTRACTION SEVERAL TIME OVER. IN THIS CASE, MANY TIME MORE THAN THA
MAGENTA'S JUST BECOME THE MOST POWERFUL MAGNET IN THE MIDWEST.
KLANNG!
KRAKKO

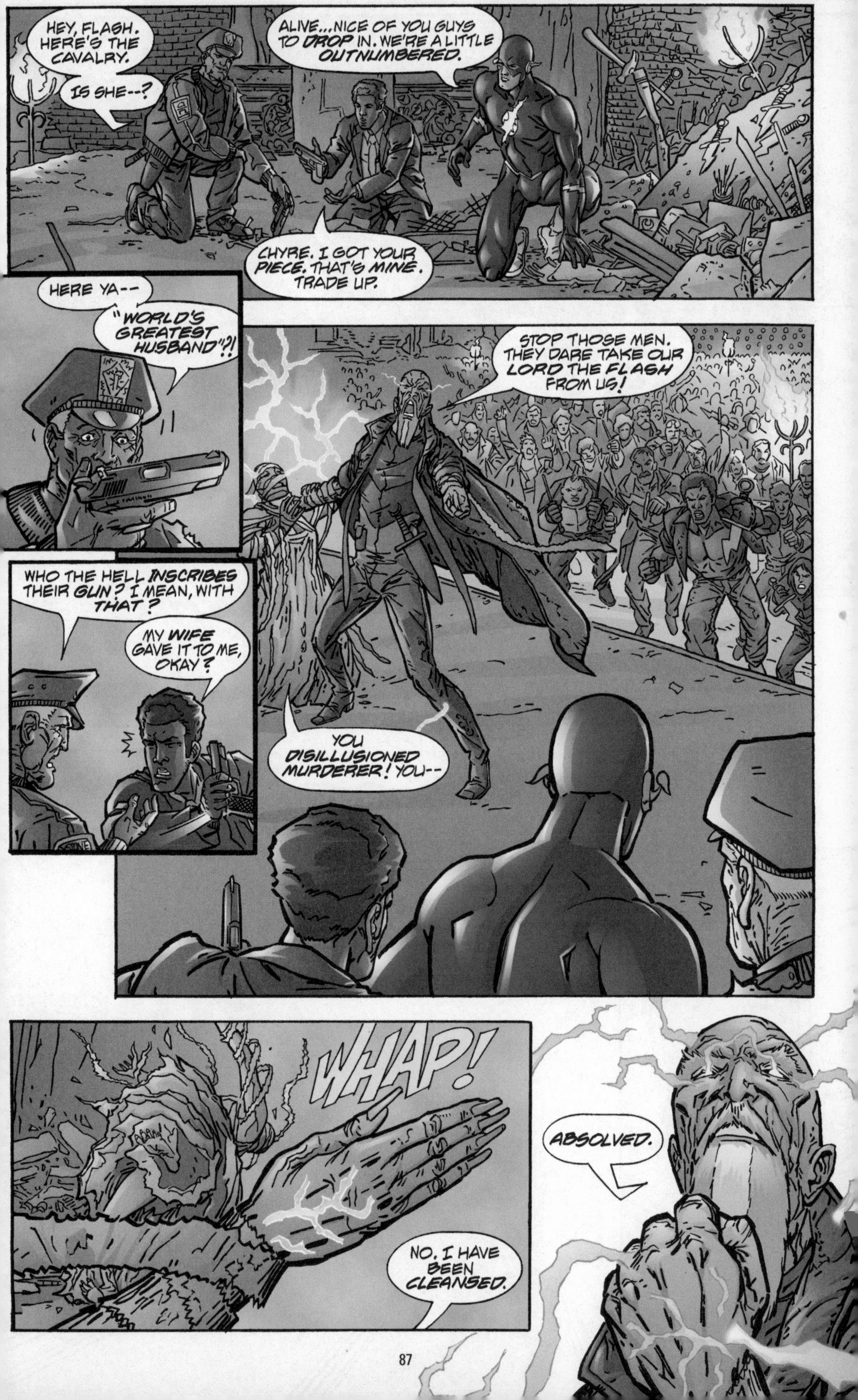
HEY, FLASH. HERE'S THE CAVALRY.
IS SHE--?
ALIVE... NICE OF YOU GUYS TO DROP IN. WE'RE A LITTLE OUTNUMBERED.
CHYRE. I GOT YOUR PIECE. THAT'S MINE. TRADE UP.
HERE YA--
"WORLD'S GREATEST HUSBAND"?!
WHO THE HELL INSCRIBES THEIR GUN? I MEAN, WITH THAT?
MY WIFE GAVE IT TO ME, OKAY?
STOP THOSE MEN. THEY DARE TAKE OUR LORD THE FLASH FROM US!
YOU DISILLUSIONED MURDERER! YOU--
WHAP!
NO. I HAVE BEEN CLEANSED.
ABSOLVED.

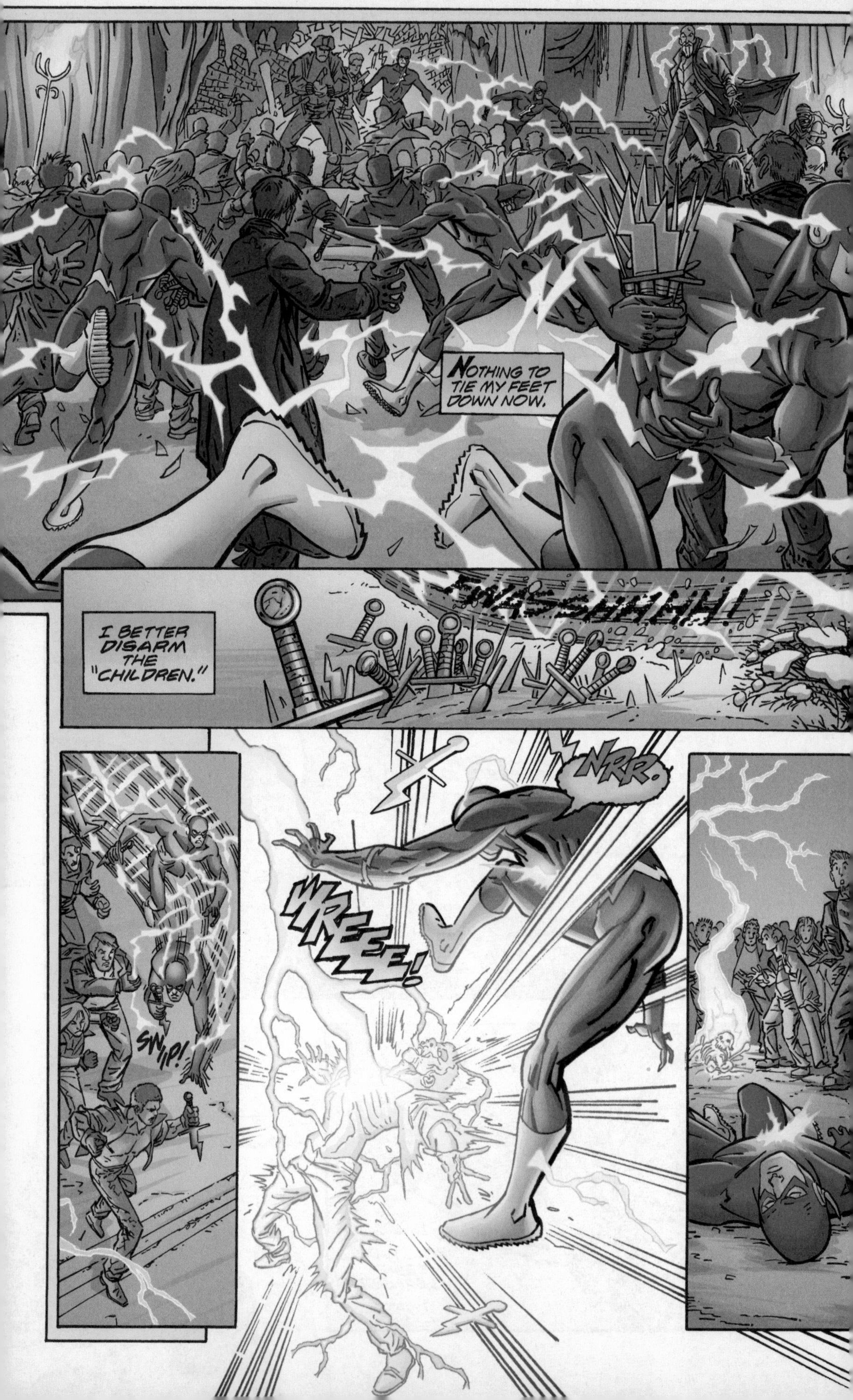
NOTHING TO TIE MY FEET DOWN NOW.
SWASSHHHH!
I BETTER DISARM THE "CHILDREN."
SNIP!
NRR.
WREEEE!

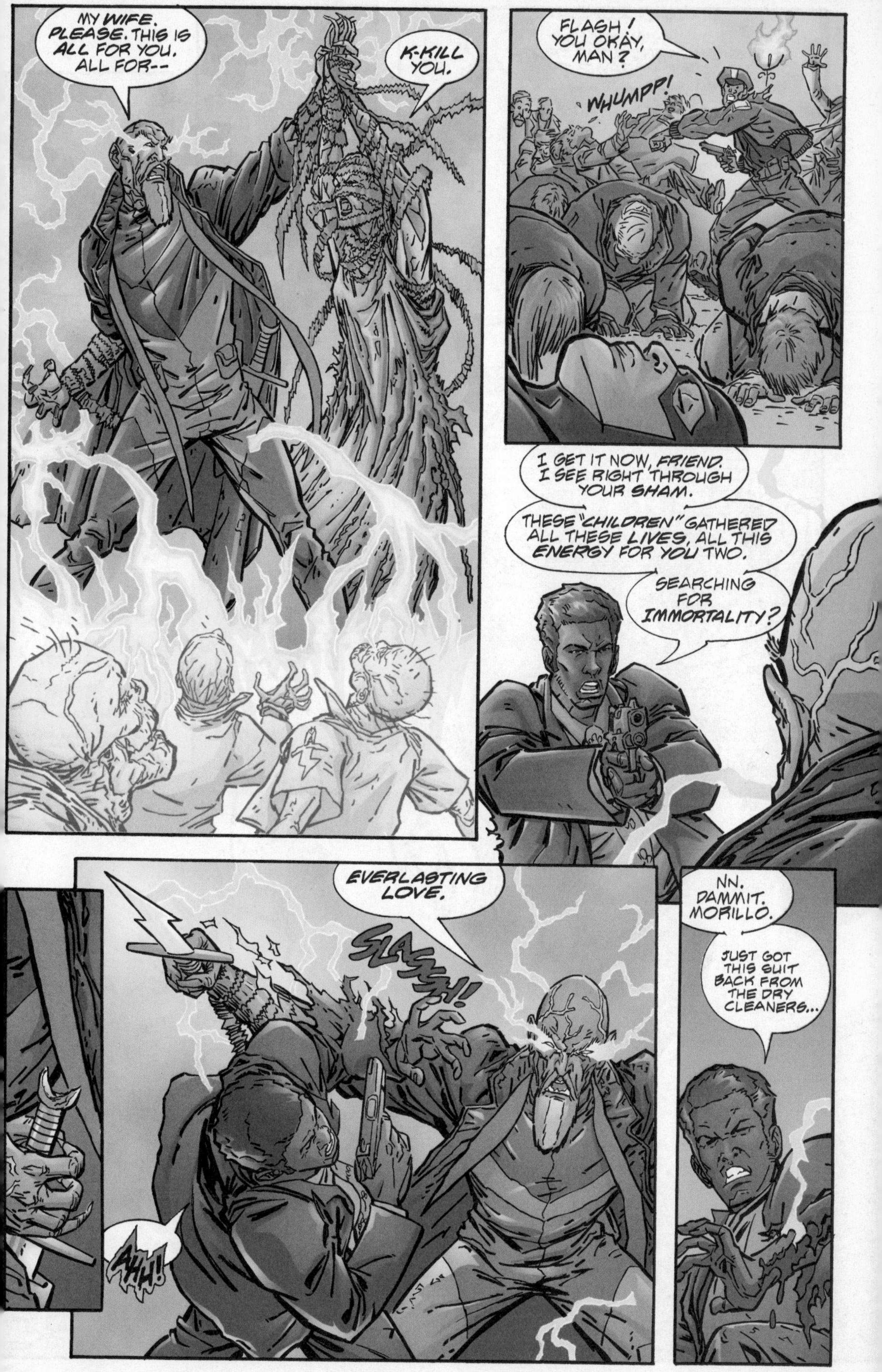
MY WIFE. PLEASE. THIS IS ALL FOR YOU. ALL FOR--
K-KILL YOU.
FLASH! YOU OKAY, MAN?
WHUMPP!
I GET IT NOW, FRIEND. I SEE RIGHT THROUGH YOUR SHAM.
THESE "CHILDREN" GATHERED ALL THESE LIVES, ALL THIS ENERGY FOR YOU TWO.
SEARCHING FOR IMMORTALITY?
EVERLASTING LOVE.
SLASSSH!
AHH!
NN. DAMMIT. MORILLO.
JUST GOT THIS SUIT BACK FROM THE DRY CLEANERS...

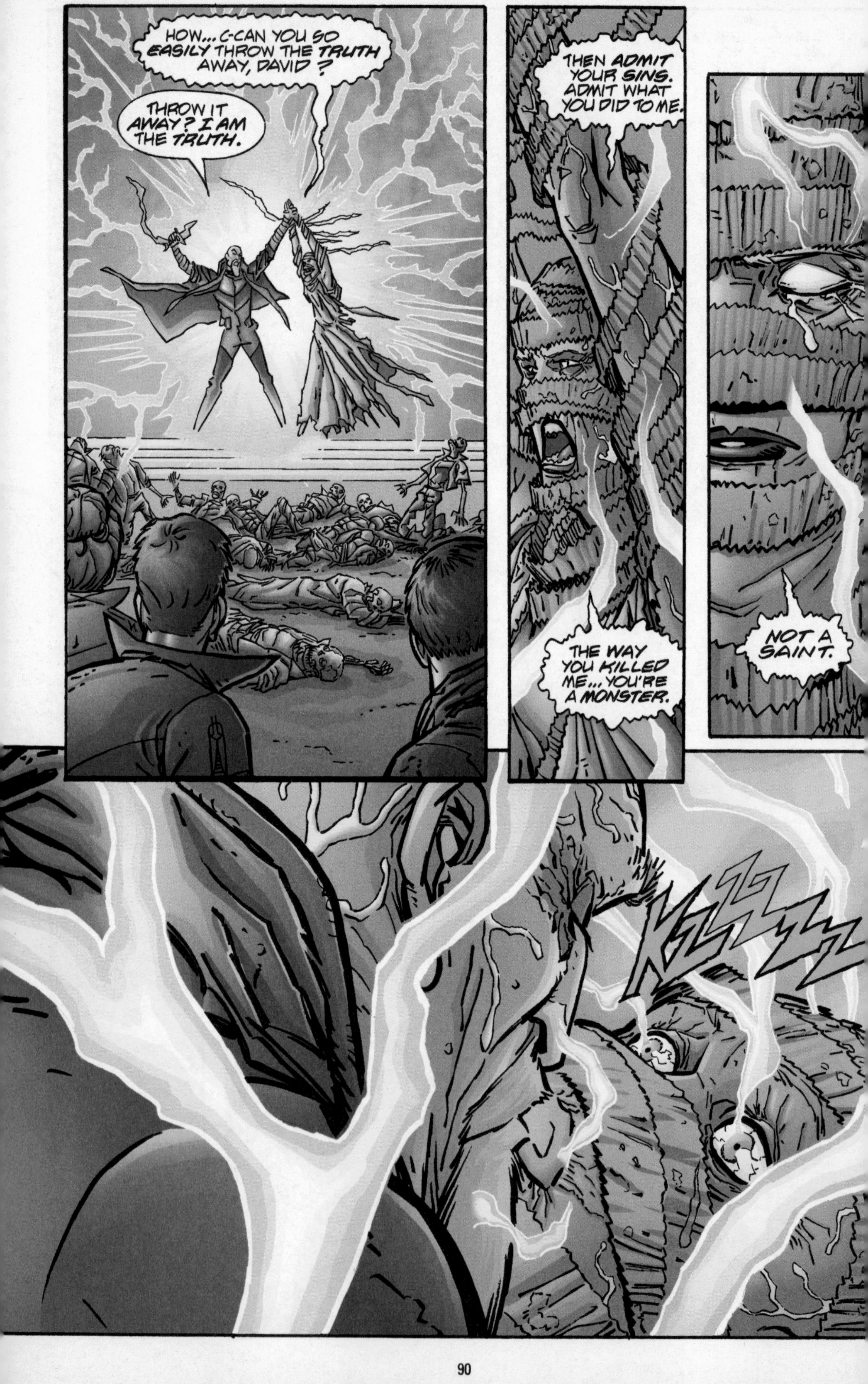
HOW... C-CAN YOU SO EASILY THROW THE TRUTH AWAY, DAVID?
THROW IT AWAY? I AM THE TRUTH.
THEN ADMIT YOUR SINS. ADMIT WHAT YOU DID TO ME.
THE WAY YOU KILLED ME... YOU'RE A MONSTER.
NOT A SAINT.
KSZZZZ

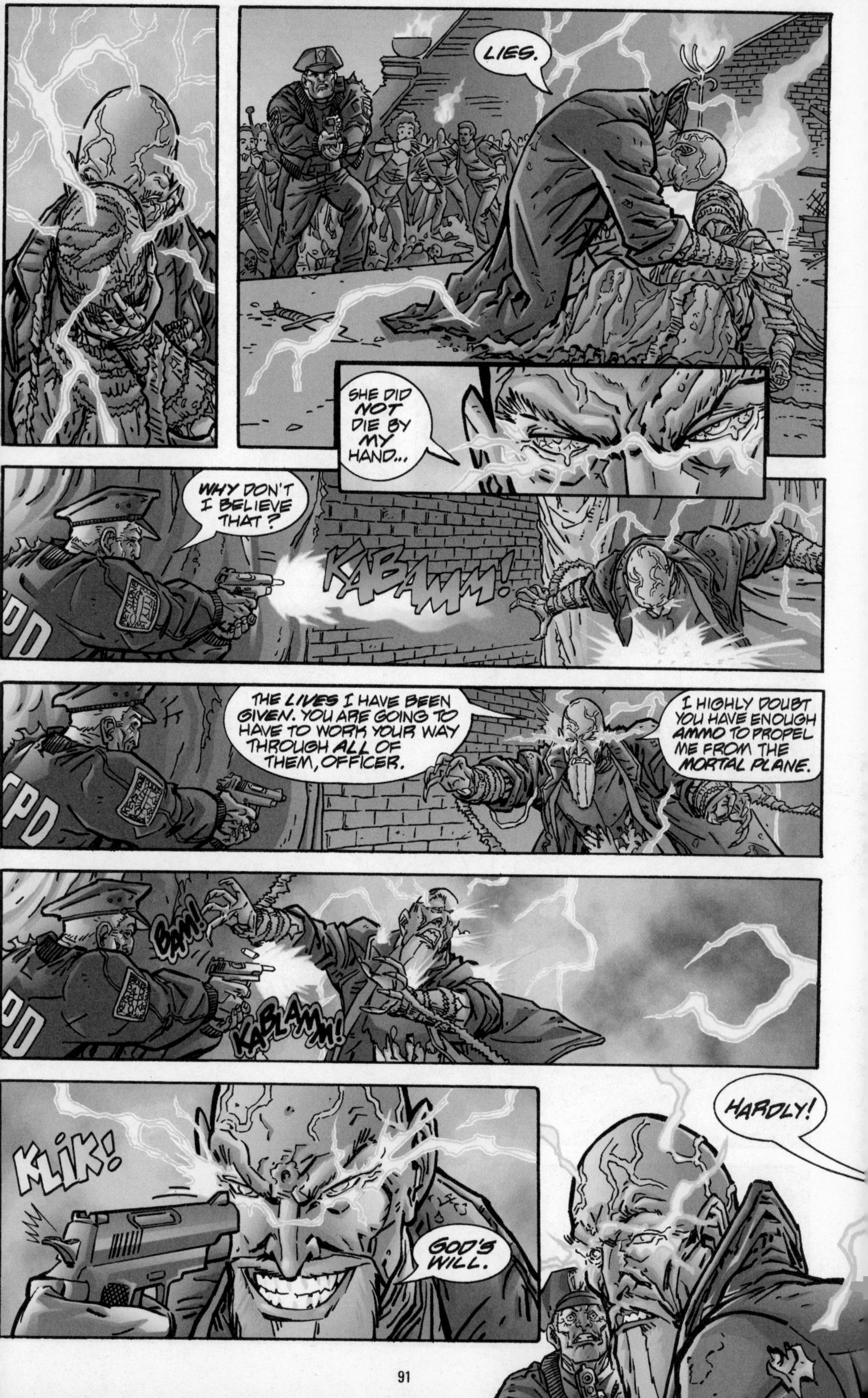
LIES.
SHE DID NOT DIE BY MY HAND...
WHY DON'T I BELIEVE THAT?
KABAMM!
THE LIVES I HAVE BEEN GIVEN. YOU ARE GOING TO HAVE TO WORK YOUR WAY THROUGH ALL OF THEM, OFFICER.
I HIGHLY DOUBT YOU HAVE ENOUGH AMMO TO PROPEL ME FROM THE MORTAL PLANE.
BAM!
KABLAMM!
KLIK!
GOD'S WILL.
HARDLY!

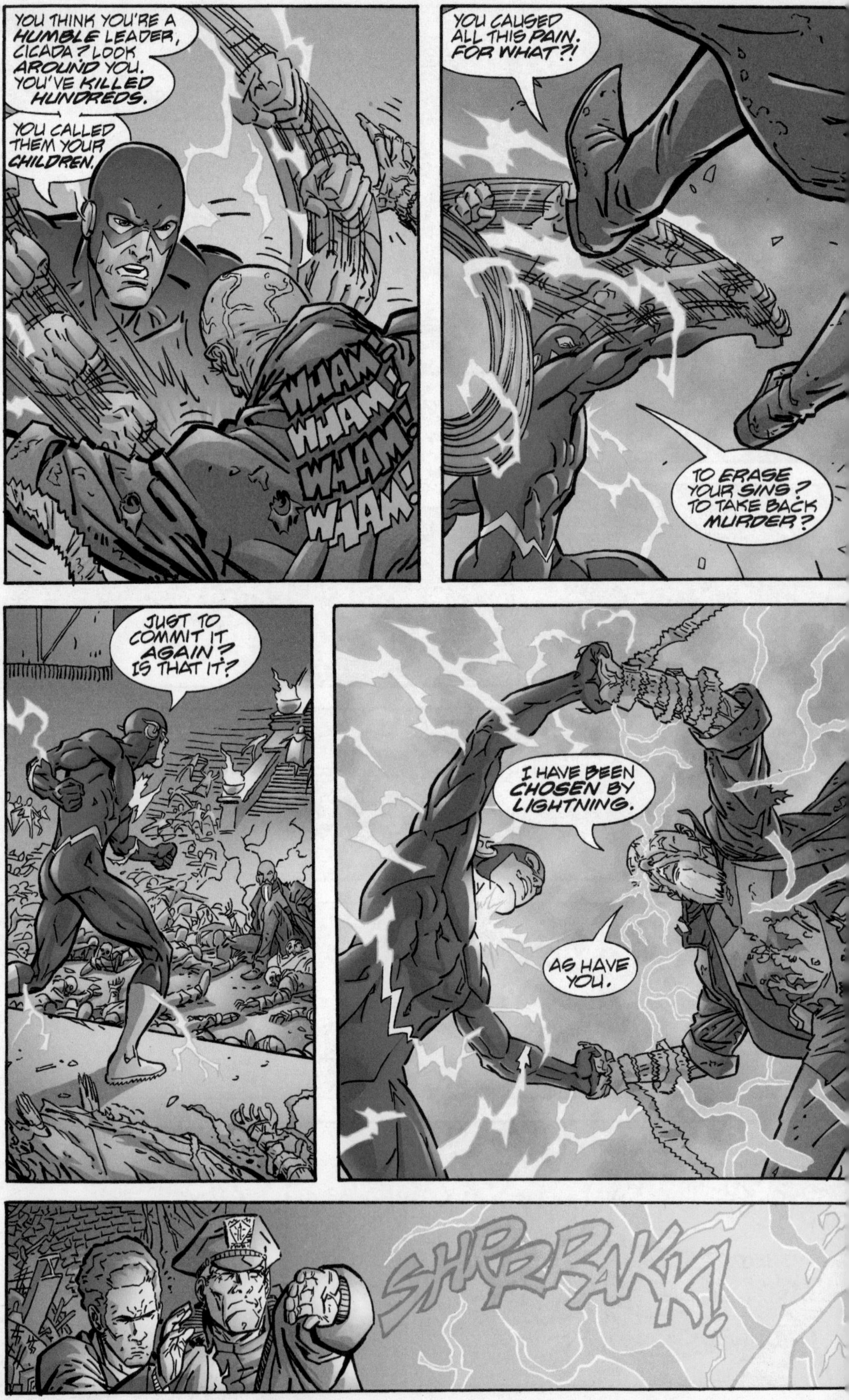
YOU THINK YOU'RE A HUMBLE LEADER, CICADA? LOOK AROUND YOU. YOU'VE KILLED HUNDREDS.
YOU CALLED THEM YOUR CHILDREN.
WHAM! WHAM! WHAM! WHAM!
YOU CAUSED ALL THIS PAIN. FOR WHAT?!
TO ERASE YOUR SINS? TO TAKE BACK MURDER?
JUST TO COMMIT IT AGAIN? IS THAT IT?
I HAVE BEEN CHOSEN BY LIGHTNING.
AS HAVE YOU.
SHRRAKK!

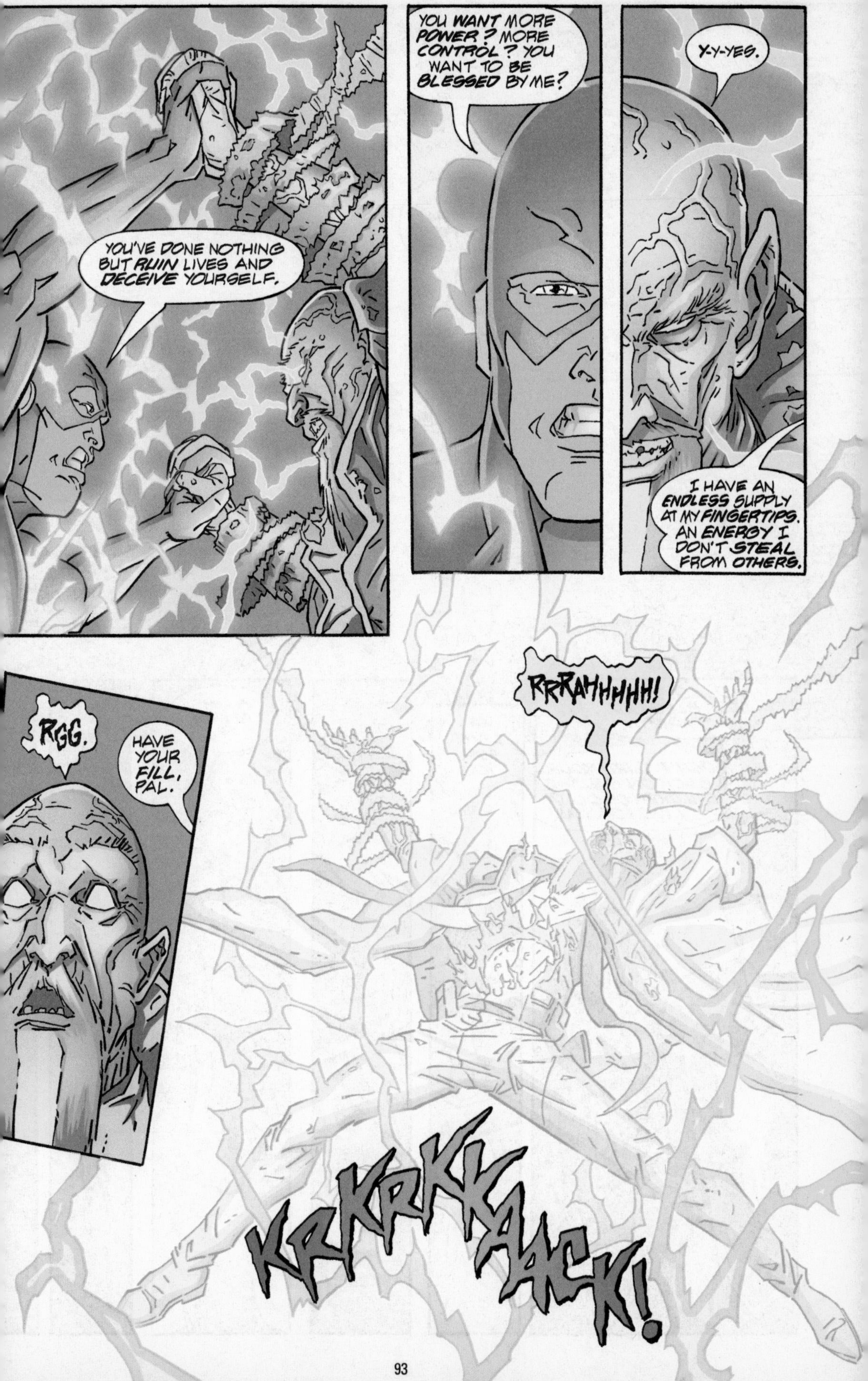
YOU'VE DONE NOTHING BUT RUIN LIVES AND DECEIVE YOURSELF.
YOU WANT MORE POWER? MORE CONTROL? YOU WANT TO BE BLESSED BY ME?
Y-Y-YES.
I HAVE AN ENDLESS SUPPLY AT MY FINGERTIPS. AN ENERGY I DON'T STEAL FROM OTHERS.
RGG.
HAVE YOUR FILL, PAL.
RRRAHHHHHH!
KRKRKKAACK!

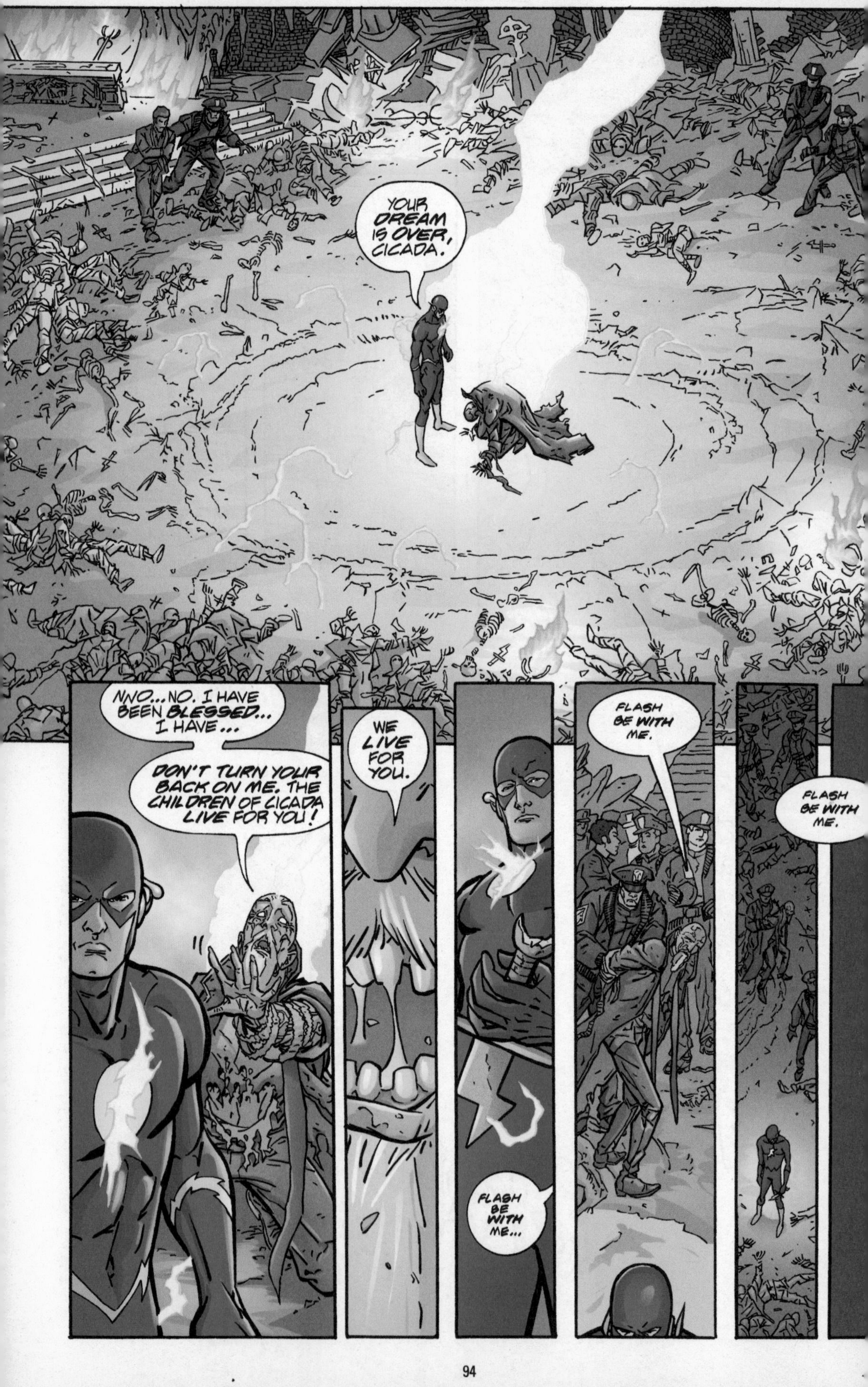
YOUR DREAM IS OVER, CICADA.
NNO... NO. I HAVE BEEN BLESSED... I HAVE...
DON'T TURN YOUR BACK ON ME. THE CHILDREN OF CICADA LIVE FOR YOU!
WE LIVE FOR YOU.
FLASH BE WITH ME...
FLASH BE WITH ME.
FLASH BE WITH ME.

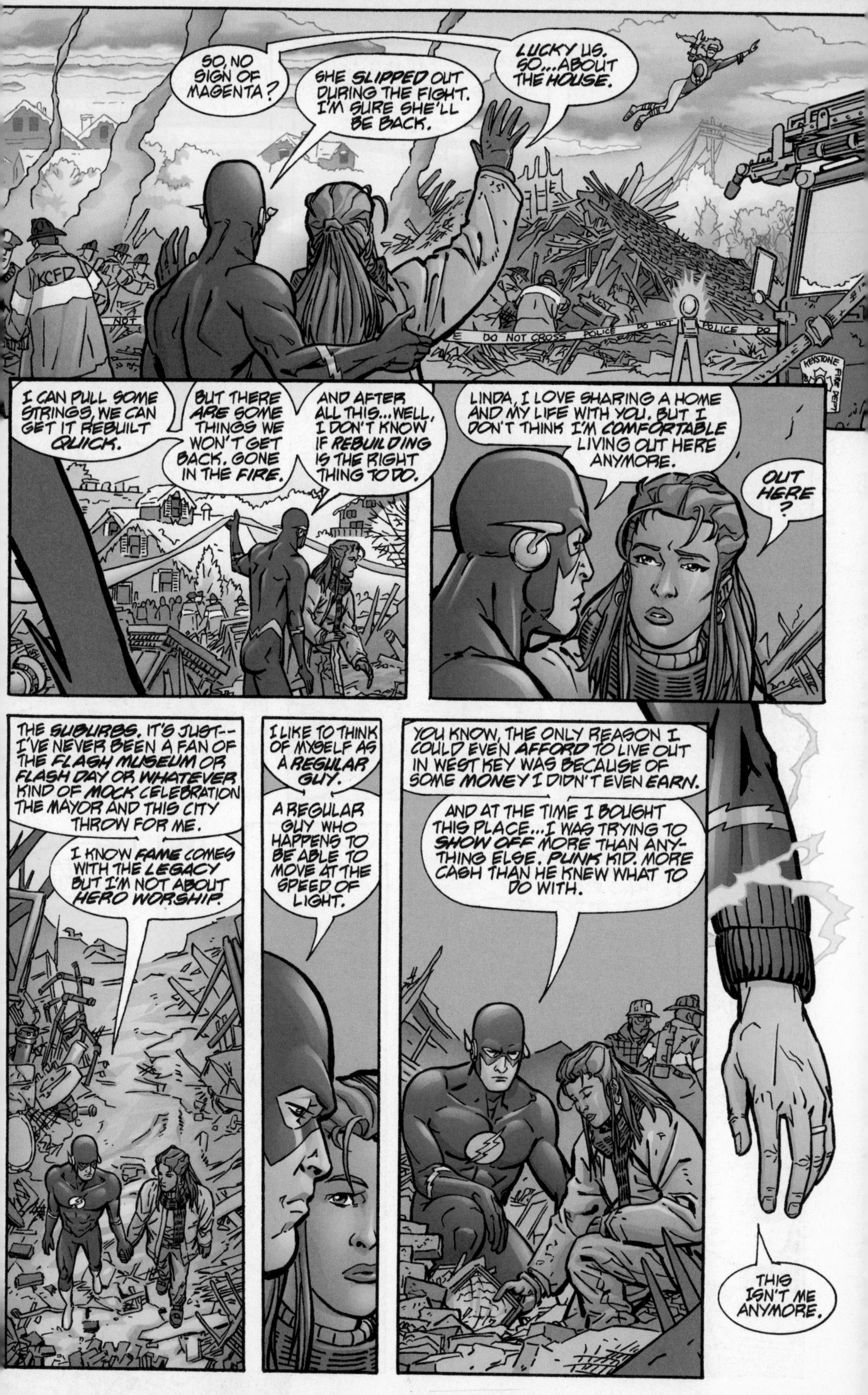
SO, NO SIGN OF MAGENTA?
SHE SLIPPED OUT DURING THE FIGHT. I'M SURE SHE'LL BE BACK.
LUCKY US. SO...ABOUT THE HOUSE.
KCFD
DO NOT CROSS POLICE DO NOT POLICE DO
KEYSTONE FIRE DEPT.
I CAN PULL SOME STRINGS, WE CAN GET IT REBUILT QUICK.
BUT THERE ARE SOME THINGS WE WON'T GET BACK. GONE IN THE FIRE.
AND AFTER ALL THIS... WELL, I DON'T KNOW IF REBUILDING IS THE RIGHT THING TO DO.
LINDA, I LOVE SHARING A HOME AND MY LIFE WITH YOU. BUT I DON'T THINK I'M COMFORTABLE LIVING OUT HERE ANYMORE.
OUT HERE?
THE SUBURBS. IT'S JUST-- I'VE NEVER BEEN A FAN OF THE FLASH MUSEUM OR FLASH DAY OR WHATEVER KIND OF MOCK CELEBRATION THE MAYOR AND THIS CITY THROW FOR ME.
I KNOW FAME COMES WITH THE LEGACY BUT I'M NOT ABOUT HERO WORSHIP.
I LIKE TO THINK OF MYSELF AS A REGULAR GUY.
A REGULAR GUY WHO HAPPENS TO BE ABLE TO MOVE AT THE SPEED OF LIGHT.
YOU KNOW, THE ONLY REASON I COULD EVEN AFFORD TO LIVE OUT IN WEST KEY WAS BECAUSE OF SOME MONEY I DIDN'T EVEN EARN.
AND AT THE TIME I BOUGHT THIS PLACE... I WAS TRYING TO SHOW OFF MORE THAN ANY-THING ELSE. PUNK KID. MORE CASH THAN HE KNEW WHAT TO DO WITH.
THIS ISN'T ME ANYMORE.

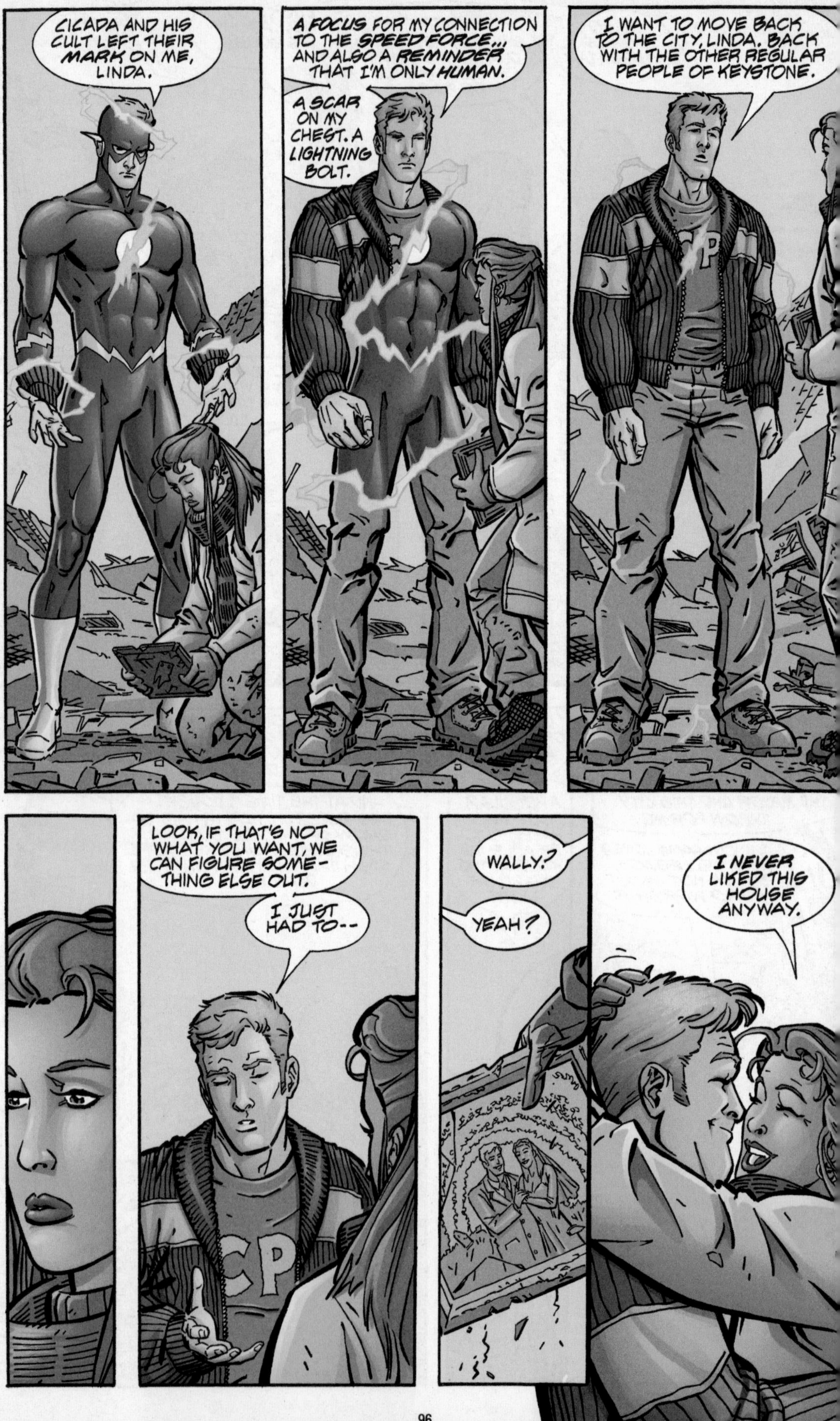
CICADA AND HIS CULT LEFT THEIR MARK ON ME, LINDA.
A SCAR ON MY CHEST. A LIGHTNING BOLT.
A FOCUS FOR MY CONNECTION TO THE SPEED FORCE... AND ALSO A REMINDER THAT I'M ONLY HUMAN.
I WANT TO MOVE BACK TO THE CITY, LINDA. BACK WITH THE OTHER REGULAR PEOPLE OF KEYSTONE.
LOOK, IF THAT'S NOT WHAT YOU WANT, WE CAN FIGURE SOME-THING ELSE OUT.
I JUST HAD TO--
WALLY?
YEAH?
I NEVER LIKED THIS HOUSE ANYWAY.

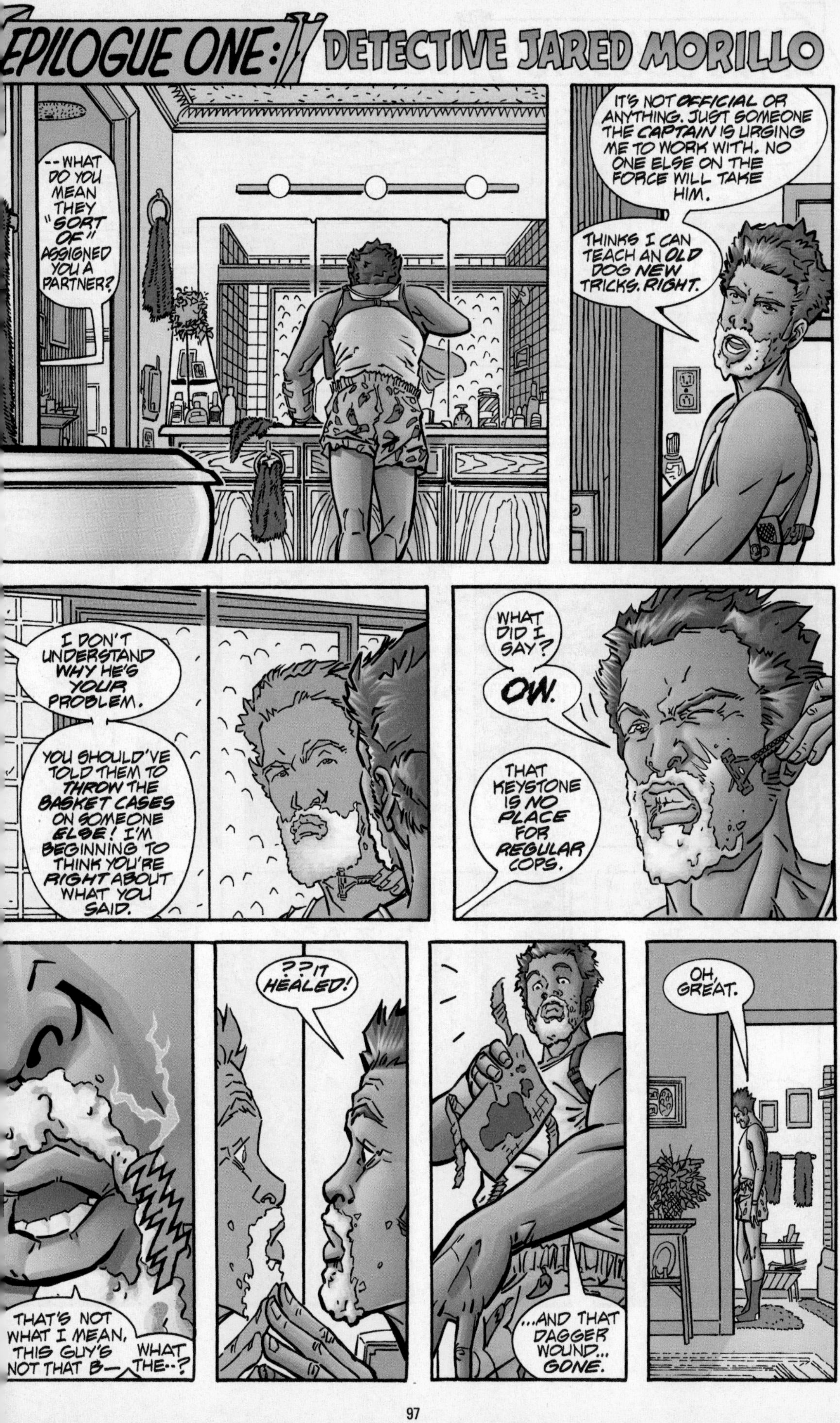
EPILOGUE ONE: DETECTIVE JARED MORILLO
--WHAT DO YOU MEAN THEY "SORT OF" ASSIGNED YOU A PARTNER?
IT'S NOT OFFICIAL OR ANYTHING. JUST SOMEONE THE CAPTAIN IS URGING ME TO WORK WITH. NO ONE ELSE ON THE FORCE WILL TAKE HIM.
THINKS I CAN TEACH AN OLD DOG NEW TRICKS. RIGHT.
I DON'T UNDERSTAND WHY HE'S YOUR PROBLEM.
YOU SHOULD'VE TOLD THEM TO THROW THE BASKET CASES ON SOMEONE ELSE! I'M BEGINNING TO THINK YOU'RE RIGHT ABOUT WHAT YOU SAID.
WHAT DID I SAY?
OW.
THAT KEYSTONE IS NO PLACE FOR REGULAR COPS.
THAT'S NOT WHAT I MEAN. THIS GUY'S NOT THAT B—
WHAT THE--?
??IT HEALED!
...AND THAT DAGGER WOUND... GONE.
OH, GREAT.

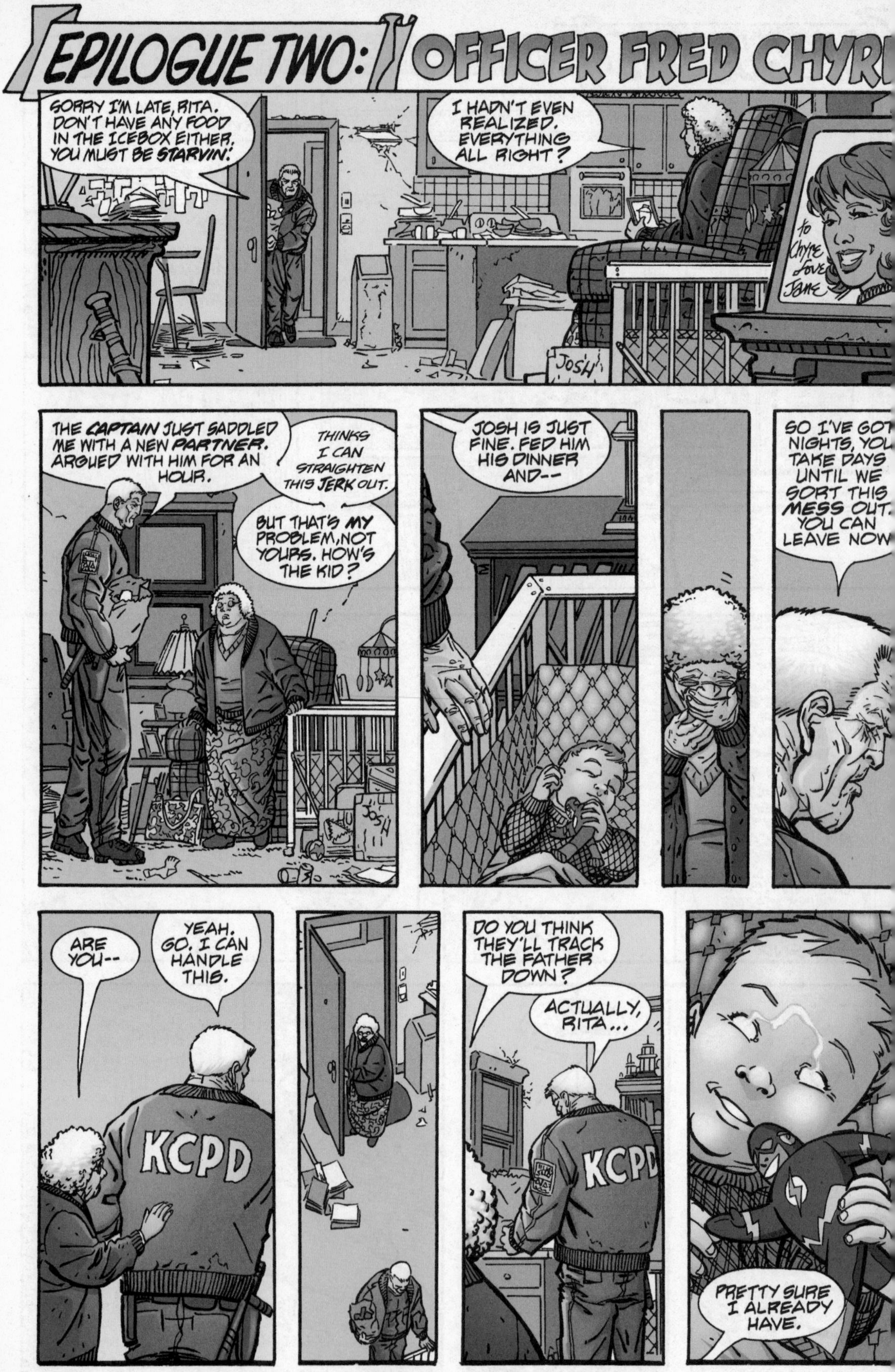
EPILOGUE TWO: OFFICER FRED CHYR
SORRY I'M LATE, RITA. DON'T HAVE ANY FOOD IN THE ICEBOX EITHER. YOU MUST BE STARVIN'.
I HADN'T EVEN REALIZED. EVERYTHING ALL RIGHT?
to Chyre Love Jane
JOSH
THE CAPTAIN JUST SADDLED ME WITH A NEW PARTNER. ARGUED WITH HIM FOR AN HOUR.
THINKS I CAN STRAIGHTEN THIS JERK OUT.
BUT THAT'S MY PROBLEM, NOT YOURS. HOW'S THE KID?
JOSH
JOSH IS JUST FINE. FED HIM HIS DINNER AND--
SO I'VE GOT NIGHTS, YOU TAKE DAYS UNTIL WE SORT THIS MESS OUT. YOU CAN LEAVE NOW
ARE YOU--
YEAH. GO. I CAN HANDLE THIS.
KCPD
DO YOU THINK THEY'LL TRACK THE FATHER DOWN?
ACTUALLY, RITA...
KCPD
PRETTY SURE I ALREADY HAVE.

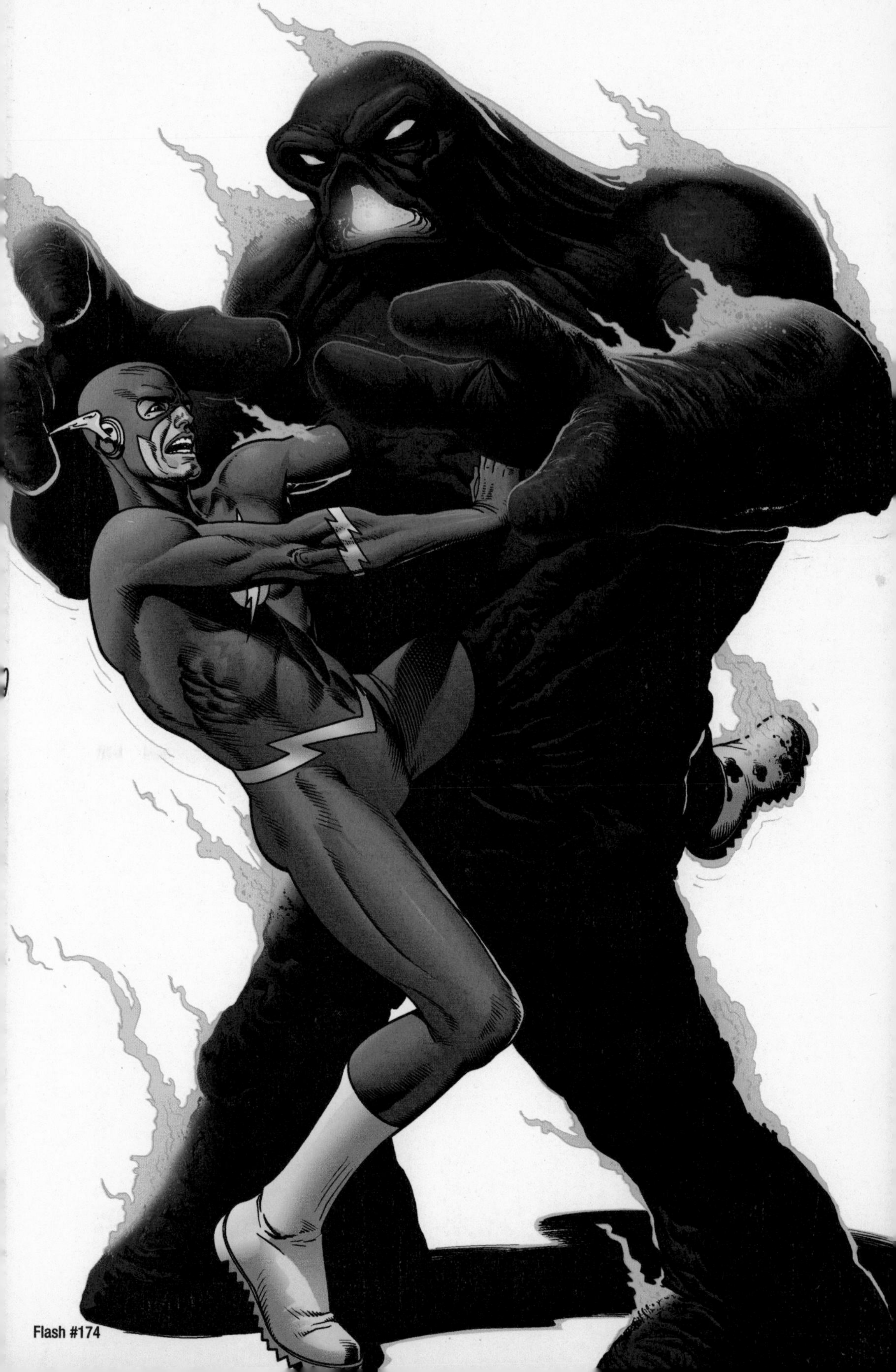

Flash #174

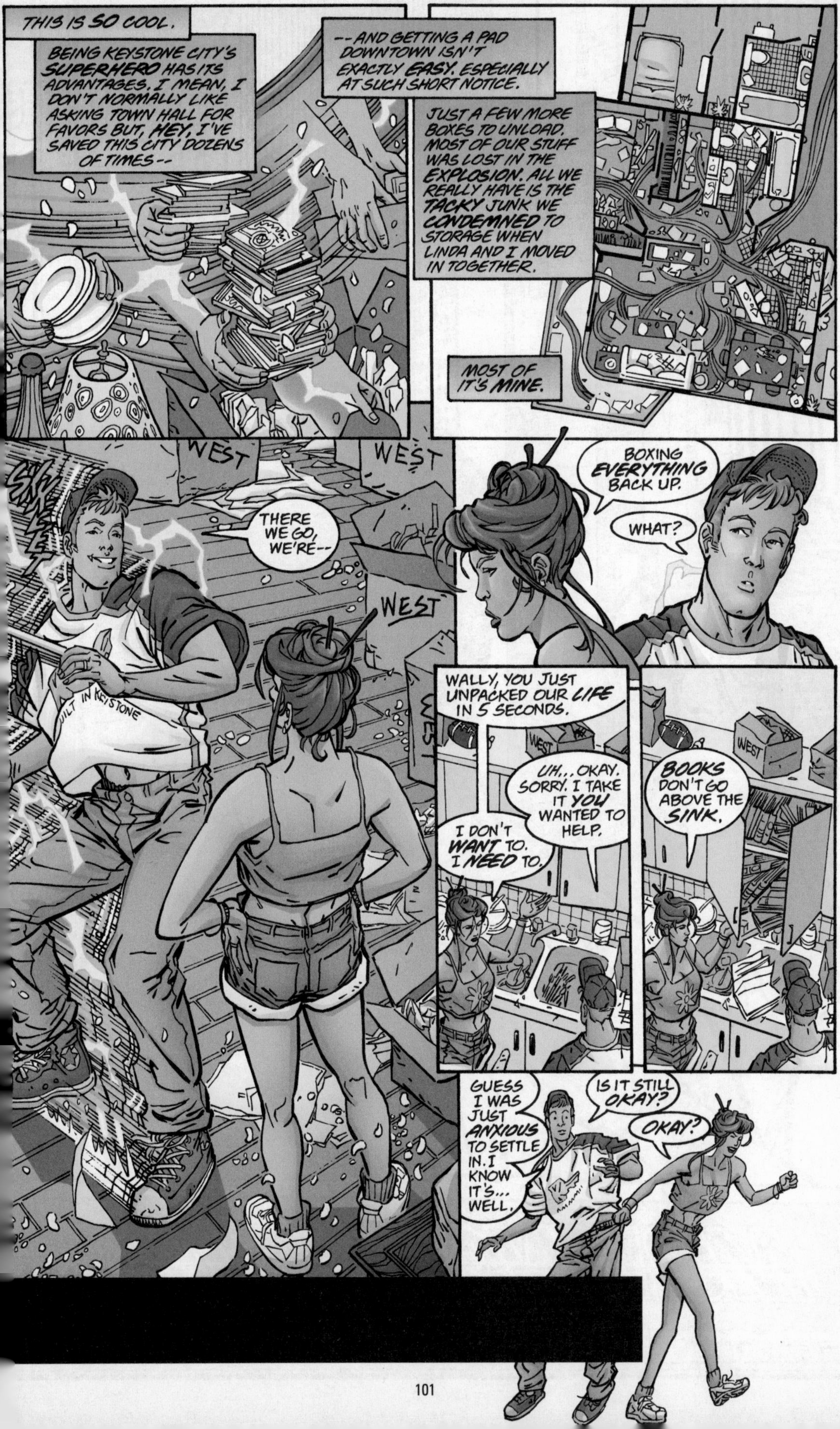

THIS IS SO COOL.
BEING KEYSTONE CITY'S SUPERHERO HAS ITS ADVANTAGES. I MEAN, I DON'T NORMALLY LIKE ASKING TOWN HALL FOR FAVORS BUT, HEY, I'VE SAVED THIS CITY DOZENS OF TIMES--
--AND GETTING A PAD DOWNTOWN ISN'T EXACTLY EASY. ESPECIALLY AT SUCH SHORT NOTICE.
JUST A FEW MORE BOXES TO UNLOAD. MOST OF OUR STUFF WAS LOST IN THE EXPLOSION. ALL WE REALLY HAVE IS THE TACKY JUNK WE CONDEMNED TO STORAGE WHEN LINDA AND I MOVED IN TOGETHER.
MOST OF IT'S MINE.
WEST
WEST
THERE WE GO, WE'RE--
WEST
BOXING EVERYTHING BACK UP.
WHAT?
WALLY, YOU JUST UNPACKED OUR LIFE IN 5 SECONDS.
UH... OKAY. SORRY. I TAKE IT YOU WANTED TO HELP.
I DON'T WANT TO. I NEED TO.
BOOKS DON'T GO ABOVE THE SINK.
GUESS I WAS JUST ANXIOUS TO SETTLE IN. I KNOW IT'S... WELL.
IS IT STILL OKAY?
OKAY?

[redacted]

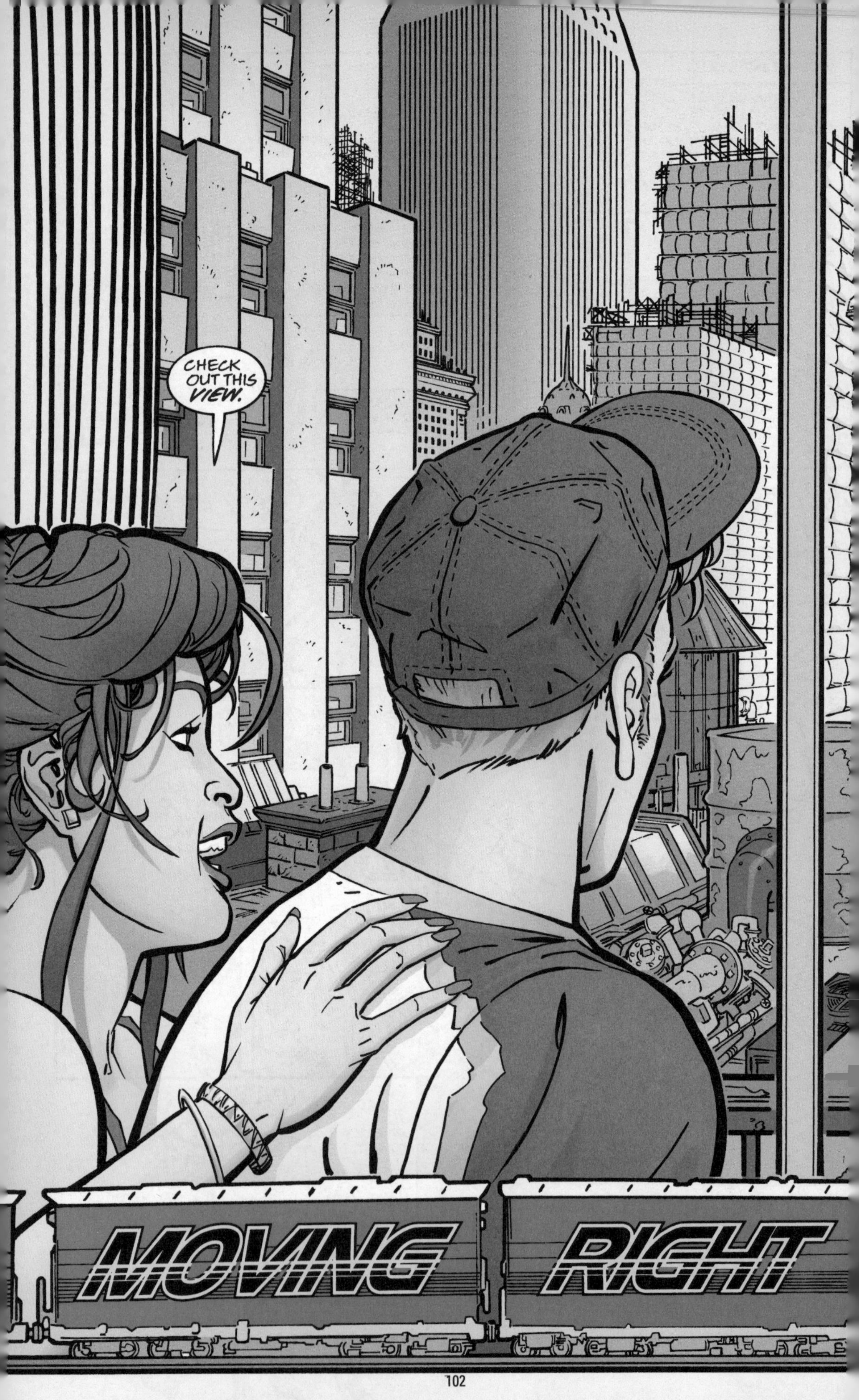
CHECK OUT THIS VIEW.
MOVING RIGHT

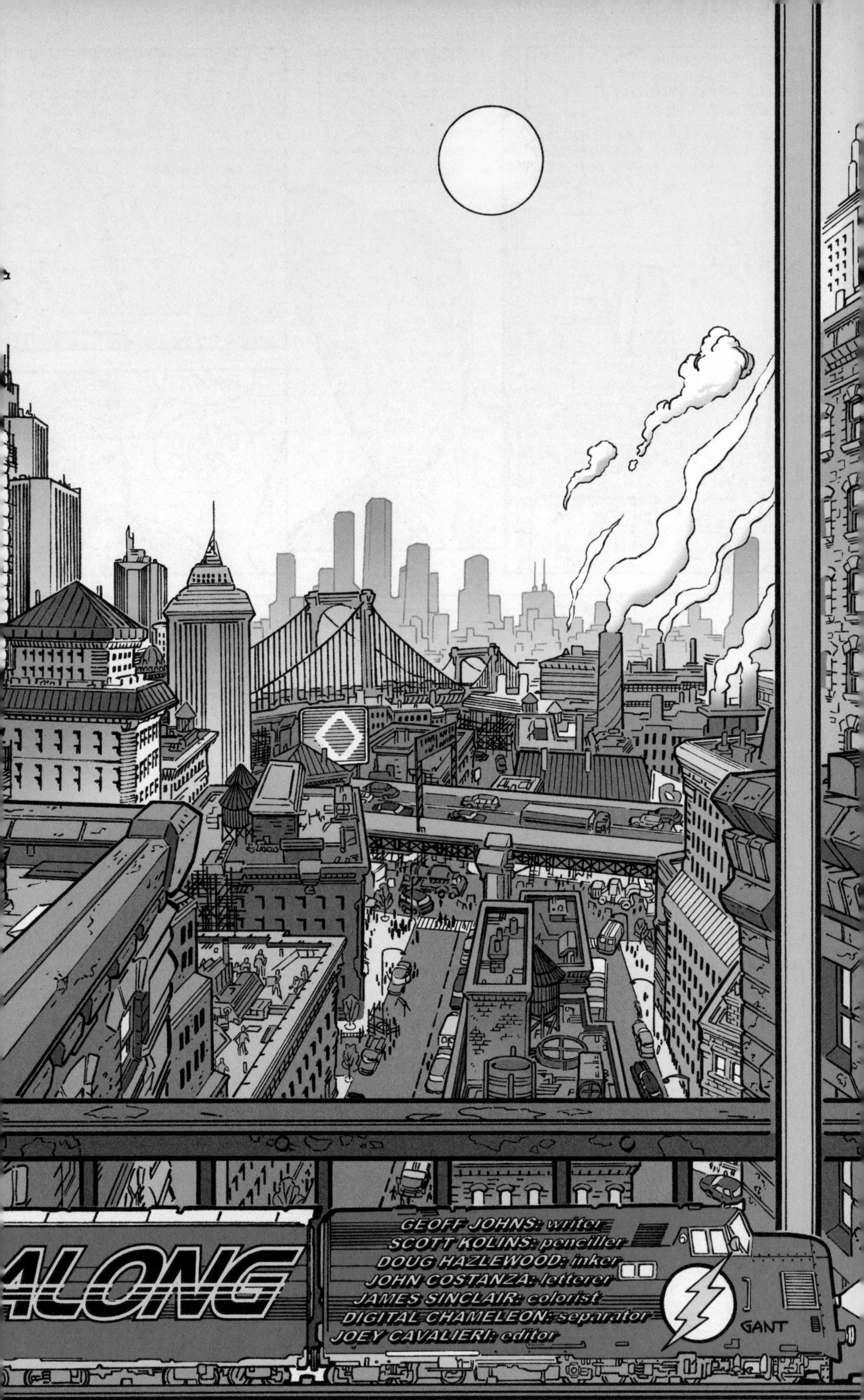

ALONG
GEOFF JOHNS: writer
SCOTT KOLINS: penciller
DOUG HAZLEWOOD: inker
JOHN COSTANZA: letterer
JAMES SINCLAIR: colorist
DIGITAL CHAMELEON: separator
JOEY CAVALIERI: editor
GANT

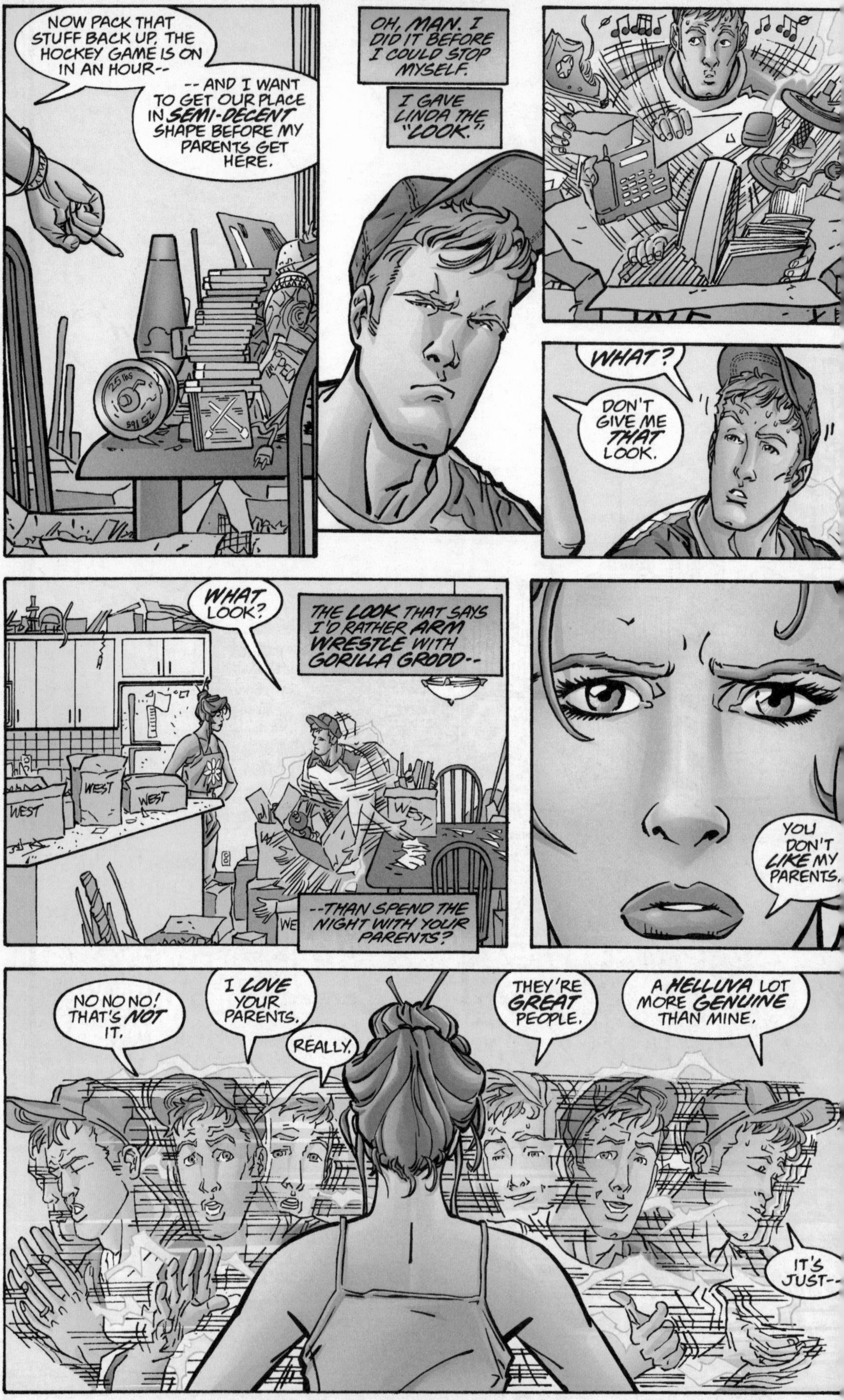
NOW PACK THAT STUFF BACK UP, THE HOCKEY GAME IS ON IN AN HOUR--
-- AND I WANT TO GET OUR PLACE IN SEMI-DECENT SHAPE BEFORE MY PARENTS GET HERE.
OH, MAN. I DID IT BEFORE I COULD STOP MYSELF.
I GAVE LINDA THE "LOOK."
WHAT?
DON'T GIVE ME THAT LOOK.
WHAT LOOK?
THE LOOK THAT SAYS I'D RATHER ARM WRESTLE WITH GORILLA GRODD--
--THAN SPEND THE NIGHT WITH YOUR PARENTS?
YOU DON'T LIKE MY PARENTS.
NO NO NO! THAT'S NOT IT.
I LOVE YOUR PARENTS.
REALLY.
THEY'RE GREAT PEOPLE.
A HELLUVA LOT MORE GENUINE THAN MINE.
IT'S JUST--

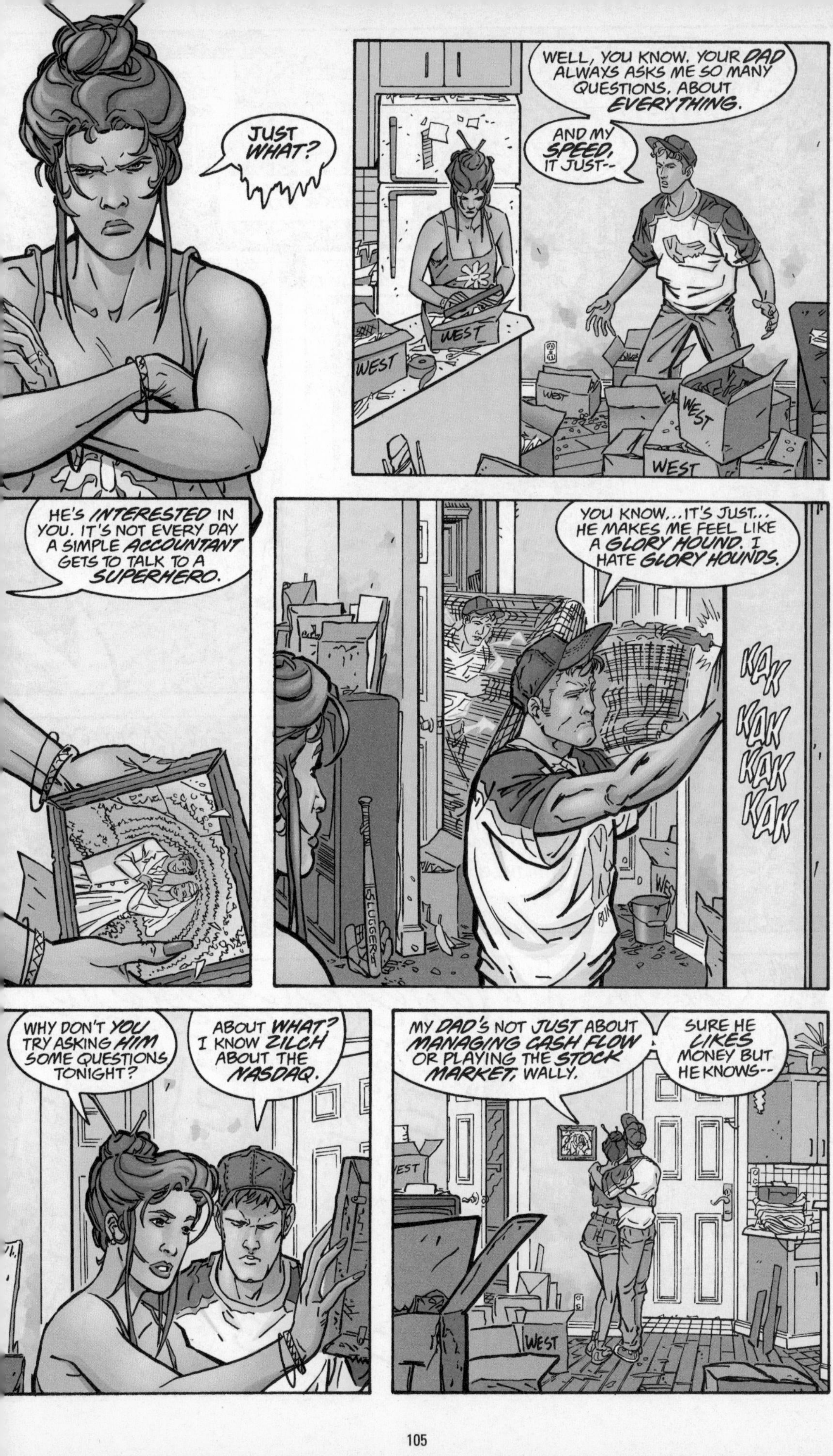
JUST WHAT?
WELL, YOU KNOW. YOUR DAD ALWAYS ASKS ME SO MANY QUESTIONS. ABOUT EVERYTHING.
AND MY SPEED, IT JUST--
WEST
HE'S INTERESTED IN YOU. IT'S NOT EVERY DAY A SIMPLE ACCOUNTANT GETS TO TALK TO A SUPERHERO.
YOU KNOW... IT'S JUST... HE MAKES ME FEEL LIKE A GLORY HOUND. I HATE GLORY HOUNDS.
KAK KAK KAK KAK
SLUGGER
WHY DON'T YOU TRY ASKING HIM SOME QUESTIONS TONIGHT?
ABOUT WHAT? I KNOW ZILCH ABOUT THE NASDAQ.
MY DAD'S NOT JUST ABOUT MANAGING CASH FLOW OR PLAYING THE STOCK MARKET, WALLY.
SURE HE LIKES MONEY BUT HE KNOWS--
WEST

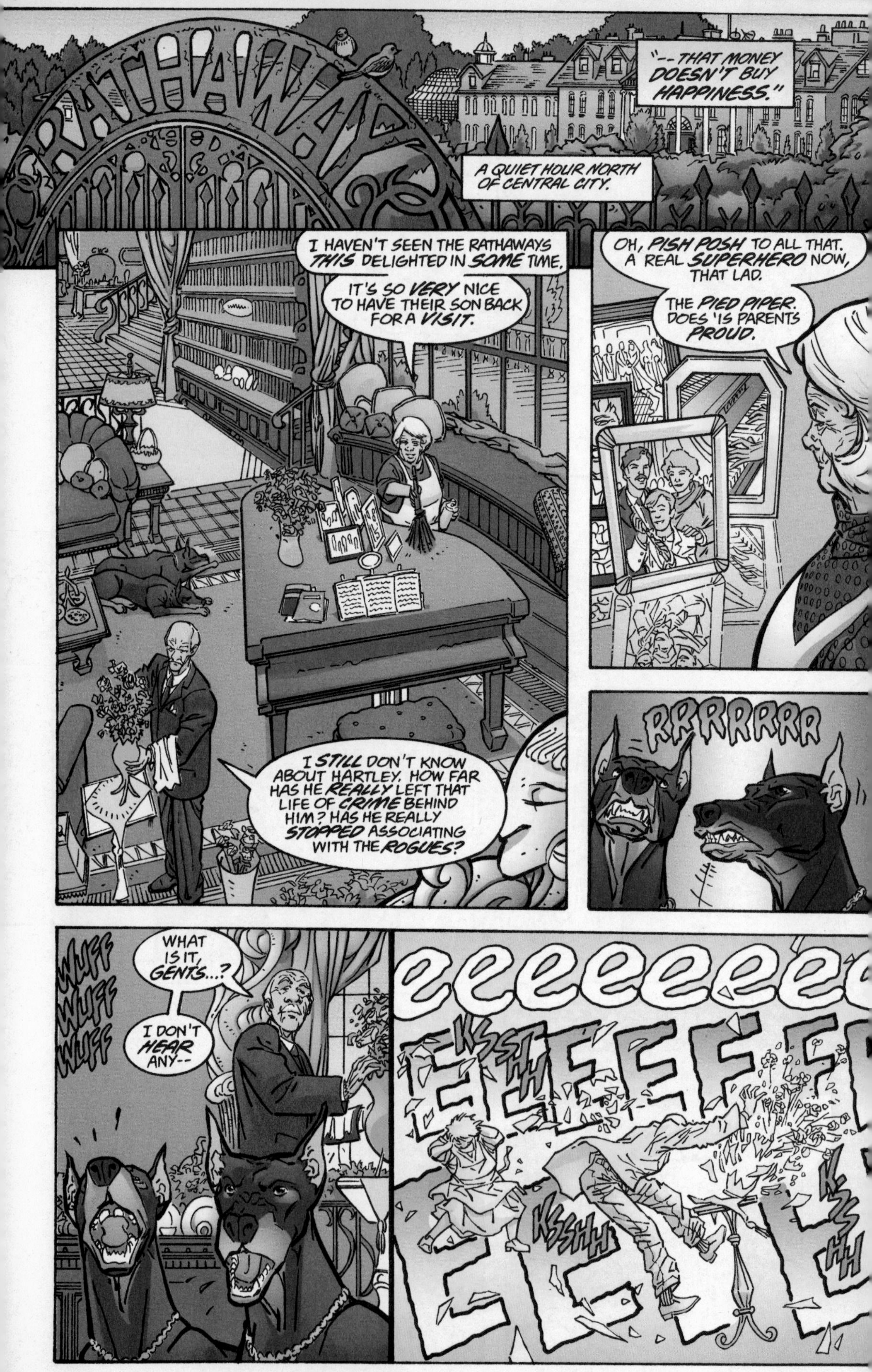
RATHAWAY
"--THAT MONEY DOESN'T BUY HAPPINESS."
A QUIET HOUR NORTH OF CENTRAL CITY.
I HAVEN'T SEEN THE RATHAWAYS THIS DELIGHTED IN SOME TIME.
IT'S SO VERY NICE TO HAVE THEIR SON BACK FOR A VISIT.
OH, PISH POSH TO ALL THAT. A REAL SUPERHERO NOW, THAT LAD.
THE PIED PIPER. DOES 'IS PARENTS PROUD.
I STILL DON'T KNOW ABOUT HARTLEY. HOW FAR HAS HE REALLY LEFT THAT LIFE OF CRIME BEHIND HIM? HAS HE REALLY STOPPED ASSOCIATING WITH THE ROGUES?
RRRRRRR
WUFF WUFF WUFF
WHAT IS IT, GENTS...?
I DON'T HEAR ANY--
eeeeeeee
EEEEEE
KSSH
KSSHH
KSSHH

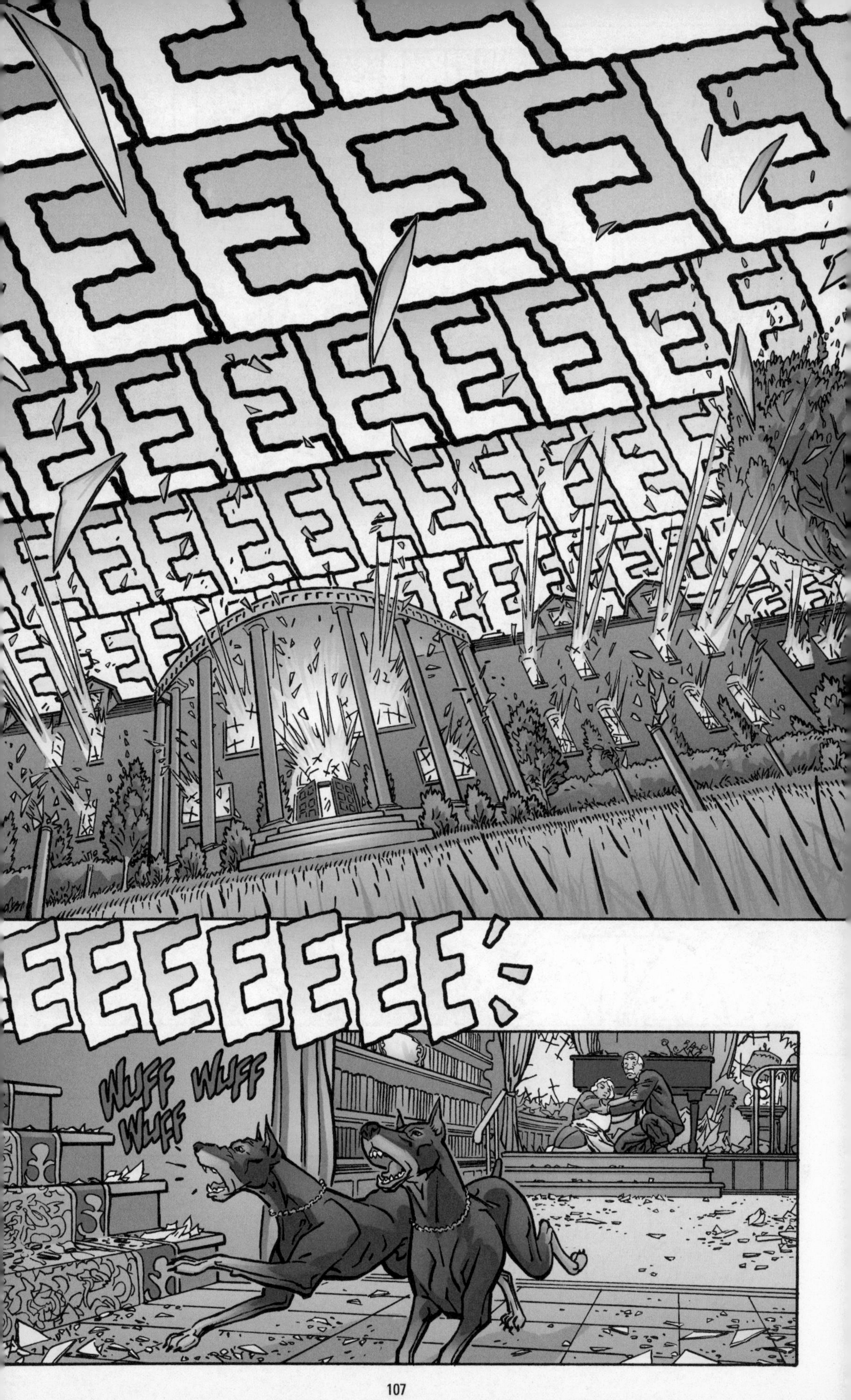
WUFF WUFF
WUFF

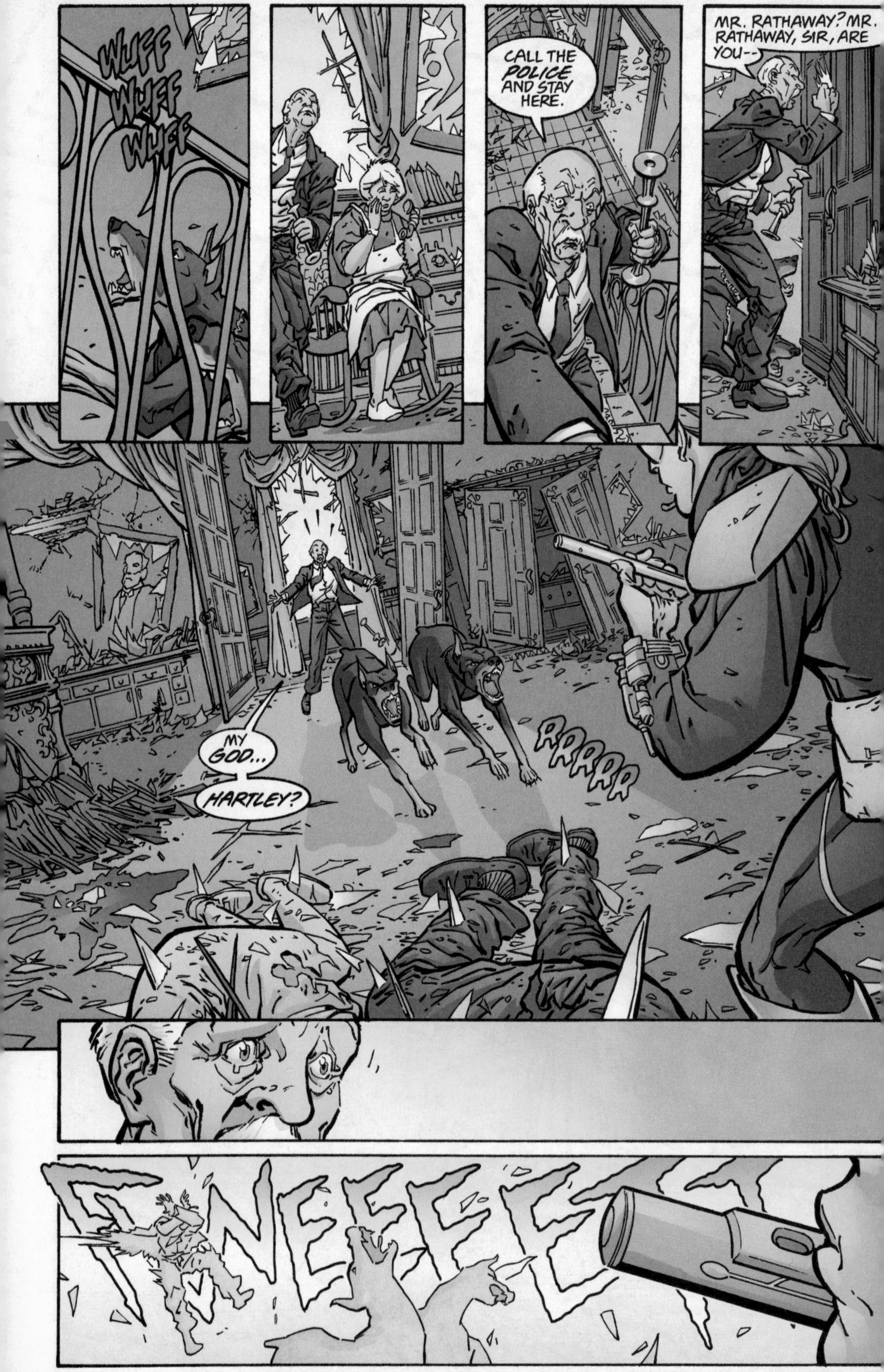
WUFF WUFF WUFF
CALL THE POLICE AND STAY HERE.
MR. RATHAWAY? MR. RATHAWAY, SIR, ARE YOU--
MY GOD...
HARTLEY?
RRRRR
FFNEFFFF

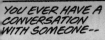

YOU EVER HAVE A CONVERSATION WITH SOMEONE--

--AND YOU DON'T HEAR A *THING* THEY'RE SAYING?

YOU JUST *STARE* OFF INTO THEIR EYES, WORDS FLYING PAST YOU.

EVERY ONCE IN AWHILE YOU NOD.

I HAVE *TWO* LEVELS OF PERCEPTION. "*NORMAL*" AND "*SPEED MODE*." I CAN SWITCH BACK AND FORTH USUALLY ANY TIME I WANT.

BUT SOMETIMES MY SPEED WILL KICK IN *AUTOMATICALLY.* UNDER HIGH DURESS OR WHEN I'M IN *DANGER.*

ONCE I WAS SHOT AT FROM BEHIND. AS SOON AS MY SKIN *FELT* THE HEAT OF THE AMMUNITION, I SHIFTED GEARS-- AND STEPPED OUT OF THE BULLET'S WAY.

BUT SOMETIMES "*SPEED MODE*" HAS ITS DISADVANTAGES TOO.

SOMETIMES IT KICKS IN WHEN I'M *BORED.* LIKE WHEN LINDA ONCE TOOK ME TO THE OPERA. I WAS THERE FOR A RELATIVE *DAY.* AND NOW...

...RIGHT WHEN I STARTED TALKING TO LINDA'S DAD MY *SPEED MODE* KICKS IN--

BONNNNNN - DDDDDDSSSSSSS...

IT'S TAKING HIM PRACTICALLY AN *HOUR* TO ASK ME ONE QUESTION.

CAN'T EVEN WATCH TV. THE *GAME* IS MOVING IN *SLOW MOTION.* THE SCREEN IS STARTING TO *STROBE* AS I WATCH THE ELECTRON GUN IN THE SET *CREATE* EVERY FRAME. PIXEL BY PIXEL.

I CAN'T TAKE MUCH MORE OF--

WHOA.

WHAT THE HELL--

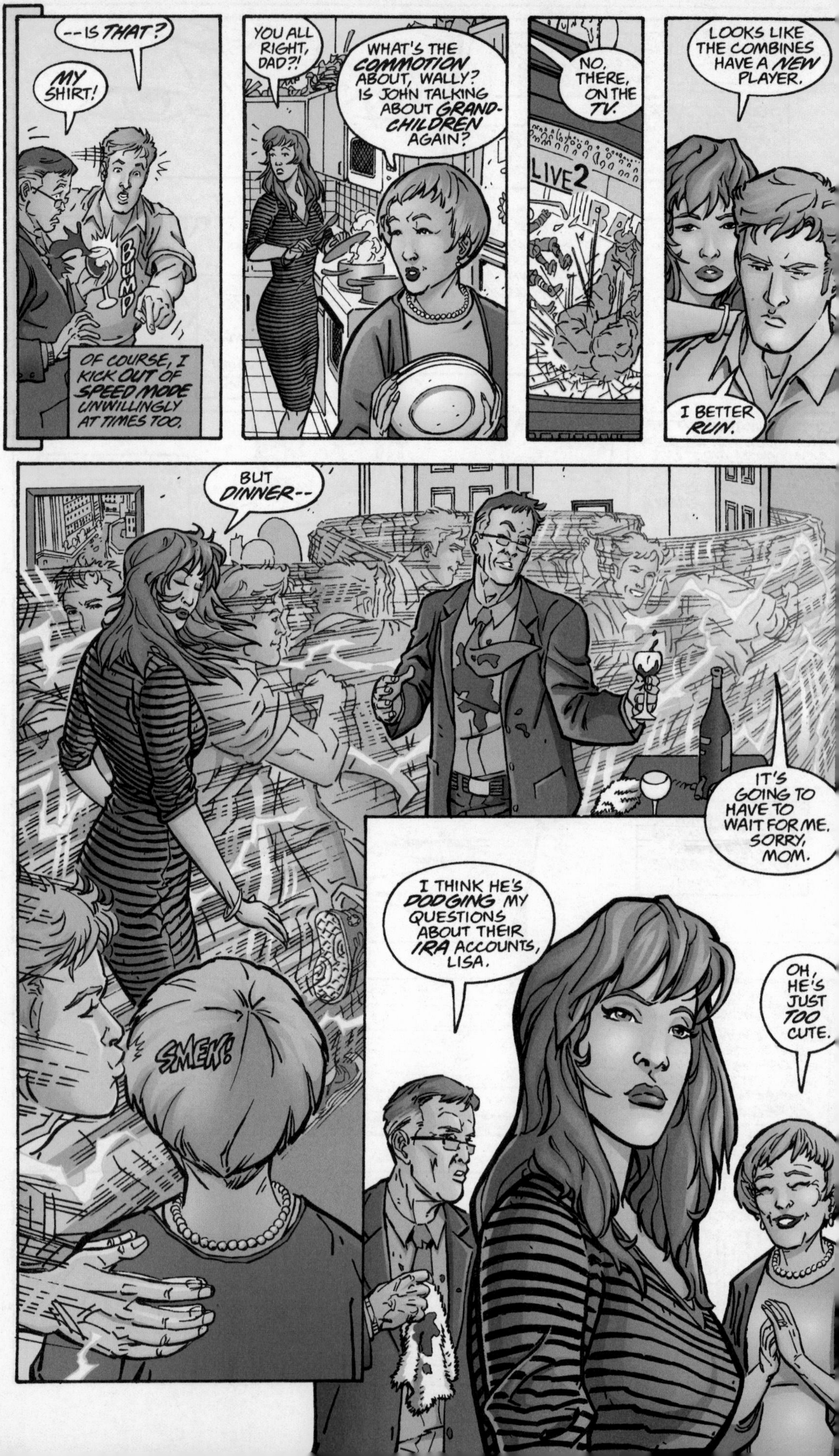
--IS THAT?
MY SHIRT!
BUMP
OF COURSE, I KICK OUT OF SPEED MODE UNWILLINGLY AT TIMES TOO.
YOU ALL RIGHT, DAD?!
WHAT'S THE COMMOTION ABOUT, WALLY? IS JOHN TALKING ABOUT GRAND-CHILDREN AGAIN?
NO, THERE, ON THE TV.
LIVE 2
LOOKS LIKE THE COMBINES HAVE A NEW PLAYER.
I BETTER RUN.
BUT DINNER--
IT'S GOING TO HAVE TO WAIT FOR ME. SORRY, MOM.
SMEK!
I THINK HE'S DODGING MY QUESTIONS ABOUT THEIR IRA ACCOUNTS, LISA.
OH, HE'S JUST TOO CUTE.

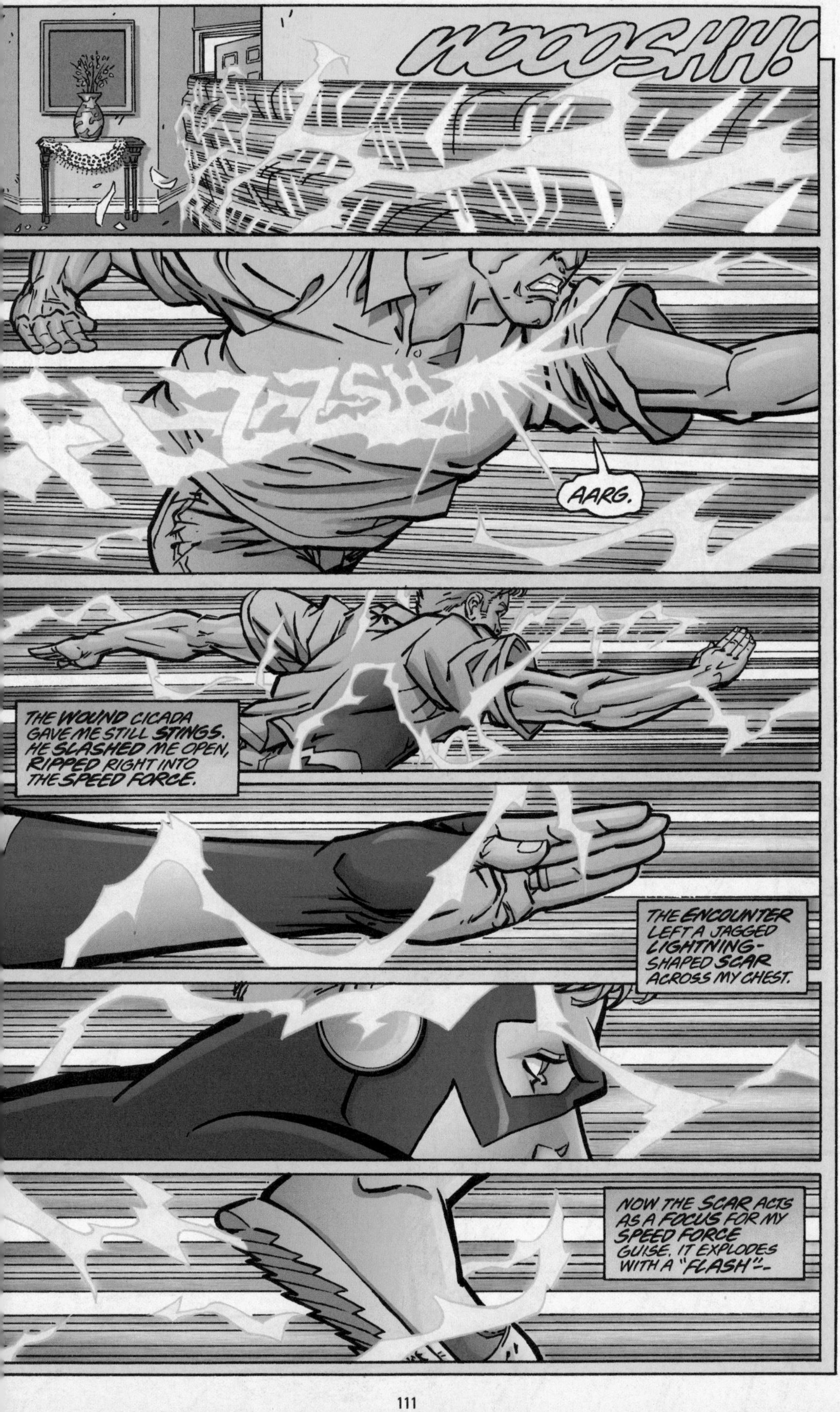
WHOOOSHH!
FZZSH
AARG.
THE WOUND CICADA GAVE ME STILL STINGS. HE SLASHED ME OPEN, RIPPED RIGHT INTO THE SPEED FORCE.
THE ENCOUNTER LEFT A JAGGED LIGHTNING-SHAPED SCAR ACROSS MY CHEST.
NOW THE SCAR ACTS AS A FOCUS FOR MY SPEED FORCE GUISE. IT EXPLODES WITH A "FLASH"--

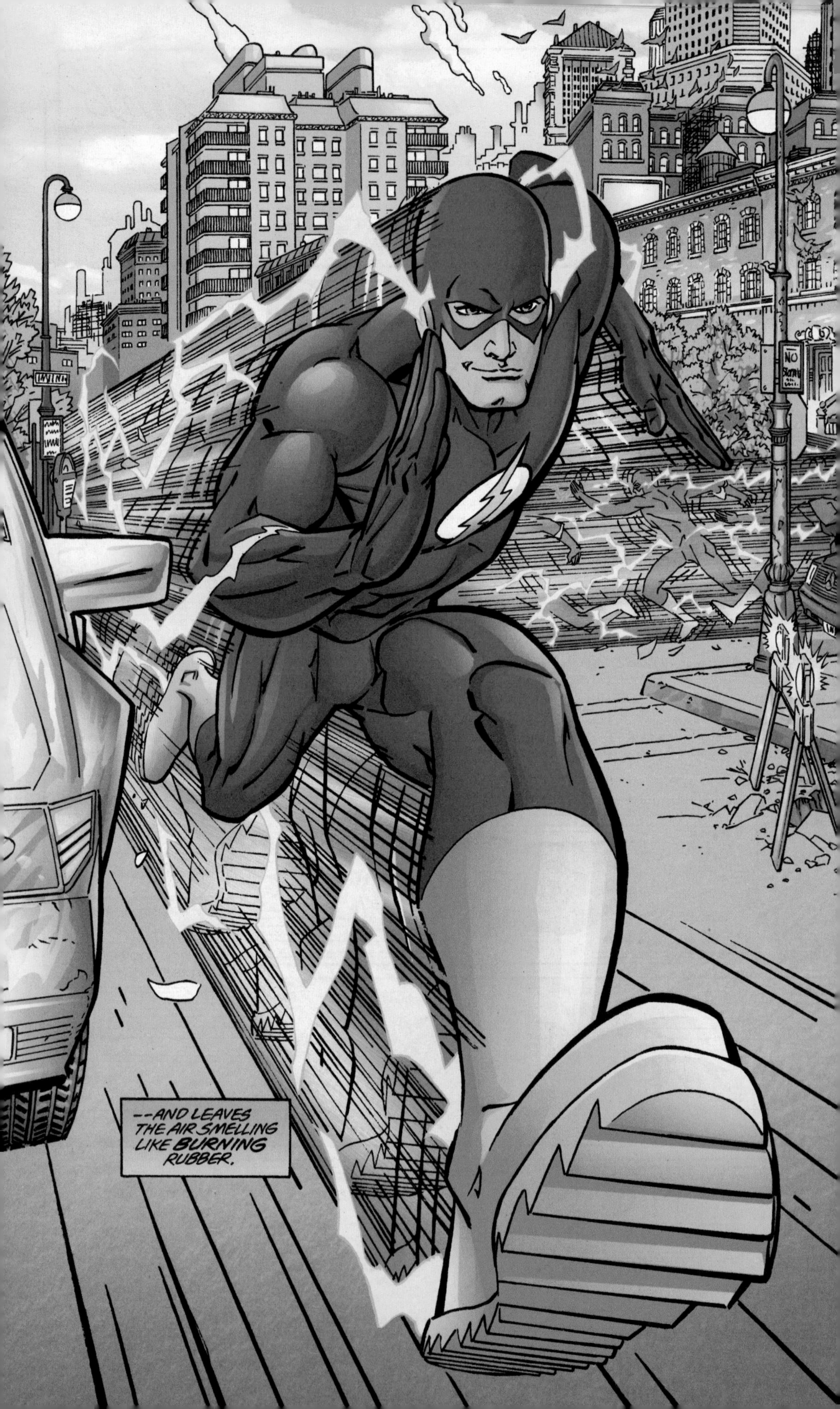
--AND LEAVES THE AIR SMELLING LIKE BURNING RUBBER.

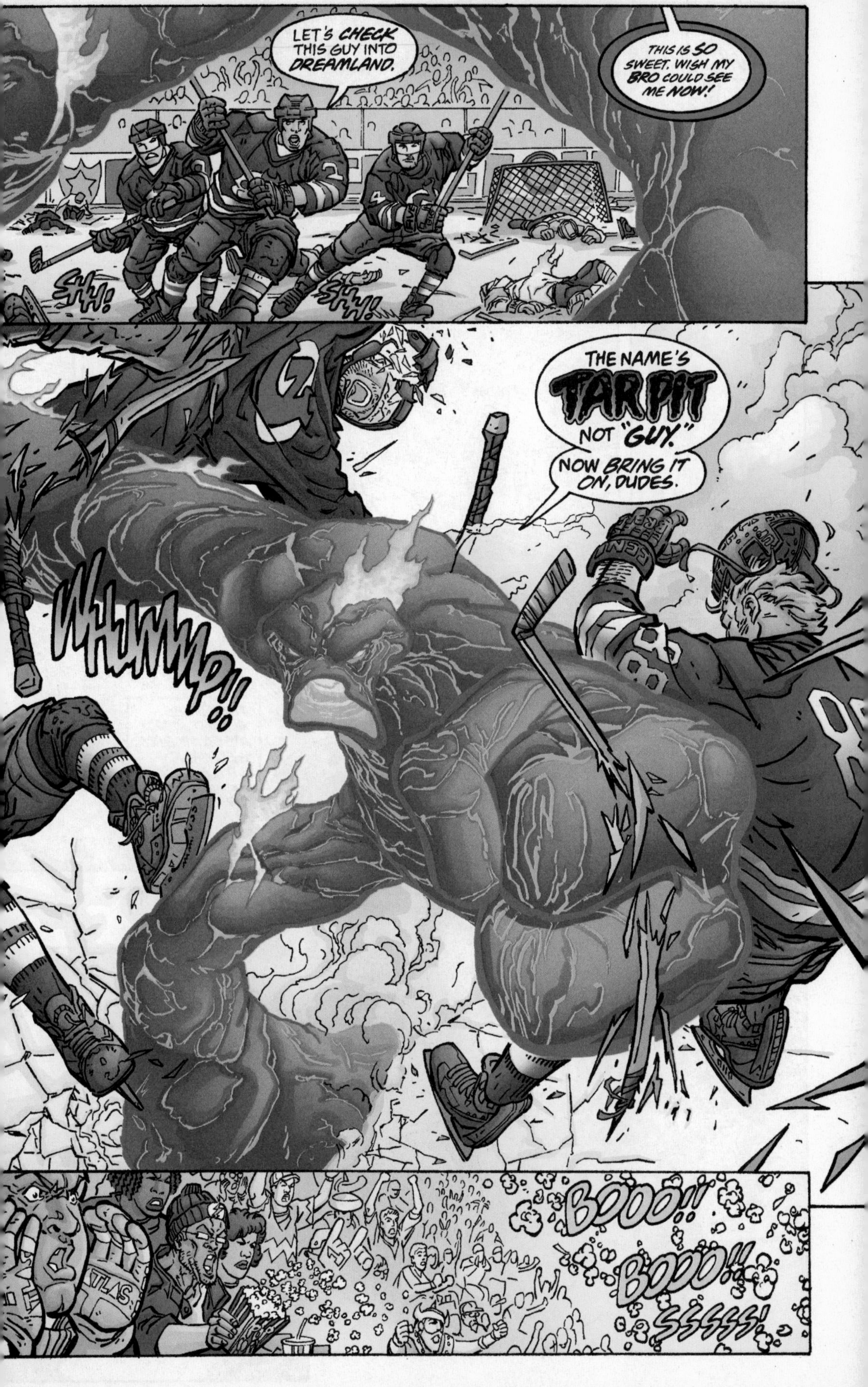

LET'S CHECK THIS GUY INTO DREAMLAND.
THIS IS SO SWEET. WISH MY BRO COULD SEE ME NOW!
SHH!
SHH!
THE NAME'S TARPIT NOT "GUY."
NOW BRING IT ON, DUDES.
WHUMMP!!
BOOO!!
BOOO!!
SSSSS!

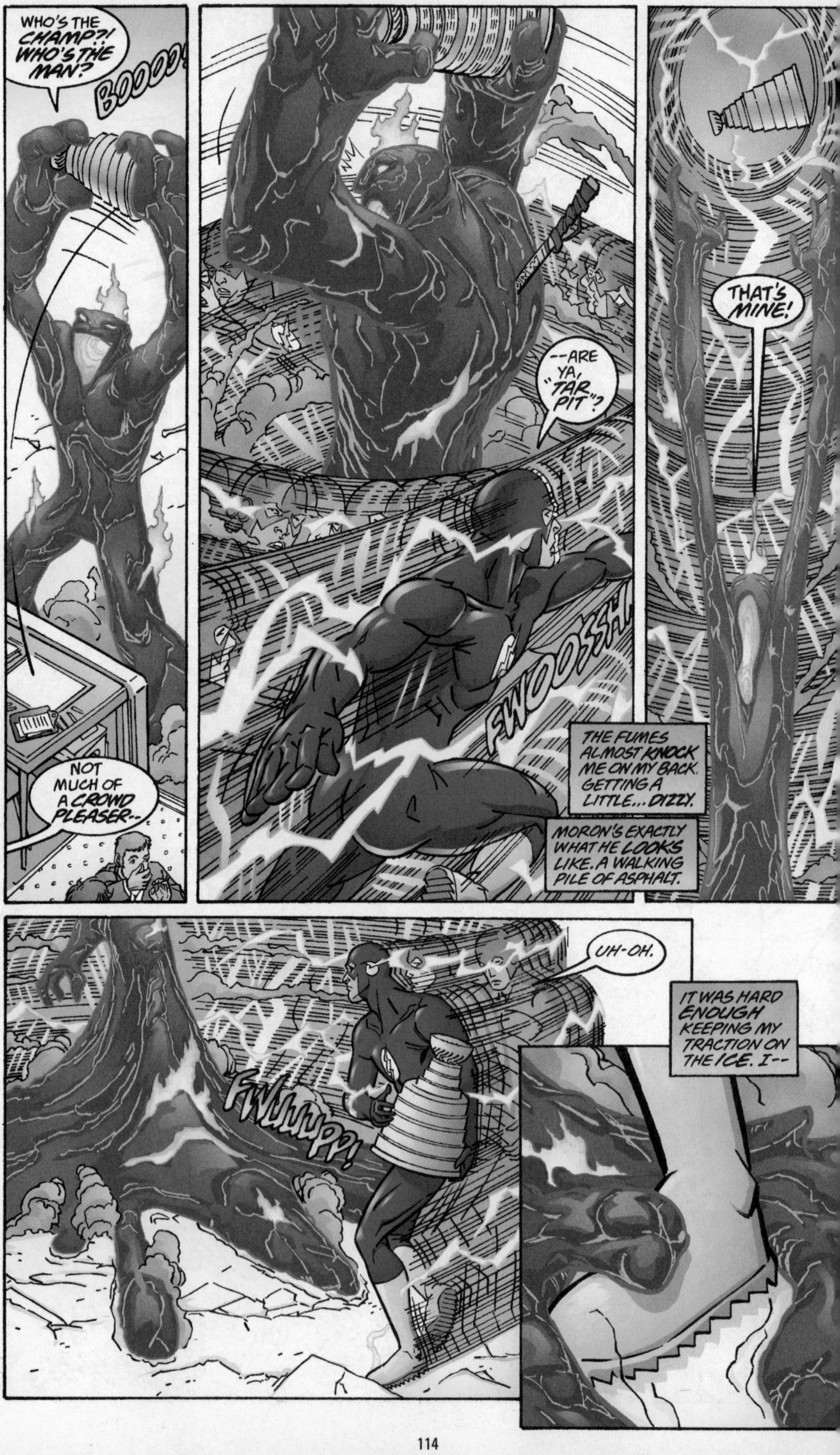

WHO'S THE CHAMP?! WHO'S THE MAN?
BOOOO!
NOT MUCH OF A CROWD PLEASER--
--ARE YA, "TAR PIT"?
FWOOSSH
THE FUMES ALMOST KNOCK ME ON MY BACK. GETTING A LITTLE... DIZZY.
MORON'S EXACTLY WHAT HE LOOKS LIKE. A WALKING PILE OF ASPHALT.
THAT'S MINE!
UH-OH.
FWUUUPP!
IT WAS HARD ENOUGH KEEPING MY TRACTION ON THE ICE. I--

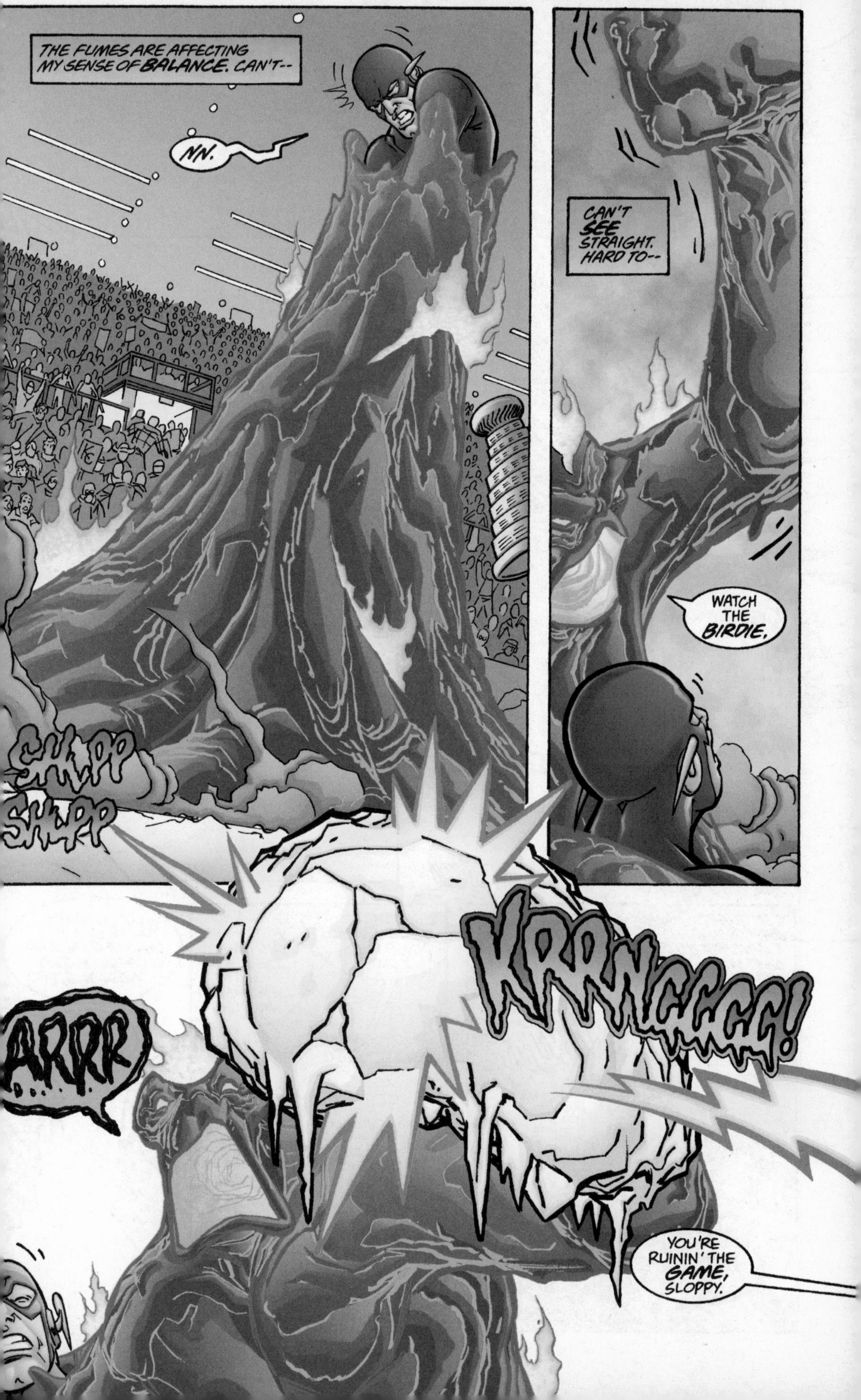
THE FUMES ARE AFFECTING MY SENSE OF BALANCE. CAN'T--
NN.
SHPP SHPP
CAN'T SEE STRAIGHT. HARD TO--
WATCH THE BIRDIE.
KRANGGGG!
ARRR...
YOU'RE RUININ' THE GAME, SLOPPY.

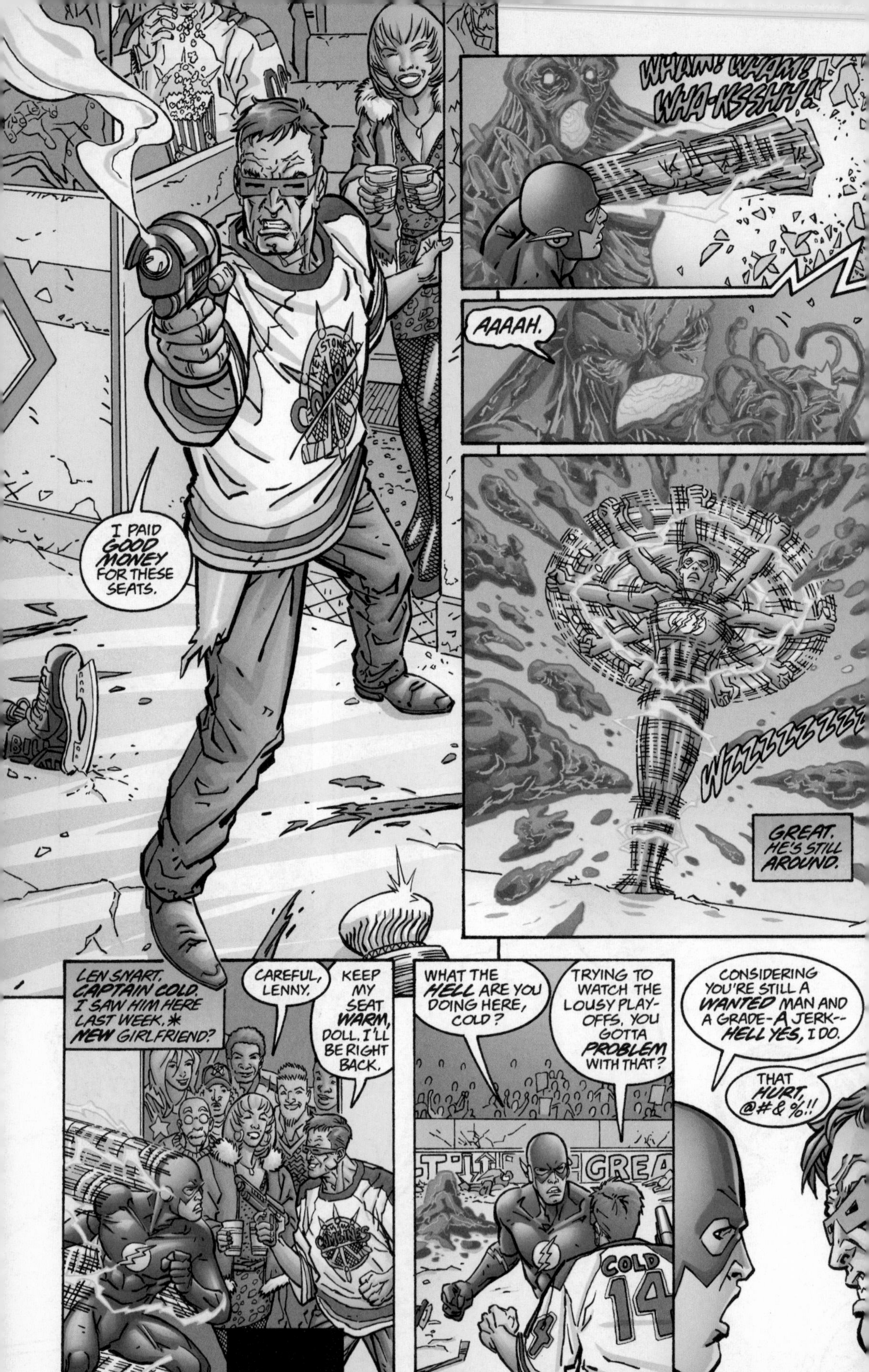

WHAM! WHAM!
WHA-KSSHH!
AAAAH.
WZZZZZZZZZ
GREAT. HE'S STILL AROUND.
I PAID GOOD MONEY FOR THESE SEATS.
LEN SNART. CAPTAIN COLD. I SAW HIM HERE LAST WEEK.* NEW GIRLFRIEND?
CAREFUL, LENNY.
KEEP MY SEAT WARM, DOLL. I'LL BE RIGHT BACK.
WHAT THE HELL ARE YOU DOING HERE, COLD?
TRYING TO WATCH THE LOUSY PLAY-OFFS. YOU GOTTA PROBLEM WITH THAT?
CONSIDERING YOU'RE STILL A WANTED MAN AND A GRADE-A JERK-- HELL YES, I DO.
THAT HURT, @#&%!!
COLD 14

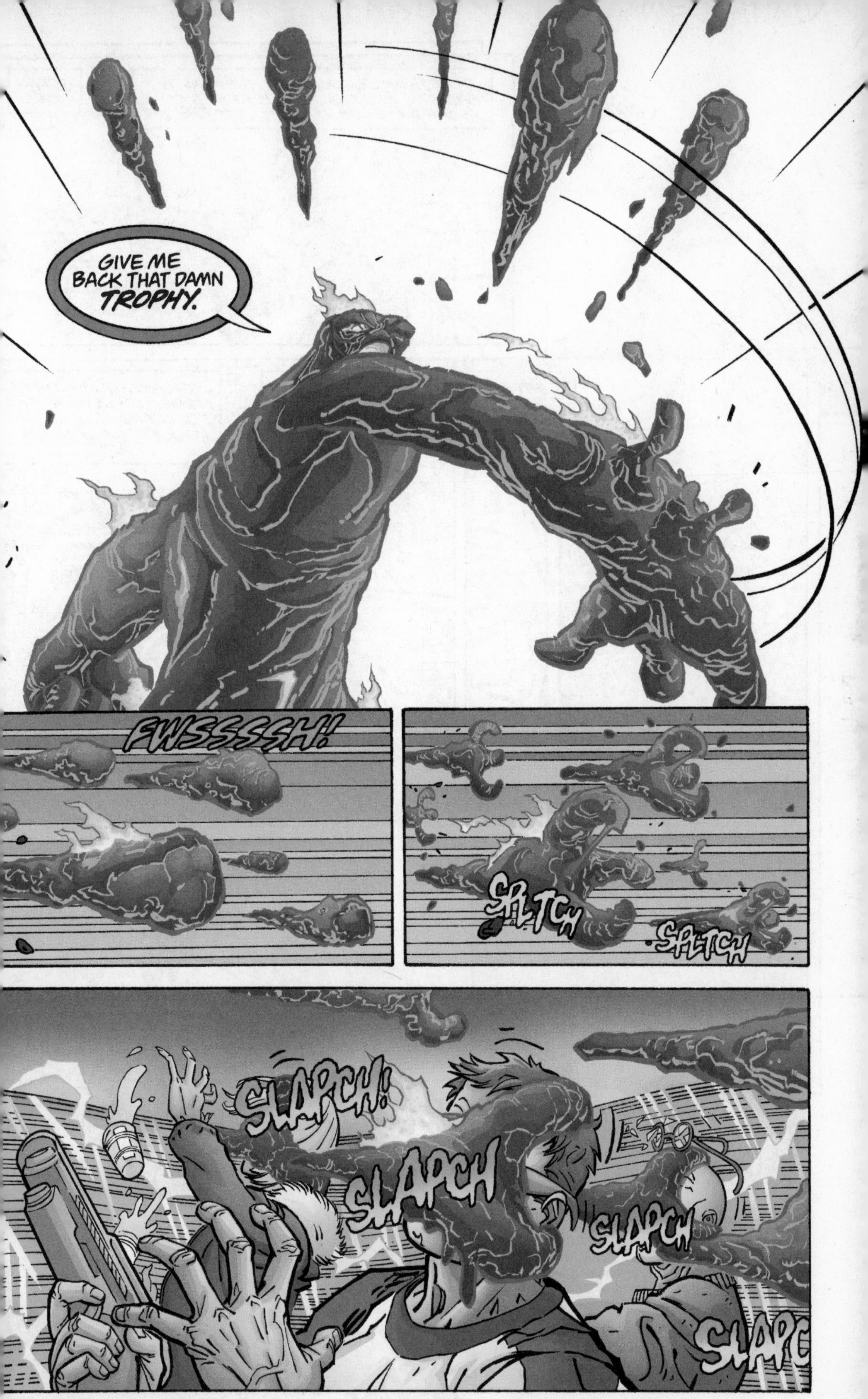
GIVE ME BACK THAT DAMN TROPHY.
FWSSSSSH!
SPLTCH
SPLTCH
SLAPCH!
SLAPCH
SLAPCH
SLAPC

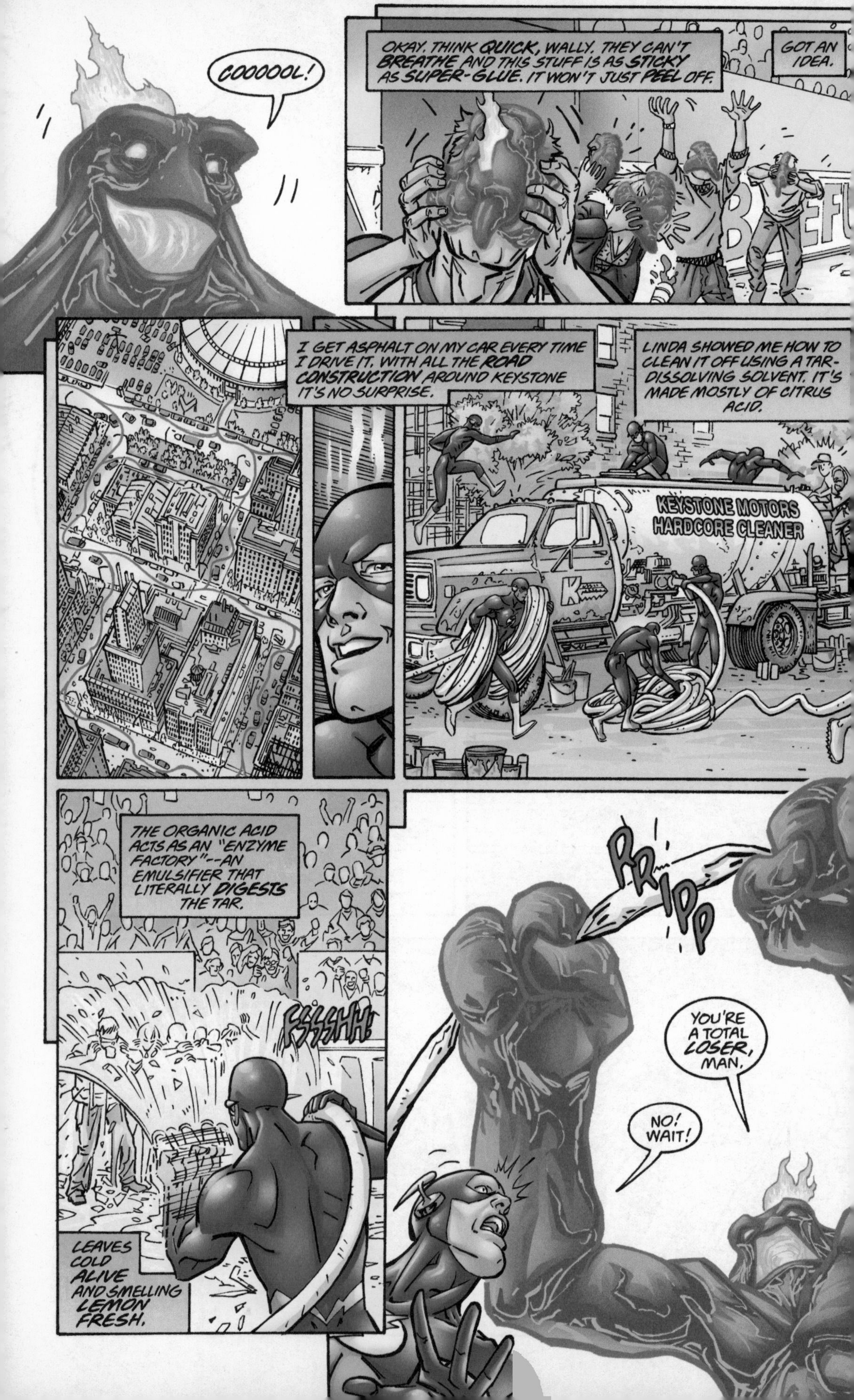

COOOOOL!
OKAY. THINK QUICK, WALLY. THEY CAN'T BREATHE AND THIS STUFF IS AS STICKY AS SUPER-GLUE. IT WON'T JUST PEEL OFF.
GOT AN IDEA.
I GET ASPHALT ON MY CAR EVERY TIME I DRIVE IT. WITH ALL THE ROAD CONSTRUCTION AROUND KEYSTONE IT'S NO SURPRISE.
LINDA SHOWED ME HOW TO CLEAN IT OFF USING A TAR-DISSOLVING SOLVENT. IT'S MADE MOSTLY OF CITRUS ACID.
KEYSTONE MOTORS
HARDCORE CLEANER
THE ORGANIC ACID ACTS AS AN "ENZYME FACTORY"--AN EMULSIFIER THAT LITERALLY DIGESTS THE TAR.
FSSSHH!
LEAVES COLD ALIVE AND SMELLING LEMON FRESH.
RRIPP
YOU'RE A TOTAL LOSER, MAN.
NO! WAIT!

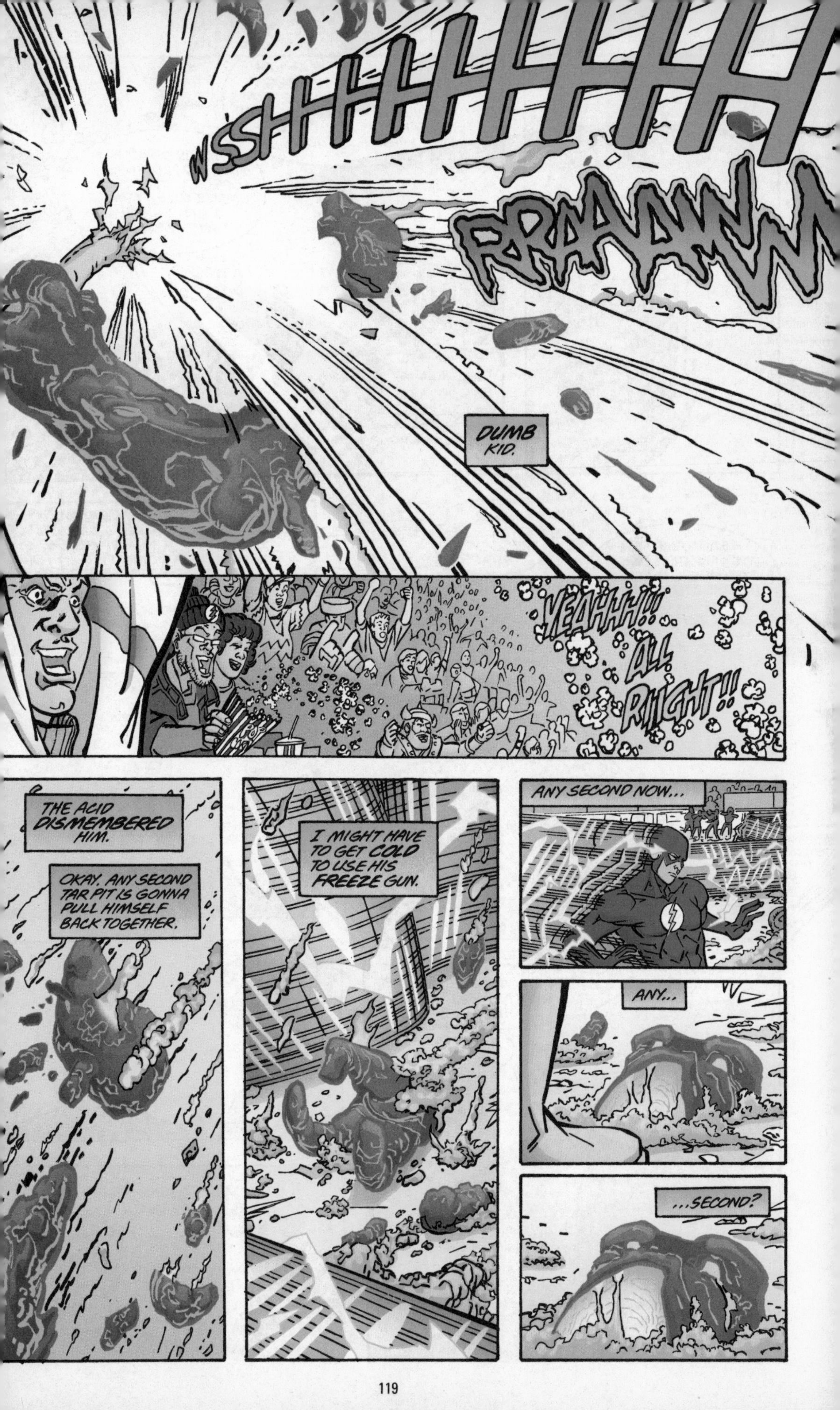
WSSHHHHHHHHHHHH
FRAAAWW
DUMB KID.
YEAHHH!! ALL RIGHT!!
THE ACID DISMEMBERED HIM.
OKAY. ANY SECOND TAR PIT IS GONNA PULL HIMSELF BACK TOGETHER.
I MIGHT HAVE TO GET COLD TO USE HIS FREEZE GUN.
ANY SECOND NOW...
ANY...
...SECOND?

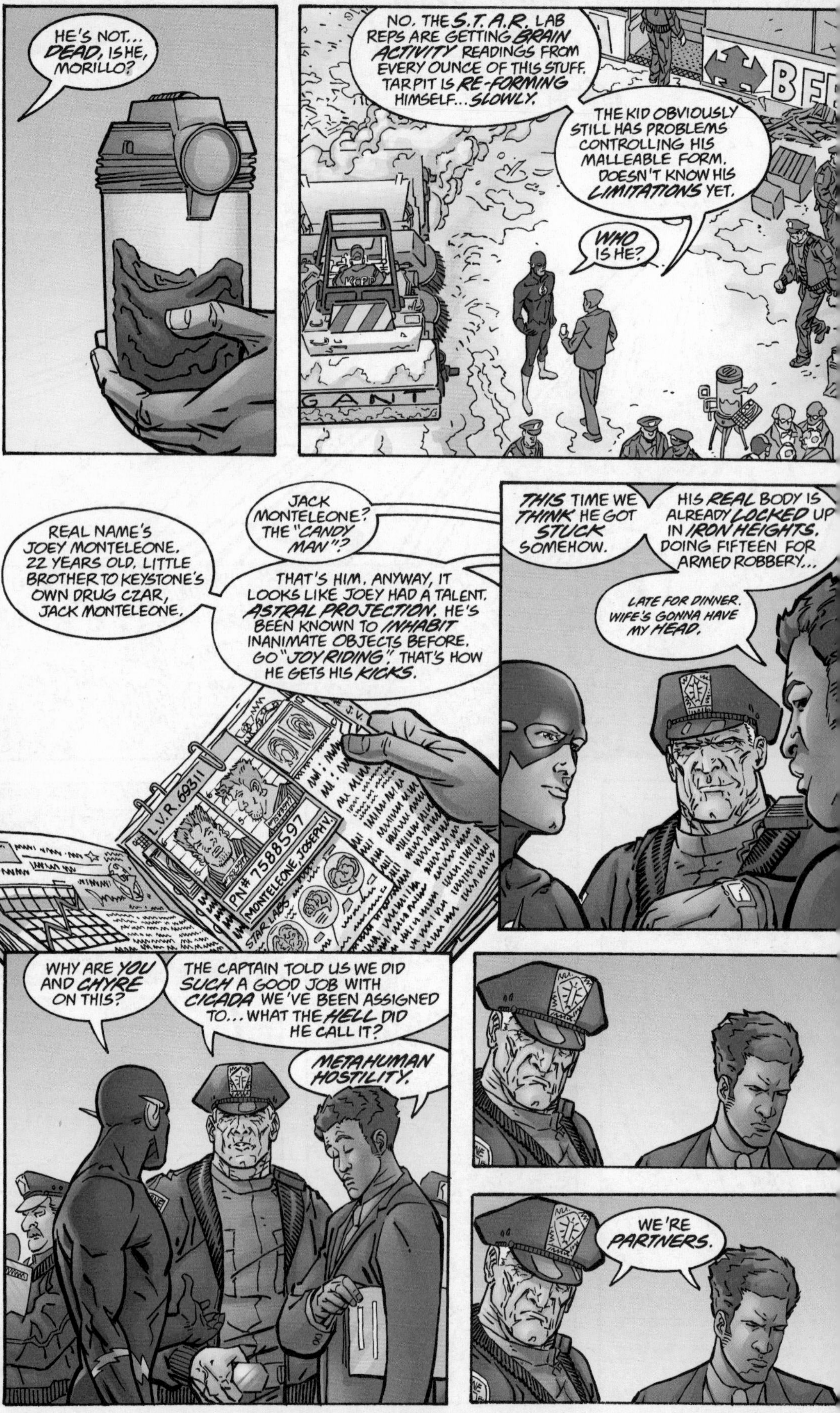

HE'S NOT... DEAD, IS HE, MORILLO?
NO. THE S.T.A.R. LAB REPS ARE GETTING BRAIN ACTIVITY READINGS FROM EVERY OUNCE OF THIS STUFF. TAR PIT IS RE-FORMING HIMSELF... SLOWLY.
THE KID OBVIOUSLY STILL HAS PROBLEMS CONTROLLING HIS MALLEABLE FORM. DOESN'T KNOW HIS LIMITATIONS YET.
WHO IS HE?
REAL NAME'S JOEY MONTELEONE, 22 YEARS OLD. LITTLE BROTHER TO KEYSTONE'S OWN DRUG CZAR, JACK MONTELEONE.
JACK MONTELEONE? THE "CANDY MAN"?
THAT'S HIM. ANYWAY, IT LOOKS LIKE JOEY HAD A TALENT. ASTRAL PROJECTION. HE'S BEEN KNOWN TO INHABIT INANIMATE OBJECTS BEFORE. GO "JOY RIDING." THAT'S HOW HE GETS HIS KICKS.
L.V.R. 69311
PN# 7588597
MONTELEONE, JOSEPH V.
STAR LABS
THIS TIME WE THINK HE GOT STUCK SOMEHOW.
HIS REAL BODY IS ALREADY LOCKED UP IN IRON HEIGHTS. DOING FIFTEEN FOR ARMED ROBBERY...
LATE FOR DINNER. WIFE'S GONNA HAVE MY HEAD.
WHY ARE YOU AND CHYRE ON THIS?
THE CAPTAIN TOLD US WE DID SUCH A GOOD JOB WITH CICADA WE'VE BEEN ASSIGNED TO... WHAT THE HELL DID HE CALL IT?
METAHUMAN HOSTILITY.
WE'RE PARTNERS.

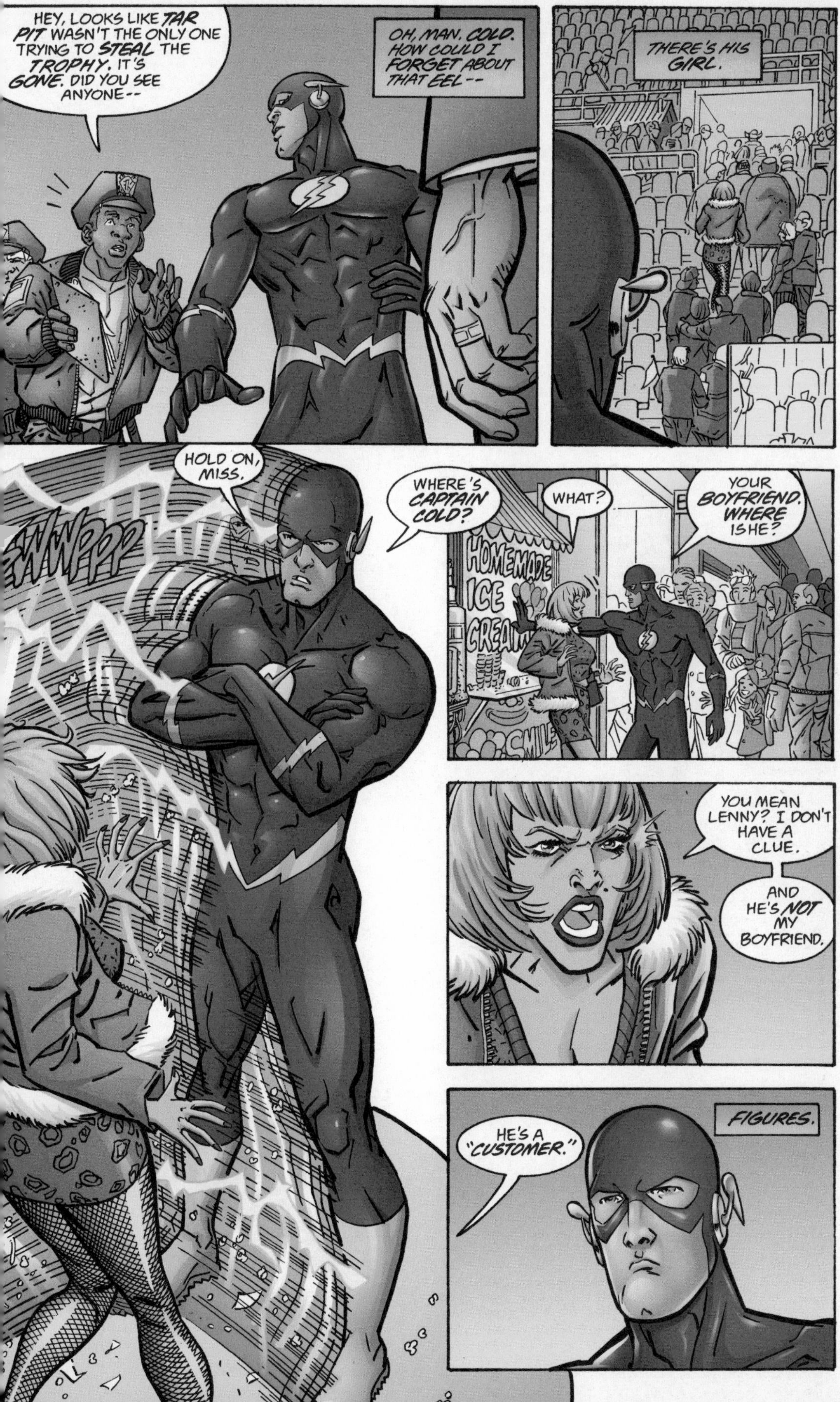

HEY, LOOKS LIKE TAR PIT WASN'T THE ONLY ONE TRYING TO STEAL THE TROPHY. IT'S GONE. DID YOU SEE ANYONE--
OH, MAN. COLD. HOW COULD I FORGET ABOUT THAT EEL--
THERE'S HIS GIRL.
SHWPPP
HOLD ON, MISS.
WHERE'S CAPTAIN COLD?
WHAT?
YOUR BOYFRIEND. WHERE IS HE?
HOMEMADE ICE CREAM
YOU MEAN LENNY? I DON'T HAVE A CLUE.
AND HE'S NOT MY BOYFRIEND.
HE'S A "CUSTOMER."
FIGURES.

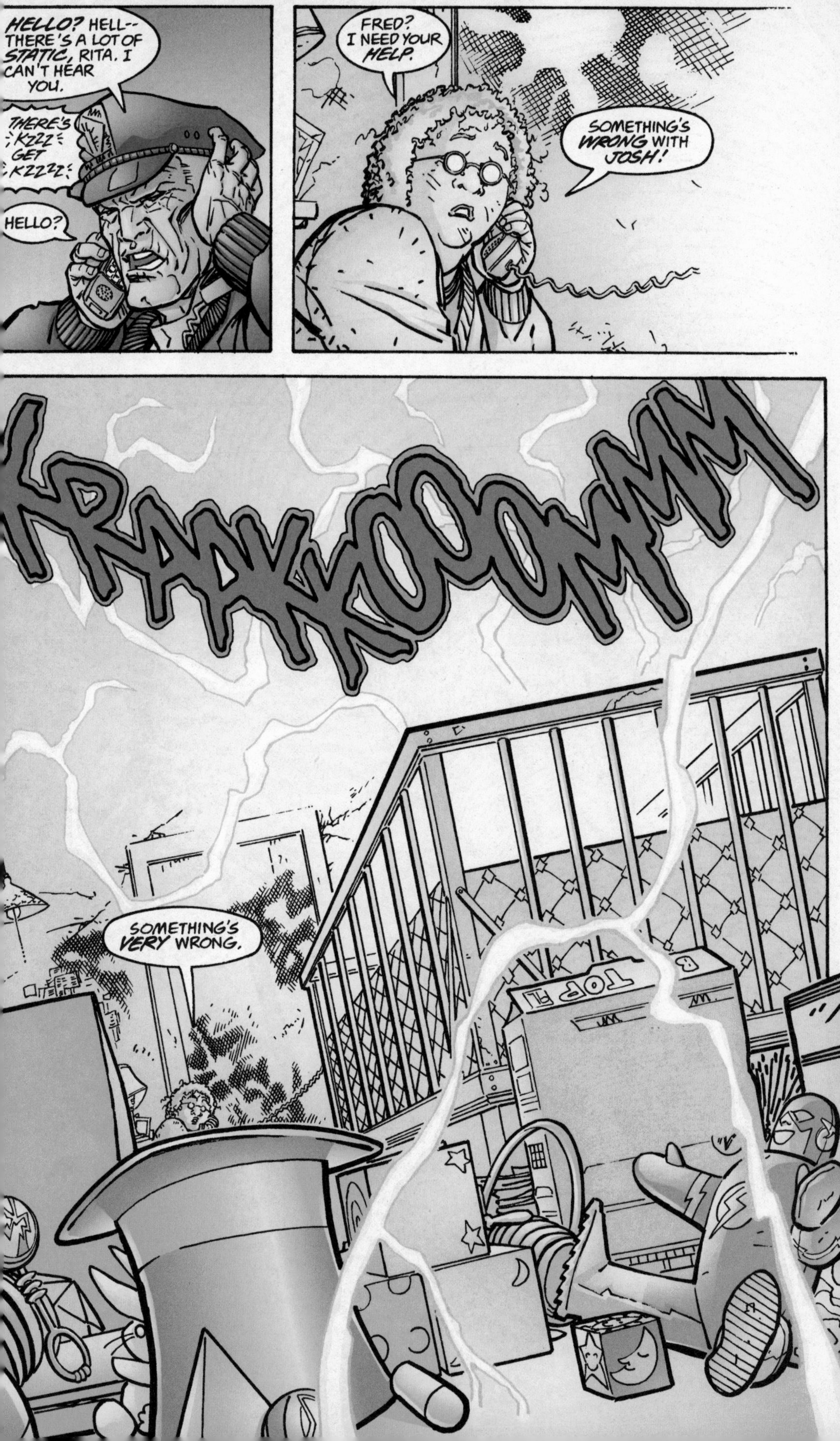
HELLO? HELL-- THERE'S A LOT OF STATIC, RITA. I CAN'T HEAR YOU.
THERE'S KZZZ GET KZZZZ
HELLO?
FRED? I NEED YOUR HELP.
SOMETHING'S WRONG WITH JOSH!
KRAKOOOMM
SOMETHING'S VERY WRONG.

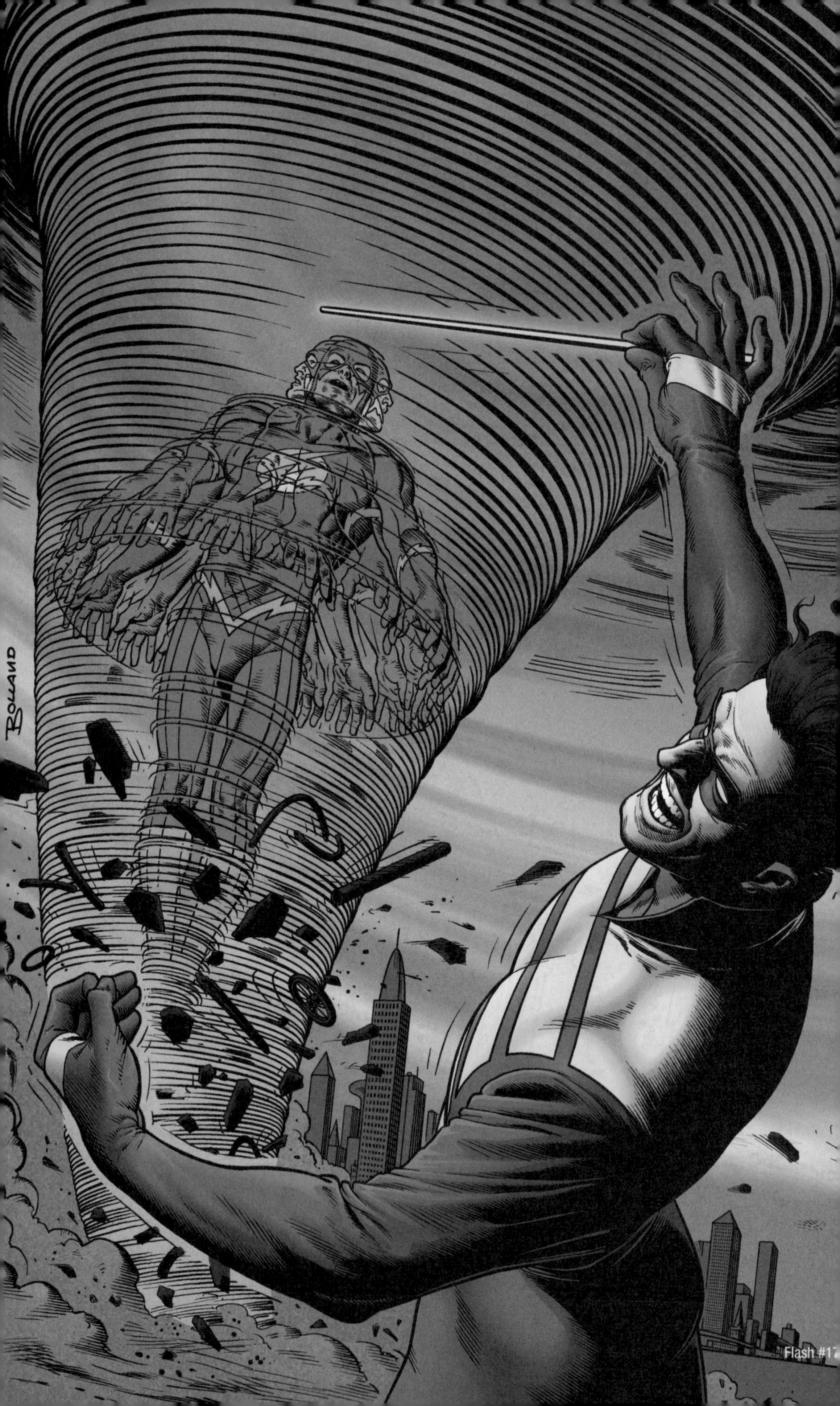
BOLLAND

Flash #17

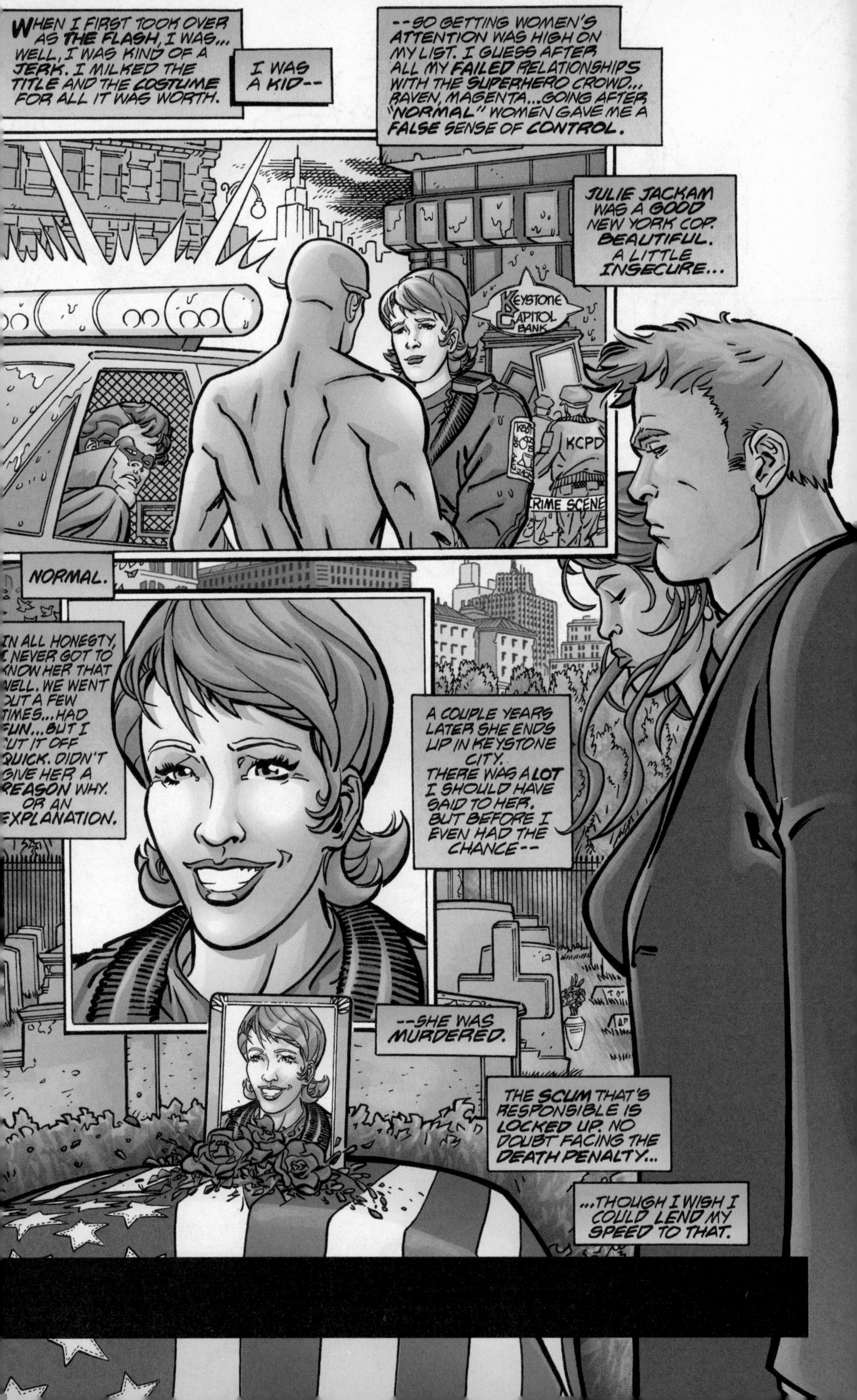

WHEN I FIRST TOOK OVER AS THE FLASH, I WAS... WELL, I WAS KIND OF A JERK. I MILKED THE TITLE AND THE COSTUME FOR ALL IT WAS WORTH.
I WAS A KID--
--SO GETTING WOMEN'S ATTENTION WAS HIGH ON MY LIST. I GUESS AFTER ALL MY FAILED RELATIONSHIPS WITH THE SUPERHERO CROWD... RAVEN, MAGENTA...GOING AFTER "NORMAL" WOMEN GAVE ME A FALSE SENSE OF CONTROL.
JULIE JACKAM WAS A GOOD NEW YORK COP. BEAUTIFUL. A LITTLE INSECURE...
KEYSTONE CAPITOL BANK
KCPD
CRIME SCENE
NORMAL.
IN ALL HONESTY, I NEVER GOT TO KNOW HER THAT WELL. WE WENT OUT A FEW TIMES...HAD FUN...BUT I CUT IT OFF QUICK. DIDN'T GIVE HER A REASON WHY. OR AN EXPLANATION.
A COUPLE YEARS LATER SHE ENDS UP IN KEYSTONE CITY. THERE WAS A LOT I SHOULD HAVE SAID TO HER. BUT BEFORE I EVEN HAD THE CHANCE--
--SHE WAS MURDERED.
THE SCUM THAT'S RESPONSIBLE IS LOCKED UP. NO DOUBT FACING THE DEATH PENALTY...
...THOUGH I WISH I COULD LEND MY SPEED TO THAT.

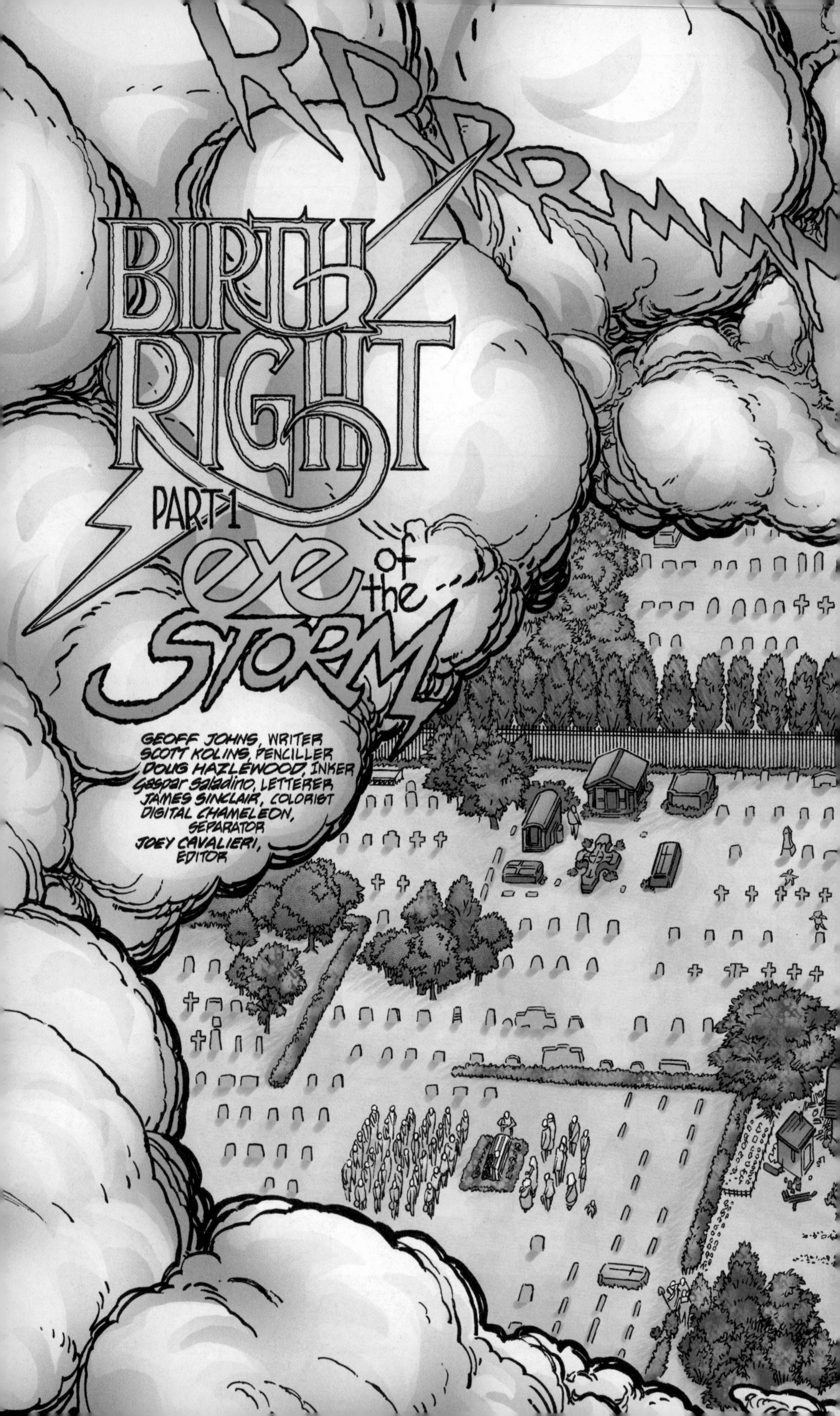
RRRRRMMM
BIRTHRIGHT
PART 1
EYE OF THE STORM
GEOFF JOHNS, WRITER
SCOTT KOLINS, PENCILLER
DOUG HAZLEWOOD, INKER
Gaspar Saladino, LETTERER
JAMES SINCLAIR, COLORIST
DIGITAL CHAMELEON, SEPARATOR
JOEY CAVALIERI, EDITOR

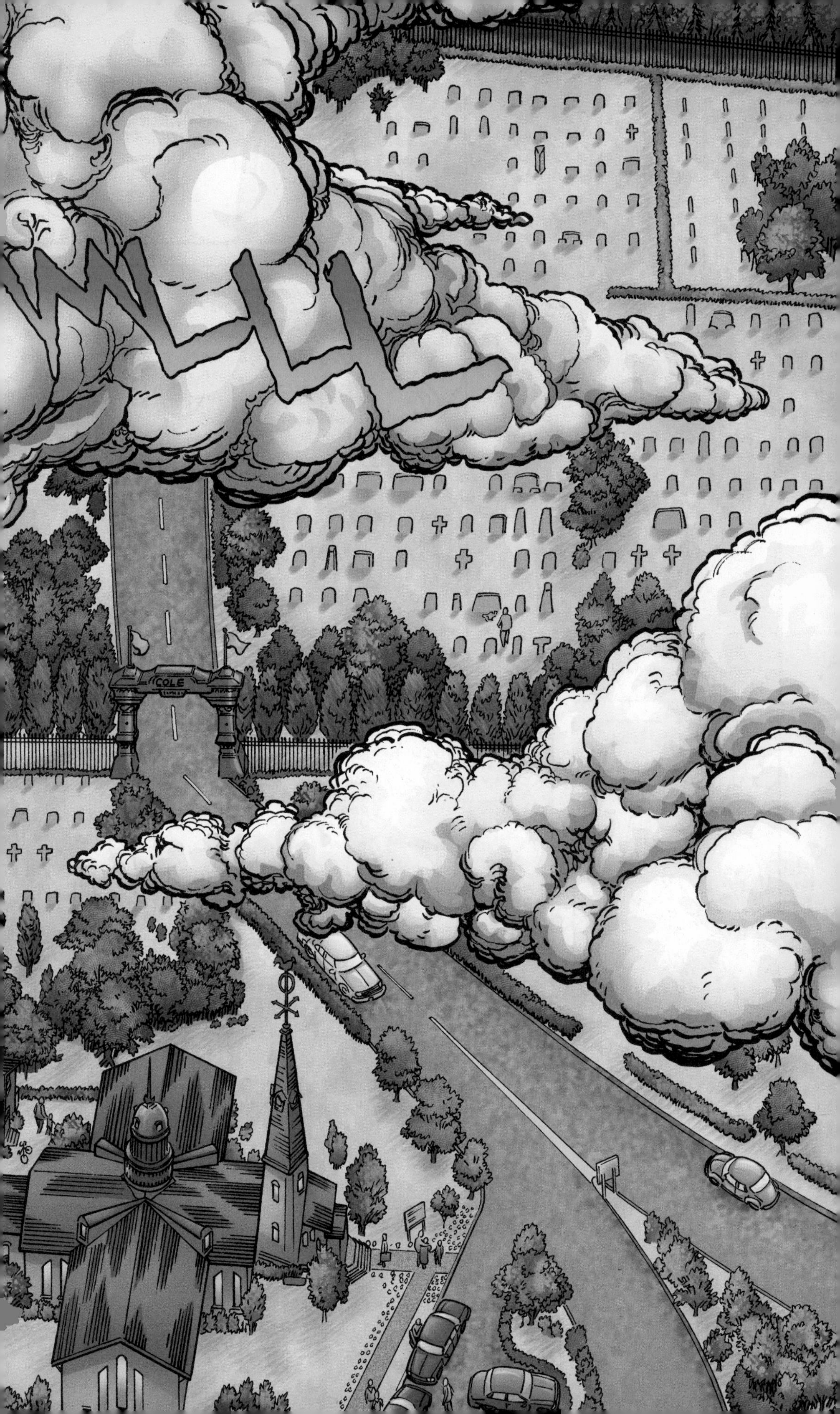
WLL
COLE

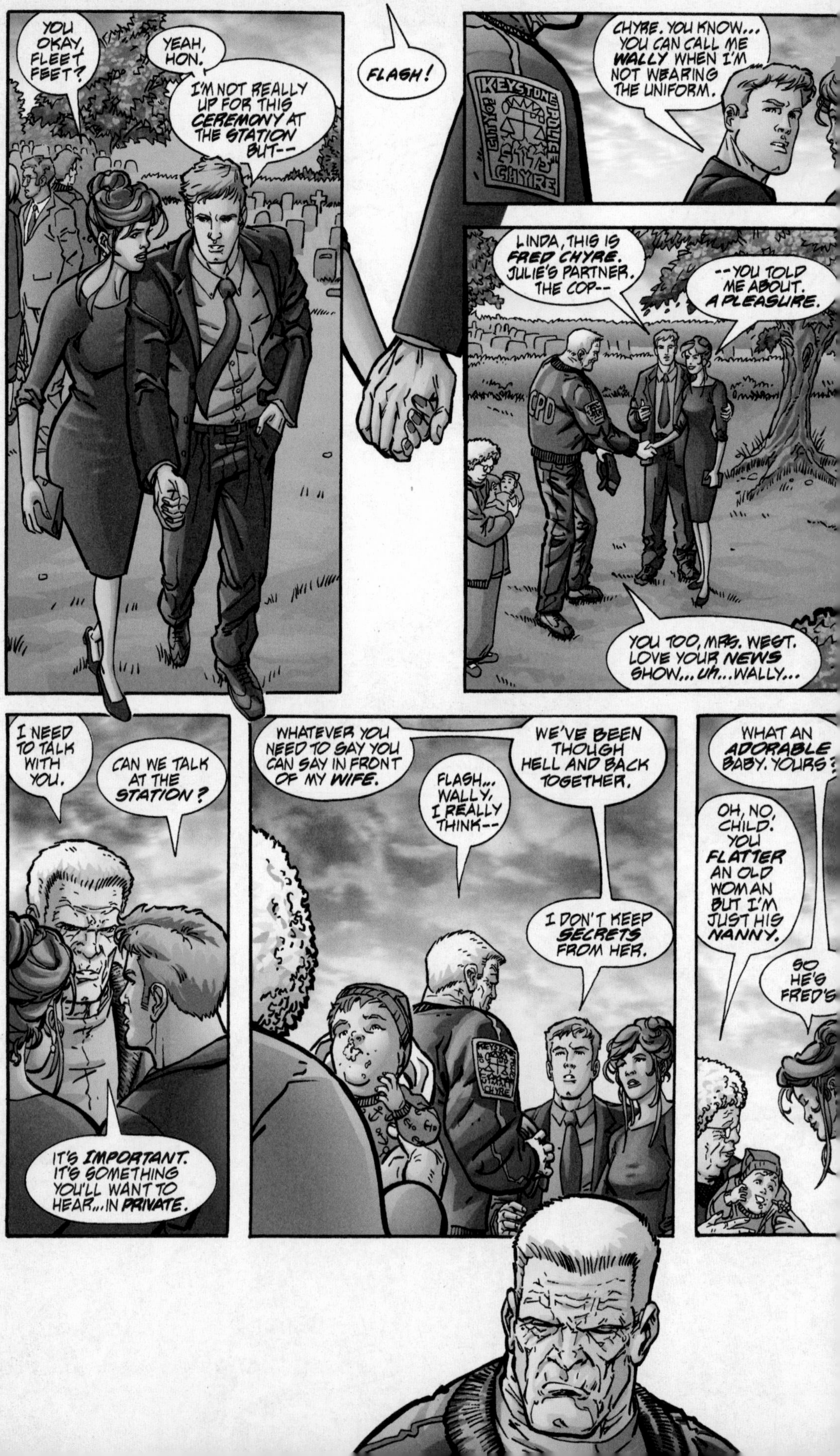
YOU OKAY, FLEET FEET?
YEAH, HON.
I'M NOT REALLY UP FOR THIS CEREMONY AT THE STATION BUT--
FLASH!
CHYRE. YOU KNOW... YOU CAN CALL ME WALLY WHEN I'M NOT WEARING THE UNIFORM.
KEYSTONE POLICE CITY 5175 CHYRE
LINDA, THIS IS FRED CHYRE. JULIE'S PARTNER. THE COP--
--YOU TOLD ME ABOUT. A PLEASURE.
CPD
YOU TOO, MRS. WEST. LOVE YOUR NEWS SHOW... UH... WALLY...
I NEED TO TALK WITH YOU.
CAN WE TALK AT THE STATION?
IT'S IMPORTANT. IT'S SOMETHING YOU'LL WANT TO HEAR... IN PRIVATE.
WHATEVER YOU NEED TO SAY YOU CAN SAY IN FRONT OF MY WIFE.
WE'VE BEEN THOUGH HELL AND BACK TOGETHER.
FLASH... WALLY, I REALLY THINK--
I DON'T KEEP SECRETS FROM HER.
WHAT AN ADORABLE BABY. YOURS?
OH, NO, CHILD. YOU FLATTER AN OLD WOMAN BUT I'M JUST HIS NANNY.
SO HE'S FRED'S

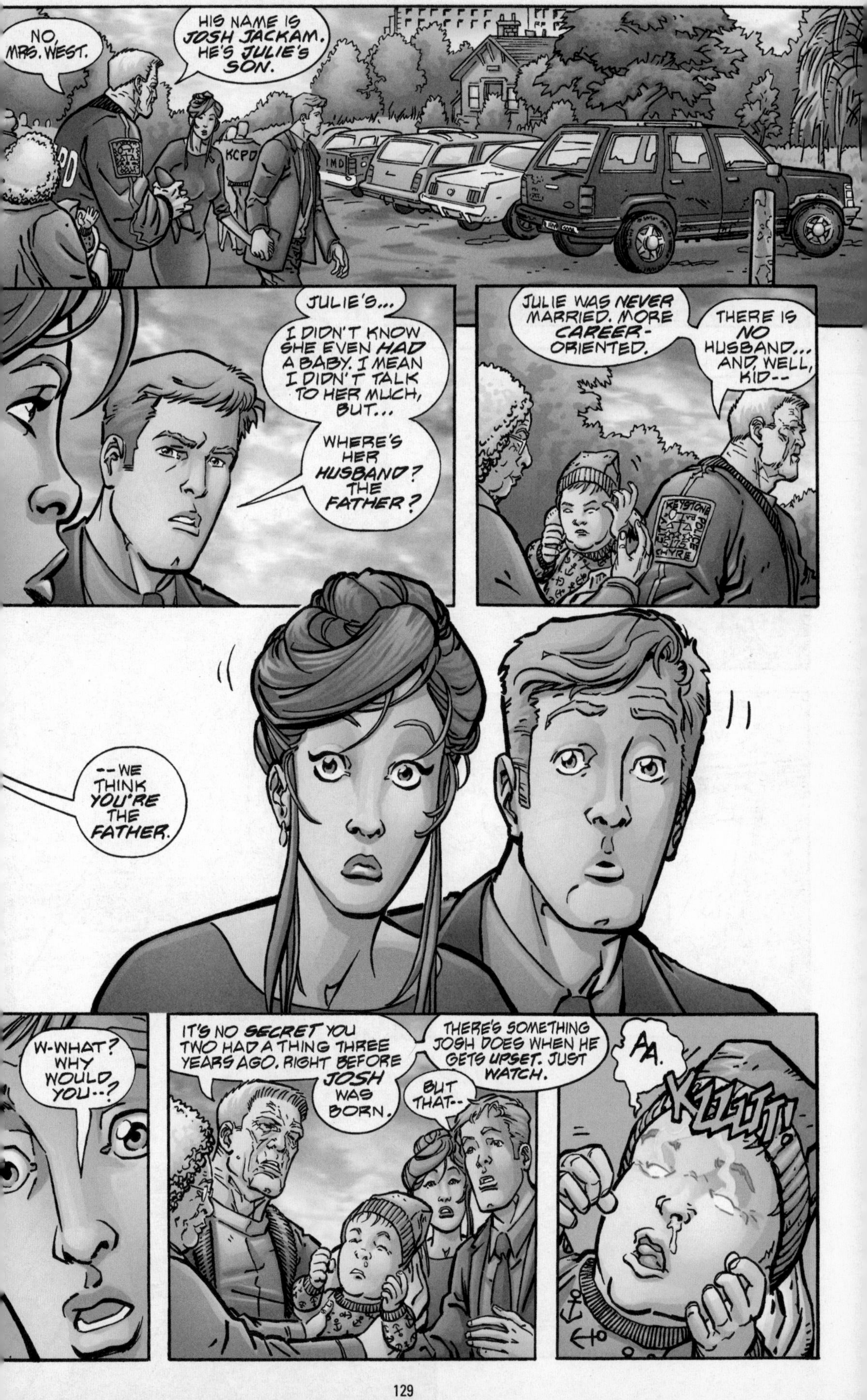

NO, MRS. WEST.
HIS NAME IS JOSH JACKAM. HE'S JULIE'S SON.
JULIE'S...
I DIDN'T KNOW SHE EVEN HAD A BABY. I MEAN I DIDN'T TALK TO HER MUCH, BUT...
WHERE'S HER HUSBAND? THE FATHER?
JULIE WAS NEVER MARRIED. MORE CAREER-ORIENTED.
THERE IS NO HUSBAND... AND, WELL, KID--
--WE THINK YOU'RE THE FATHER.
W-WHAT? WHY WOULD YOU--?
IT'S NO SECRET YOU TWO HAD A THING THREE YEARS AGO. RIGHT BEFORE JOSH WAS BORN.
BUT THAT--
THERE'S SOMETHING JOSH DOES WHEN HE GETS UPSET. JUST WATCH.
AA.
XZUTT!

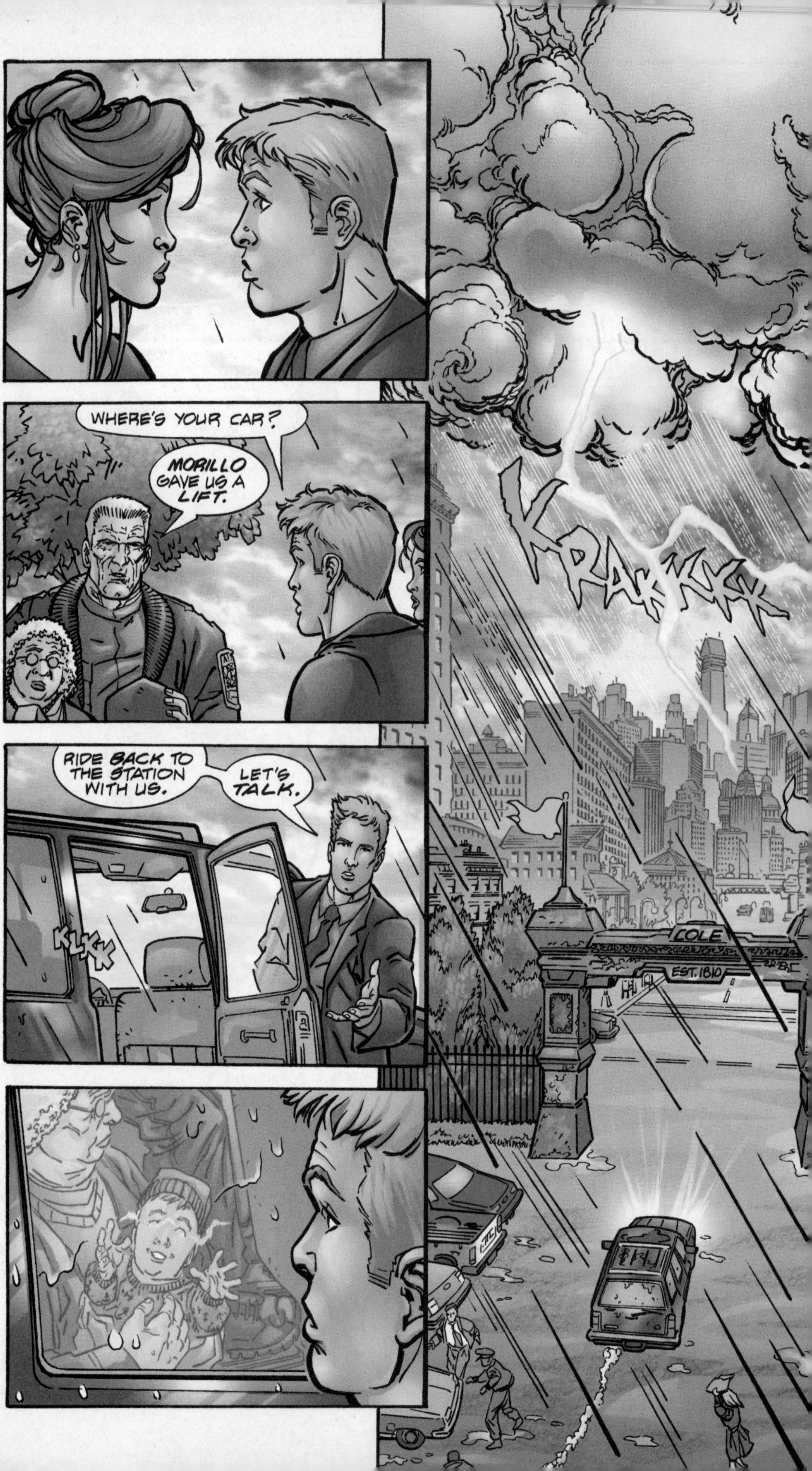

WHERE'S YOUR CAR?
MORILLO GAVE US A LIFT.
RIDE BACK TO THE STATION WITH US.
LET'S TALK.
KLIKK
KRAKKKK
COLE
EST. 1810

NOT GOING TO
BREAK OUT IF THAT'S
WHAT YOU'RE WAITING
FOR. WE BOTH HAVE
HAD RELATIONSHIPS.
I'M *DIVORCED.*
YOU'VE PLAYED
THE FIELD--

--I'M
JUST ASKING
YOU TO *THINK,*
WALLY.

IT'S...*POSSIBLE.*
I DON'T KNOW.

SHE
WOULD'VE
TOLD
ME.

YOU *SURE*
ABOUT THAT,
FLASH?

HOW DO YOU
EXPLAIN HIS...
TANTRUMS? THE
LIGHTNING
AND--

WAAAAA!

P'KAZZT!!

WHAT'S WRONG?
IS HE ALL RIGHT?

SHNK!

SHNK!
SHNK!
SHNK!

131

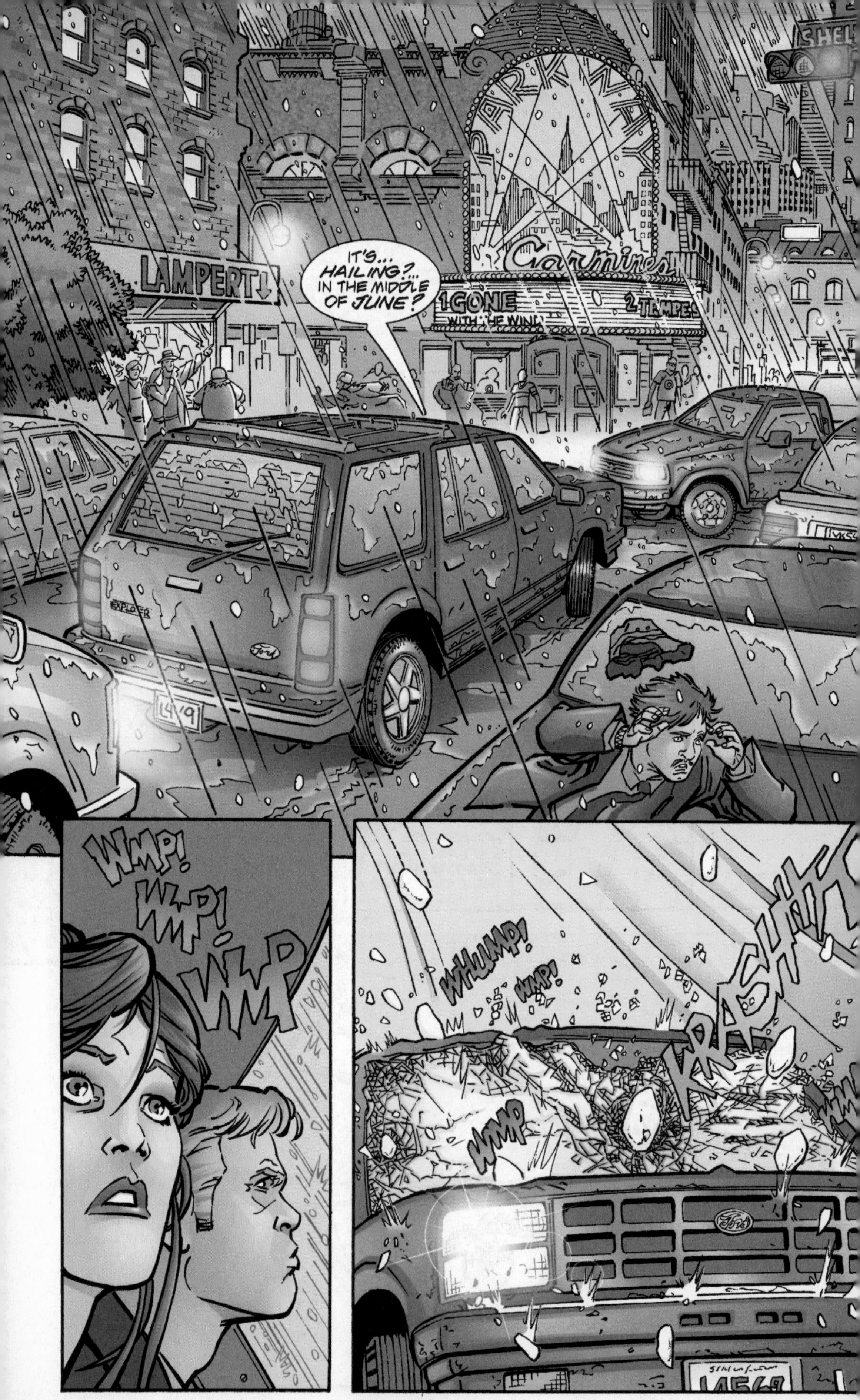
LAMPERT
IT'S... HAILING?... IN THE MIDDLE OF JUNE?
Carmine's
1 GONE WITH THE WIND
WMP!
WMP!
WMP
WHUMP!
WMP!
KRASH!
WMP

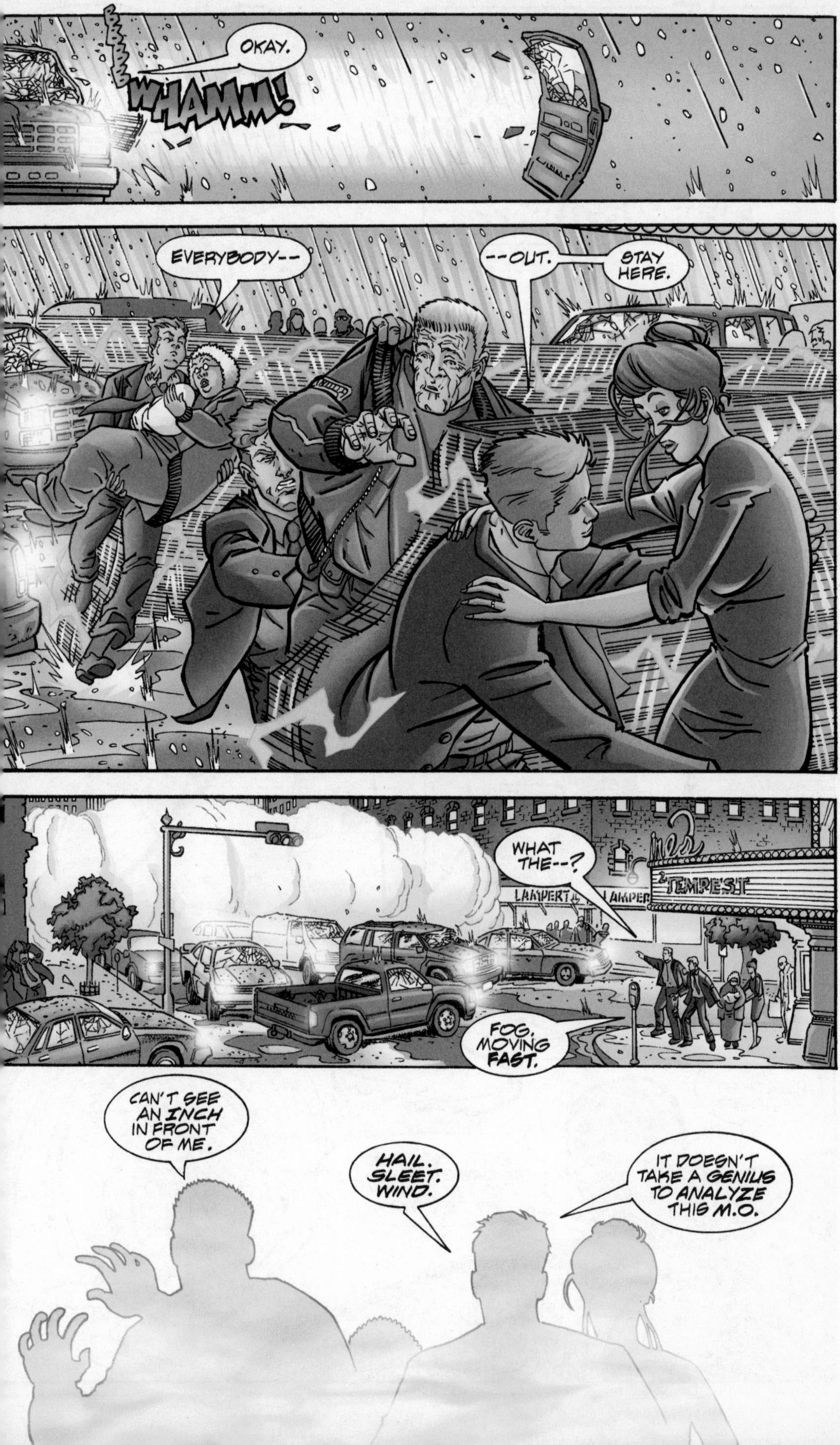
OKAY.
WHAMM!
EVERYBODY--
--OUT.
STAY HERE.
WHAT THE--?
LAMPERT
TEMPEST
FOG. MOVING FAST.
CAN'T SEE AN INCH IN FRONT OF ME.
HAIL. SLEET. WIND.
IT DOESN'T TAKE A GENIUS TO ANALYZE THIS M.O.

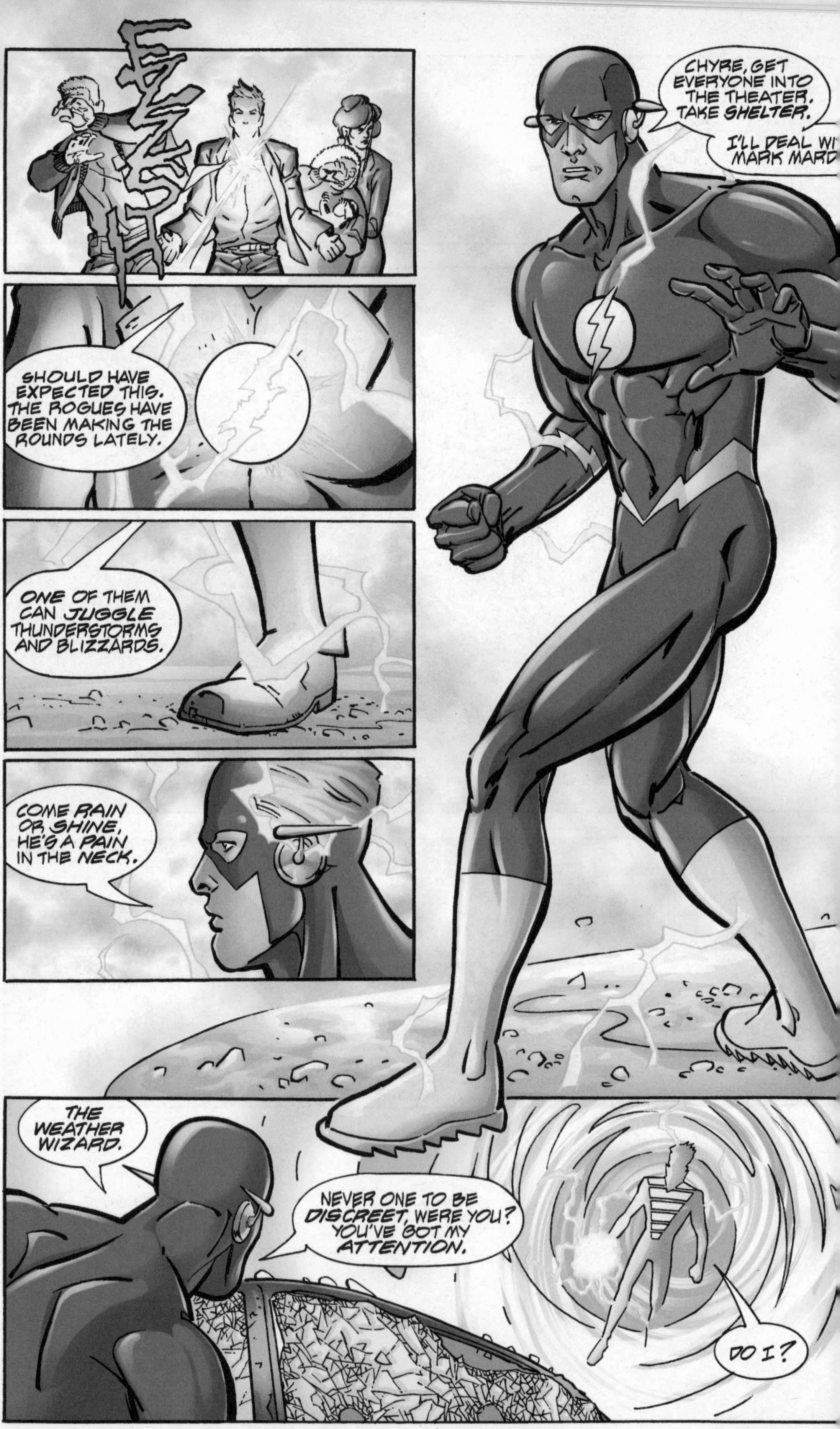
FLASH
CHYRE, GET EVERYONE INTO THE THEATER. TAKE SHELTER.
I'LL DEAL WI MARK MARD
SHOULD HAVE EXPECTED THIS. THE ROGUES HAVE BEEN MAKING THE ROUNDS LATELY.
ONE OF THEM CAN JUGGLE THUNDERSTORMS AND BLIZZARDS.
COME RAIN OR SHINE, HE'S A PAIN IN THE NECK.
THE WEATHER WIZARD.
NEVER ONE TO BE DISCREET, WERE YOU? YOU'VE GOT MY ATTENTION.
DO I?

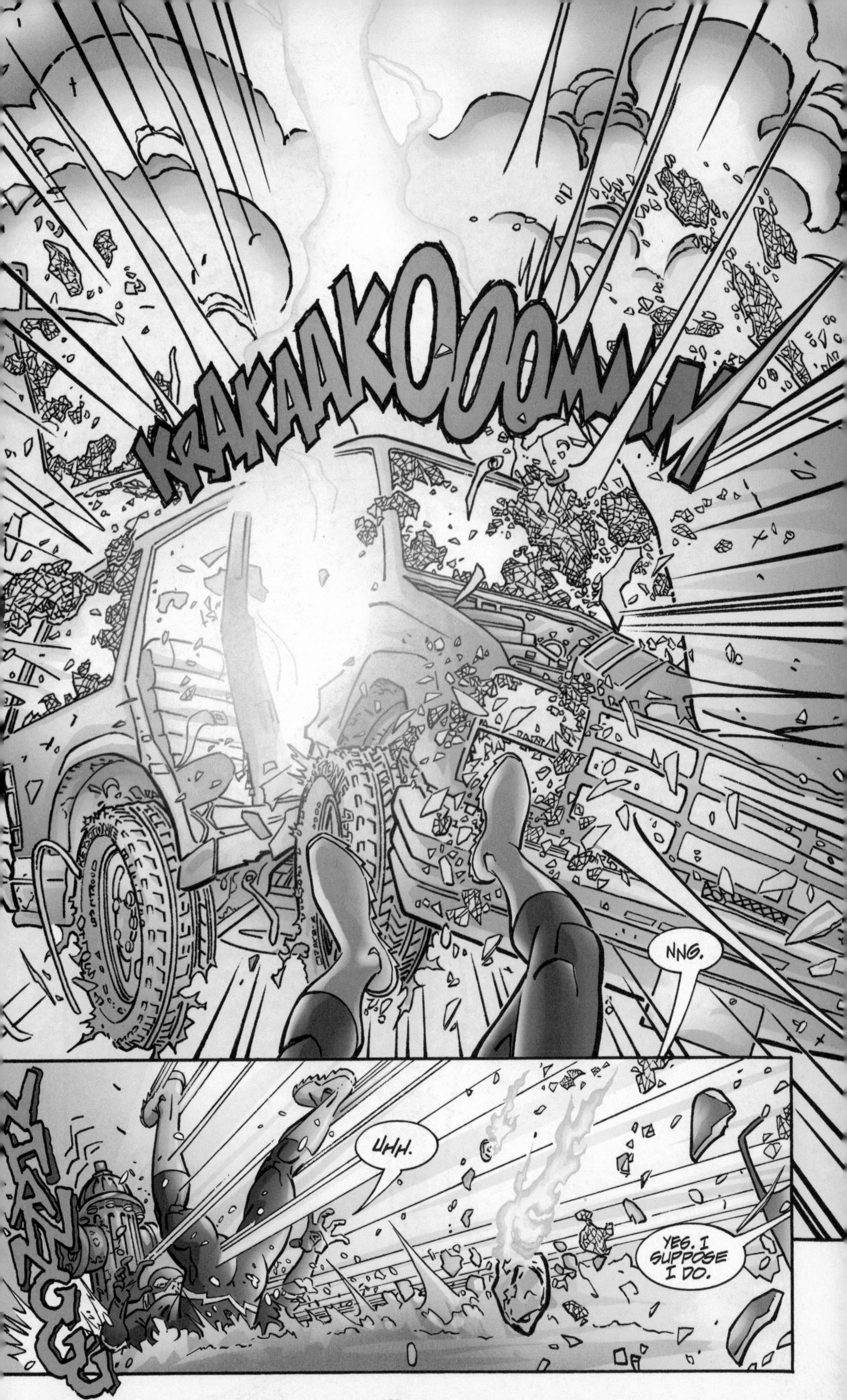
KRAKAAKOOOMMM
NNG.
YANNGG
UHH.
YES. I SUPPOSE I DO.

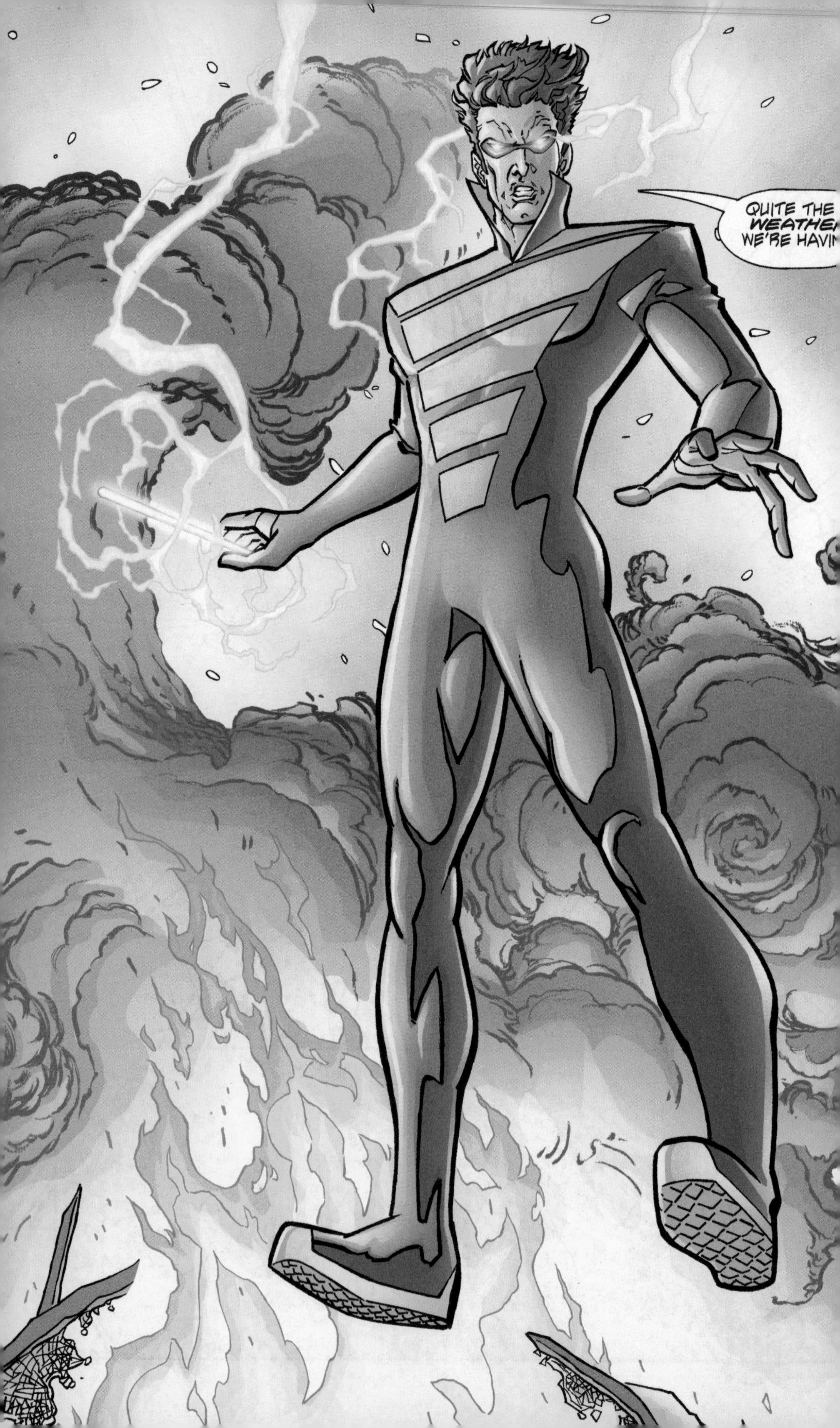
QUITE THE WEATHE WE'RE HAVIN

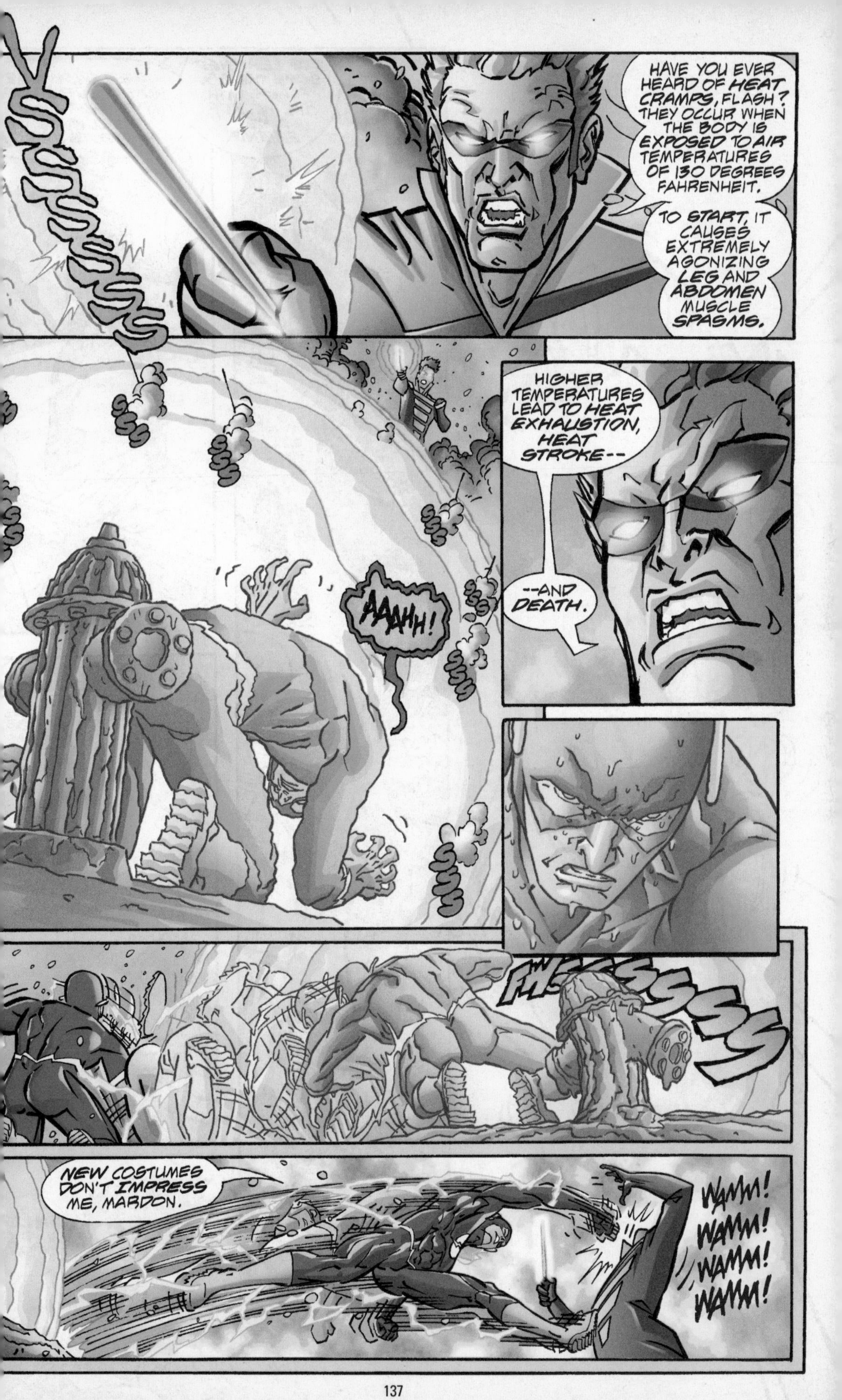
SSSSSSSSS
HAVE YOU EVER HEARD OF HEAT CRAMPS, FLASH? THEY OCCUR WHEN THE BODY IS EXPOSED TO AIR TEMPERATURES OF 130 DEGREES FAHRENHEIT.
TO START, IT CAUSES EXTREMELY AGONIZING LEG AND ABDOMEN MUSCLE SPASMS.
SSS
SSS
SSS
AAAHH!
HIGHER TEMPERATURES LEAD TO HEAT EXHAUSTION, HEAT STROKE--
--AND DEATH.
FWSSSSSSS
NEW COSTUMES DON'T IMPRESS ME, MARDON.
WAMM!
WAMM!
WAMM!
WAMM!

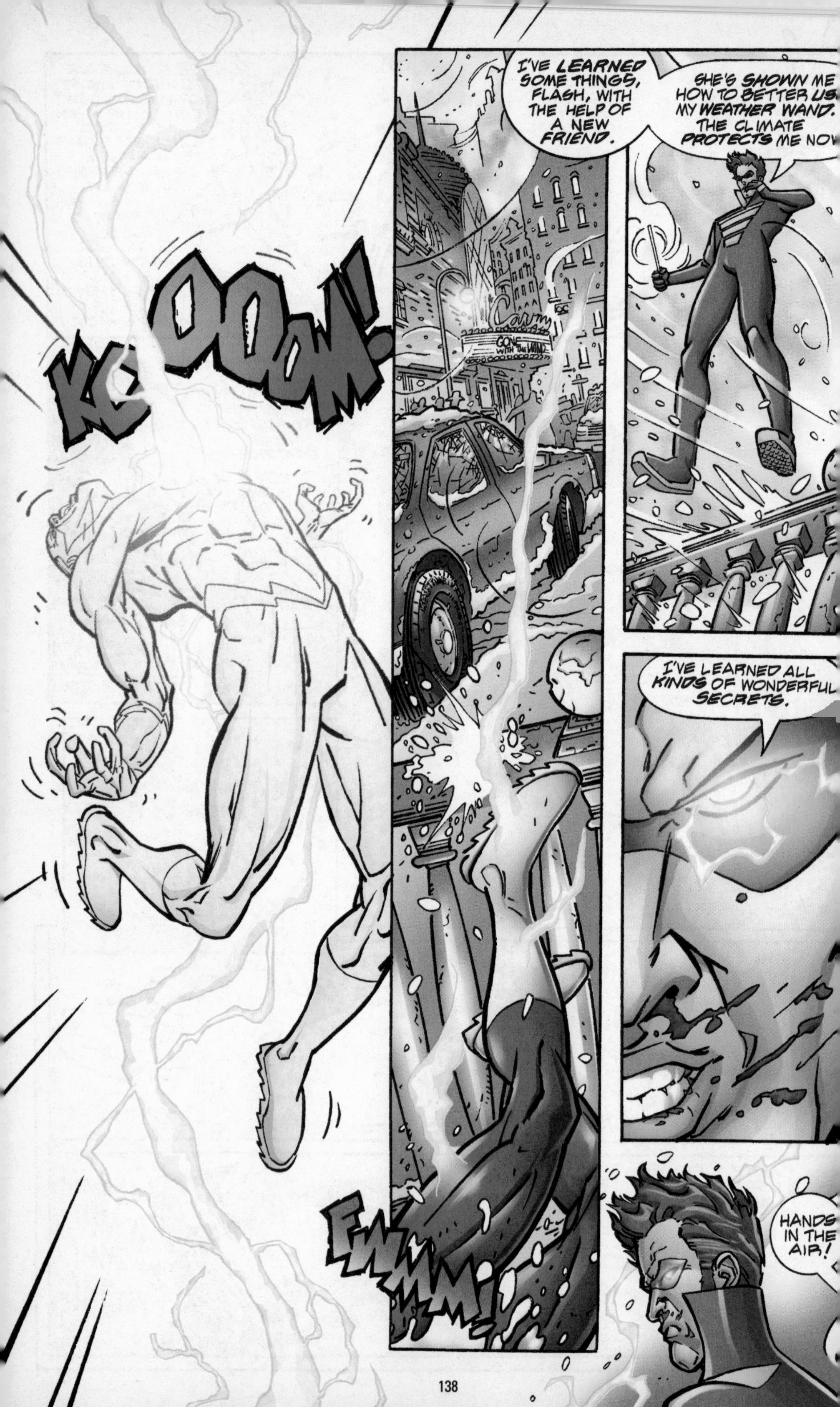

KROOOM!
I'VE LEARNED SOME THINGS, FLASH, WITH THE HELP OF A NEW FRIEND.
SHE'S SHOWN ME HOW TO BETTER US MY WEATHER WAND. THE CLIMATE PROTECTS ME NOW
GONE WITH THE WIND
I'VE LEARNED ALL KINDS OF WONDERFUL SECRETS.
FWAM!
HANDS IN THE AIR!

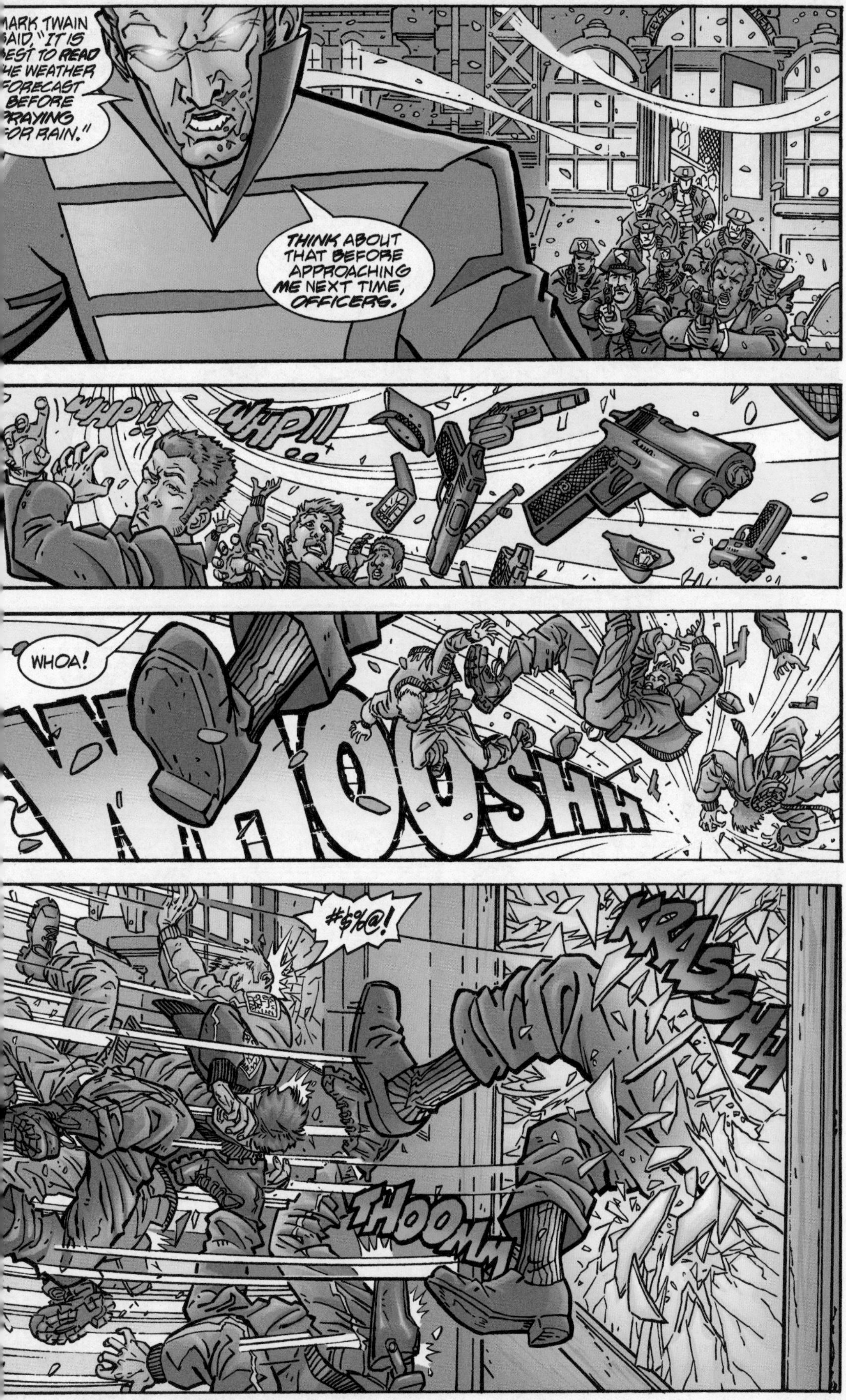
MARK TWAIN SAID, "IT IS BEST TO READ THE WEATHER FORECAST BEFORE PRAYING FOR RAIN."
THINK ABOUT THAT BEFORE APPROACHING ME NEXT TIME, OFFICERS.
WHP!!
WHP!!
WHOA!
OOSHH
#$%@!
KRASSHH
THOOMM

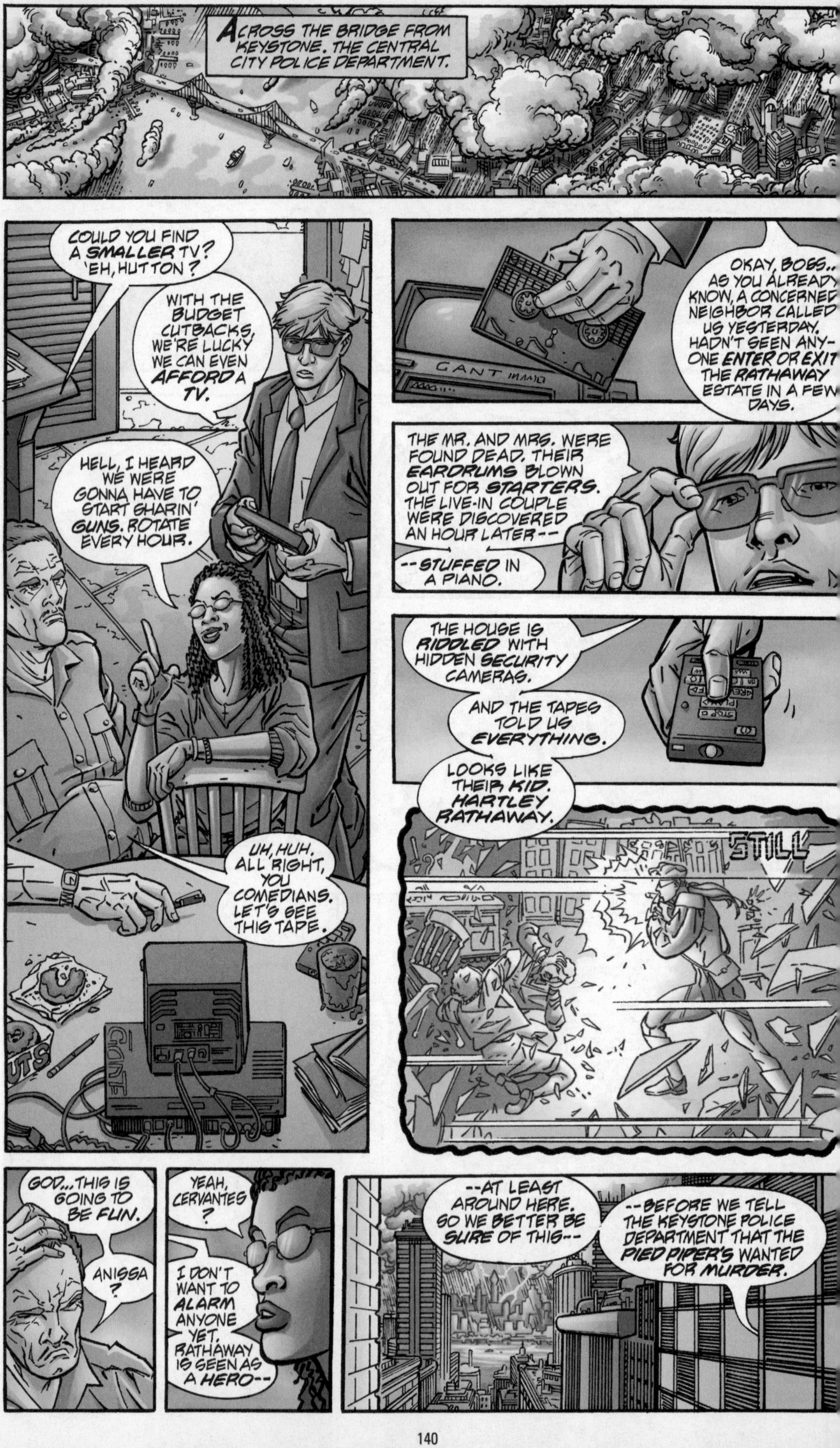
ACROSS THE BRIDGE FROM KEYSTONE. THE CENTRAL CITY POLICE DEPARTMENT.
COULD YOU FIND A SMALLER TV? 'EH, HUTTON?
WITH THE BUDGET CUTBACKS, WE'RE LUCKY WE CAN EVEN AFFORD A TV.
HELL, I HEARD WE WERE GONNA HAVE TO START SHARIN' GUNS. ROTATE EVERY HOUR.
UH, HUH. ALL RIGHT, YOU COMEDIANS. LET'S SEE THIS TAPE.
OKAY, BOSS... AS YOU ALREADY KNOW, A CONCERNED NEIGHBOR CALLED US YESTERDAY. HADN'T SEEN ANYONE ENTER OR EXIT THE RATHAWAY ESTATE IN A FEW DAYS.
THE MR. AND MRS. WERE FOUND DEAD. THEIR EARDRUMS BLOWN OUT FOR STARTERS. THE LIVE-IN COUPLE WERE DISCOVERED AN HOUR LATER--
--STUFFED IN A PIANO.
THE HOUSE IS RIDDLED WITH HIDDEN SECURITY CAMERAS.
AND THE TAPES TOLD US EVERYTHING.
LOOKS LIKE THEIR KID. HARTLEY RATHAWAY.
STILL
GOD... THIS IS GOING TO BE FUN.
ANISSA?
YEAH, CERVANTES?
I DON'T WANT TO ALARM ANYONE YET. RATHAWAY IS SEEN AS A HERO--
--AT LEAST AROUND HERE. SO WE BETTER BE SURE OF THIS--
--BEFORE WE TELL THE KEYSTONE POLICE DEPARTMENT THAT THE PIED PIPER'S WANTED FOR MURDER.

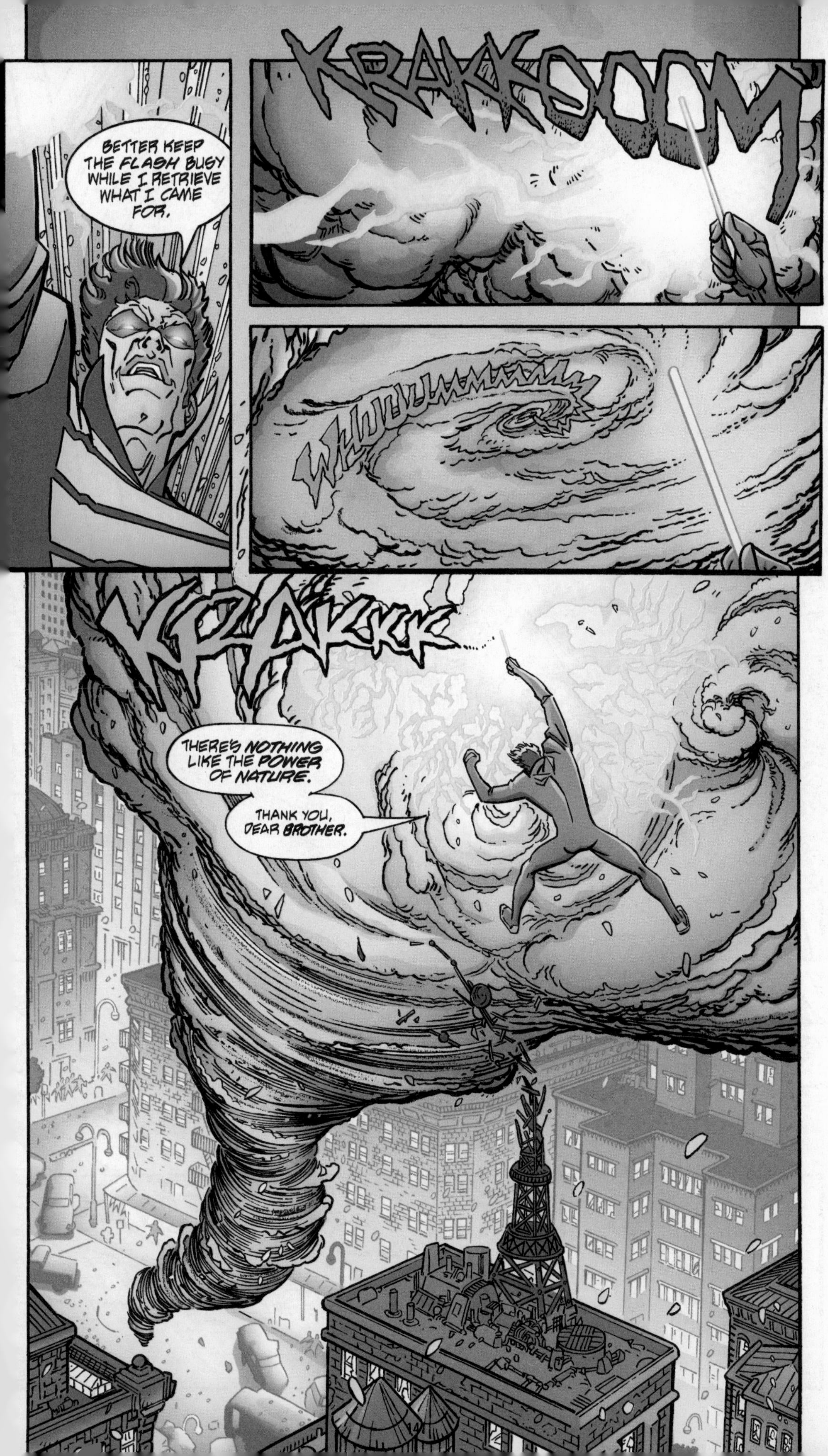
BETTER KEEP THE FLASH BUSY WHILE I RETRIEVE WHAT I CAME FOR.
KRAKKOOOM
KRAKKKK
THERE'S NOTHING LIKE THE POWER OF NATURE.
THANK YOU, DEAR BROTHER.

WSHH SSSHHHH

WHAT THE--?

OH GREAT.

I'VE OUTRACED TORNADOES BEFORE. USUALLY, I CAN RUN AGAINST ITS WIND VORTEX AND CANCEL THE SUCKER OUT.

BUT THIS TWISTER ISN'T JUST POWERED BY 300 MILE PER HOUR WINDS AND A SUPERCELL THUNDERSTORM--IT'S BACKED BY THE WEATHER WIZARD'S RAGE.

WHAT COULD DRIVE HIM TO CAUSE THIS MUCH DAMAGE? WHO SHOWED HIM HOW TO--

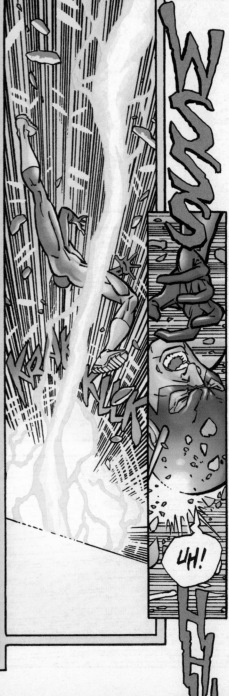

UH!

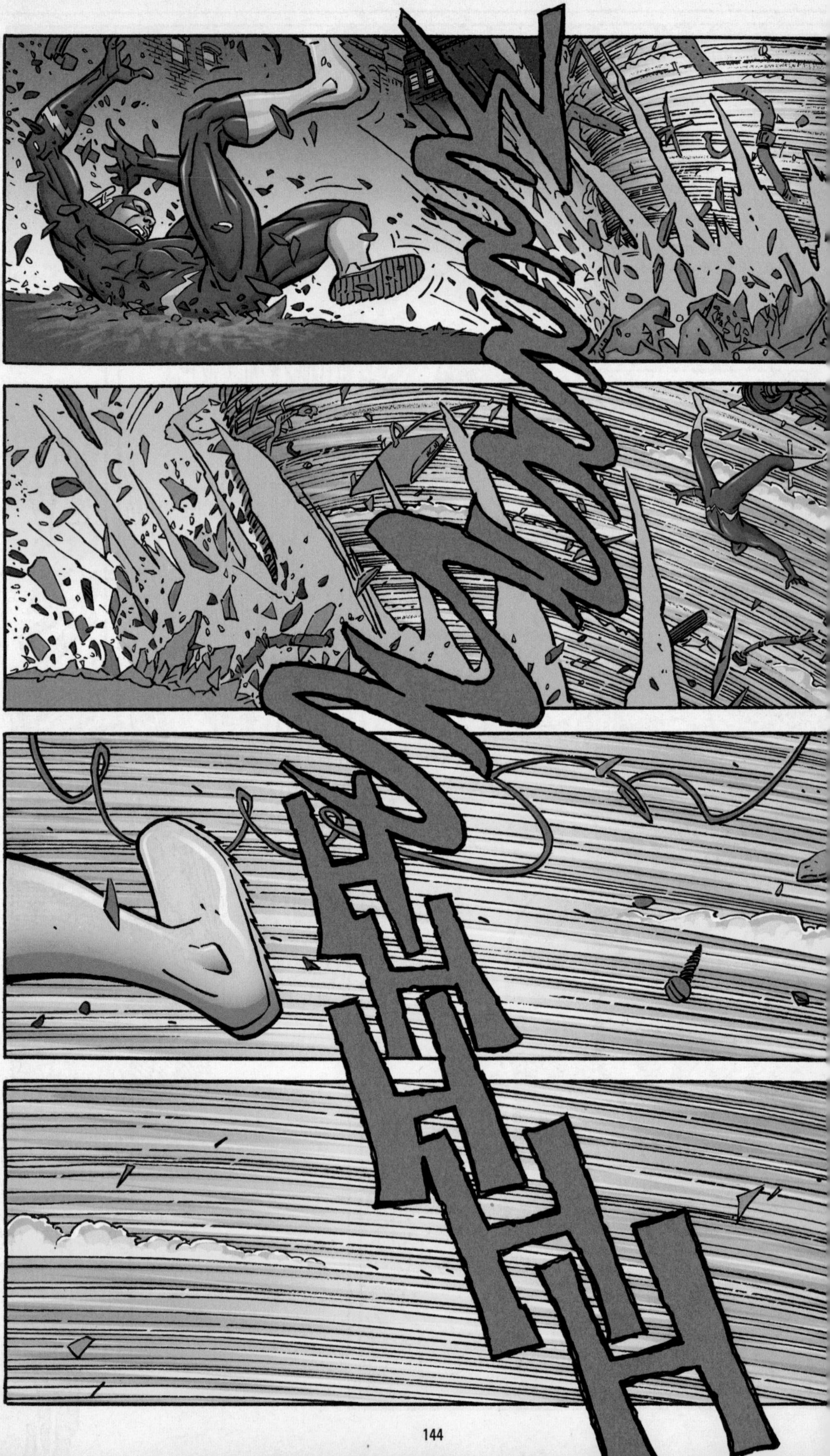
WOOOOOSHHHHHH

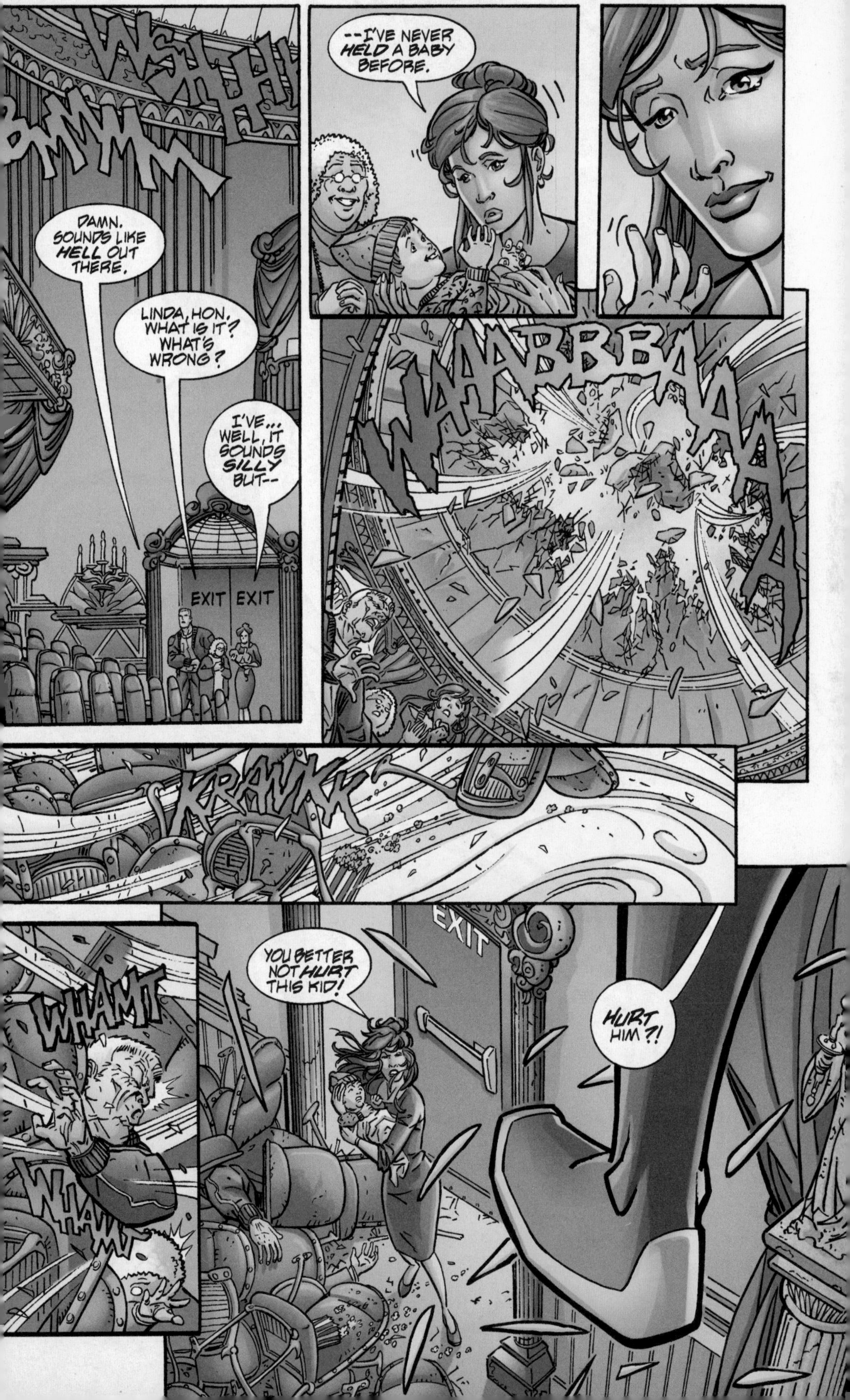
WSHHH
BMMMM
DAMN. SOUNDS LIKE HELL OUT THERE.
LINDA, HON. WHAT IS IT? WHAT'S WRONG?
I'VE... WELL, IT SOUNDS SILLY BUT--
EXIT EXIT
--I'VE NEVER HELD A BABY BEFORE.
WAABBBAAAA
KRANKK
WHAMT
WHAMT
EXIT
YOU BETTER NOT HURT THIS KID!
HURT HIM?!

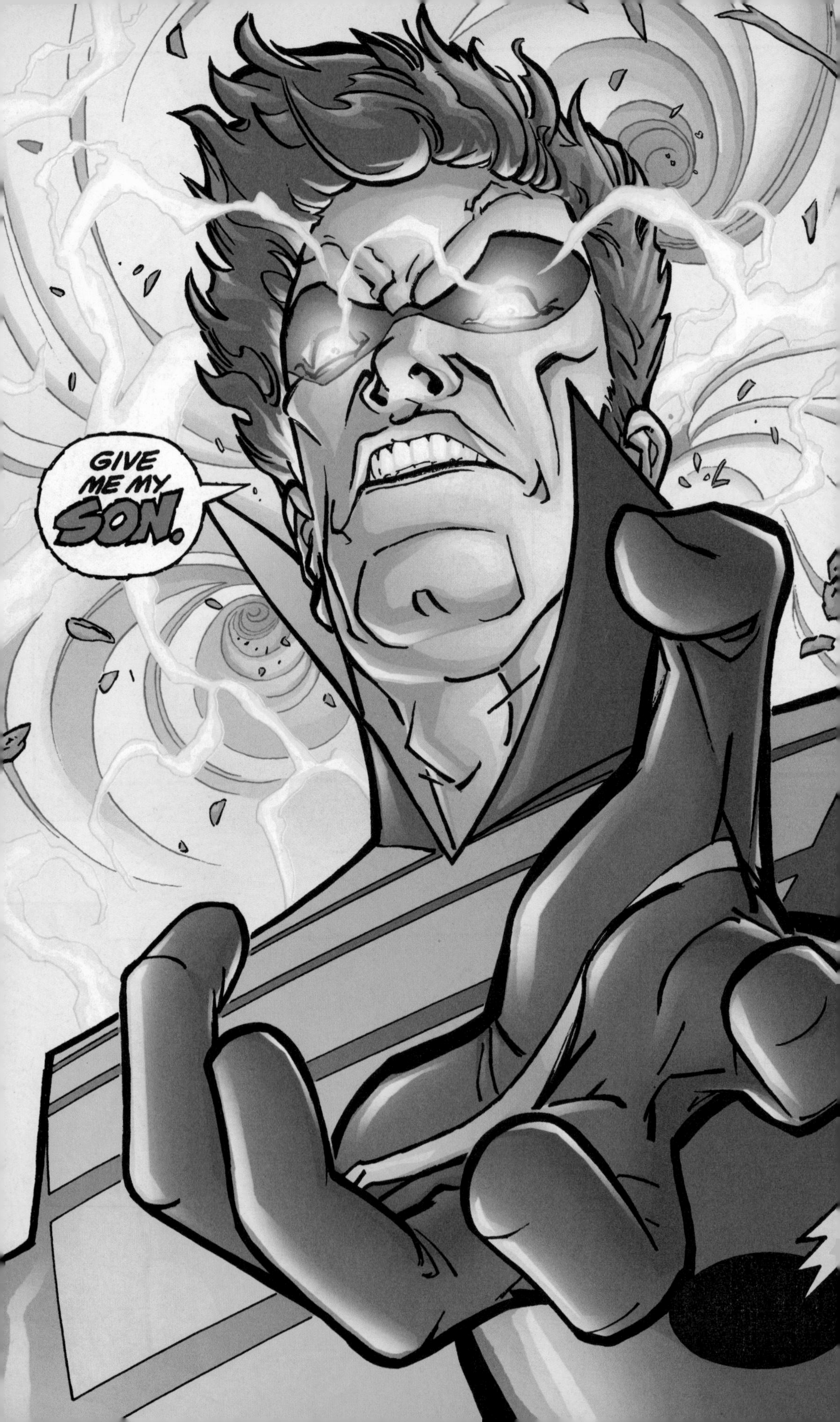
GIVE ME MY SON.

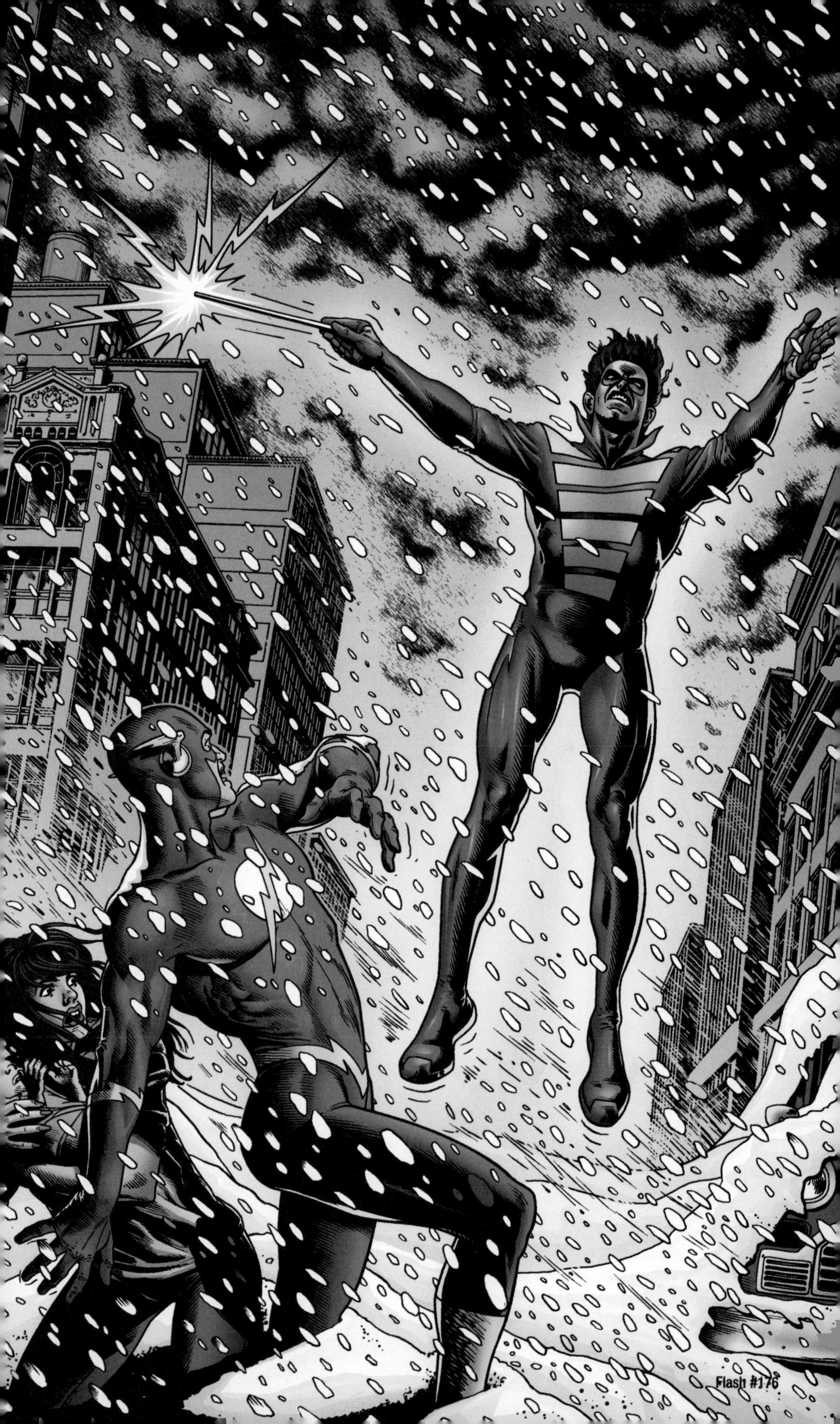

Flash #176

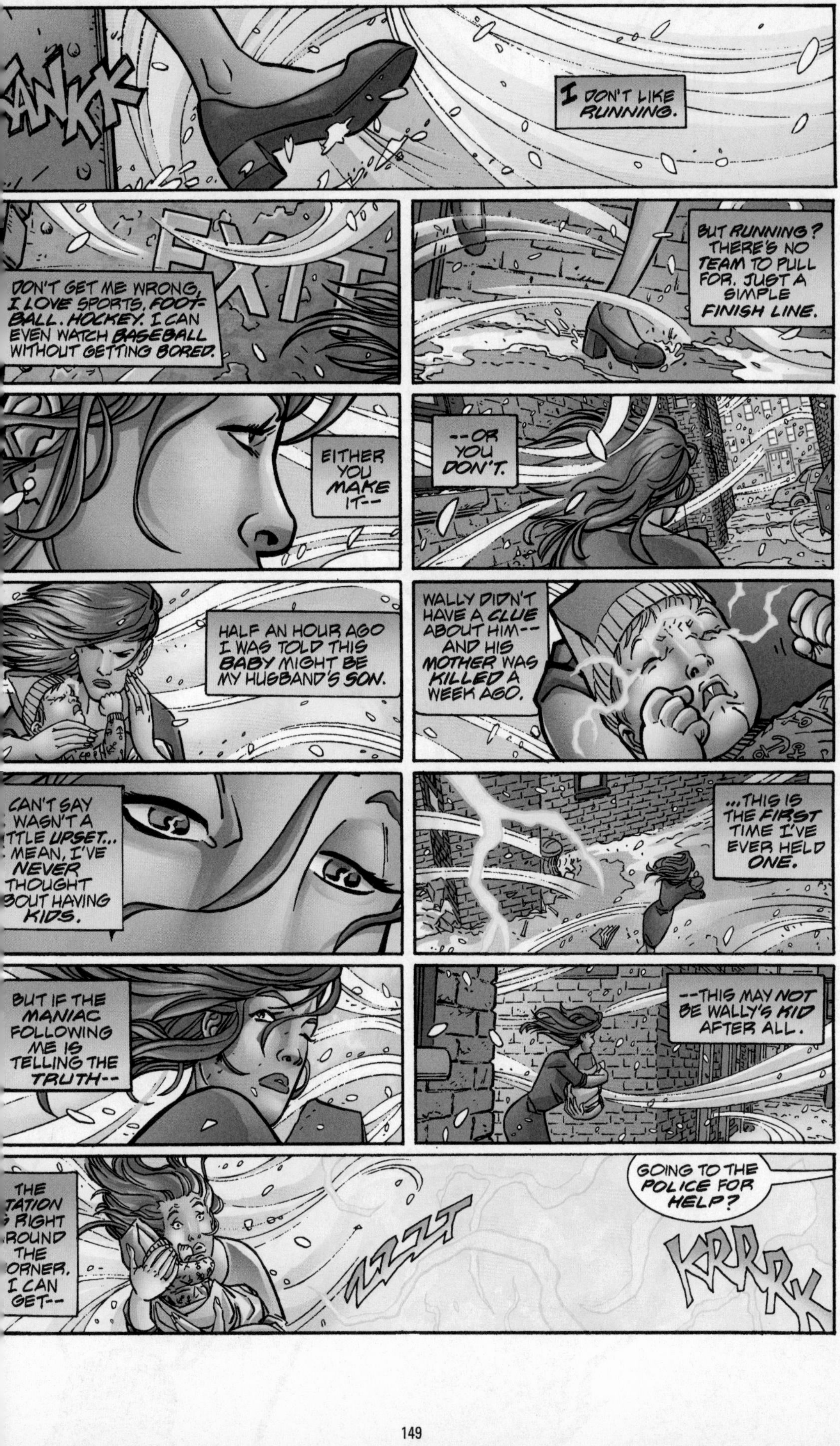
ANKK
I DON'T LIKE RUNNING.
EXIT
DON'T GET ME WRONG, I LOVE SPORTS. FOOTBALL. HOCKEY. I CAN EVEN WATCH BASEBALL WITHOUT GETTING BORED.
BUT RUNNING? THERE'S NO TEAM TO PULL FOR. JUST A SIMPLE FINISH LINE.
EITHER YOU MAKE IT--
--OR YOU DON'T.
HALF AN HOUR AGO I WAS TOLD THIS BABY MIGHT BE MY HUSBAND'S SON.
WALLY DIDN'T HAVE A CLUE ABOUT HIM-- AND HIS MOTHER WAS KILLED A WEEK AGO.
CAN'T SAY WASN'T A TTLE UPSET... MEAN, I'VE NEVER THOUGHT BOUT HAVING KIDS.
...THIS IS THE FIRST TIME I'VE EVER HELD ONE.
BUT IF THE MANIAC FOLLOWING ME IS TELLING THE TRUTH--
--THIS MAY NOT BE WALLY'S KID AFTER ALL.
THE TATION S RIGHT ROUND THE ORNER. I CAN GET--
ZZZT
GOING TO THE POLICE FOR HELP?
KRRRK

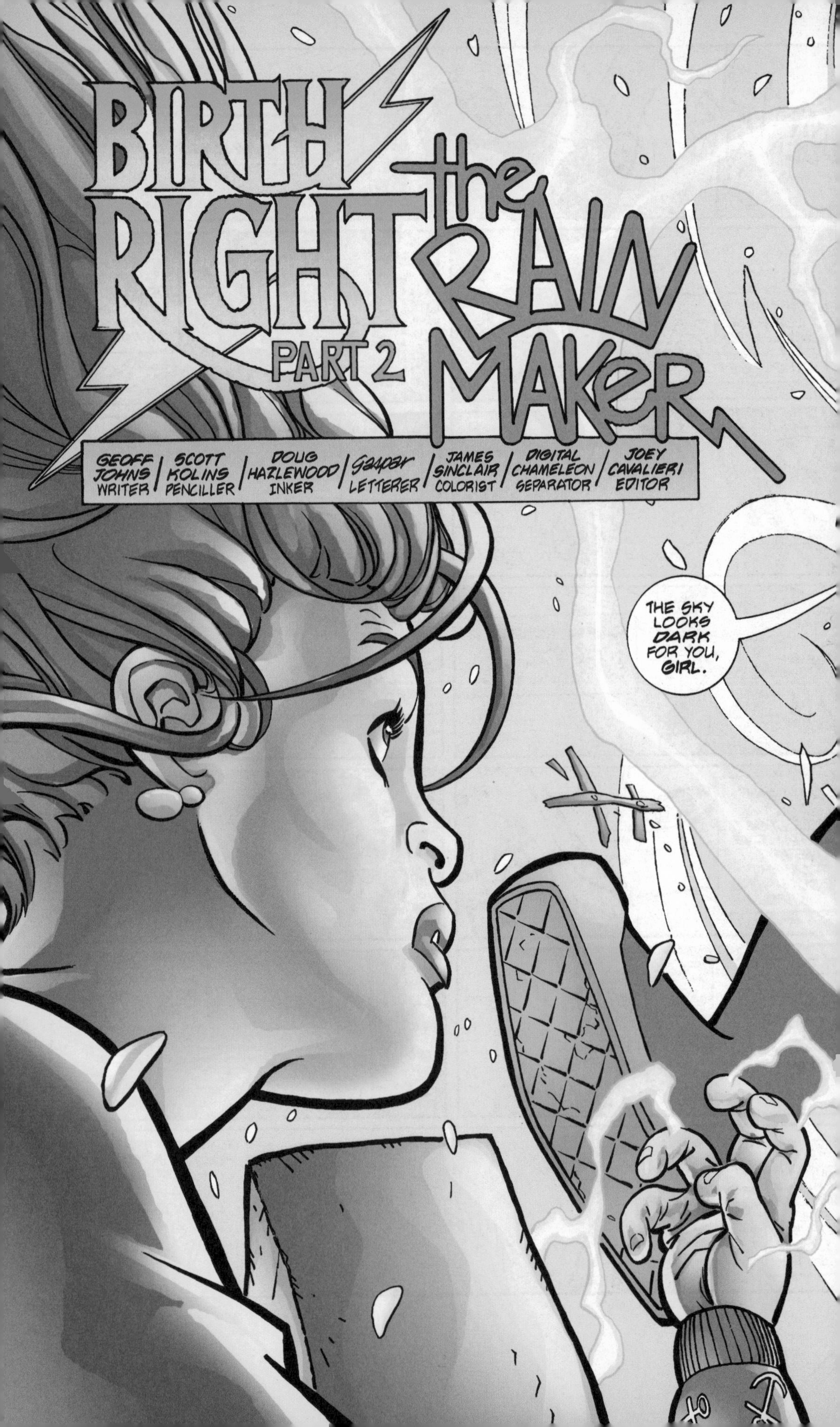
BIRTHRIGHT PART 2
the RAIN MAKER
GEOFF JOHNS WRITER
SCOTT KOLINS PENCILLER
DOUG HAZLEWOOD INKER
Gaspar LETTERER
JAMES SINCLAIR COLORIST
DIGITAL CHAMELEON SEPARATOR
JOEY CAVALIERI EDITOR
THE SKY LOOKS DARK FOR YOU, GIRL.

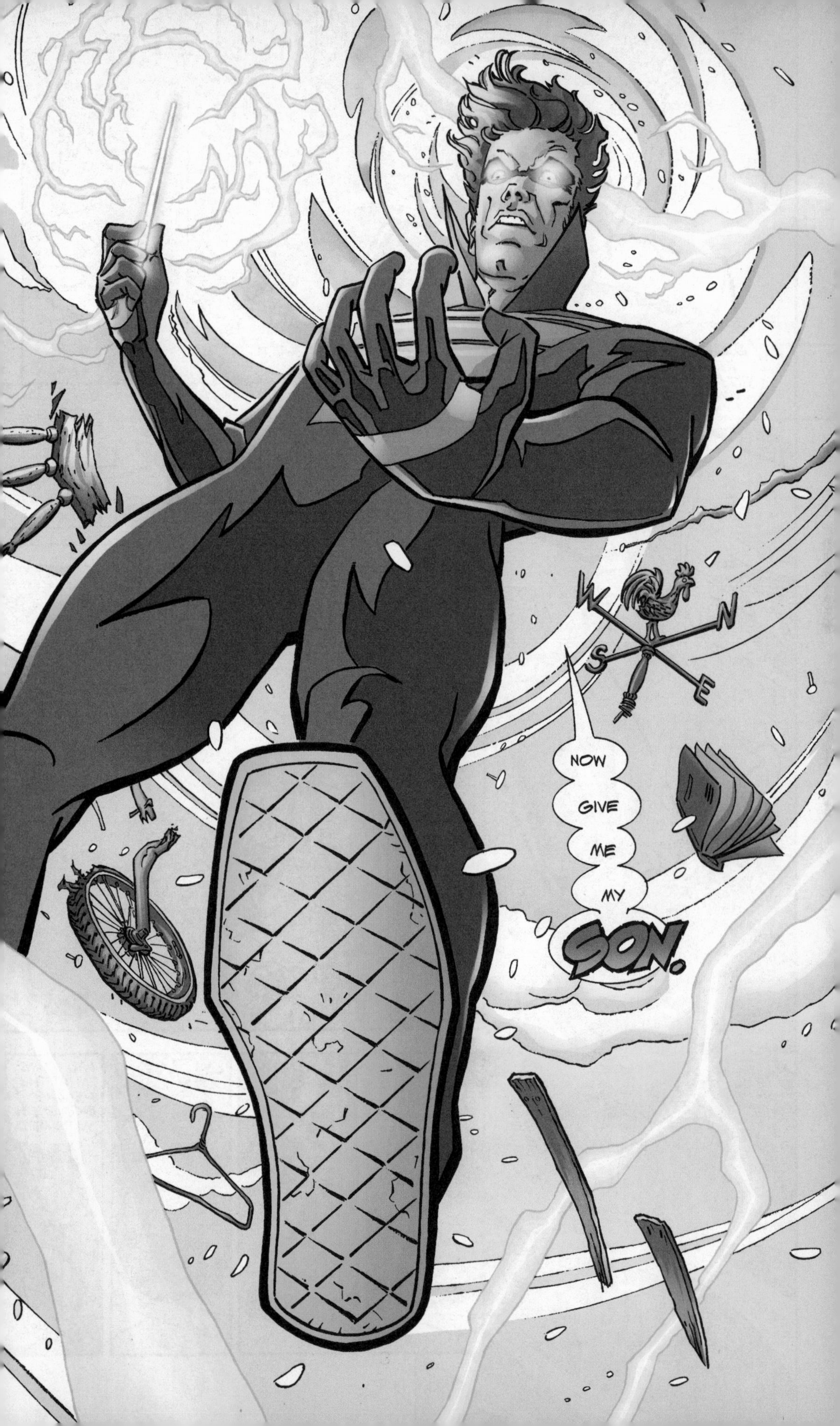
W
N
S
E
NOW GIVE ME MY SON.

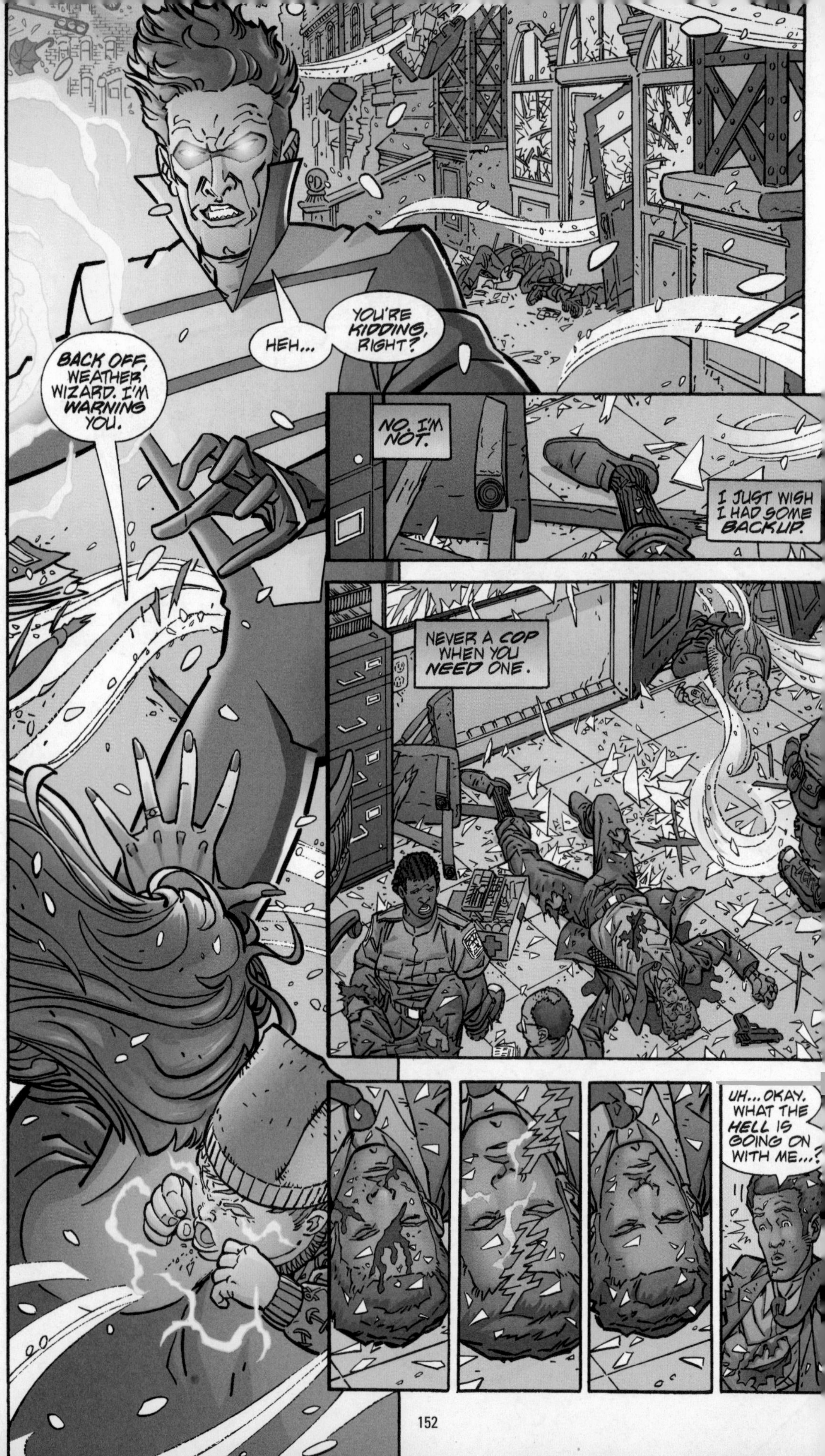

BACK OFF, WEATHER WIZARD. I'M WARNING YOU.
HEH...
YOU'RE KIDDING, RIGHT?
NO. I'M NOT.
I JUST WISH I HAD SOME BACKUP.
NEVER A COP WHEN YOU NEED ONE.
UH...OKAY. WHAT THE HELL IS GOING ON WITH ME...?

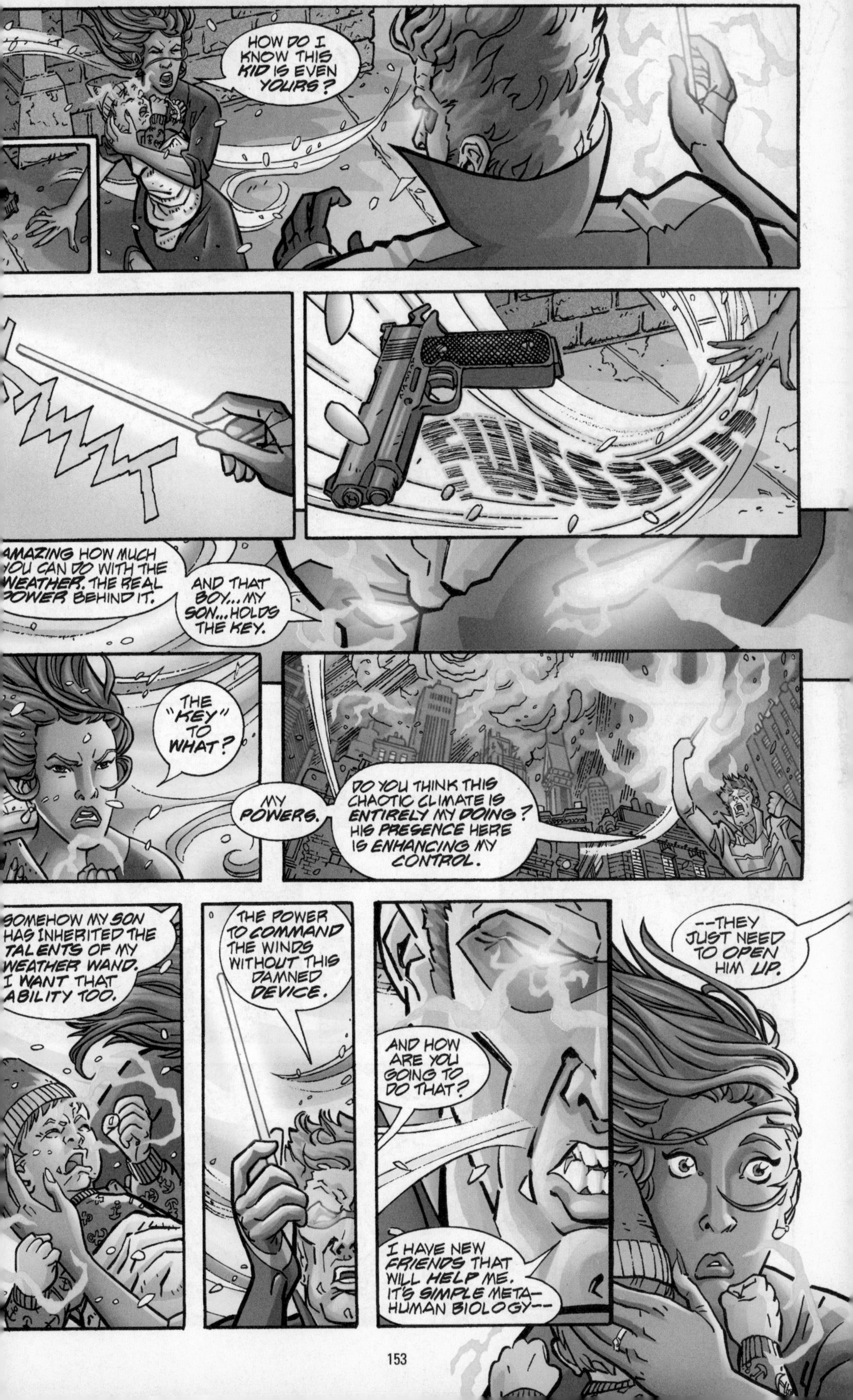
HOW DO I KNOW THIS KID IS EVEN YOURS?
AMAZING HOW MUCH YOU CAN DO WITH THE WEATHER. THE REAL POWER BEHIND IT.
AND THAT BOY... MY SON... HOLDS THE KEY.
THE "KEY" TO WHAT?
MY POWERS.
DO YOU THINK THIS CHAOTIC CLIMATE IS ENTIRELY MY DOING? HIS PRESENCE HERE IS ENHANCING MY CONTROL.
SOMEHOW MY SON HAS INHERITED THE TALENTS OF MY WEATHER WAND. I WANT THAT ABILITY TOO.
THE POWER TO COMMAND THE WINDS WITHOUT THIS DAMNED DEVICE.
AND HOW ARE YOU GOING TO DO THAT?
I HAVE NEW FRIENDS THAT WILL HELP ME. IT'S SIMPLE META-HUMAN BIOLOGY--
--THEY JUST NEED TO OPEN HIM UP.

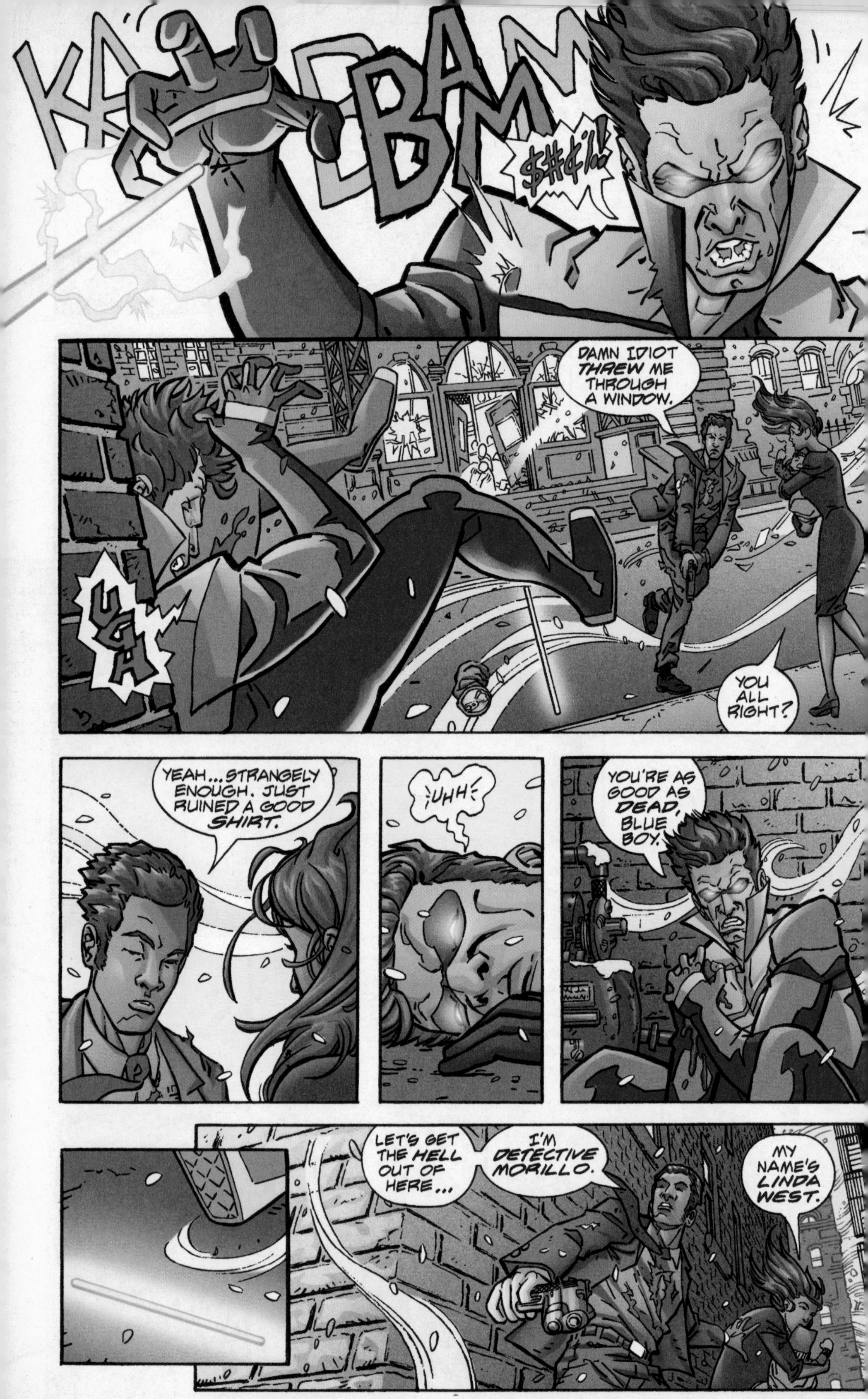
KA-DBAMM
$#¢!!
DAMN IDIOT THREW ME THROUGH A WINDOW.
UGA
YOU ALL RIGHT?
YEAH...STRANGELY ENOUGH. JUST RUINED A GOOD SHIRT.
UHH
YOU'RE AS GOOD AS DEAD, BLUE BOY.
LET'S GET THE HELL OUT OF HERE...
I'M DETECTIVE MORILLO.
MY NAME'S LINDA WEST.

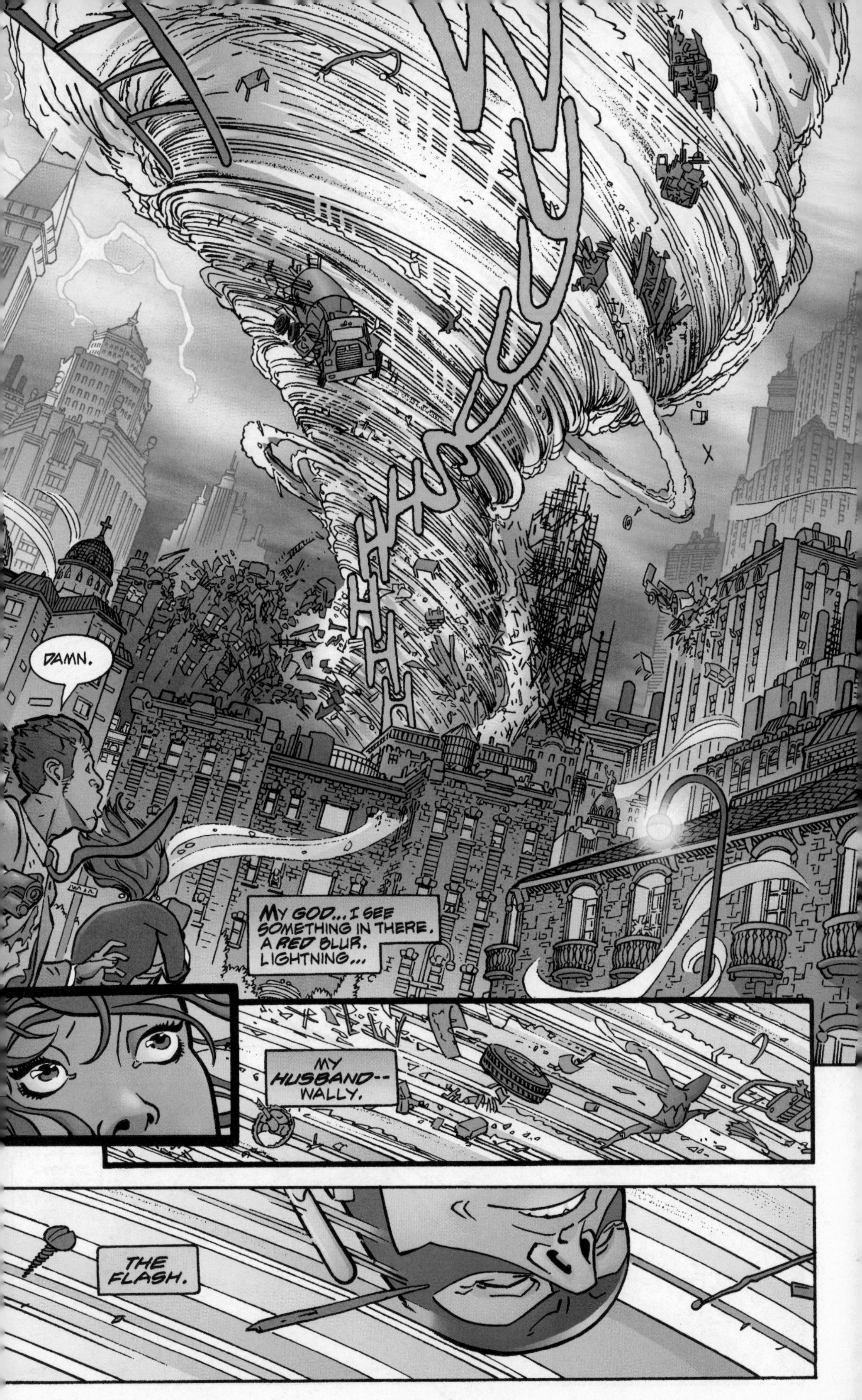
DAMN.
MY GOD... I SEE SOMETHING IN THERE. A RED BLUR. LIGHTNING...
MY HUSBAND--WALLY.
THE FLASH.

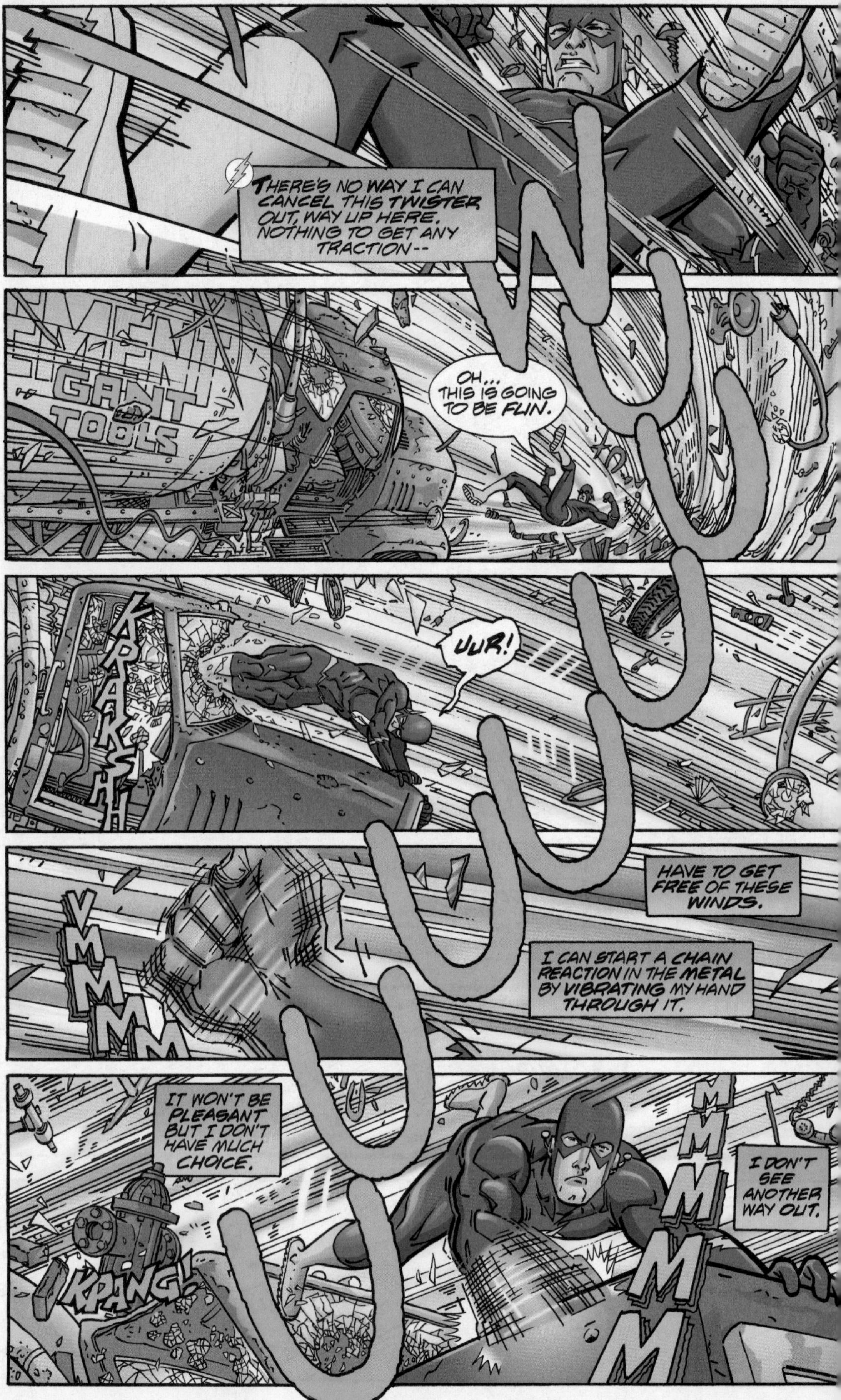
THERE'S NO WAY I CAN CANCEL THIS TWISTER OUT, WAY UP HERE. NOTHING TO GET ANY TRACTION--
WUUUUUUUU
GANT TOOLS
OH... THIS IS GOING TO BE FUN.
KRAKSH!
UUR!
HAVE TO GET FREE OF THESE WINDS.
I CAN START A CHAIN REACTION IN THE METAL BY VIBRATING MY HAND THROUGH IT.
VMMMMM
IT WON'T BE PLEASANT BUT I DON'T HAVE MUCH CHOICE.
I DON'T SEE ANOTHER WAY OUT.
MMMMMM
KRANG!

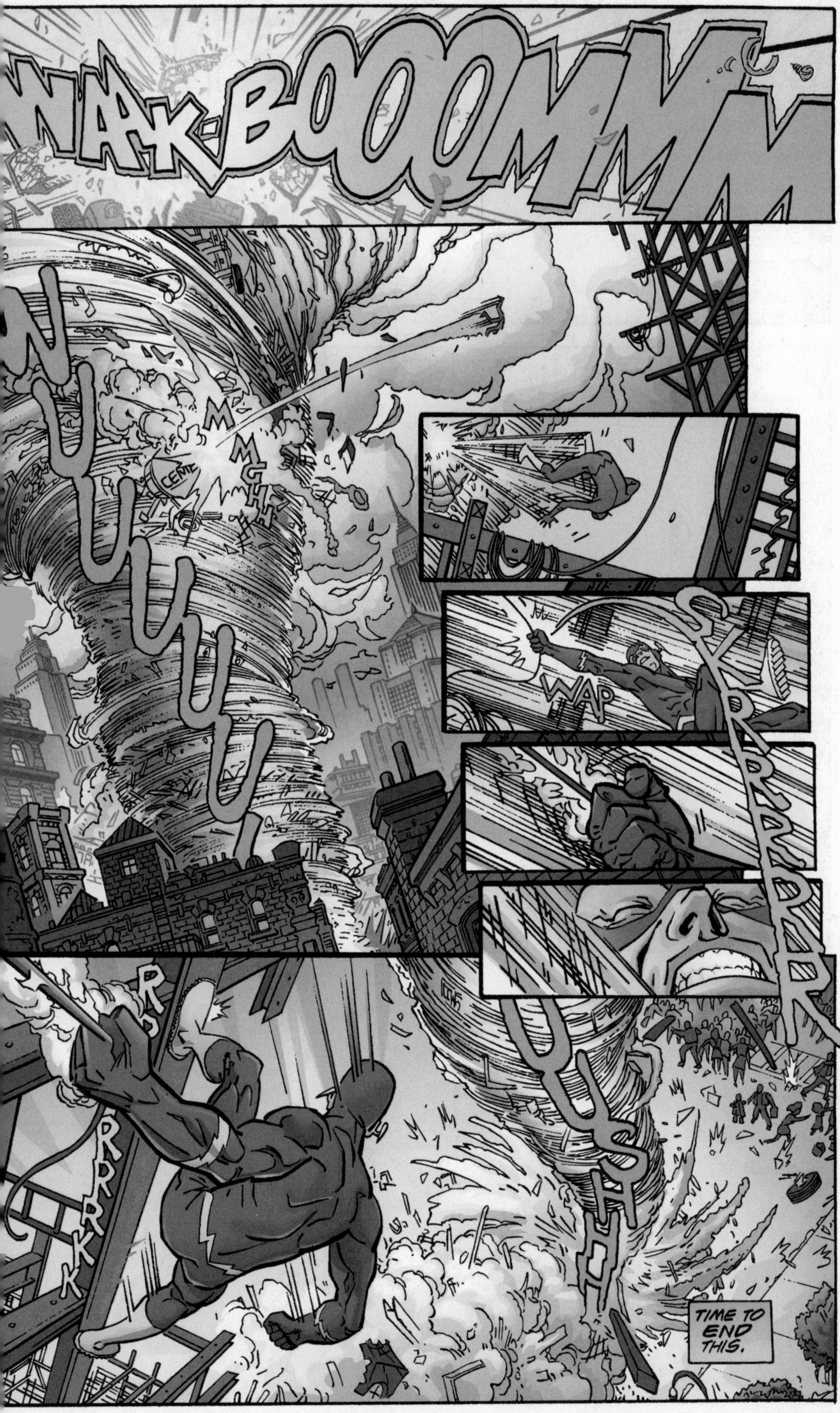
BOOOMMM
WAP
RRRRK
TIME TO END THIS.

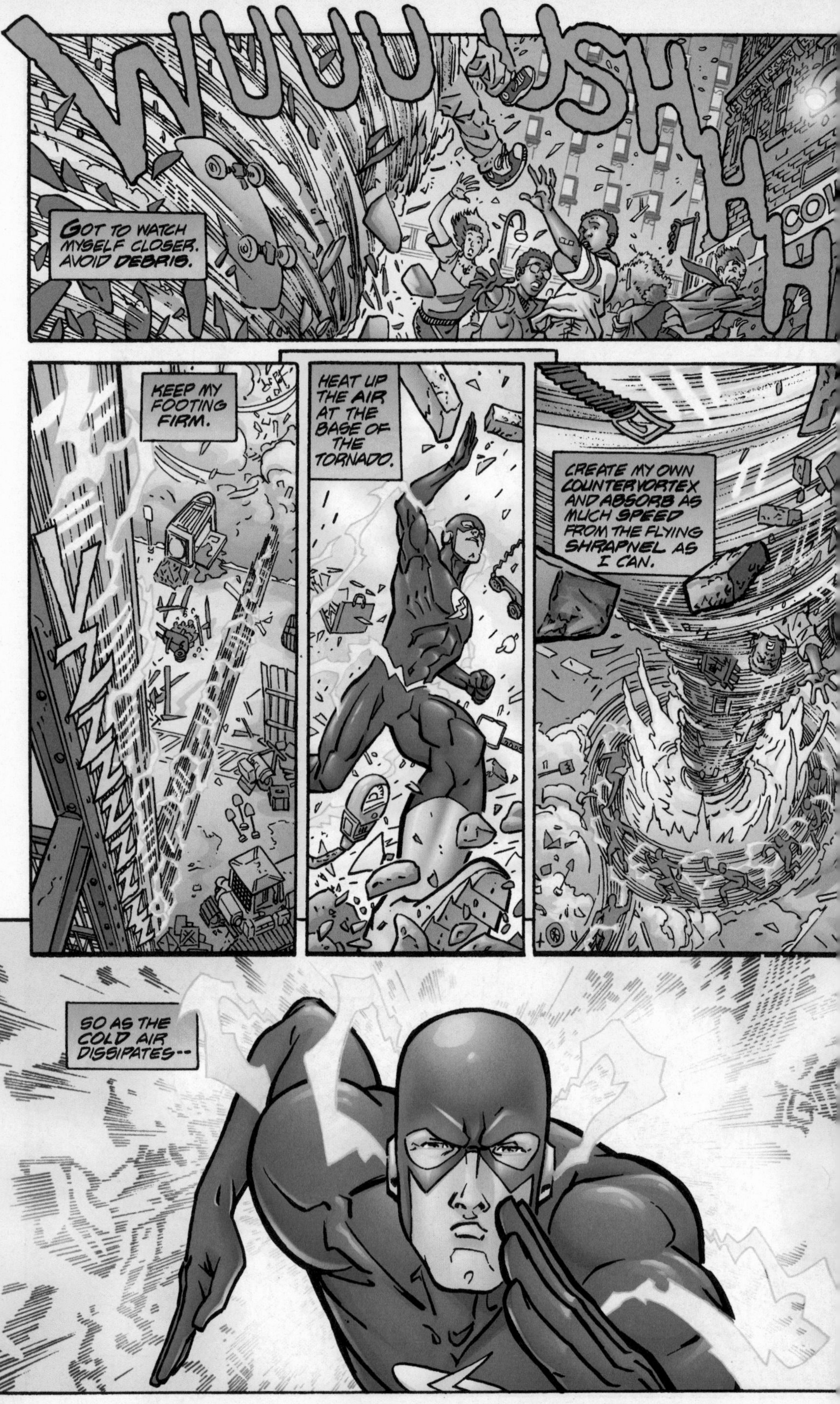
WUUUUSHHH
GOT TO WATCH MYSELF CLOSER. AVOID DEBRIS.
KEEP MY FOOTING FIRM.
VZZZZZZZ
HEAT UP THE AIR AT THE BASE OF THE TORNADO.
CREATE MY OWN COUNTERVORTEX AND ABSORB AS MUCH SPEED FROM THE FLYING SHRAPNEL AS I CAN.
SO AS THE COLD AIR DISSIPATES--

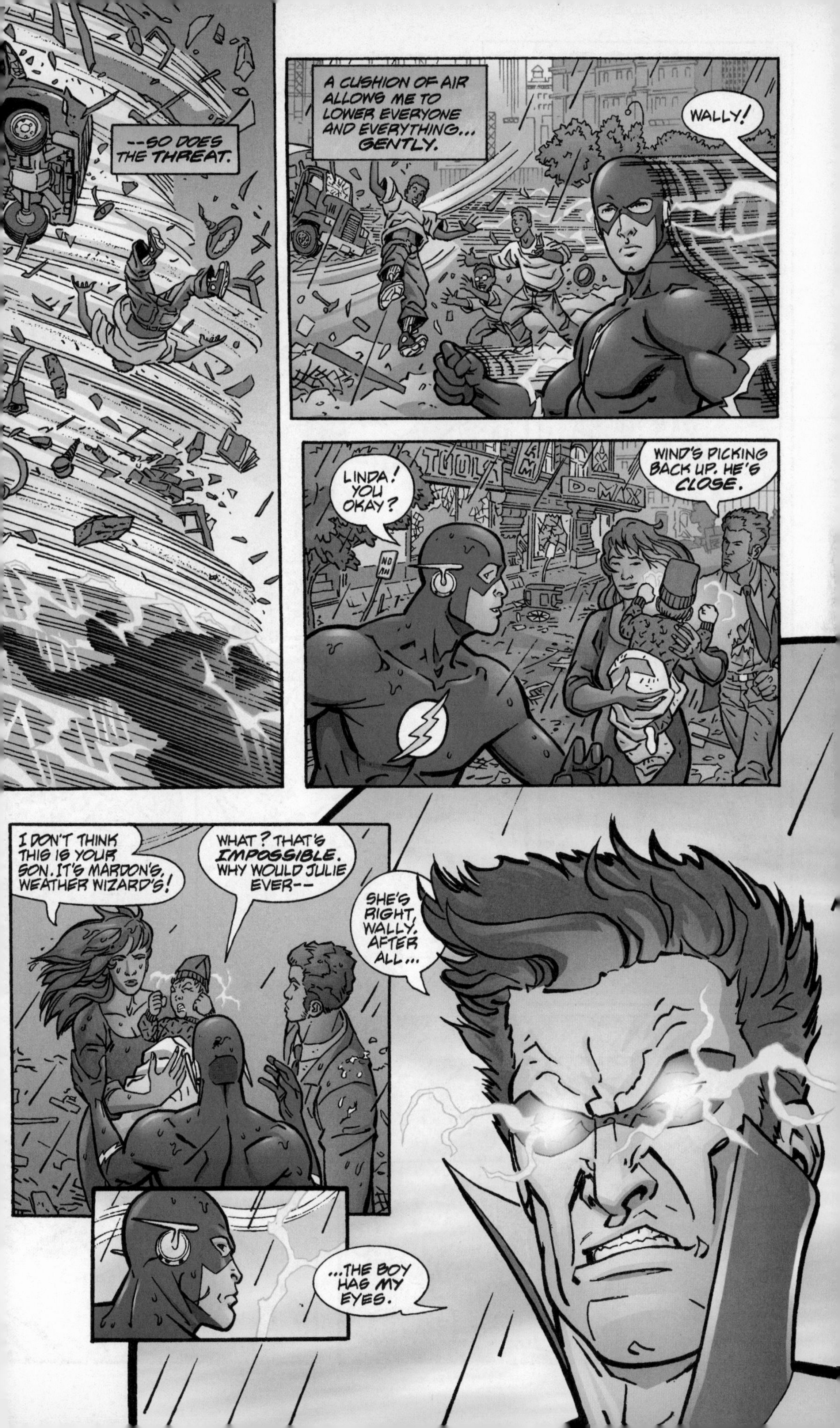

--SO DOES THE THREAT.
A CUSHION OF AIR ALLOWS ME TO LOWER EVERYONE AND EVERYTHING... GENTLY.
WALLY!
LINDA! YOU OKAY?
WIND'S PICKING BACK UP. HE'S CLOSE.
D-MAX
NO
I DON'T THINK THIS IS YOUR SON. IT'S MARDON'S. WEATHER WIZARD'S!
WHAT? THAT'S IMPOSSIBLE. WHY WOULD JULIE EVER--
SHE'S RIGHT, WALLY. AFTER ALL...
...THE BOY HAS MY EYES.

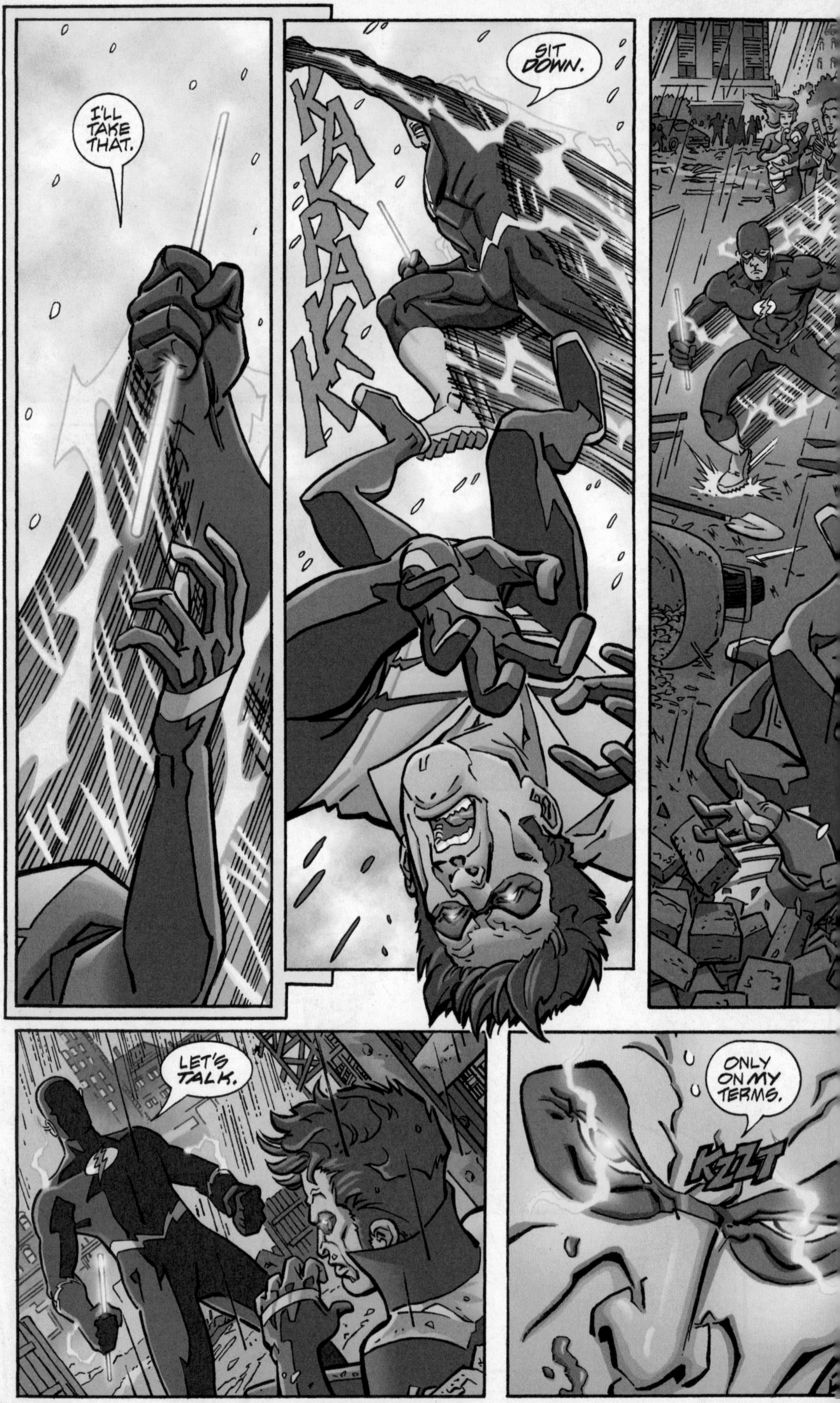
I'LL TAKE THAT.
KAKRAKK
SIT DOWN.
LET'S TALK.
ONLY ON MY TERMS.
KZZT

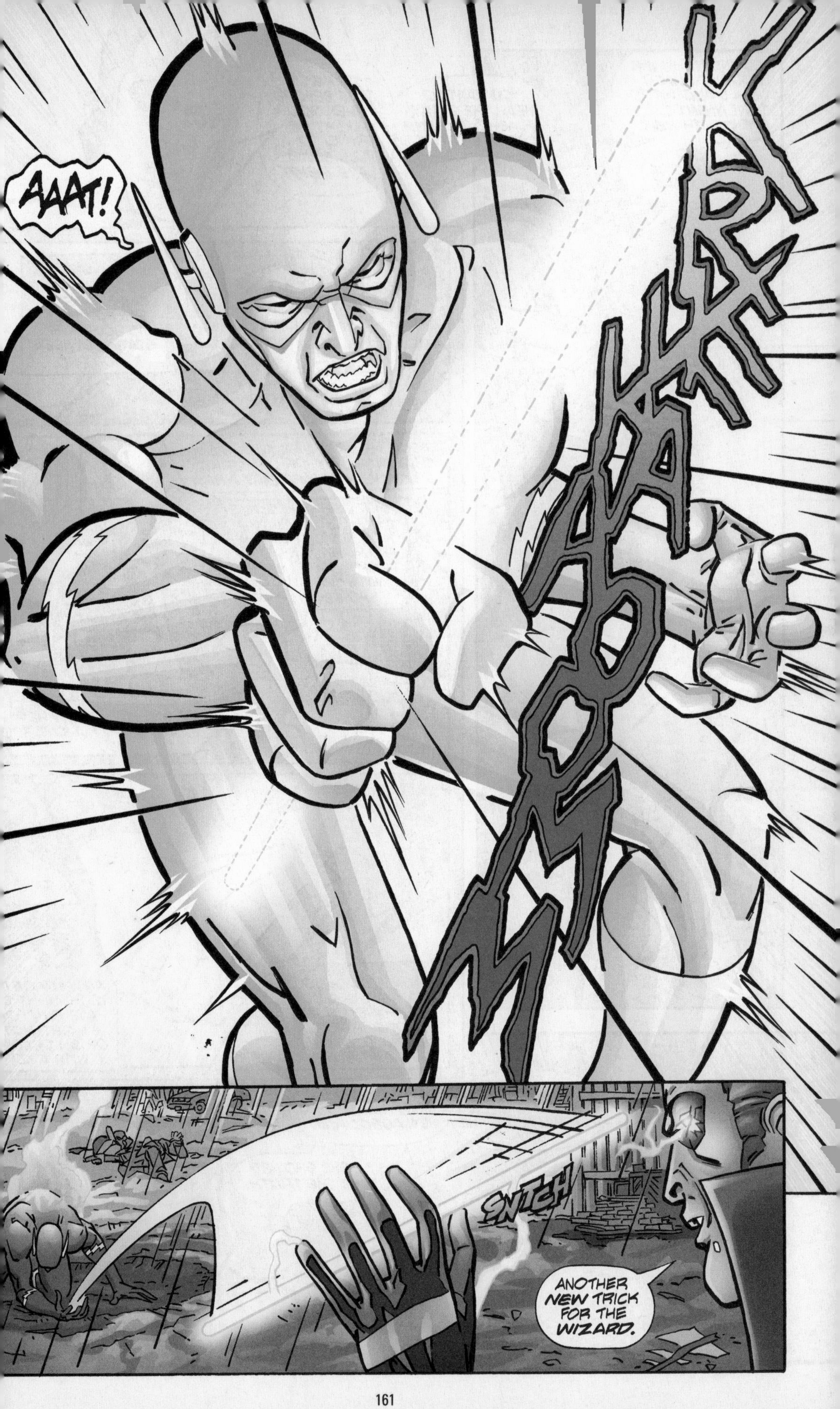
AAAT!
SNTCH
ANOTHER NEW TRICK FOR THE WIZARD.

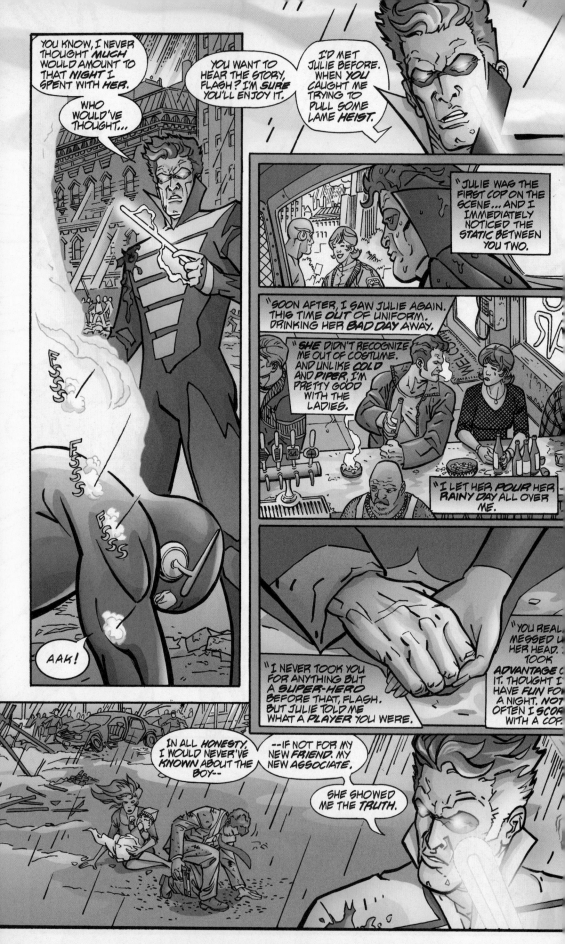

YOU KNOW, I NEVER THOUGHT *MUCH* WOULD AMOUNT TO THAT *NIGHT* I SPENT WITH *HER.*

WHO WOULD'VE THOUGHT...

YOU WANT TO HEAR THE STORY, FLASH? I'M *SURE* YOU'LL ENJOY IT.

I'D MET JULIE BEFORE. WHEN *YOU* CAUGHT ME TRYING TO PULL SOME LAME *HEIST.*

"JULIE WAS THE FIRST COP ON THE SCENE... AND I IMMEDIATELY NOTICED THE *STATIC* BETWEEN YOU TWO.

"SOON AFTER, I SAW JULIE AGAIN. THIS TIME *OUT* OF UNIFORM. DRINKING HER *BAD DAY* AWAY.

"SHE DIDN'T RECOGNIZE ME OUT OF COSTUME. AND UNLIKE *COLD* AND *PIPER,* I'M PRETTY GOOD WITH THE LADIES.

"I LET HER *POUR* HER RAINY DAY ALL OVER ME.

AAK!

"I NEVER TOOK YOU FOR ANYTHING BUT A *SUPER-HERO* BEFORE THAT, FLASH. BUT JULIE TOLD ME WHAT A *PLAYER* YOU WERE.

"YOU REAL... MESSED U... HER HEAD. ... TOOK *ADVANTAGE* O... IT. THOUGHT I... HAVE *FUN* FO... A NIGHT. *NOT...* OFTEN I SCOR... WITH A COP.

IN ALL *HONESTY,* I WOULD NEVER'VE KNOWN ABOUT THE BOY--

--IF NOT FOR MY NEW *FRIEND.* MY NEW ASSOCIATE.

SHE SHOWED ME THE *TRUTH.*

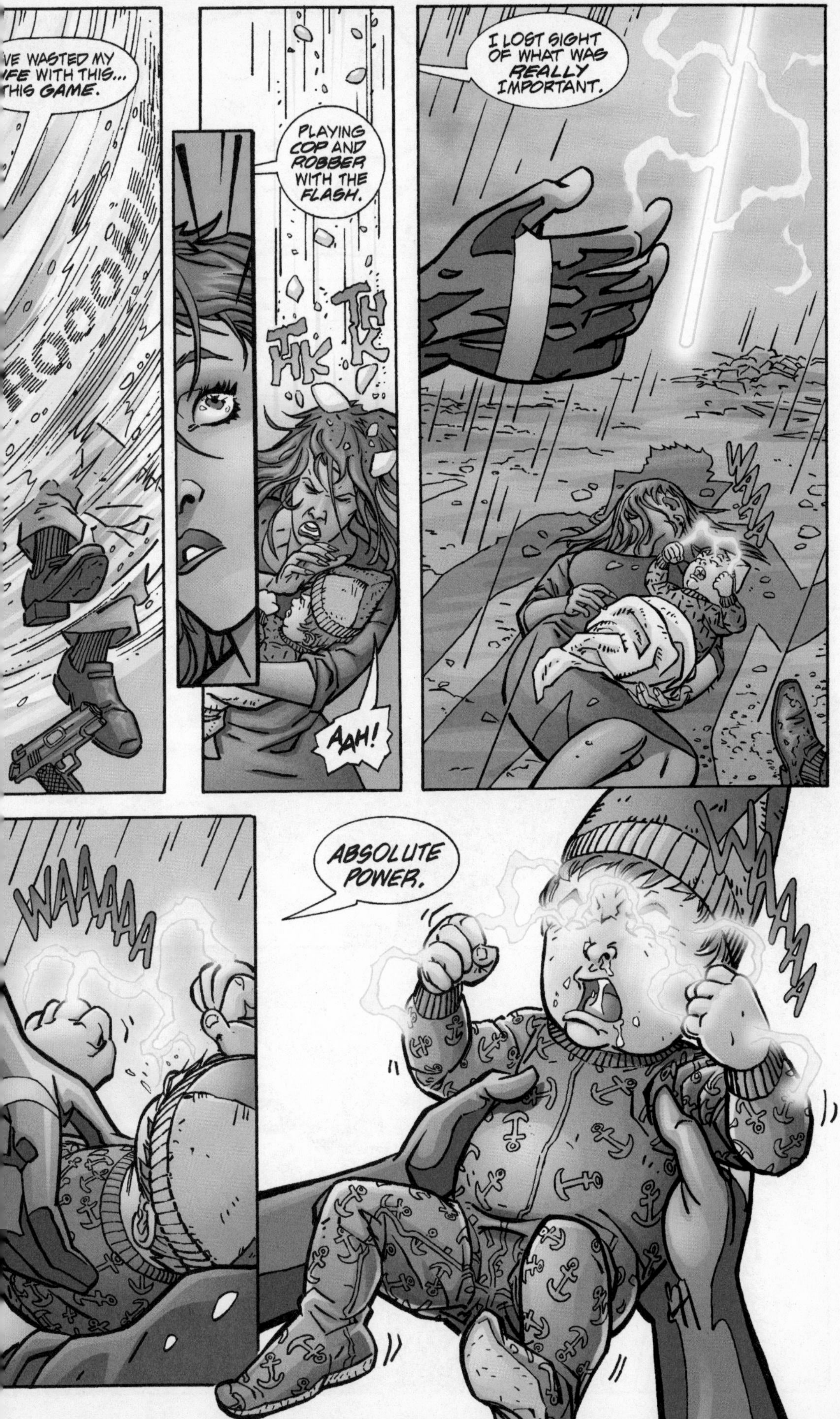
VE WASTED MY
LIFE WITH THIS...
THIS GAME.
ROOOOM
PLAYING
COP AND
ROBBER
WITH THE
FLASH.
THK
THK
AAH!
I LOST SIGHT
OF WHAT WAS
REALLY
IMPORTANT.
WAAAA
WAAAAA
ABSOLUTE
POWER.
WAAAAA

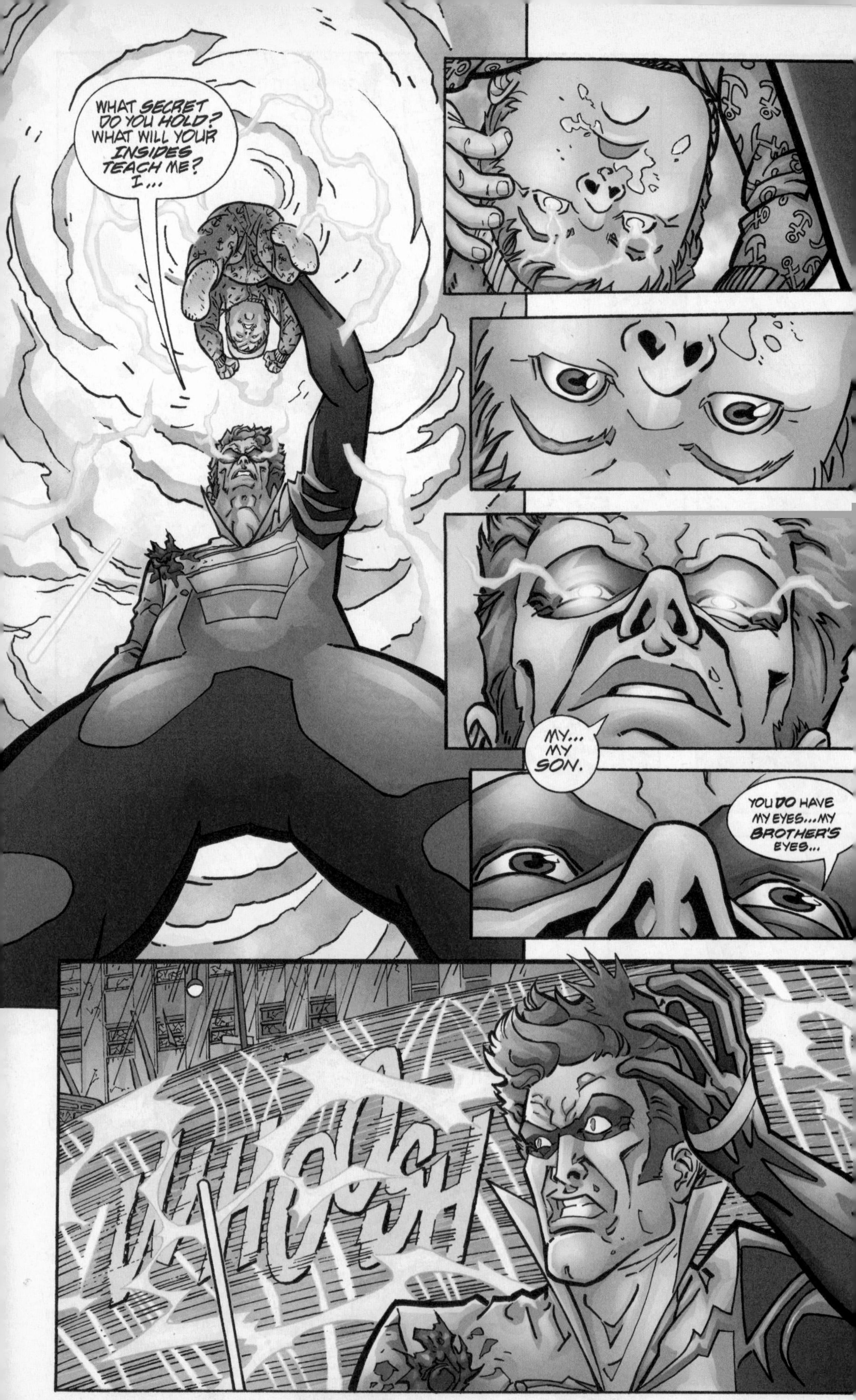
WHAT SECRET DO YOU HOLD? WHAT WILL YOUR INSIDES TEACH ME? I...
MY... MY SON.
YOU DO HAVE MY EYES...MY BROTHER'S EYES...
WHOOSH

WHA-?

BE RIGHT BACK.

GIVE HIM TO ME.

SAVE IT, WIZARD. I'M NOT PUTTING THAT CHILD IN HARM'S WAY.

NOW YOU BETTER DROP THAT WAND.

NO!

DAMN YOU, FLASH!

KSHRK!

WHA-KABOOOM

KR KR KRK KRK KRK

KRK KRK

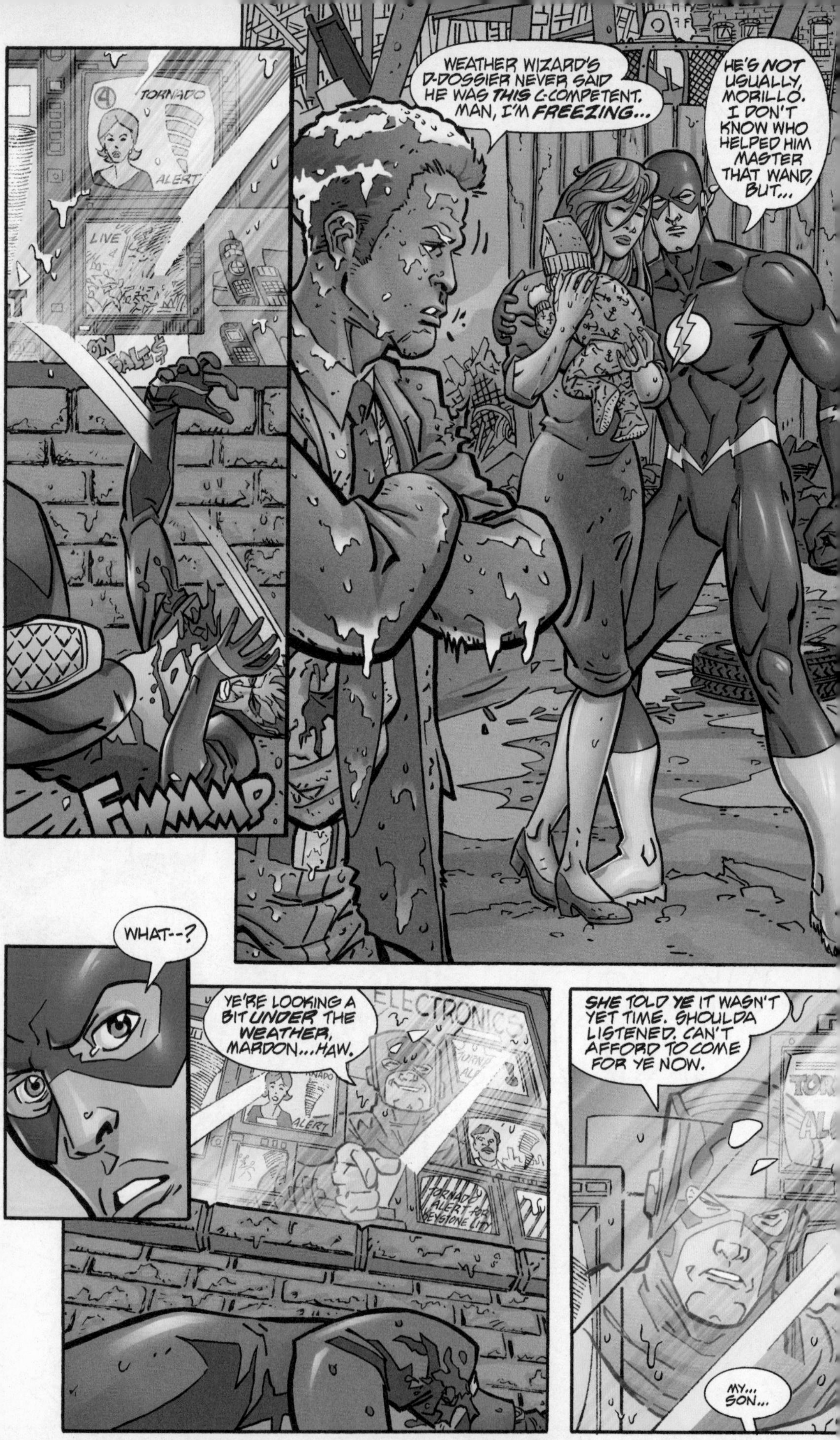

TORNADO
ALERT
LIVE
ON SALE$
FWMMP
WEATHER WIZARD'S D-DOSSIER NEVER SAID HE WAS THIS C-COMPETENT. MAN, I'M FREEZING...
HE'S NOT USUALLY, MORILLO. I DON'T KNOW WHO HELPED HIM MASTER THAT WAND, BUT...
WHAT--?
YE'RE LOOKING A BIT UNDER THE WEATHER, MARDON...HAW.
ELECTRONICS
TORNADO ALERT FOR KEYSTONE CITY
SHE TOLD YE IT WASN'T YET TIME. SHOULDA LISTENED. CAN'T AFFORD TO COME FOR YE NOW.
MY... SON...

McCULLOCH!

FLASHER...

GONNA *ARREST* ME, THEN? HEH.

TA.

DAMMIT, MIRROR MASTER! WHAT ARE YOU--

GROUND ZERO ELECTRONICS

TORNADO ALERT CANCELED. REPEAT--

ALERT OVER

OPEN

KRASHH

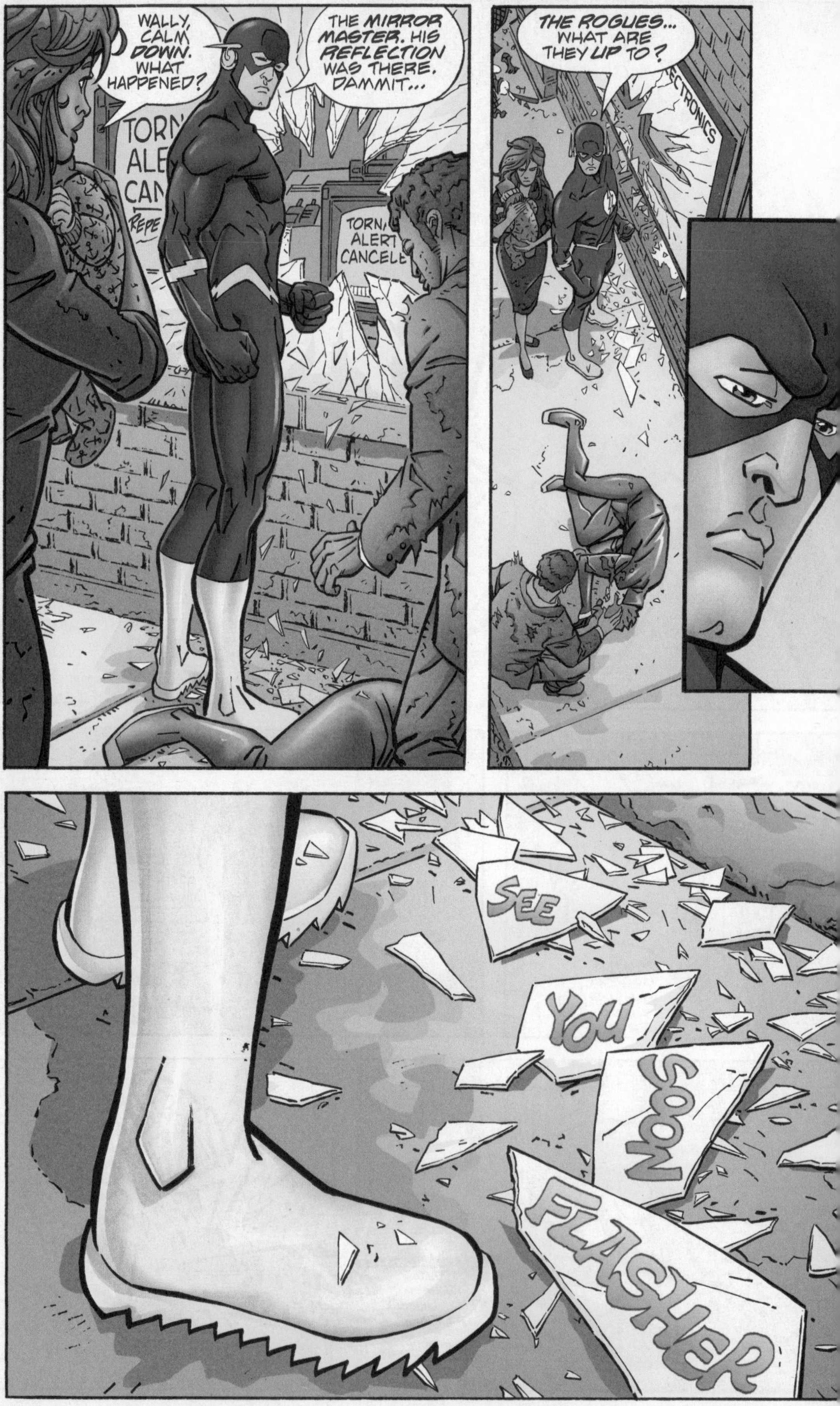

WALLY, CALM DOWN. WHAT HAPPENED?
THE MIRROR MASTER. HIS REFLECTION WAS THERE. DAMMIT...
TORN ALERT CANCELE
THE ROGUES... WHAT ARE THEY UP TO?
ECTRONICS
SEE
YOU
SOON
FLASHER

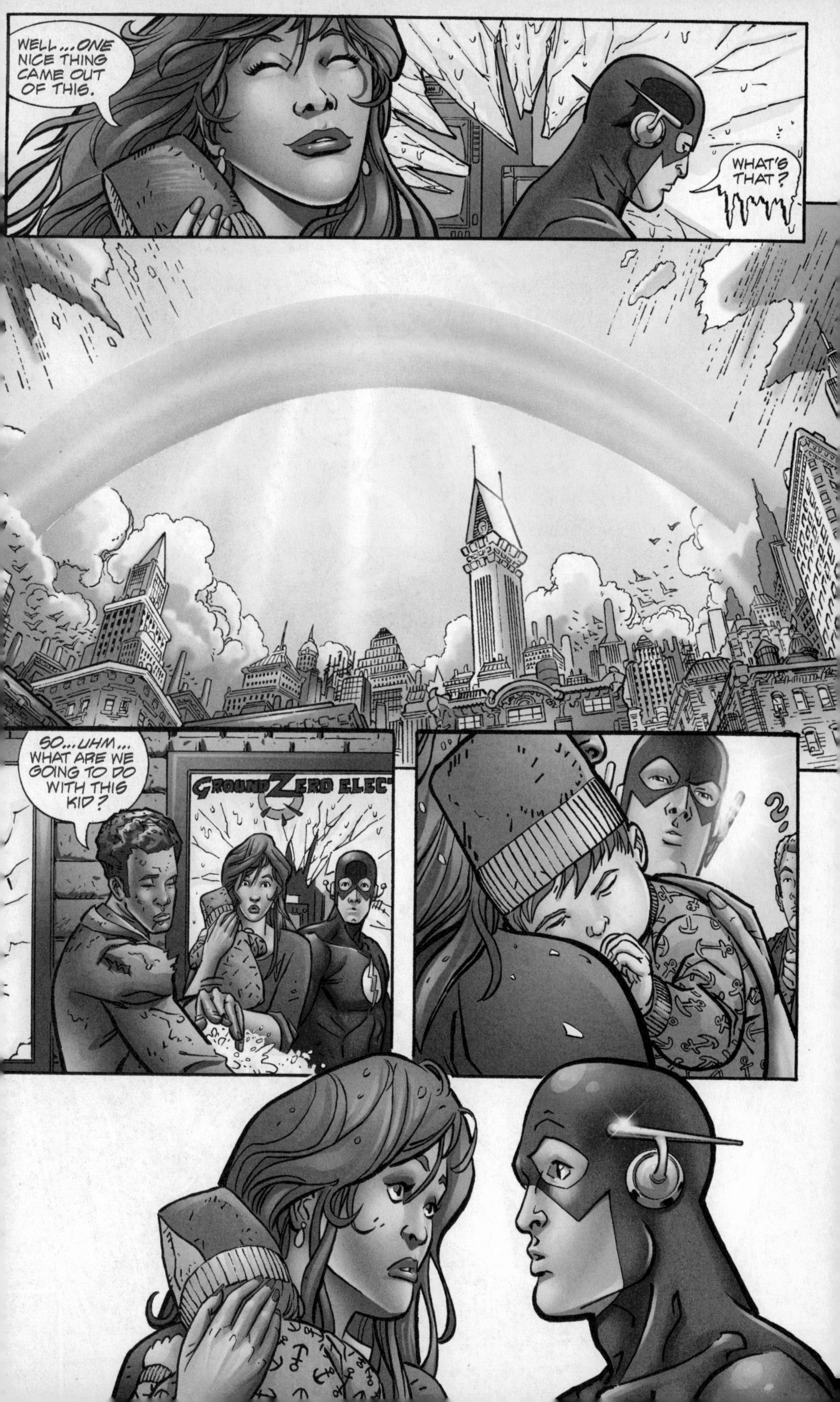
WELL... ONE NICE THING CAME OUT OF THIS.
WHAT'S THAT?
SO... UHM... WHAT ARE WE GOING TO DO WITH THIS KID?
GROUND ZERO ELEC
?

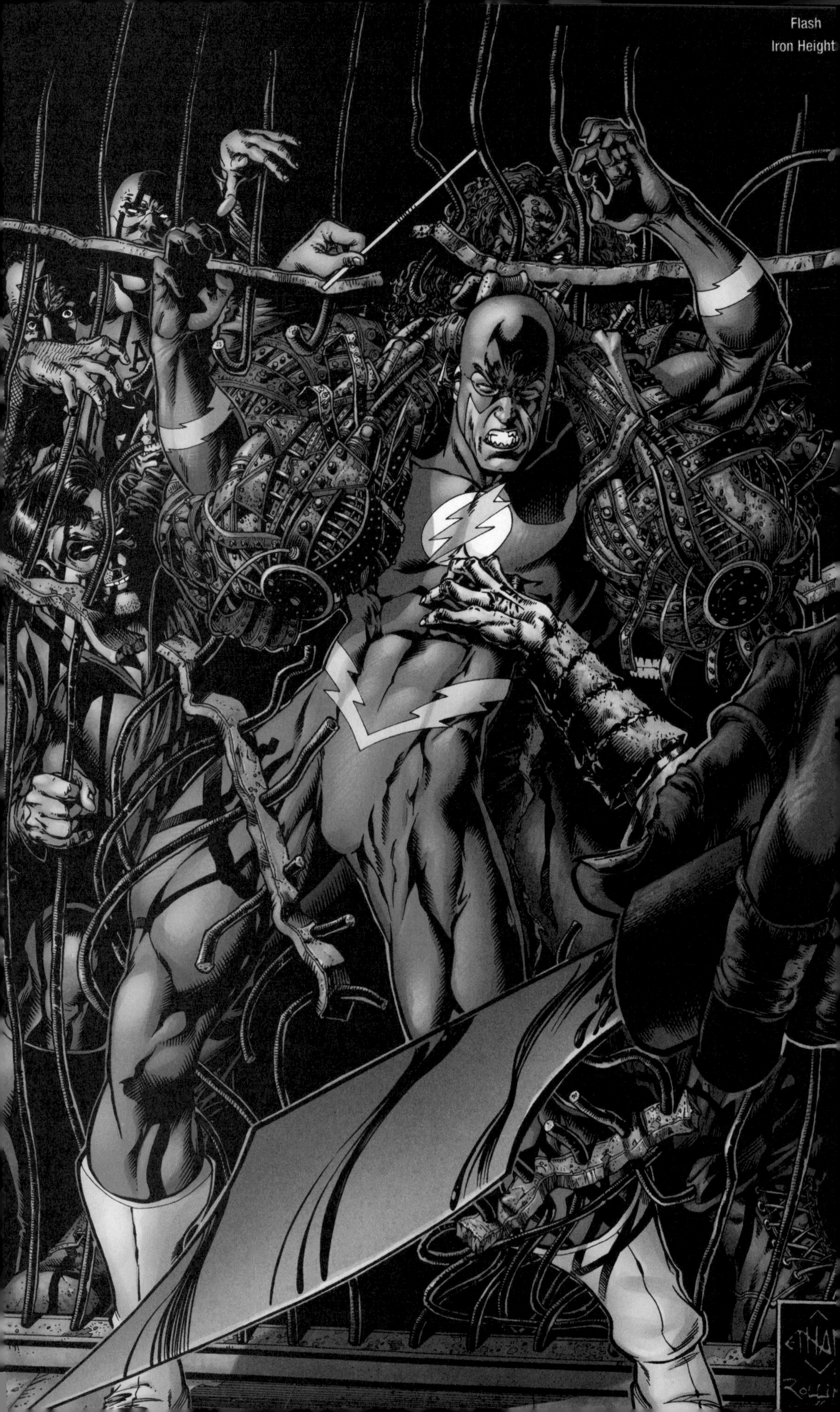

Flash
Iron Height

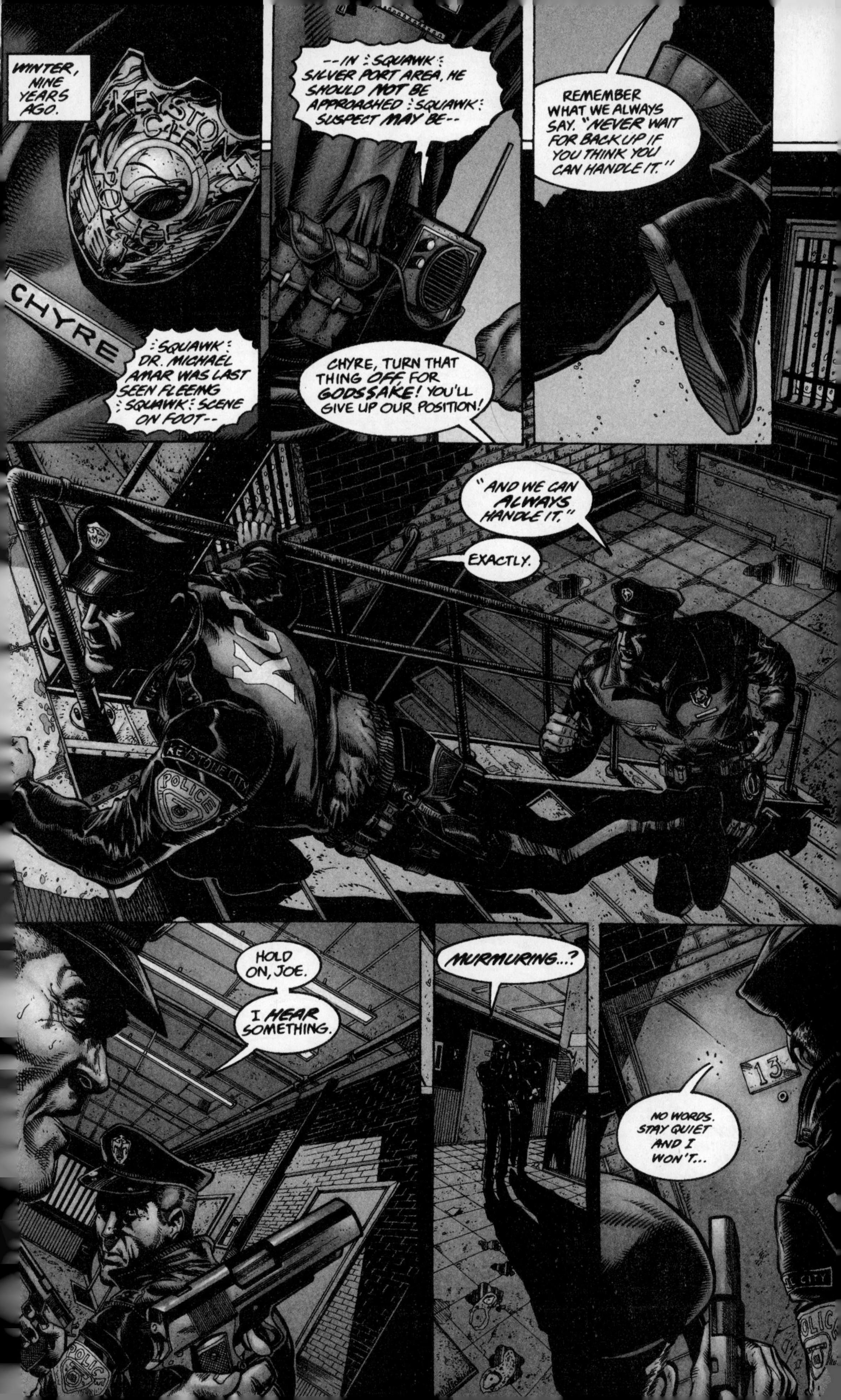
WINTER, NINE YEARS AGO.
KEYSTONE CITY POLICE
CHYRE
:SQUAWK: DR. MICHAEL AMAR WAS LAST SEEN FLEEING :SQUAWK: SCENE ON FOOT--
--IN :SQUAWK: SILVER PORT AREA. HE SHOULD NOT BE APPROACHED :SQUAWK: SUSPECT MAY BE--
CHYRE, TURN THAT THING OFF FOR GODSSAKE! YOU'LL GIVE UP OUR POSITION!
REMEMBER WHAT WE ALWAYS SAY. "NEVER WAIT FOR BACK UP IF YOU THINK YOU CAN HANDLE IT."
"AND WE CAN ALWAYS HANDLE IT."
EXACTLY.
KEYSTONE CITY POLICE
HOLD ON, JOE.
I HEAR SOMETHING.
POLICE
MURMURING...?
13
NO WORDS. STAY QUIET AND I WON'T...
POLICE

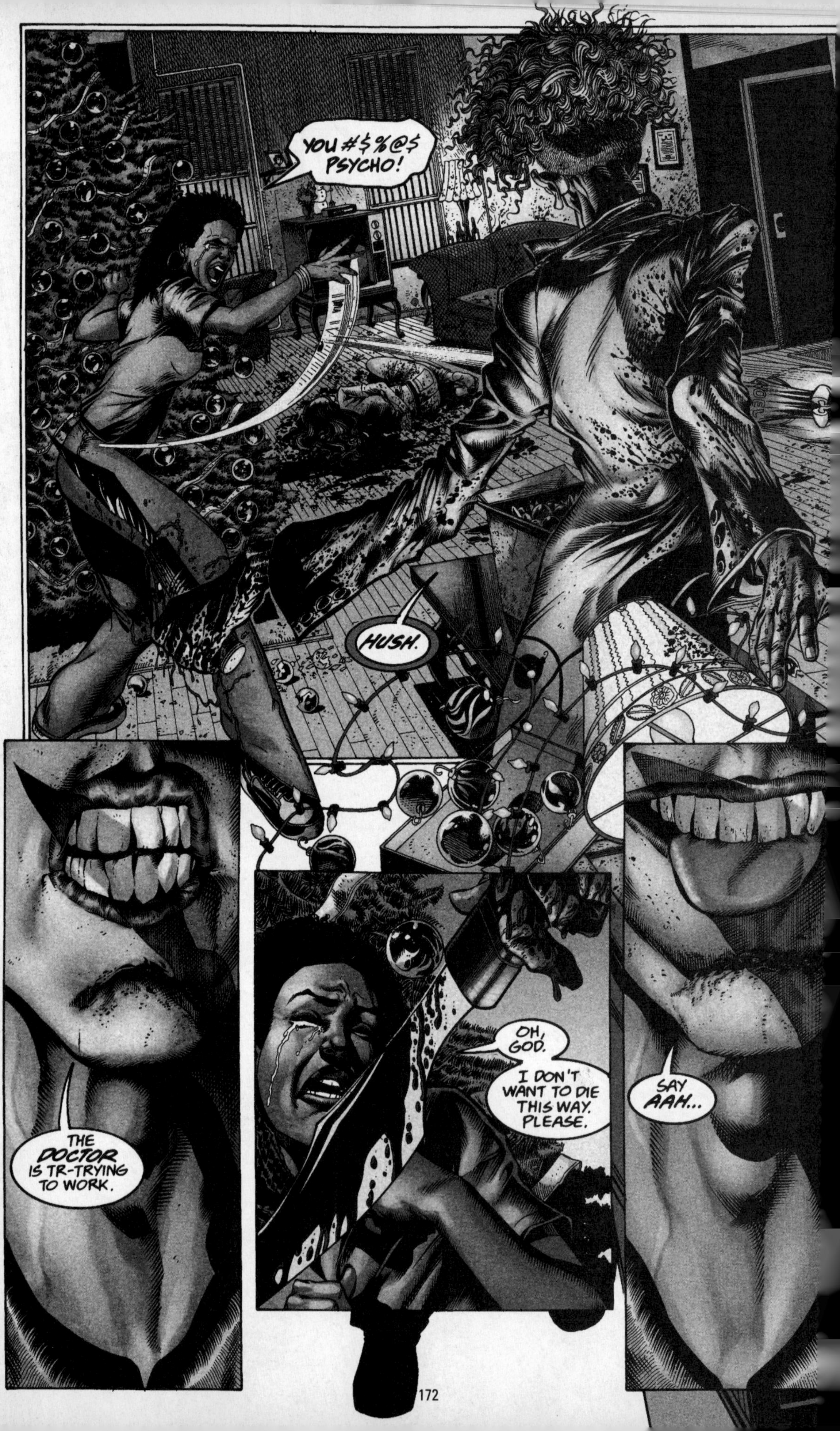
YOU #$%@$ PSYCHO!
HUSH.
THE DOCTOR IS TR-TRYING TO WORK.
OH, GOD.
I DON'T WANT TO DIE THIS WAY. PLEASE.
SAY AAH...

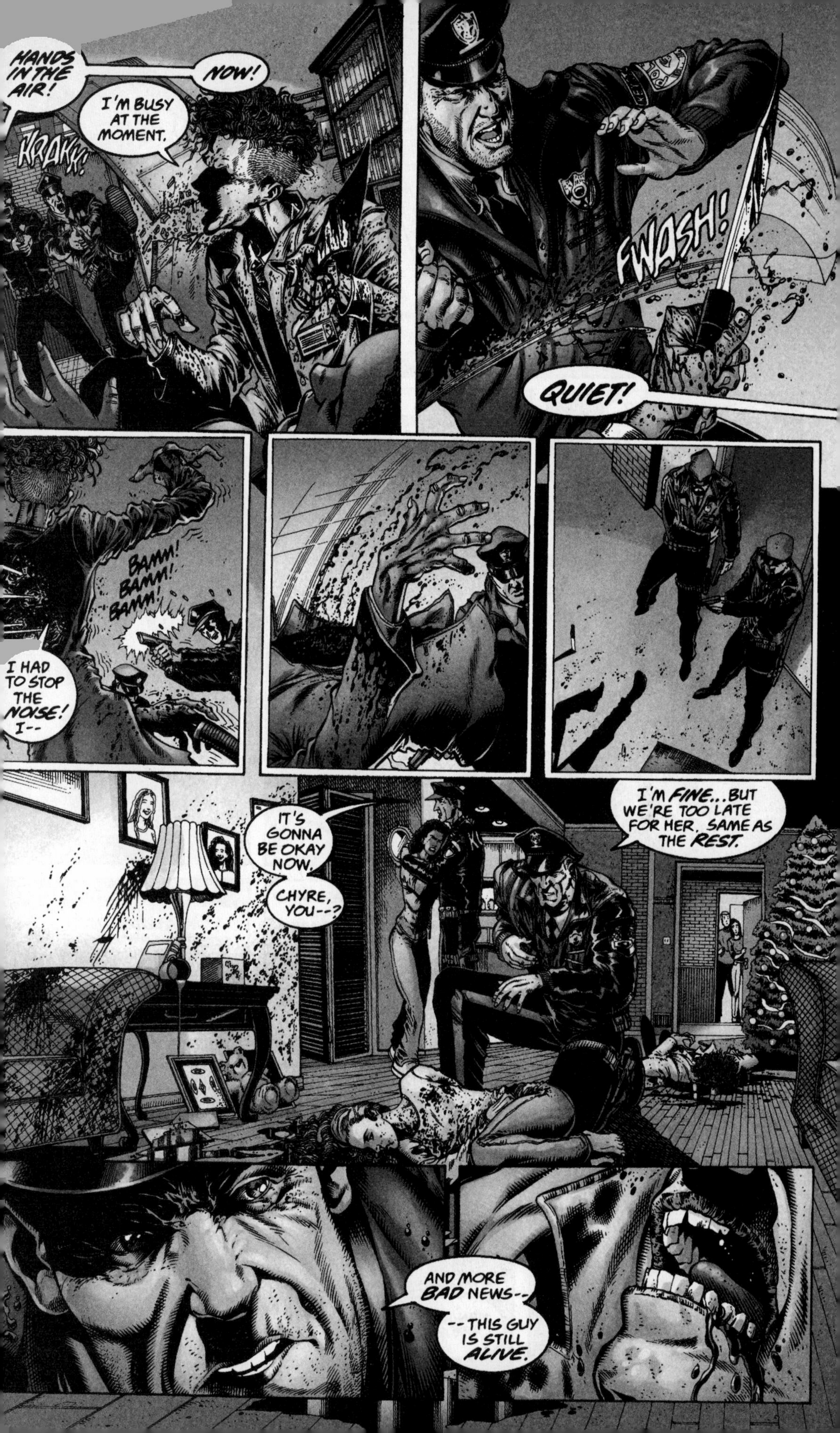
HANDS IN THE AIR!
NOW!
I'M BUSY AT THE MOMENT.
KRAKK!
FWASH!
QUIET!
BAMM! BAMM! BAMM!
I HAD TO STOP THE NOISE! I--
IT'S GONNA BE OKAY NOW.
CHYRE, YOU--?
I'M FINE...BUT WE'RE TOO LATE FOR HER, SAME AS THE REST.
AND MORE BAD NEWS--
--THIS GUY IS STILL ALIVE.

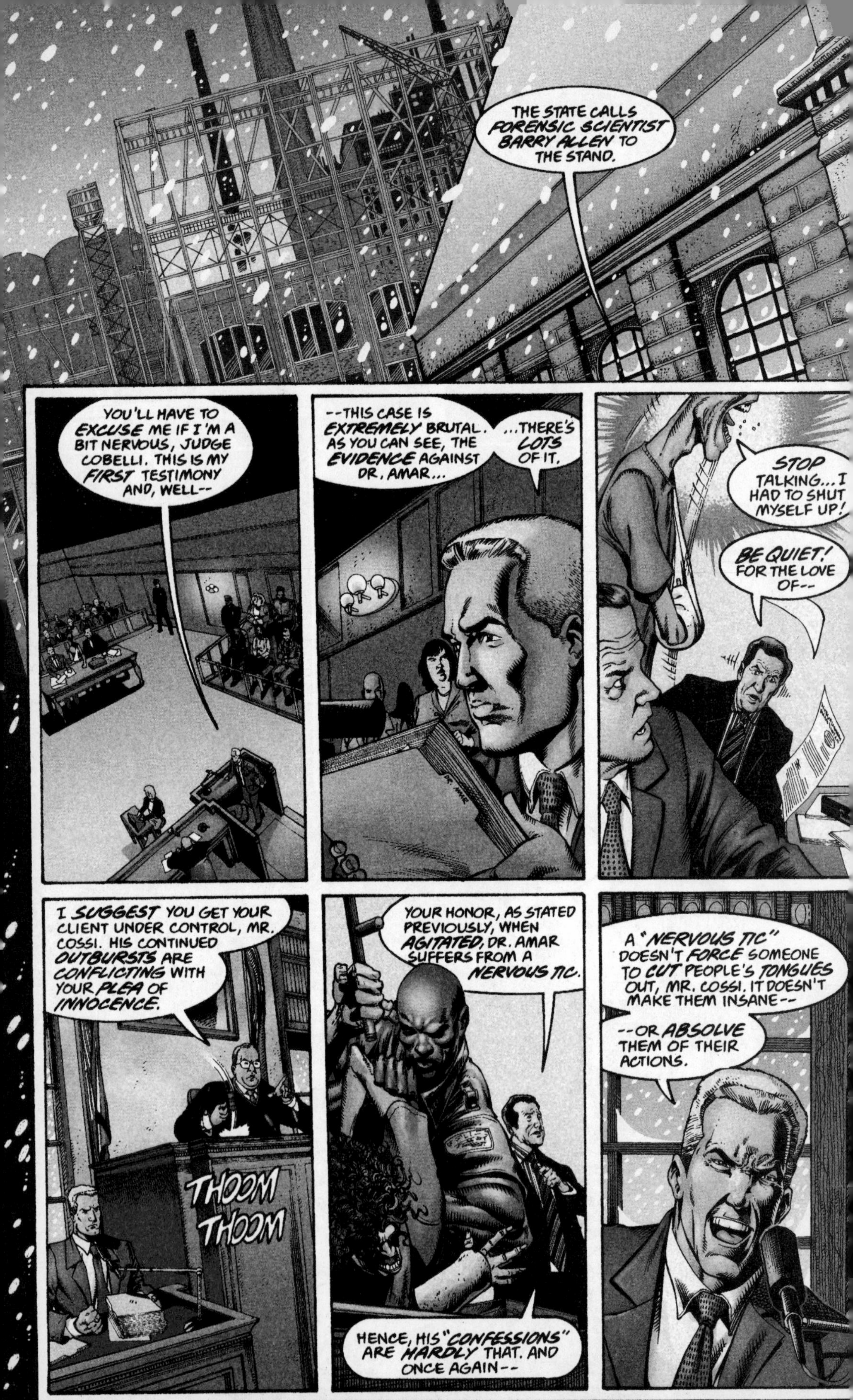
THE STATE CALLS FORENSIC SCIENTIST BARRY ALLEN TO THE STAND.
YOU'LL HAVE TO EXCUSE ME IF I'M A BIT NERVOUS, JUDGE COBELLI. THIS IS MY FIRST TESTIMONY AND, WELL--
--THIS CASE IS EXTREMELY BRUTAL. AS YOU CAN SEE, THE EVIDENCE AGAINST DR. AMAR...
...THERE'S LOTS OF IT.
DR. AMAR
STOP TALKING... I HAD TO SHUT MYSELF UP!
BE QUIET! FOR THE LOVE OF--
I SUGGEST YOU GET YOUR CLIENT UNDER CONTROL, MR. COSSI. HIS CONTINUED OUTBURSTS ARE CONFLICTING WITH YOUR PLEA OF INNOCENCE.
THOOM THOOM
YOUR HONOR, AS STATED PREVIOUSLY, WHEN AGITATED, DR. AMAR SUFFERS FROM A NERVOUS TIC.
HENCE, HIS "CONFESSIONS" ARE HARDLY THAT. AND ONCE AGAIN--
A "NERVOUS TIC" DOESN'T FORCE SOMEONE TO CUT PEOPLE'S TONGUES OUT, MR. COSSI. IT DOESN'T MAKE THEM INSANE--
--OR ABSOLVE THEM OF THEIR ACTIONS.

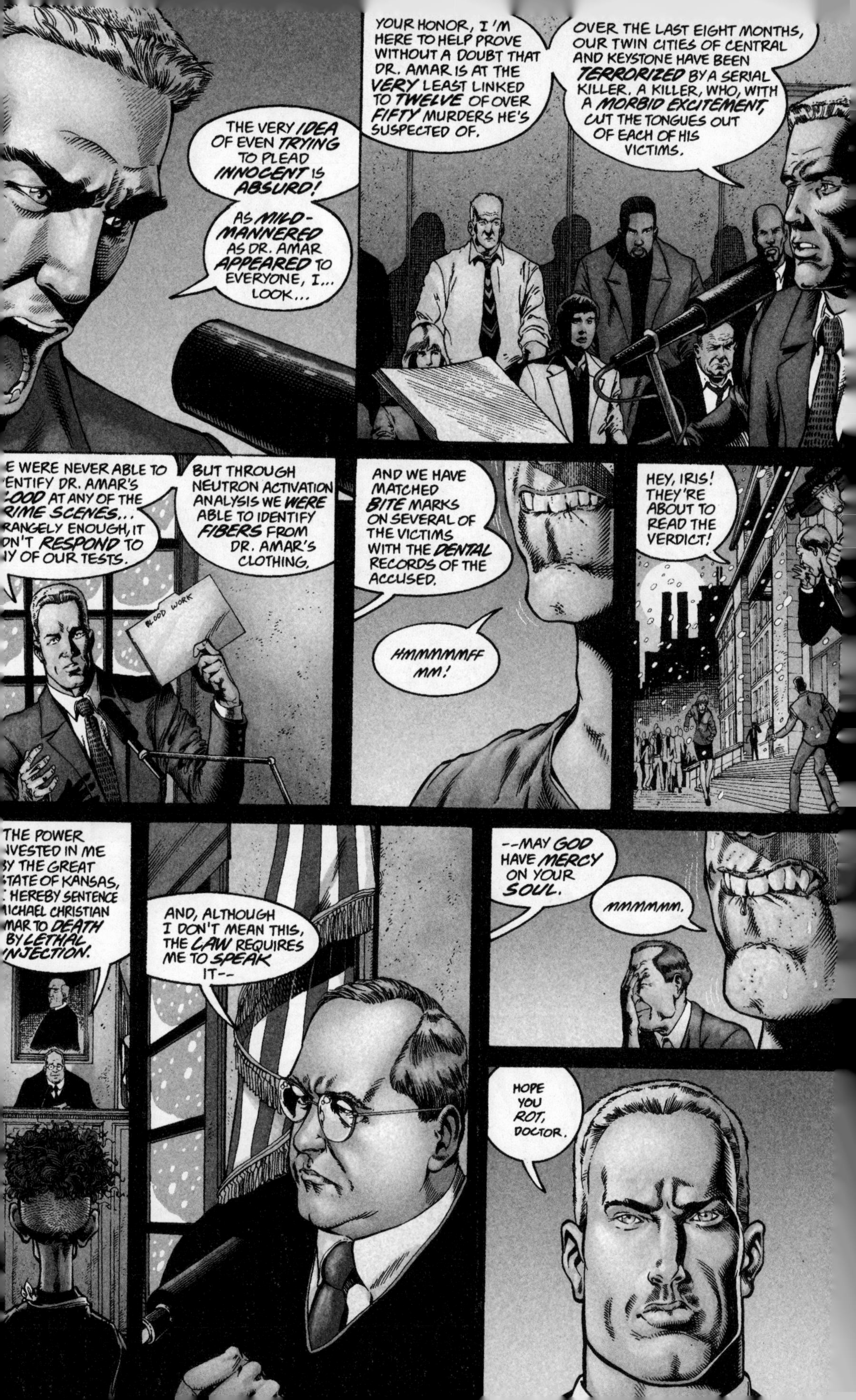
THE VERY IDEA OF EVEN TRYING TO PLEAD INNOCENT IS ABSURD!
AS MILD-MANNERED AS DR. AMAR APPEARED TO EVERYONE, I... LOOK...
YOUR HONOR, I'M HERE TO HELP PROVE WITHOUT A DOUBT THAT DR. AMAR IS AT THE VERY LEAST LINKED TO TWELVE OF OVER FIFTY MURDERS HE'S SUSPECTED OF.
OVER THE LAST EIGHT MONTHS, OUR TWIN CITIES OF CENTRAL AND KEYSTONE HAVE BEEN TERRORIZED BY A SERIAL KILLER. A KILLER, WHO, WITH A MORBID EXCITEMENT, CUT THE TONGUES OUT OF EACH OF HIS VICTIMS.
E WERE NEVER ABLE TO ENTIFY DR. AMAR'S LOOD AT ANY OF THE RIME SCENES... RANGELY ENOUGH, IT DN'T RESPOND TO IY OF OUR TESTS.
BUT THROUGH NEUTRON ACTIVATION ANALYSIS WE WERE ABLE TO IDENTIFY FIBERS FROM DR. AMAR'S CLOTHING.
BLOOD WORK
AND WE HAVE MATCHED BITE MARKS ON SEVERAL OF THE VICTIMS WITH THE DENTAL RECORDS OF THE ACCUSED.
HMMMMMFF MM!
HEY, IRIS! THEY'RE ABOUT TO READ THE VERDICT!
THE POWER VESTED IN ME Y THE GREAT STATE OF KANSAS, HEREBY SENTENCE MICHAEL CHRISTIAN MAR TO DEATH BY LETHAL INJECTION.
AND, ALTHOUGH I DON'T MEAN THIS, THE LAW REQUIRES ME TO SPEAK IT--
--MAY GOD HAVE MERCY ON YOUR SOUL.
MMMMMM.
HOPE YOU ROT, DOCTOR.

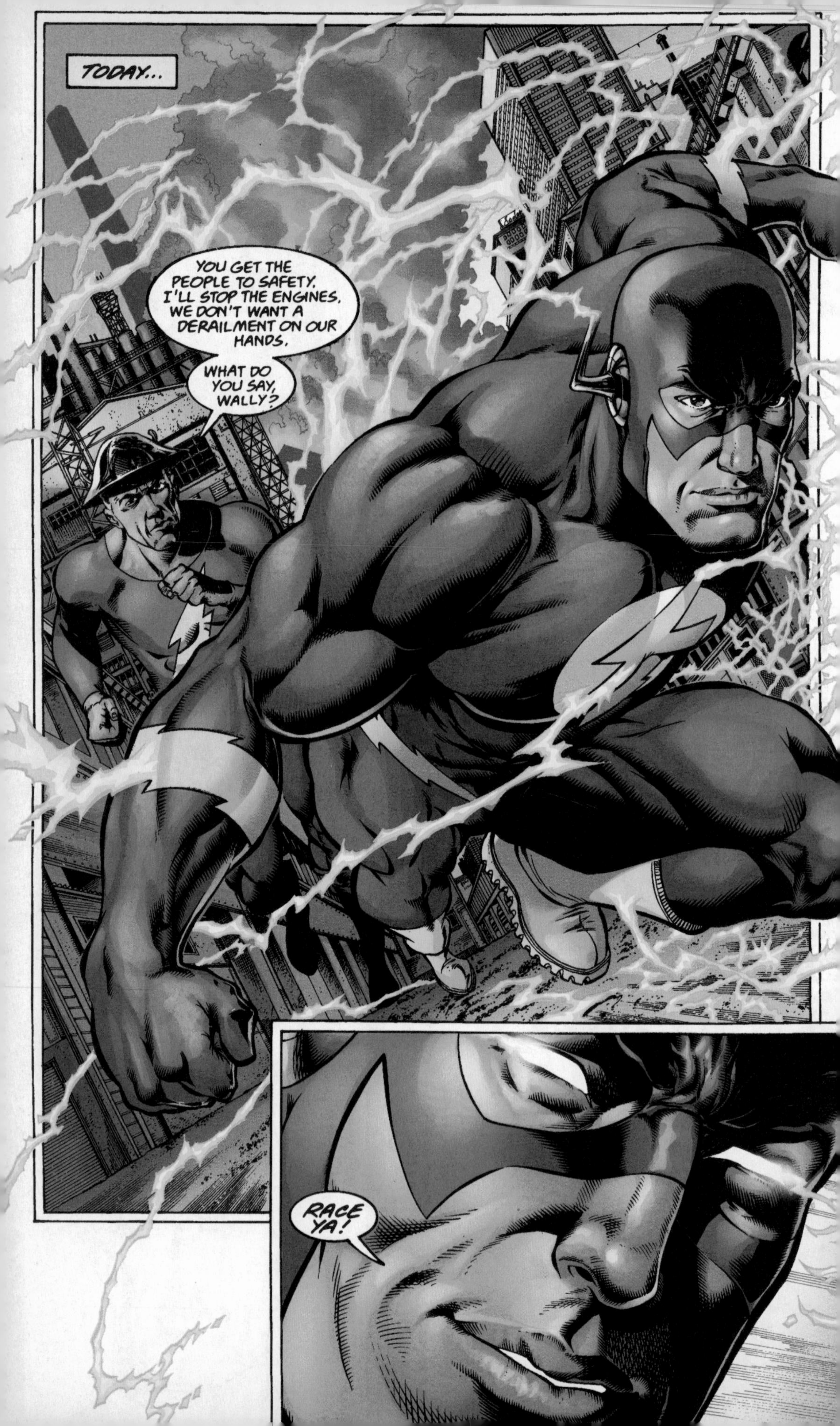
TODAY...
YOU GET THE PEOPLE TO SAFETY. I'LL STOP THE ENGINES. WE DON'T WANT A DERAILMENT ON OUR HANDS.
WHAT DO YOU SAY, WALLY?
RACE YA!

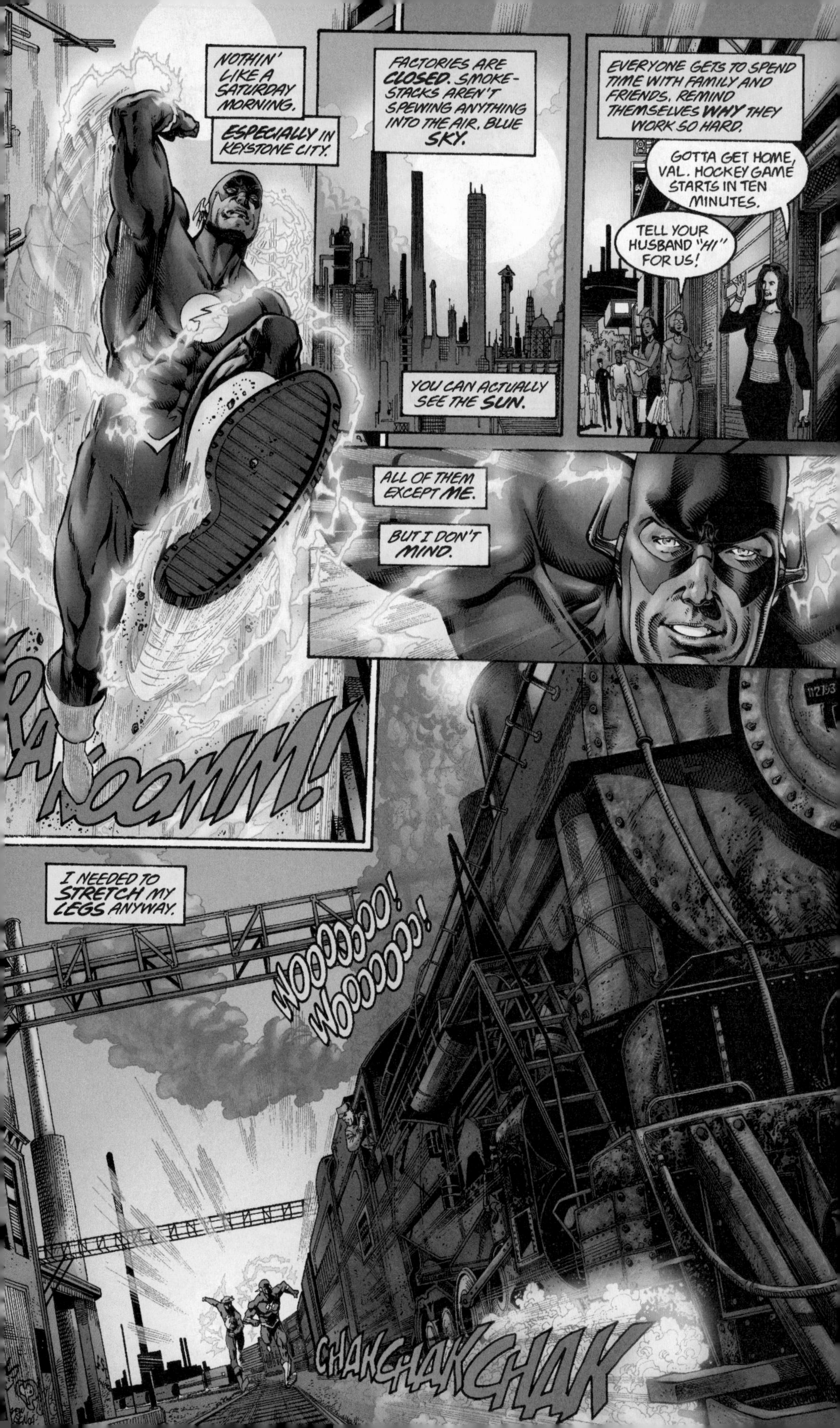
NOTHIN' LIKE A SATURDAY MORNING.
ESPECIALLY IN KEYSTONE CITY.
FACTORIES ARE CLOSED. SMOKE-STACKS AREN'T SPEWING ANYTHING INTO THE AIR. BLUE SKY.
YOU CAN ACTUALLY SEE THE SUN.
EVERYONE GETS TO SPEND TIME WITH FAMILY AND FRIENDS, REMIND THEMSELVES WHY THEY WORK SO HARD.
GOTTA GET HOME, VAL. HOCKEY GAME STARTS IN TEN MINUTES.
TELL YOUR HUSBAND "HI" FOR US!
ALL OF THEM EXCEPT ME.
BUT I DON'T MIND.
RA-BOOMM!
I NEEDED TO STRETCH MY LEGS ANYWAY.
WOOOOOOO! WOOOOOOO!
CHAKCHAKCHAK

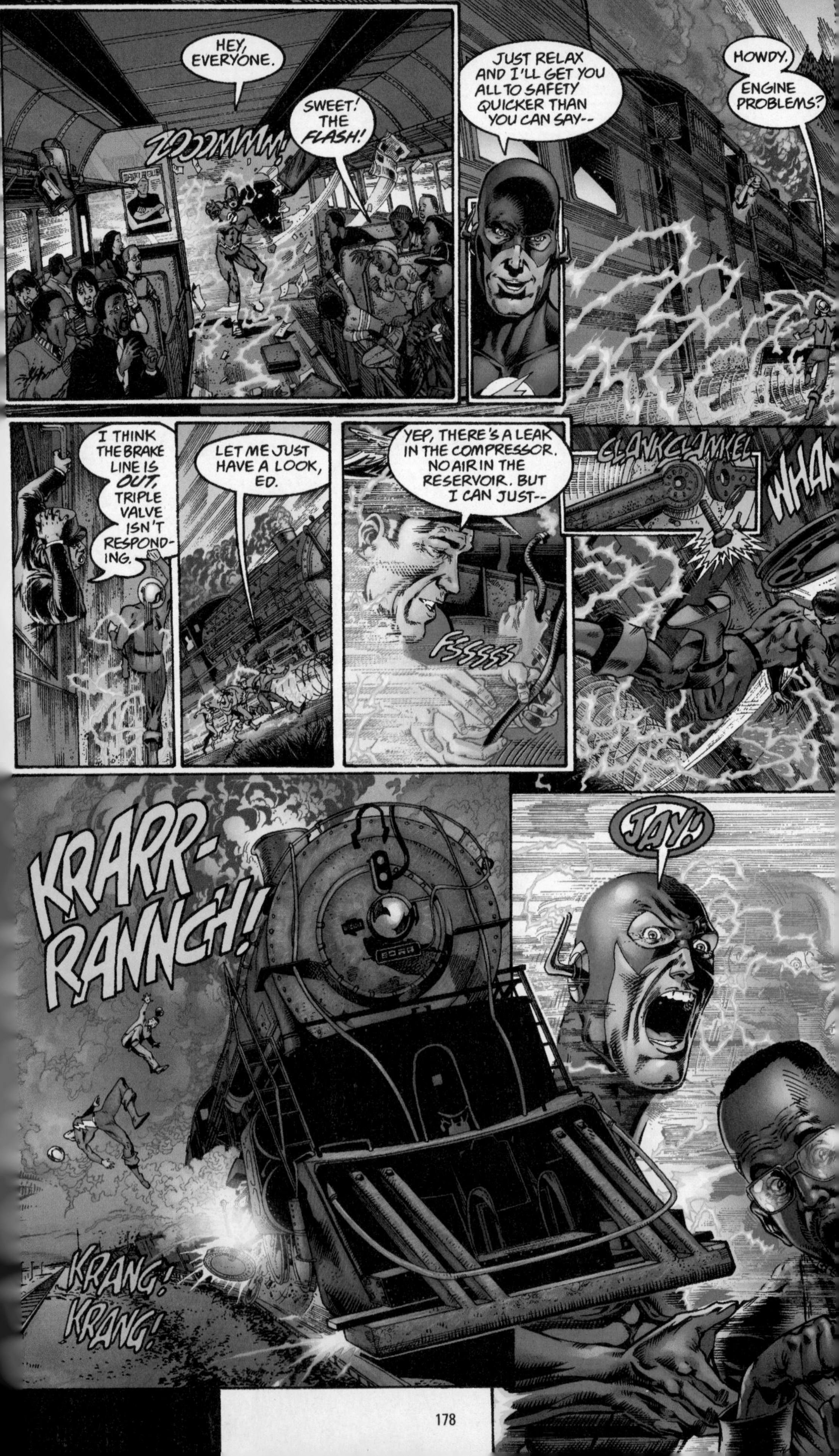
HEY, EVERYONE.
ZOOOMMM!
SWEET! THE FLASH!
JUST RELAX AND I'LL GET YOU ALL TO SAFETY QUICKER THAN YOU CAN SAY--
HOWDY.
ENGINE PROBLEMS?
I THINK THE BRAKE LINE IS OUT, TRIPLE VALVE ISN'T RESPONDING.
LET ME JUST HAVE A LOOK, ED.
YEP, THERE'S A LEAK IN THE COMPRESSOR. NO AIR IN THE RESERVOIR. BUT I CAN JUST--
FSSSSS
CLANKCLANKEL
KRARR-RANNCH!
JAY!
KRANG! KRANG!

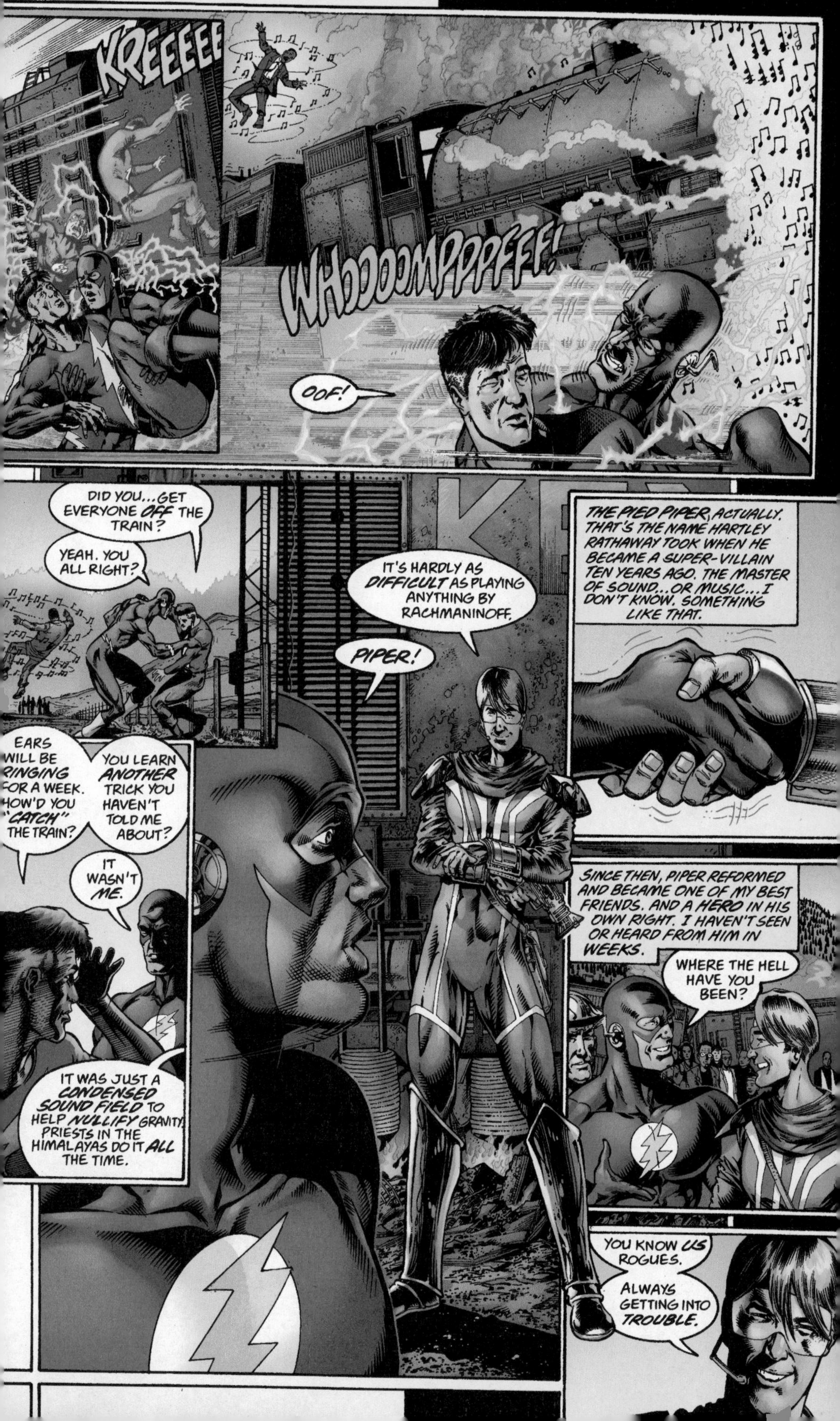
KREEEEE
WHOOOOMPPPFFF!
OOF!
DID YOU...GET EVERYONE OFF THE TRAIN?
YEAH. YOU ALL RIGHT?
IT'S HARDLY AS DIFFICULT AS PLAYING ANYTHING BY RACHMANINOFF.
PIPER!
THE PIED PIPER, ACTUALLY. THAT'S THE NAME HARTLEY RATHAWAY TOOK WHEN HE BECAME A SUPER-VILLAIN TEN YEARS AGO. THE MASTER OF SOUND...OR MUSIC...I DON'T KNOW. SOMETHING LIKE THAT.
EARS WILL BE RINGING FOR A WEEK. HOW'D YOU "CATCH" THE TRAIN?
YOU LEARN ANOTHER TRICK YOU HAVEN'T TOLD ME ABOUT?
IT WASN'T ME.
IT WAS JUST A CONDENSED SOUND FIELD TO HELP NULLIFY GRAVITY. PRIESTS IN THE HIMALAYAS DO IT ALL THE TIME.
SINCE THEN, PIPER REFORMED AND BECAME ONE OF MY BEST FRIENDS. AND A HERO IN HIS OWN RIGHT. I HAVEN'T SEEN OR HEARD FROM HIM IN WEEKS.
WHERE THE HELL HAVE YOU BEEN?
YOU KNOW US ROGUES.
ALWAYS GETTING INTO TROUBLE.

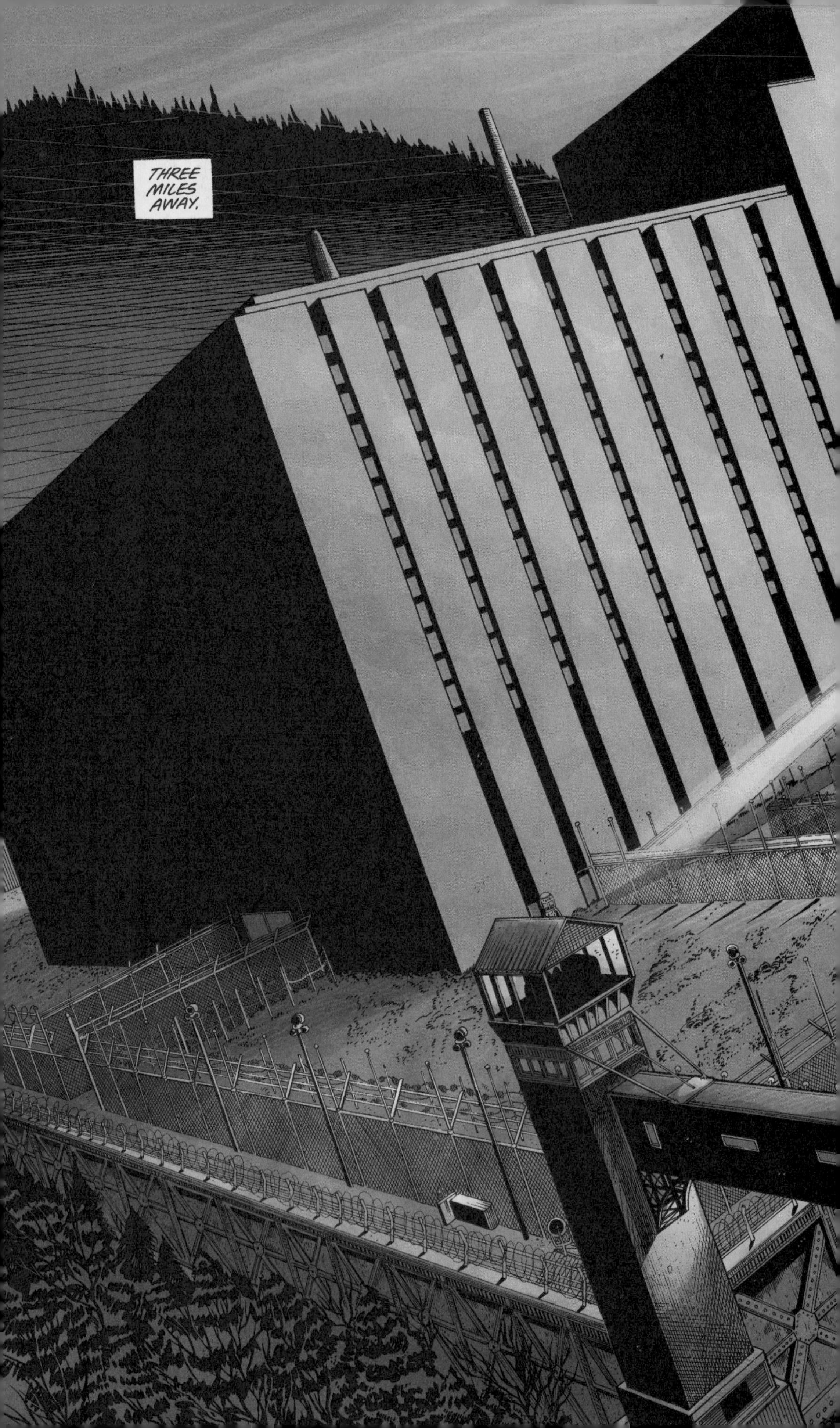
THREE MILES AWAY.

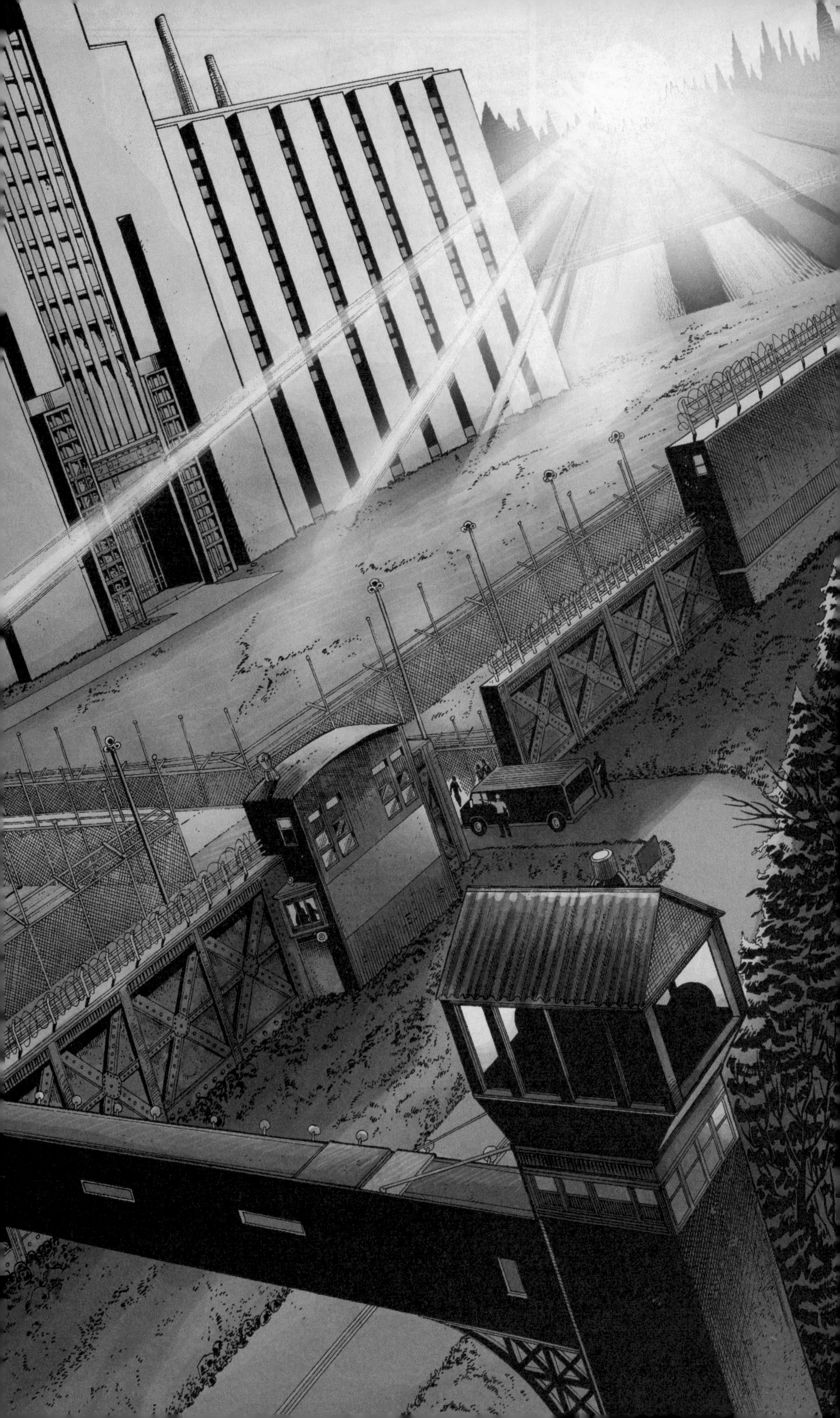

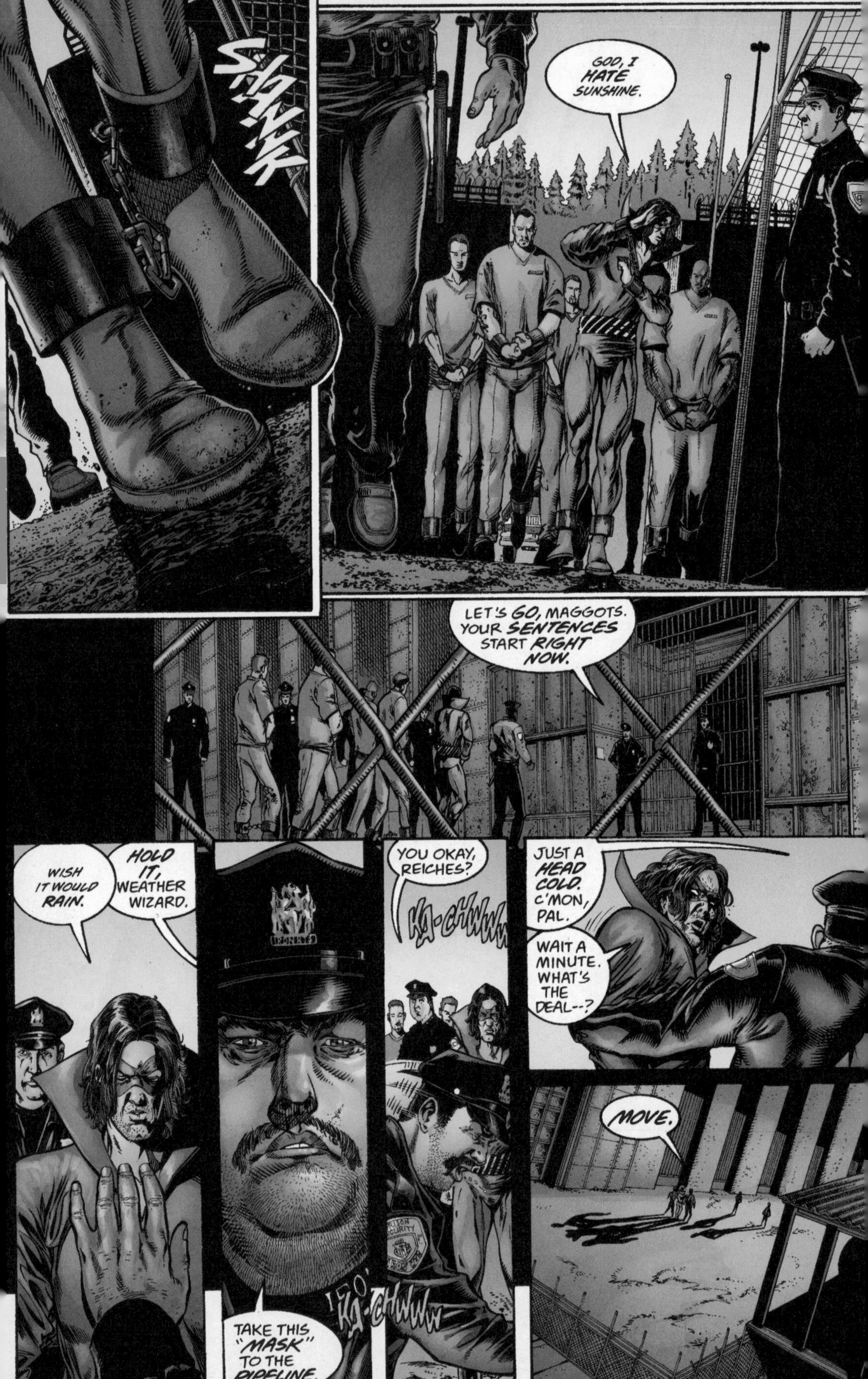
SHNK
GOD, I HATE SUNSHINE.
LET'S GO, MAGGOTS. YOUR SENTENCES START RIGHT NOW.
WISH IT WOULD RAIN.
HOLD IT, WEATHER WIZARD.
TAKE THIS "MASK" TO THE PIPELINE.
YOU OKAY, REICHES?
KA-CHWWW
KA-CHWWW
JUST A HEAD COLD. C'MON, PAL.
WAIT A MINUTE. WHAT'S THE DEAL--?
MOVE.

RRRANK

WHAT THE HELL *IS* THIS?

KLANK

GOOD MORNING, *MR. MARK MARDON.*

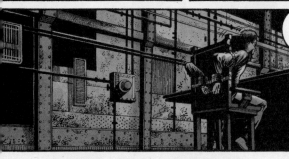

OR DO YOU PREFER YOUR *OTHER* NAME, *WEATHER WIZARD?*

AND *WHO* THE *HELL* ARE YOU?

A BIT *SILLY,* DON'T YOU THINK? LIKE YOUR *COSTUME. NICE* OF US TO PUT YOU BACK IN YOUR *OLD* ONE FOR THE DURATION OF YOUR *STAY.*

NAME IS EGORY OLFE.

I'M THE *WARDEN* OF THIS *FINE* ESTABLISHMENT.

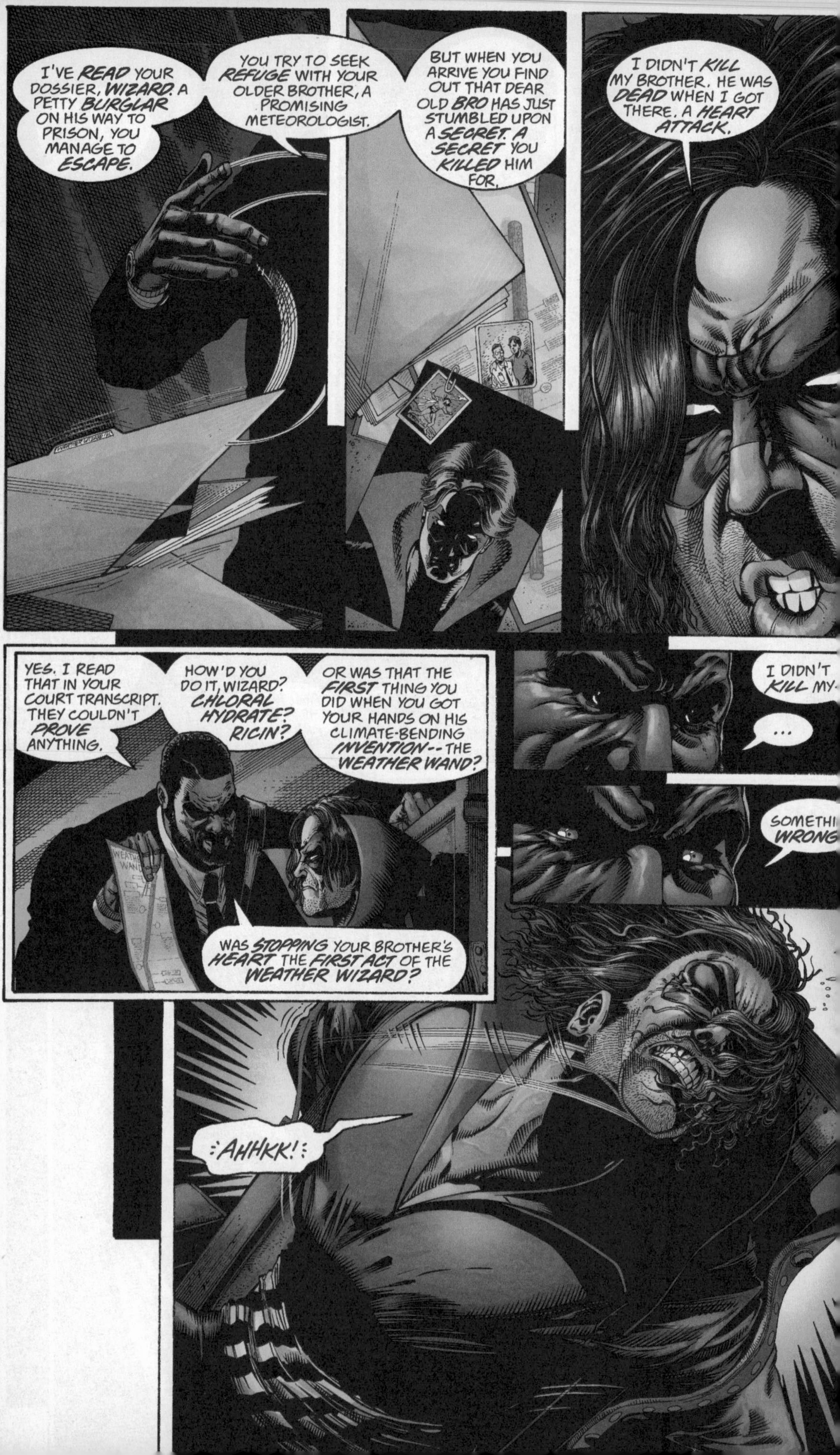
I'VE READ YOUR DOSSIER, WIZARD. A PETTY BURGLAR ON HIS WAY TO PRISON, YOU MANAGE TO ESCAPE.
YOU TRY TO SEEK REFUGE WITH YOUR OLDER BROTHER, A PROMISING METEOROLOGIST.
BUT WHEN YOU ARRIVE YOU FIND OUT THAT DEAR OLD BRO HAS JUST STUMBLED UPON A SECRET. A SECRET YOU KILLED HIM FOR.
I DIDN'T KILL MY BROTHER. HE WAS DEAD WHEN I GOT THERE. A HEART ATTACK.
YES. I READ THAT IN YOUR COURT TRANSCRIPT. THEY COULDN'T PROVE ANYTHING.
HOW'D YOU DO IT, WIZARD? CHLORAL HYDRATE? RICIN?
OR WAS THAT THE FIRST THING YOU DID WHEN YOU GOT YOUR HANDS ON HIS CLIMATE-BENDING INVENTION--THE WEATHER WAND?
WAS STOPPING YOUR BROTHER'S HEART THE FIRST ACT OF THE WEATHER WIZARD?
I DIDN'T KILL MY-
...
SOMETHI
WRONG
AHHKK!

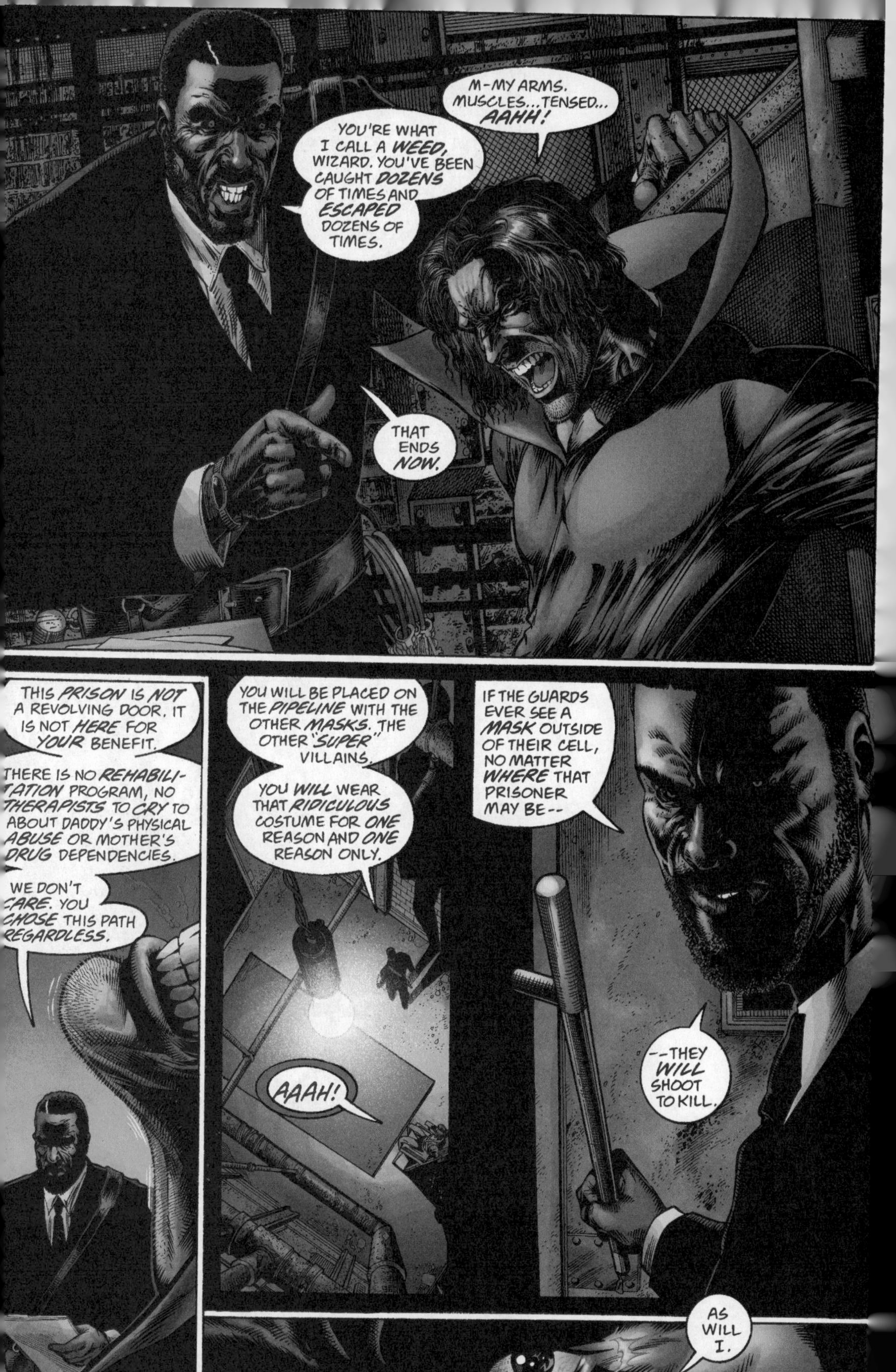
YOU'RE WHAT I CALL A WEED, WIZARD. YOU'VE BEEN CAUGHT DOZENS OF TIMES AND ESCAPED DOZENS OF TIMES.
M-MY ARMS. MUSCLES...TENSED... AAHH!
THAT ENDS NOW.
THIS PRISON IS NOT A REVOLVING DOOR. IT IS NOT HERE FOR YOUR BENEFIT.
THERE IS NO REHABILITATION PROGRAM, NO THERAPISTS TO CRY TO ABOUT DADDY'S PHYSICAL ABUSE OR MOTHER'S DRUG DEPENDENCIES.
WE DON'T CARE. YOU CHOSE THIS PATH REGARDLESS.
YOU WILL BE PLACED ON THE PIPELINE WITH THE OTHER MASKS. THE OTHER "SUPER" VILLAINS.
YOU WILL WEAR THAT RIDICULOUS COSTUME FOR ONE REASON AND ONE REASON ONLY.
AAAH!
IF THE GUARDS EVER SEE A MASK OUTSIDE OF THEIR CELL, NO MATTER WHERE THAT PRISONER MAY BE--
--THEY WILL SHOOT TO KILL.
AS WILL I.

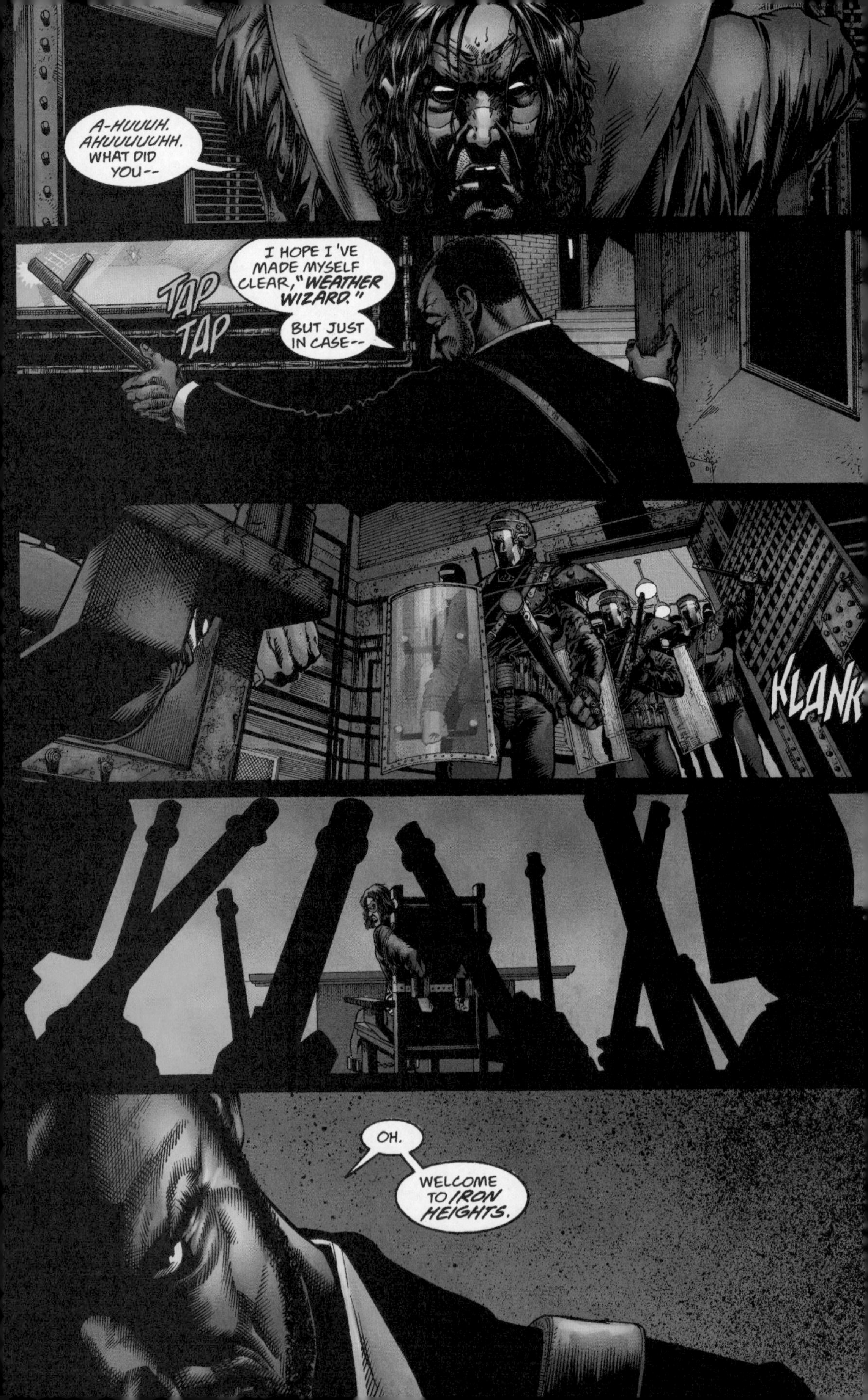
A-HUUUH. AHUUUUUUHH. WHAT DID YOU--
TAP TAP
I HOPE I'VE MADE MYSELF CLEAR, "WEATHER WIZARD."
BUT JUST IN CASE--
KLANK
OH.
WELCOME TO IRON HEIGHTS.

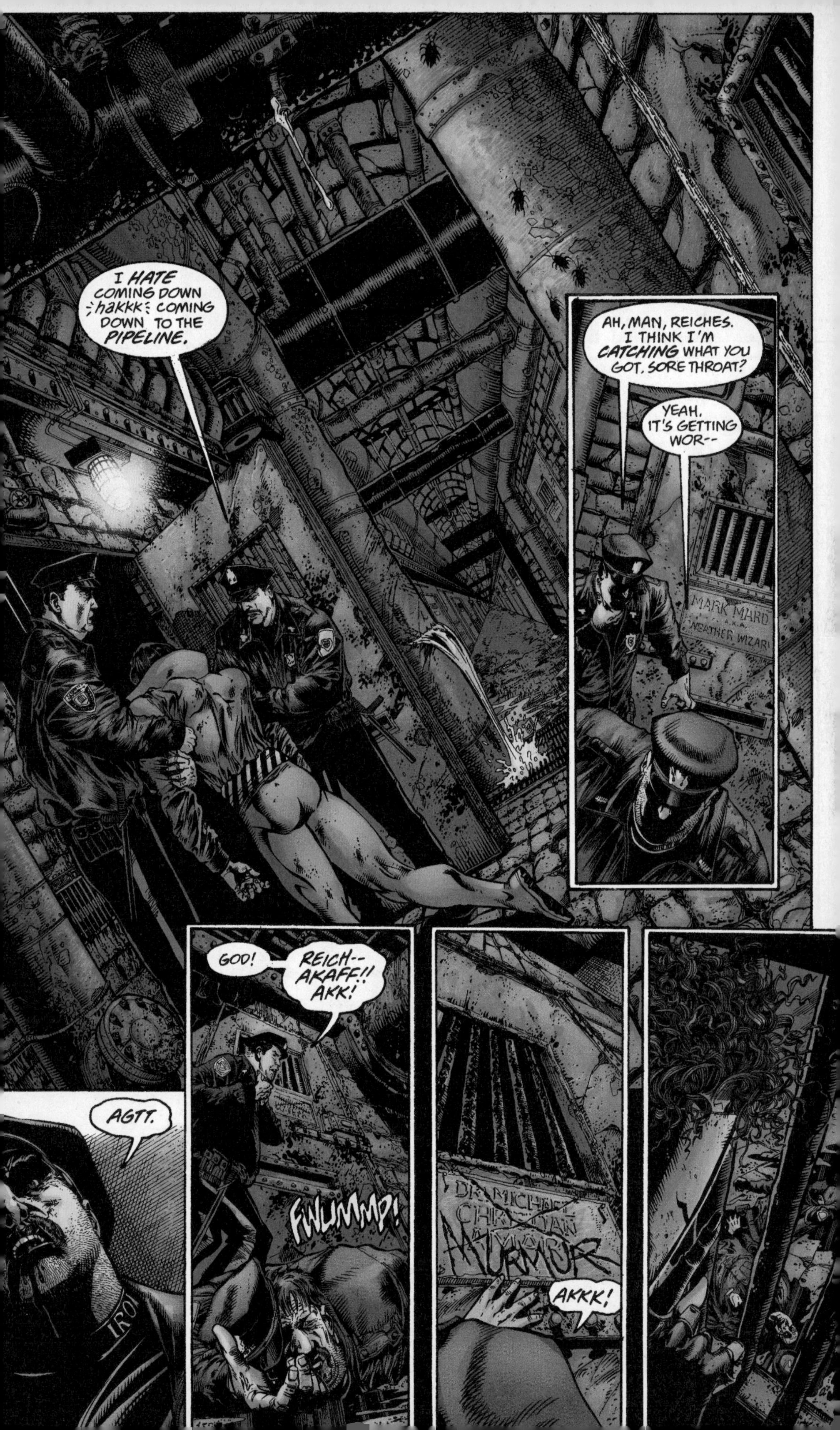

I HATE COMING DOWN -hakkk- COMING DOWN TO THE PIPELINE.
AH, MAN, REICHES. I THINK I'M CATCHING WHAT YOU GOT. SORE THROAT?
YEAH. IT'S GETTING WOR--
MARK MARDON A.K.A. WEATHER WIZARD
AGTT.
GOD!
REICH-- AKAFF!! AKK!
FWUMMP!
AKKK!

C'MON!
C'MON!

YEAH!
SCORE!

CAN THIS *GET* ANY BETTER? IS IT *POSSIBLE?*

WHAT

DIDN'T KNOW YOU WERE SUCH A *SPORTS* FAN! OR ARE YOU USING THE *GAME* TO AVOID TELLING US WHERE YOU'VE BEEN?

WALLY?... C'MERE.

LINDA...

NOW, SWEETHEART.

RELAX. ENJOY THE GAME, 'KAY?

PIPER TOLD YOU HE HAD TO SORT OUT *FAMILY* PROBLEMS. *DON'T* PUSH IT. IF HE WANTS TO *TALK* ABOUT IT SOME MORE HE *WILL.*

I KNOW...

HEY, I'M JUST ASKING YOU TO *ENJOY* YOURSELF. WE'RE HANGING OUT WITH FRIENDS, YOUR JUSTICE LEAGUE BEEPER IS QUIET. HOW *OFTEN* DO YOU SIT ON THE SIDELINES ANYMORE, *HUH?*

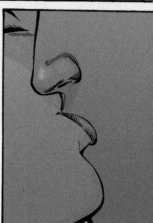

SHE'S *RIGHT. OF COURSE.*

SHE'S *ALWAYS* RIGHT.

RRING

RRINGGG

UGH. I HAD TO SAY SOMETHING...

WHAT IS IT?

BETTER SUIT UP.

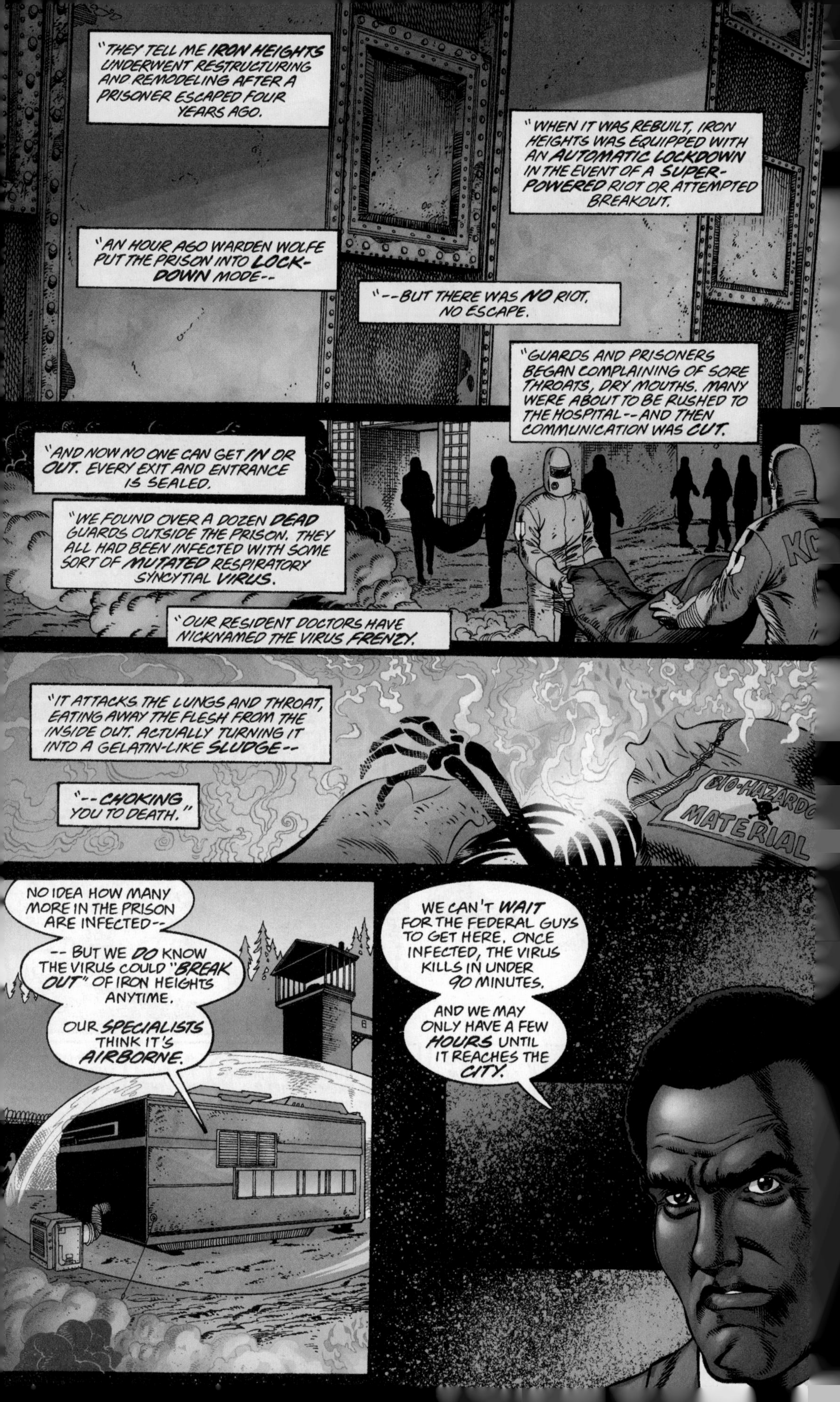
"THEY TELL ME IRON HEIGHTS UNDERWENT RESTRUCTURING AND REMODELING AFTER A PRISONER ESCAPED FOUR YEARS AGO.
"WHEN IT WAS REBUILT, IRON HEIGHTS WAS EQUIPPED WITH AN AUTOMATIC LOCKDOWN IN THE EVENT OF A SUPER-POWERED RIOT OR ATTEMPTED BREAKOUT.
"AN HOUR AGO WARDEN WOLFE PUT THE PRISON INTO LOCK-DOWN MODE--
"--BUT THERE WAS NO RIOT. NO ESCAPE.
"GUARDS AND PRISONERS BEGAN COMPLAINING OF SORE THROATS, DRY MOUTHS. MANY WERE ABOUT TO BE RUSHED TO THE HOSPITAL--AND THEN COMMUNICATION WAS CUT.
"AND NOW NO ONE CAN GET IN OR OUT. EVERY EXIT AND ENTRANCE IS SEALED.
"WE FOUND OVER A DOZEN DEAD GUARDS OUTSIDE THE PRISON. THEY ALL HAD BEEN INFECTED WITH SOME SORT OF MUTATED RESPIRATORY SYNCYTIAL VIRUS.
"OUR RESIDENT DOCTORS HAVE NICKNAMED THE VIRUS FRENZY.
"IT ATTACKS THE LUNGS AND THROAT, EATING AWAY THE FLESH FROM THE INSIDE OUT. ACTUALLY TURNING IT INTO A GELATIN-LIKE SLUDGE--
"--CHOKING YOU TO DEATH."
BIO-HAZARDO MATERIAL
NO IDEA HOW MANY MORE IN THE PRISON ARE INFECTED--
--BUT WE DO KNOW THE VIRUS COULD "BREAK OUT" OF IRON HEIGHTS ANYTIME.
OUR SPECIALISTS THINK IT'S AIRBORNE.
WE CAN'T WAIT FOR THE FEDERAL GUYS TO GET HERE. ONCE INFECTED, THE VIRUS KILLS IN UNDER 90 MINUTES.
AND WE MAY ONLY HAVE A FEW HOURS UNTIL IT REACHES THE CITY.

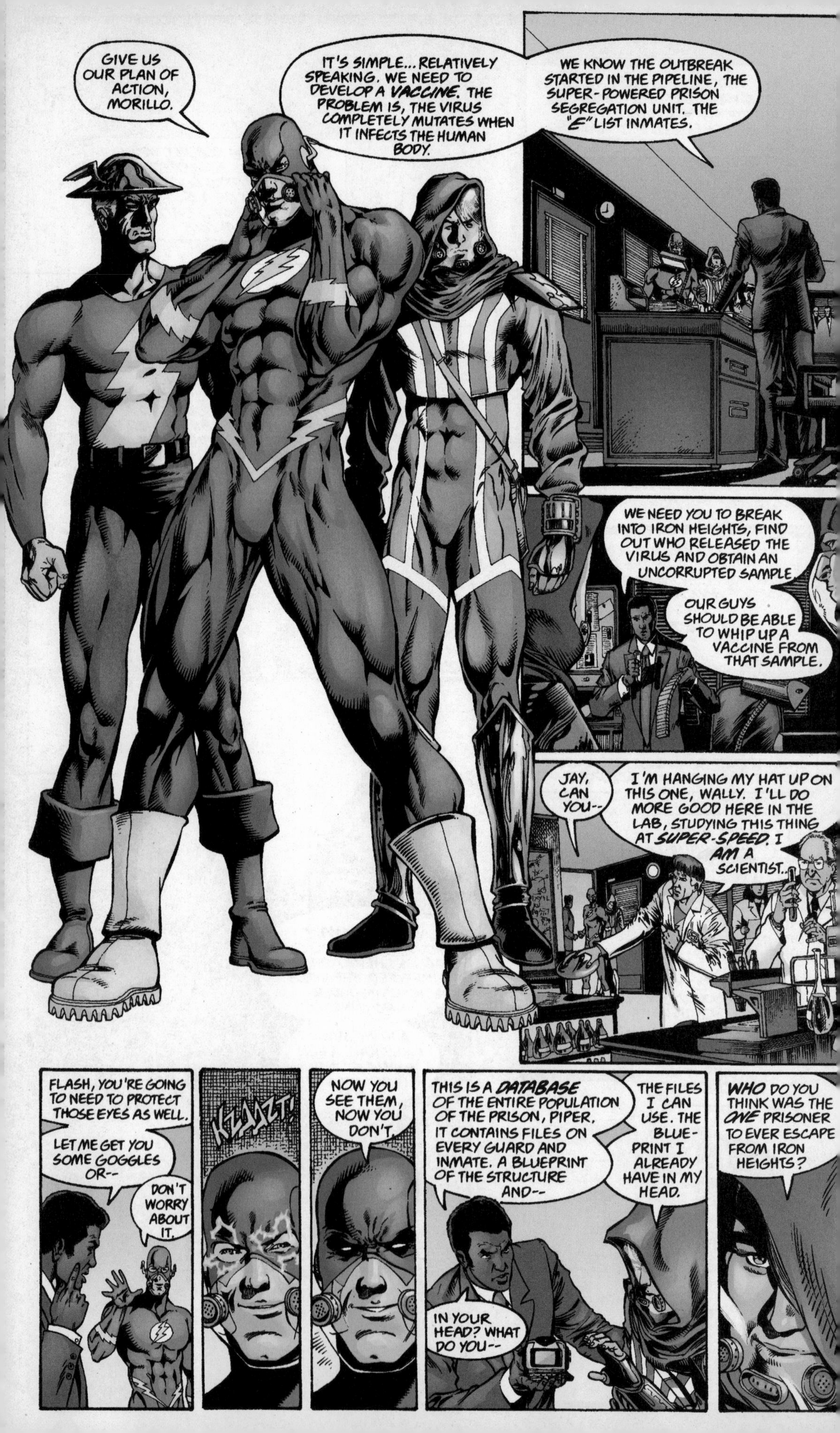
GIVE US OUR PLAN OF ACTION, MORILLO.
IT'S SIMPLE... RELATIVELY SPEAKING. WE NEED TO DEVELOP A VACCINE. THE PROBLEM IS, THE VIRUS COMPLETELY MUTATES WHEN IT INFECTS THE HUMAN BODY.
WE KNOW THE OUTBREAK STARTED IN THE PIPELINE, THE SUPER-POWERED PRISON SEGREGATION UNIT. THE "E" LIST INMATES.
WE NEED YOU TO BREAK INTO IRON HEIGHTS, FIND OUT WHO RELEASED THE VIRUS AND OBTAIN AN UNCORRUPTED SAMPLE.
OUR GUYS SHOULD BE ABLE TO WHIP UP A VACCINE FROM THAT SAMPLE.
JAY, CAN YOU--
I'M HANGING MY HAT UP ON THIS ONE, WALLY. I'LL DO MORE GOOD HERE IN THE LAB, STUDYING THIS THING AT SUPER-SPEED. I AM A SCIENTIST.
FLASH, YOU'RE GOING TO NEED TO PROTECT THOSE EYES AS WELL.
LET ME GET YOU SOME GOGGLES OR--
DON'T WORRY ABOUT IT.
KZZZZT!
NOW YOU SEE THEM, NOW YOU DON'T.
THIS IS A DATABASE OF THE ENTIRE POPULATION OF THE PRISON, PIPER. IT CONTAINS FILES ON EVERY GUARD AND INMATE. A BLUEPRINT OF THE STRUCTURE AND--
THE FILES I CAN USE. THE BLUEPRINT I ALREADY HAVE IN MY HEAD.
IN YOUR HEAD? WHAT DO YOU--
WHO DO YOU THINK WAS THE ONE PRISONER TO EVER ESCAPE FROM IRON HEIGHTS?

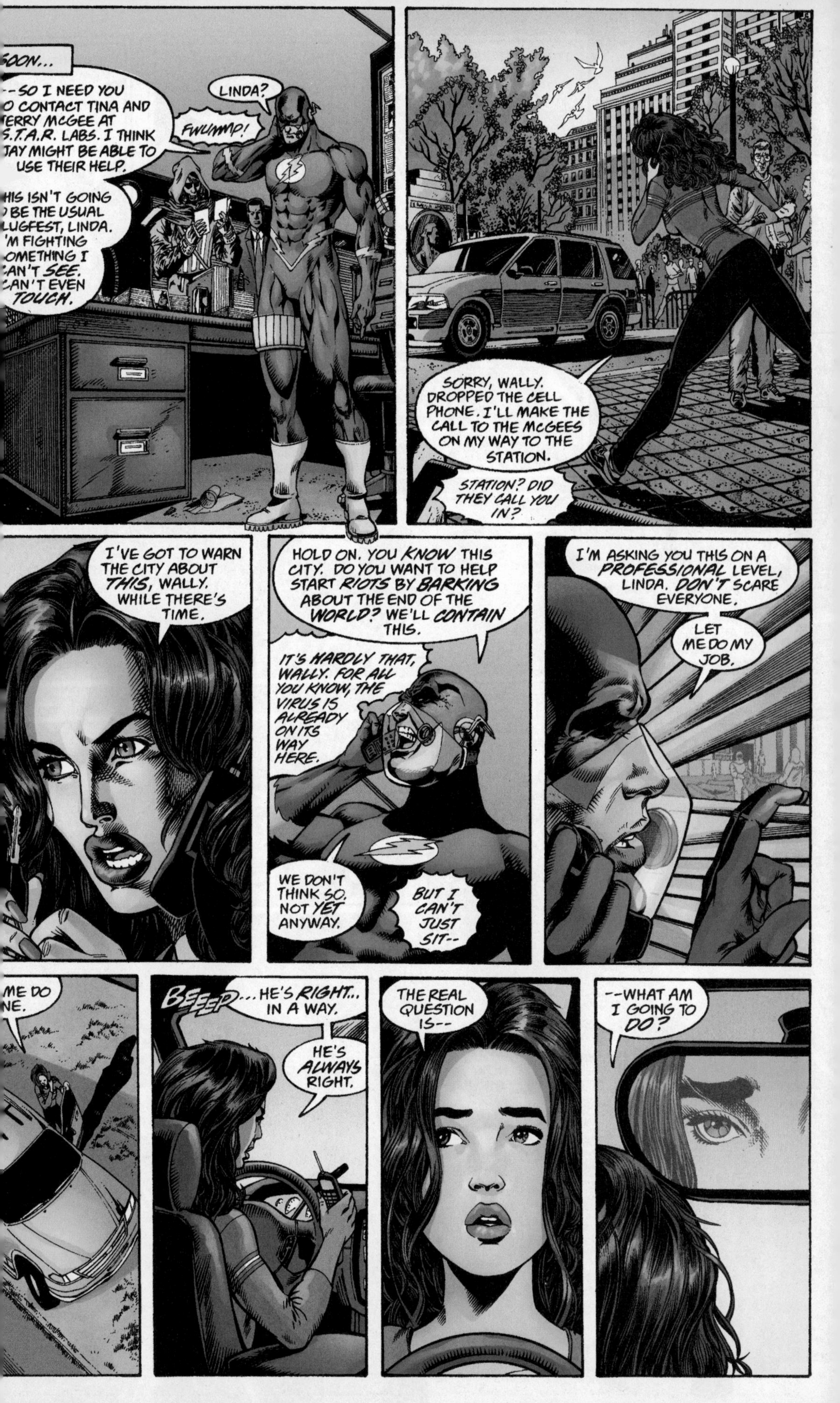
SOON...
--SO I NEED YOU TO CONTACT TINA AND JERRY McGEE AT S.T.A.R. LABS. I THINK JAY MIGHT BE ABLE TO USE THEIR HELP.
THIS ISN'T GOING TO BE THE USUAL SLUGFEST, LINDA. I'M FIGHTING SOMETHING I CAN'T SEE. CAN'T EVEN TOUCH.
FWUMMP!
LINDA?
SORRY, WALLY. DROPPED THE CELL PHONE. I'LL MAKE THE CALL TO THE McGEES ON MY WAY TO THE STATION.
STATION? DID THEY CALL YOU IN?
I'VE GOT TO WARN THE CITY ABOUT THIS, WALLY. WHILE THERE'S TIME.
HOLD ON. YOU KNOW THIS CITY. DO YOU WANT TO HELP START RIOTS BY BARKING ABOUT THE END OF THE WORLD? WE'LL CONTAIN THIS.
IT'S HARDLY THAT, WALLY. FOR ALL YOU KNOW, THE VIRUS IS ALREADY ON ITS WAY HERE.
WE DON'T THINK SO. NOT YET ANYWAY.
BUT I CAN'T JUST SIT--
I'M ASKING YOU THIS ON A PROFESSIONAL LEVEL, LINDA. DON'T SCARE EVERYONE.
LET ME DO MY JOB.
ME DO NE.
BEEEP... HE'S RIGHT... IN A WAY.
HE'S ALWAYS RIGHT.
THE REAL QUESTION IS--
--WHAT AM I GOING TO DO?

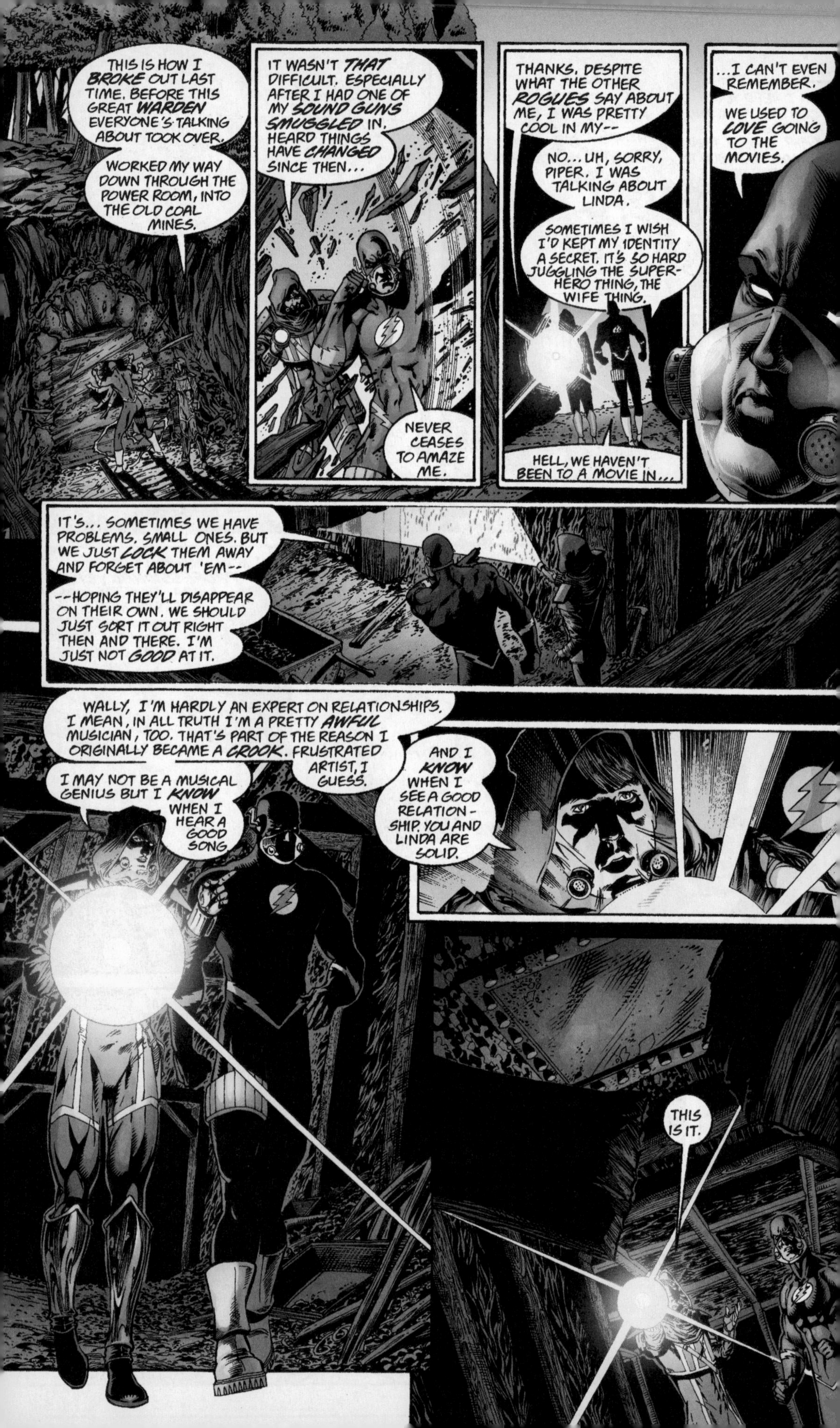
THIS IS HOW I BROKE OUT LAST TIME. BEFORE THIS GREAT WARDEN EVERYONE'S TALKING ABOUT TOOK OVER.
WORKED MY WAY DOWN THROUGH THE POWER ROOM, INTO THE OLD COAL MINES.
IT WASN'T THAT DIFFICULT. ESPECIALLY AFTER I HAD ONE OF MY SOUND GUNS SMUGGLED IN. HEARD THINGS HAVE CHANGED SINCE THEN...
NEVER CEASES TO AMAZE ME.
THANKS. DESPITE WHAT THE OTHER ROGUES SAY ABOUT ME, I WAS PRETTY COOL IN MY--
NO... UH, SORRY, PIPER. I WAS TALKING ABOUT LINDA.
SOMETIMES I WISH I'D KEPT MY IDENTITY A SECRET. IT'S SO HARD JUGGLING THE SUPER-HERO THING, THE WIFE THING.
HELL, WE HAVEN'T BEEN TO A MOVIE IN...
...I CAN'T EVEN REMEMBER.
WE USED TO LOVE GOING TO THE MOVIES.
IT'S... SOMETIMES WE HAVE PROBLEMS. SMALL ONES. BUT WE JUST LOCK THEM AWAY AND FORGET ABOUT 'EM--
--HOPING THEY'LL DISAPPEAR ON THEIR OWN. WE SHOULD JUST SORT IT OUT RIGHT THEN AND THERE. I'M JUST NOT GOOD AT IT.
WALLY, I'M HARDLY AN EXPERT ON RELATIONSHIPS. I MEAN, IN ALL TRUTH I'M A PRETTY AWFUL MUSICIAN, TOO. THAT'S PART OF THE REASON I ORIGINALLY BECAME A CROOK. FRUSTRATED ARTIST, I GUESS.
I MAY NOT BE A MUSICAL GENIUS BUT I KNOW WHEN I HEAR A GOOD SONG
AND I KNOW WHEN I SEE A GOOD RELATION-SHIP. YOU AND LINDA ARE SOLID.
THIS IS IT.

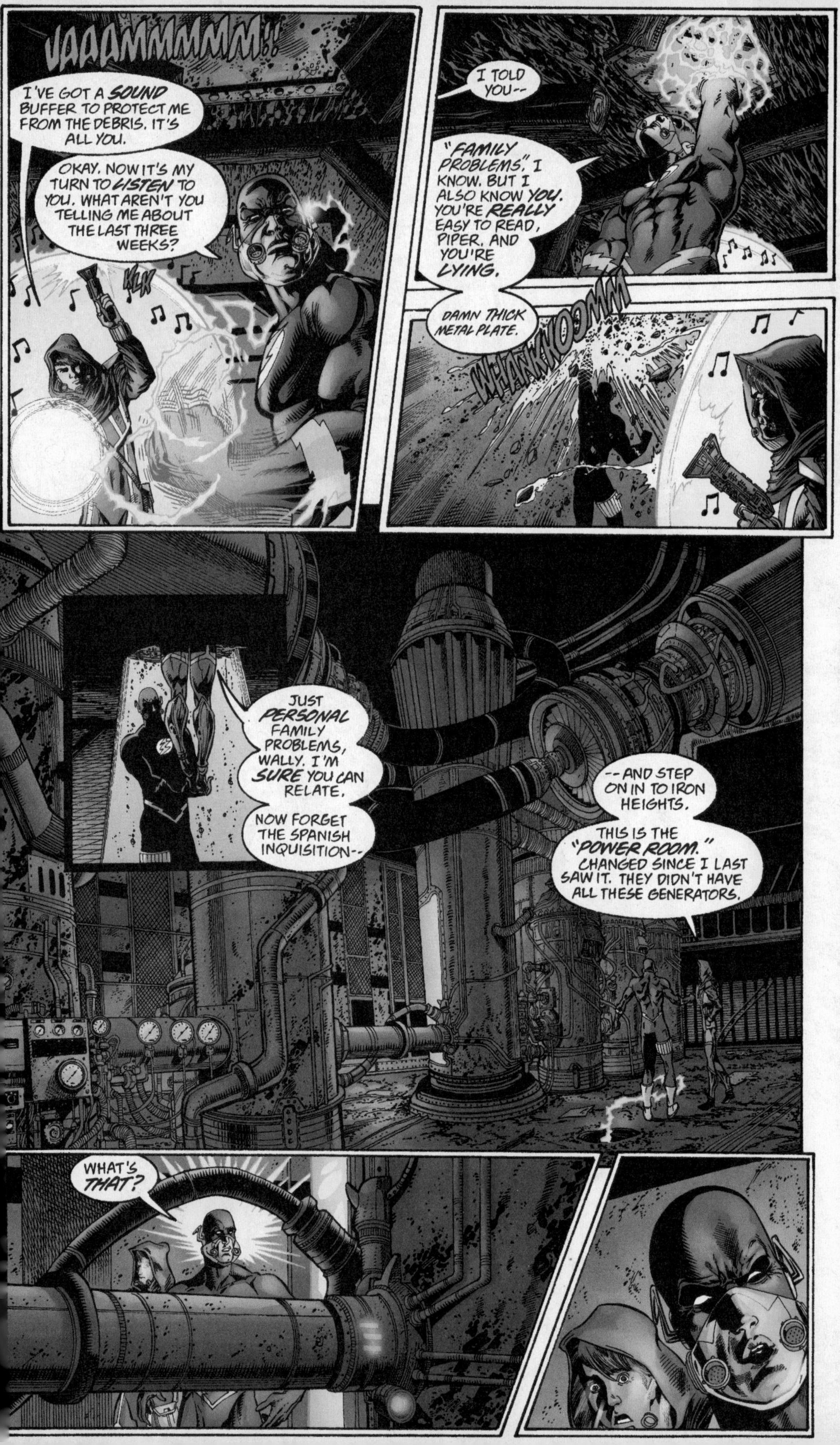
VAAAMMMMMM!!
I'VE GOT A SOUND BUFFER TO PROTECT ME FROM THE DEBRIS. IT'S ALL YOU.
OKAY. NOW IT'S MY TURN TO LISTEN TO YOU. WHAT AREN'T YOU TELLING ME ABOUT THE LAST THREE WEEKS?
KLIK
I TOLD YOU--
"FAMILY PROBLEMS." I KNOW. BUT I ALSO KNOW YOU. YOU'RE REALLY EASY TO READ, PIPER. AND YOU'RE LYING.
DAMN THICK METAL PLATE.
WHANKOOMM
JUST PERSONAL FAMILY PROBLEMS, WALLY. I'M SURE YOU CAN RELATE.
NOW FORGET THE SPANISH INQUISITION--
--AND STEP ON IN TO IRON HEIGHTS.
THIS IS THE "POWER ROOM." CHANGED SINCE I LAST SAW IT. THEY DIDN'T HAVE ALL THESE GENERATORS.
WHAT'S THAT?

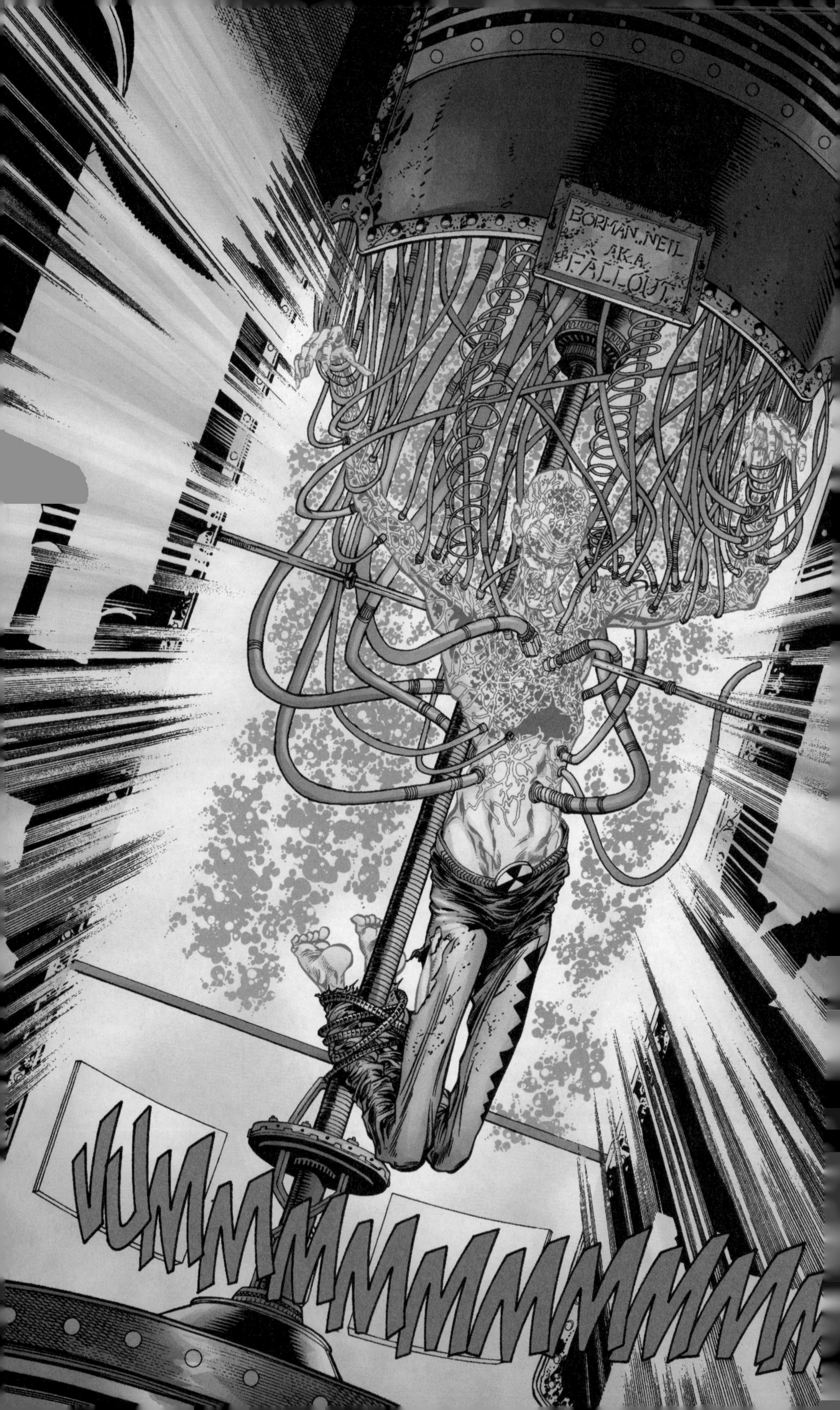

BORMAN, NEIL
A.K.A.
FALLOUT
VUMMMMMMMMMMMM

BORMAN,
NEIL
PRISONER
IH 420
ALTER EGO:
FALL OUT

FORMER OCCUPATION: MASON
METAHUMAN ABILITIES: GENERATES A SEEMINGLY UNLIMITED AMOUNT OF RADIOACTIVITY, ENHANCED STRENGTH.
SENTENCE: 20 YEARS FOR ARMED ROBBERY, RE-SENTENCED 11/23/97 FOR MURDERING A FELLOW INMATE--LIFE WITHOUT PAROLE.

FILE SAYS *BORMAN* WAS THE ONLY SURVIVOR OF THE BRADDOCK ACCIDENT 10 YEARS AGO.

WHEN THEY WERE TRYING TO BUILD THAT *NUCLEAR PLANT* NORTH OF THE CITY? KEYSTONE ALMOST HAD A *THREE MILE ISLAND* OF THEIR OWN.

BUT WHAT THE HELL IS BORMAN DOING LOCKED UP DOWN--

--I THINK ...GOD, I THINK THEY'RE POWERING THIS *PRISON* OFF *HIM*.

WHAT ARE THEY TRYING TO DO? SAVE *TAX DOLLARS*?

WHAPTT!

C'MON. NOTHING WE CAN DO FOR HIM RIGHT NOW. HE'S NOT THE ONE WE'RE LOOKING FOR.

WAIT. HE'S TRYING TO TELL US SOMETHING.

YEAH, HOW MUCH HE'D LOVE TO WRAP HIS *MOLTEN HANDS* AROUND OUR *THROATS.* LET'S GO.

BAM! BAM!

HELP ME, DAMN YOU.

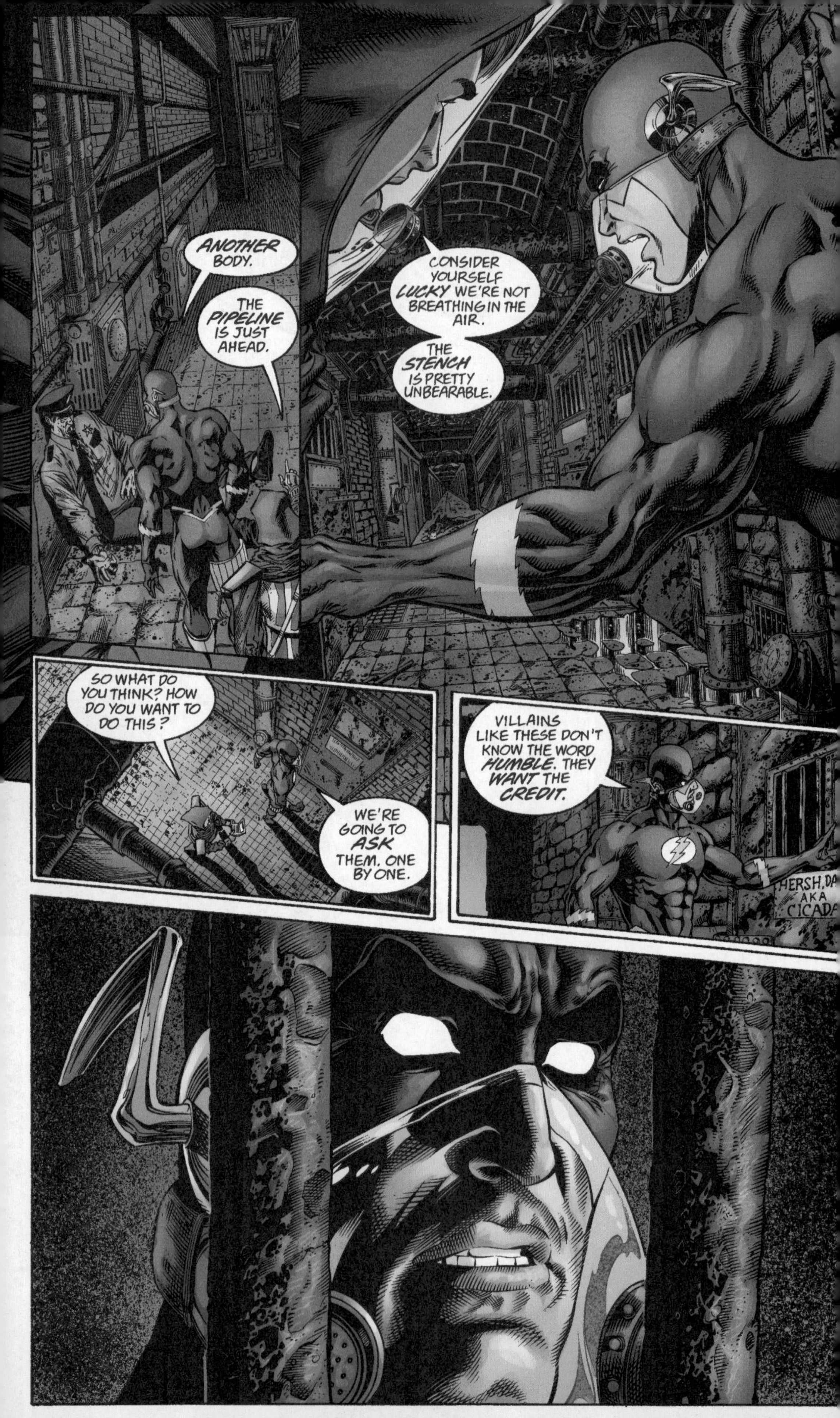
ANOTHER BODY.
THE PIPELINE IS JUST AHEAD.
CONSIDER YOURSELF LUCKY WE'RE NOT BREATHING IN THE AIR.
THE STENCH IS PRETTY UNBEARABLE.
SO WHAT DO YOU THINK? HOW DO YOU WANT TO DO THIS?
WE'RE GOING TO ASK THEM. ONE BY ONE.
VILLAINS LIKE THESE DON'T KNOW THE WORD HUMBLE. THEY WANT THE CREDIT.
HERSH, DA
AKA
CICADA

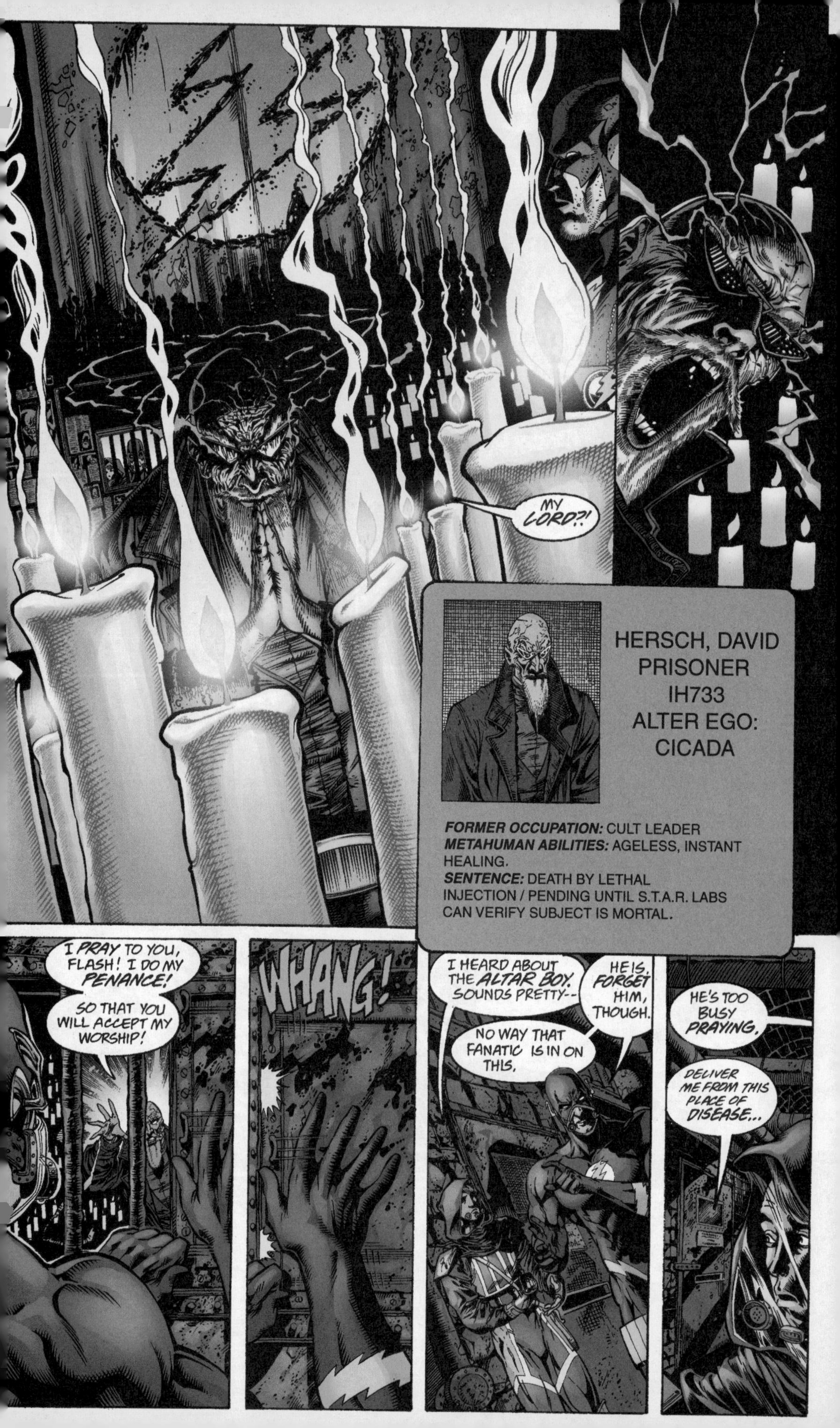
MY LORD?!
HERSCH, DAVID
PRISONER
IH733
ALTER EGO:
CICADA
FORMER OCCUPATION: CULT LEADER
METAHUMAN ABILITIES: AGELESS, INSTANT HEALING.
SENTENCE: DEATH BY LETHAL INJECTION / PENDING UNTIL S.T.A.R. LABS CAN VERIFY SUBJECT IS MORTAL.
I PRAY TO YOU, FLASH! I DO MY PENANCE!
SO THAT YOU WILL ACCEPT MY WORSHIP!
WHANG!
I HEARD ABOUT THE ALTAR BOY. SOUNDS PRETTY--
HE IS. FORGET HIM, THOUGH.
NO WAY THAT FANATIC IS IN ON THIS.
HE'S TOO BUSY PRAYING.
DELIVER ME FROM THIS PLACE OF DISEASE...

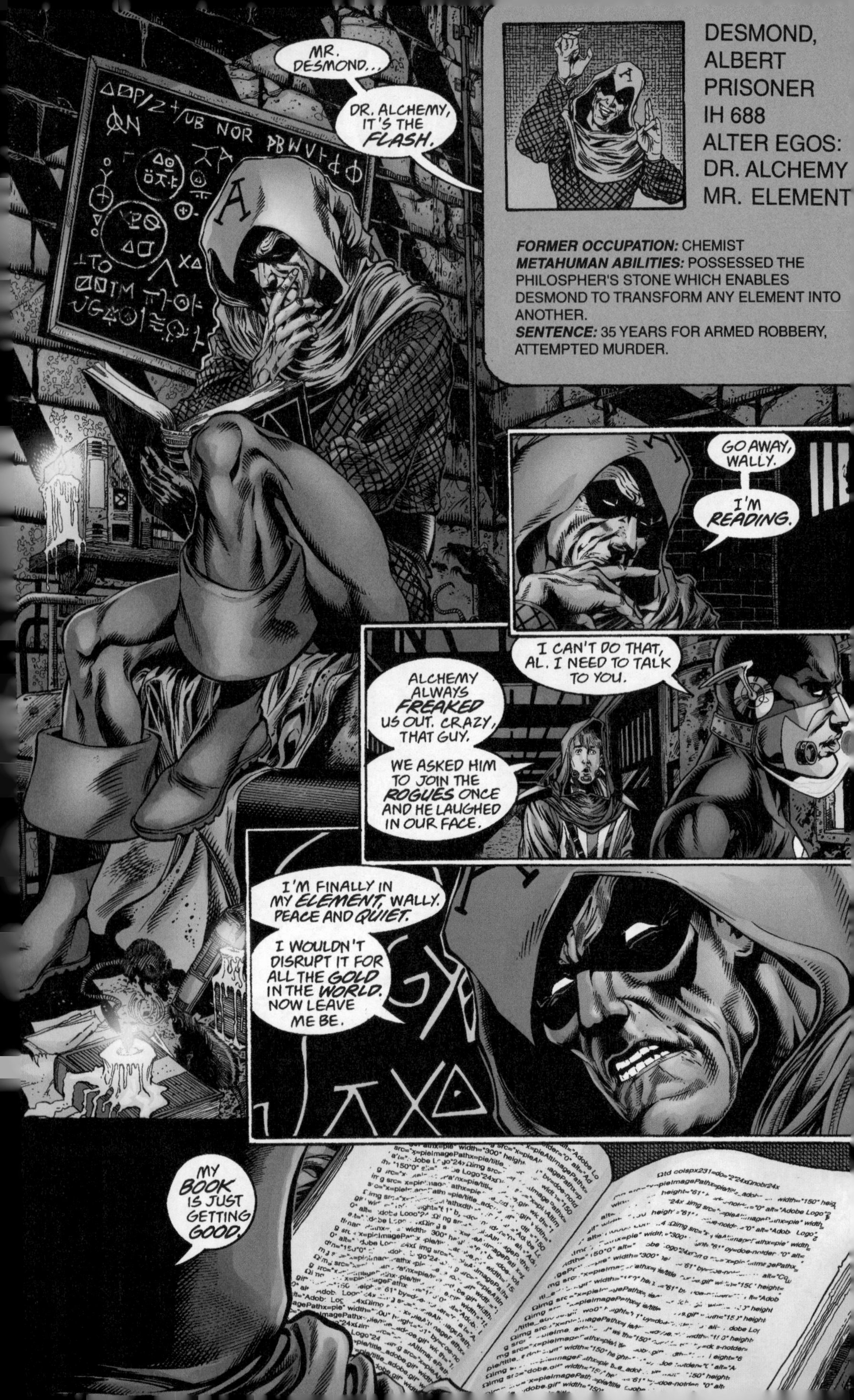
MR. DESMOND...
DR. ALCHEMY, IT'S THE FLASH.
DESMOND, ALBERT
PRISONER IH 688
ALTER EGOS: DR. ALCHEMY MR. ELEMENT
FORMER OCCUPATION: CHEMIST
METAHUMAN ABILITIES: POSSESSED THE PHILOSPHER'S STONE WHICH ENABLES DESMOND TO TRANSFORM ANY ELEMENT INTO ANOTHER.
SENTENCE: 35 YEARS FOR ARMED ROBBERY, ATTEMPTED MURDER.
GO AWAY, WALLY.
I'M READING.
I CAN'T DO THAT, AL. I NEED TO TALK TO YOU.
ALCHEMY ALWAYS FREAKED US OUT. CRAZY, THAT GUY.
WE ASKED HIM TO JOIN THE ROGUES ONCE AND HE LAUGHED IN OUR FACE.
I'M FINALLY IN MY ELEMENT, WALLY. PEACE AND QUIET.
I WOULDN'T DISRUPT IT FOR ALL THE GOLD IN THE WORLD. NOW LEAVE ME BE.
MY BOOK IS JUST GETTING GOOD.

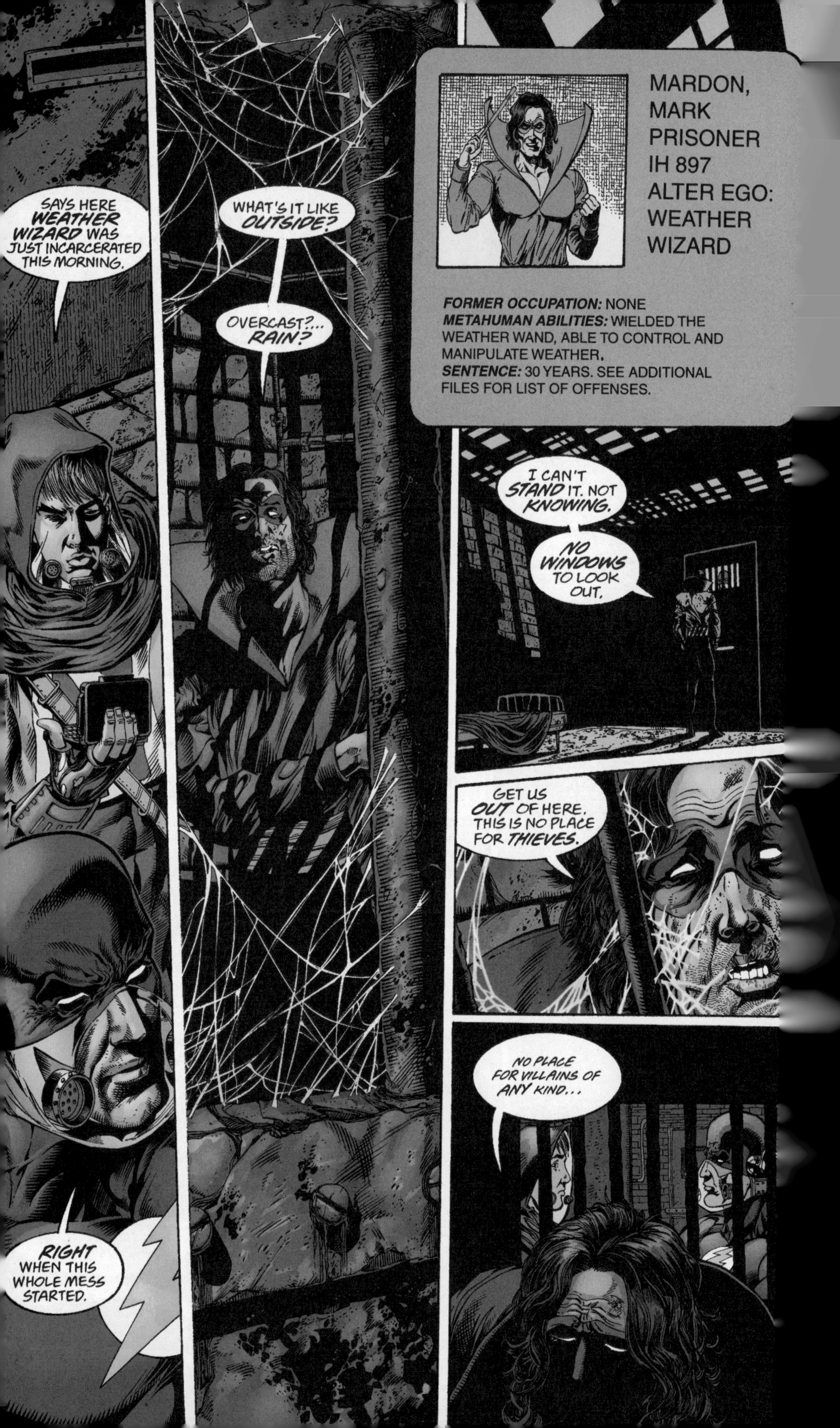
SAYS HERE WEATHER WIZARD WAS JUST INCARCERATED THIS MORNING.
RIGHT WHEN THIS WHOLE MESS STARTED.
WHAT'S IT LIKE OUTSIDE?
OVERCAST?... RAIN?
MARDON, MARK PRISONER IH 897 ALTER EGO: WEATHER WIZARD
FORMER OCCUPATION: NONE
METAHUMAN ABILITIES: WIELDED THE WEATHER WAND, ABLE TO CONTROL AND MANIPULATE WEATHER.
SENTENCE: 30 YEARS. SEE ADDITIONAL FILES FOR LIST OF OFFENSES.
I CAN'T STAND IT. NOT KNOWING.
NO WINDOWS TO LOOK OUT.
GET US OUT OF HERE. THIS IS NO PLACE FOR THIEVES.
NO PLACE FOR VILLAINS OF ANY KIND...

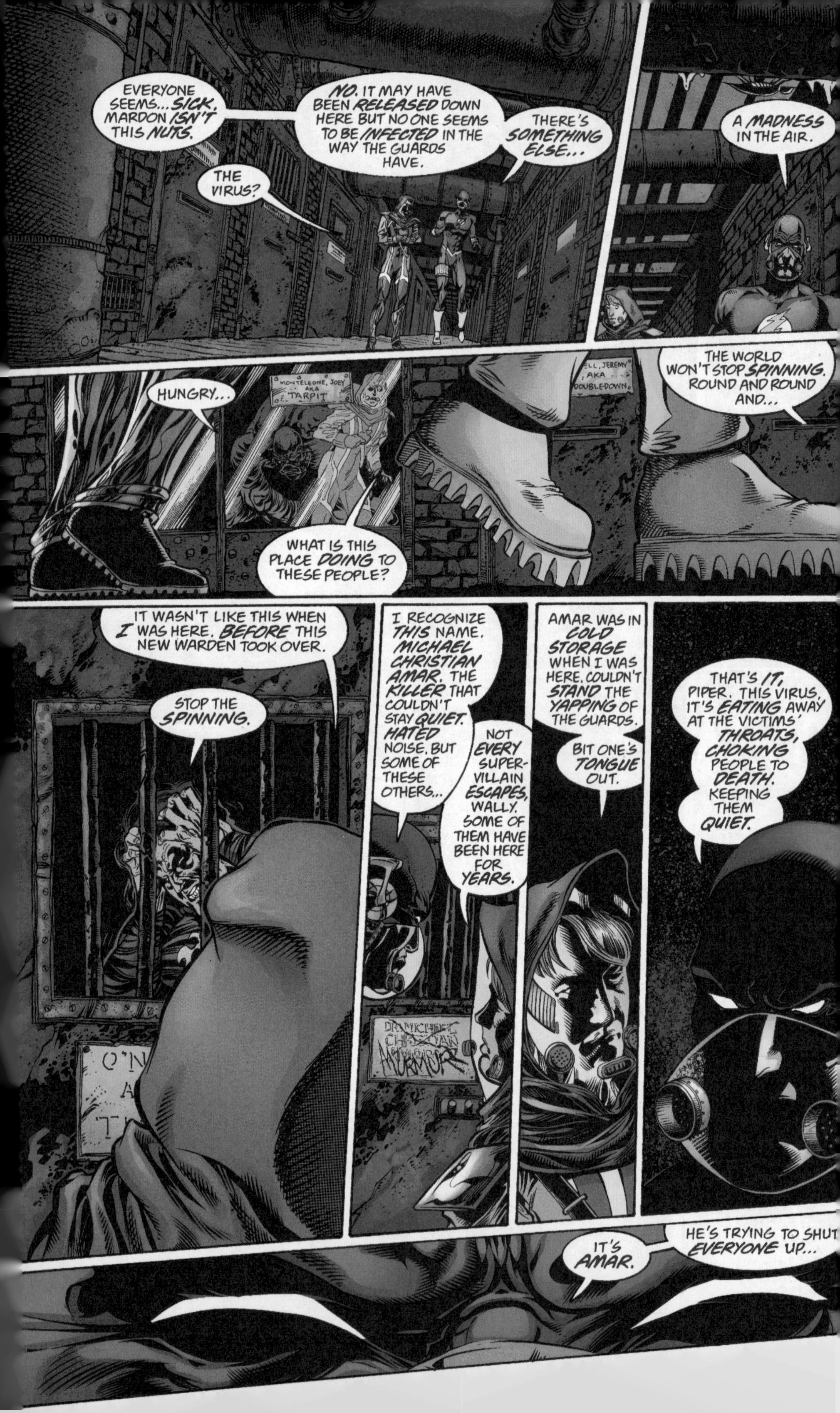
EVERYONE SEEMS... SICK. MARDON ISN'T THIS NUTS.
THE VIRUS?
NO. IT MAY HAVE BEEN RELEASED DOWN HERE BUT NO ONE SEEMS TO BE INFECTED IN THE WAY THE GUARDS HAVE.
THERE'S SOMETHING ELSE...
A MADNESS IN THE AIR.
MONTELEONE, JOEY AKA TARPIT
HUNGRY...
ELL, JEREMY AKA DOUBLEDOWN
THE WORLD WON'T STOP SPINNING. ROUND AND ROUND AND...
WHAT IS THIS PLACE DOING TO THESE PEOPLE?
IT WASN'T LIKE THIS WHEN I WAS HERE. BEFORE THIS NEW WARDEN TOOK OVER.
STOP THE SPINNING.
I RECOGNIZE THIS NAME. MICHAEL CHRISTIAN AMAR. THE KILLER THAT COULDN'T STAY QUIET. HATED NOISE, BUT SOME OF THESE OTHERS...
NOT EVERY SUPER-VILLAIN ESCAPES, WALLY. SOME OF THEM HAVE BEEN HERE FOR YEARS.
AMAR WAS IN COLD STORAGE WHEN I WAS HERE. COULDN'T STAND THE YAPPING OF THE GUARDS.
BIT ONE'S TONGUE OUT.
THAT'S IT, PIPER. THIS VIRUS, IT'S EATING AWAY AT THE VICTIMS' THROATS, CHOKING PEOPLE TO DEATH. KEEPING THEM QUIET.
IT'S AMAR.
HE'S TRYING TO SHUT EVERYONE UP...

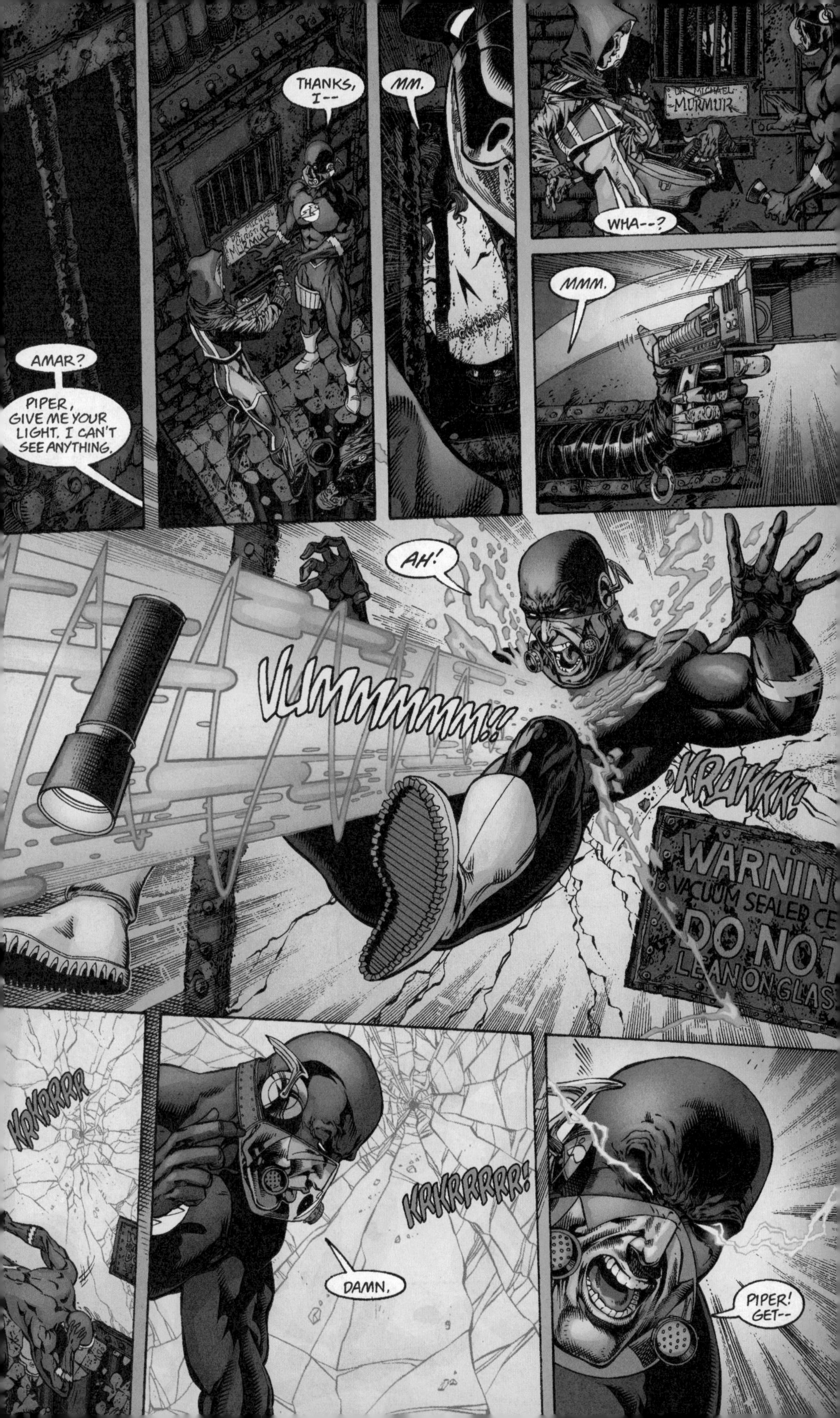
AMAR?
PIPER, GIVE ME YOUR LIGHT. I CAN'T SEE ANYTHING.
THANKS, I--
MM.
DR. MICHAEL MURMUR
WHA--?
MMM.
AH!
VUMMMMMM!!
KRAKKK!
WARNING
VACUUM SEALED CE
DO NOT
LEAN ON GLAS
KRKRRRR
KRKRRRRR!
DAMN.
PIPER! GET--

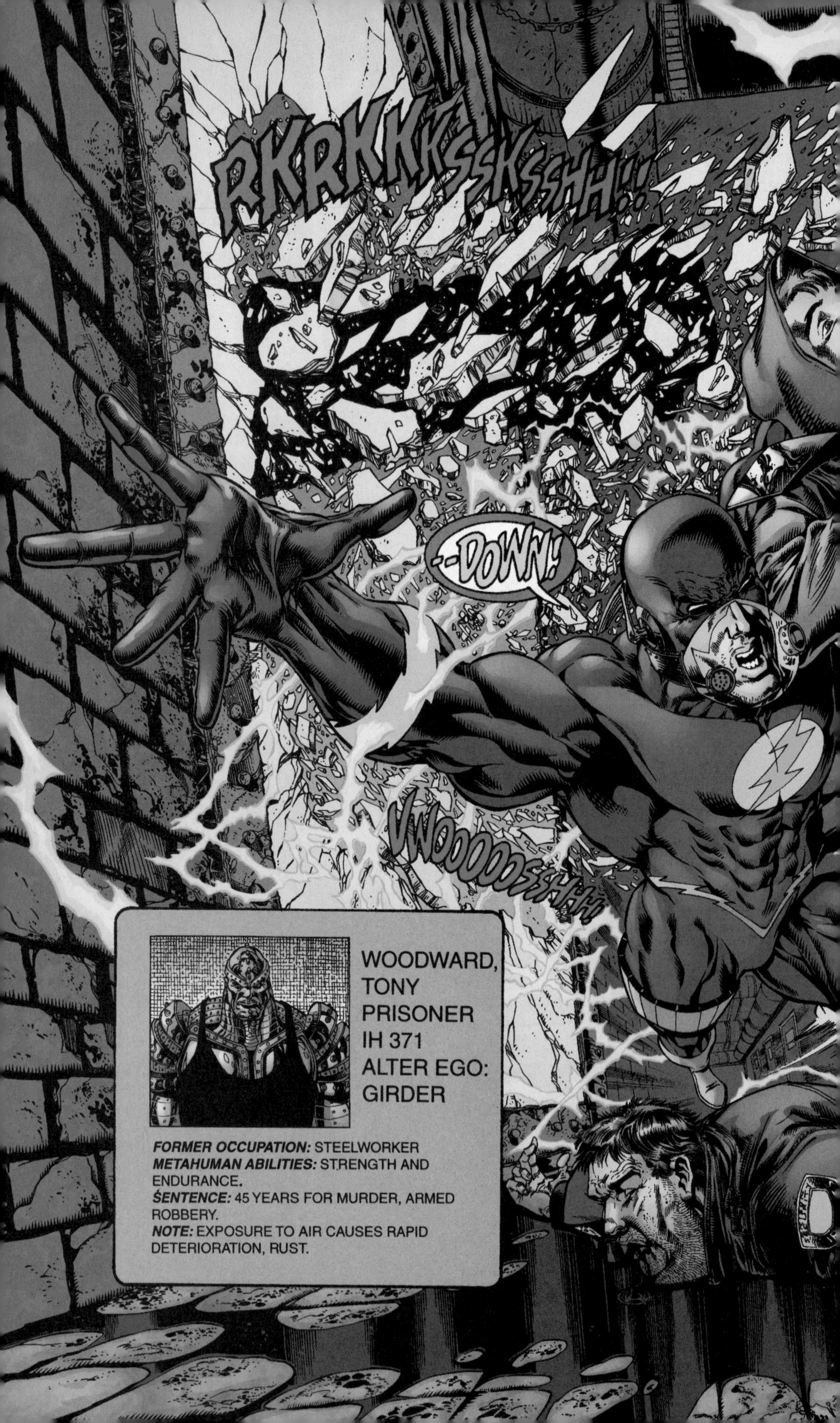
RKRKKKSSKSSHH!!
--DOWN!
VWOOOOOOSSHHH
WOODWARD, TONY
PRISONER IH 371
ALTER EGO: GIRDER
FORMER OCCUPATION: STEELWORKER
METAHUMAN ABILITIES: STRENGTH AND ENDURANCE.
SENTENCE: 45 YEARS FOR MURDER, ARMED ROBBERY.
NOTE: EXPOSURE TO AIR CAUSES RAPID DETERIORATION, RUST.

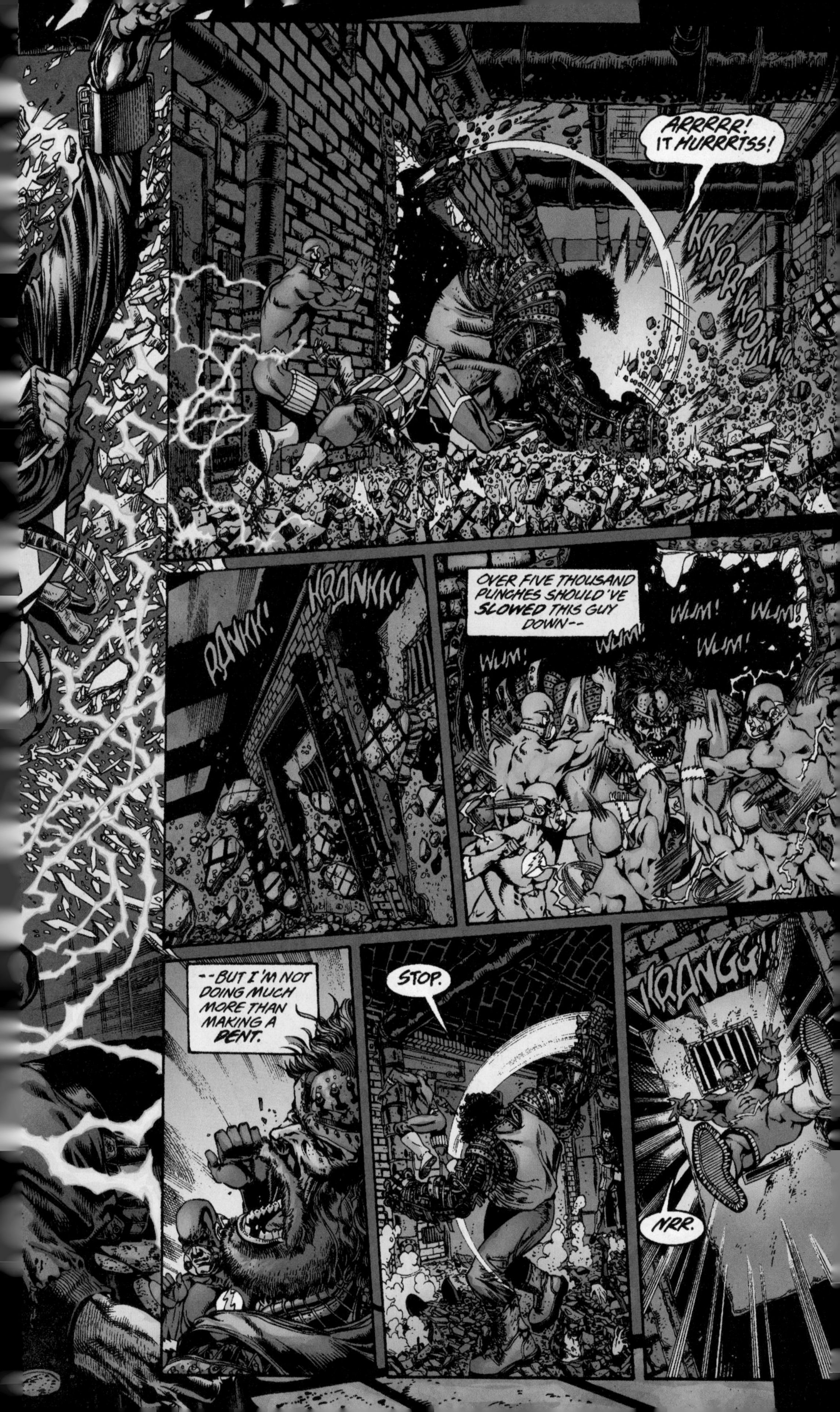
ARRRRR! IT HURRRTSS!
KKRRAKOOMM
RANKK!
KRANKK!
OVER FIVE THOUSAND PUNCHES SHOULD'VE SLOWED THIS GUY DOWN--
WUM!
WUM!
WUM!
WUM!
WUM!
--BUT I'M NOT DOING MUCH MORE THAN MAKING A DENT.
STOP.
KRANGG!
NRR.

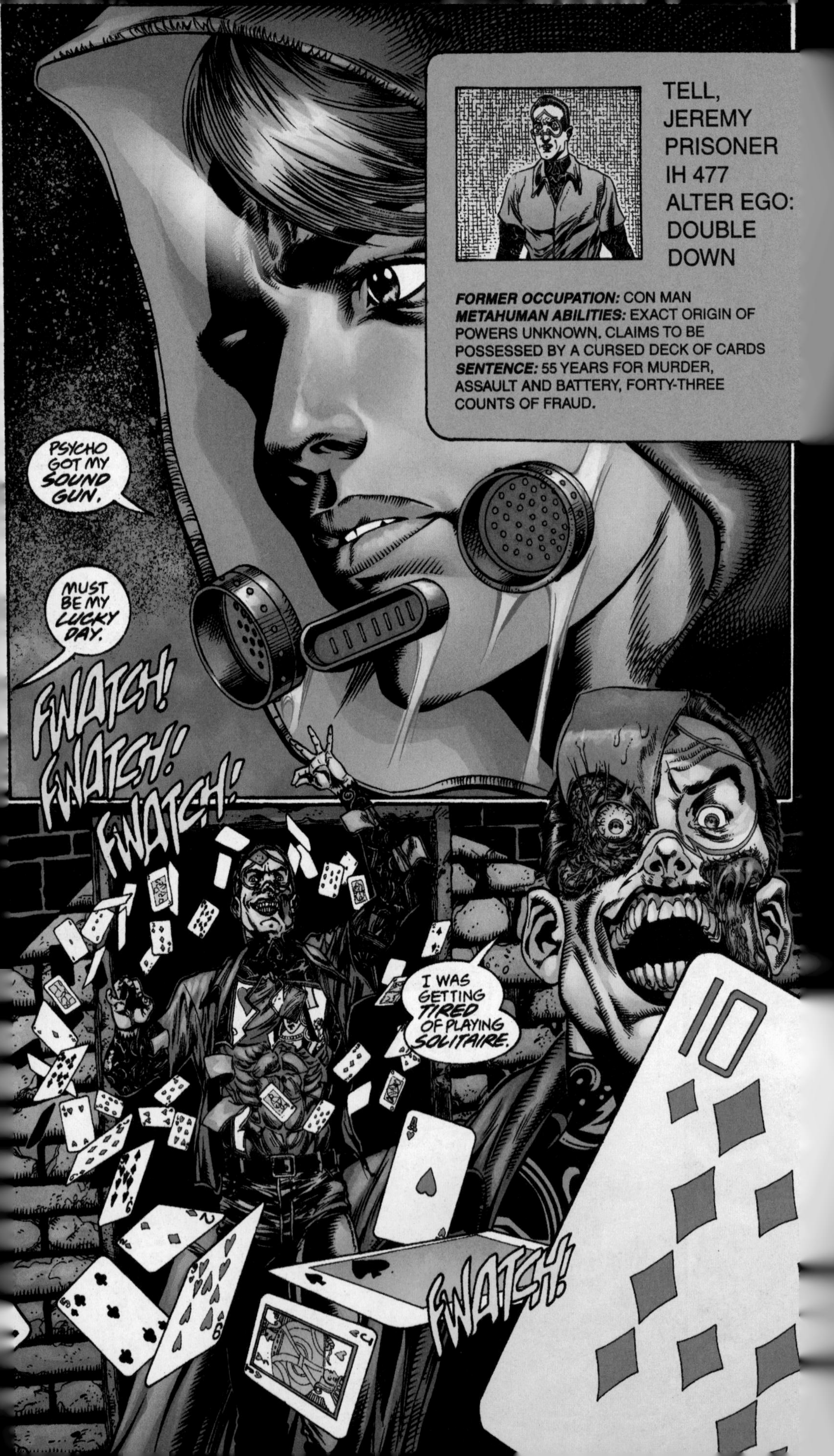

TELL, JEREMY
PRISONER IH 477
ALTER EGO: DOUBLE DOWN
FORMER OCCUPATION: CON MAN
METAHUMAN ABILITIES: EXACT ORIGIN OF POWERS UNKNOWN. CLAIMS TO BE POSSESSED BY A CURSED DECK OF CARDS
SENTENCE: 55 YEARS FOR MURDER, ASSAULT AND BATTERY, FORTY-THREE COUNTS OF FRAUD.
PSYCHO GOT MY SOUND GUN.
MUST BE MY LUCKY DAY.
FWATCH! FWATCH! FWATCH!
I WAS GETTING TIRED OF PLAYING SOLITAIRE.
FWATCH!

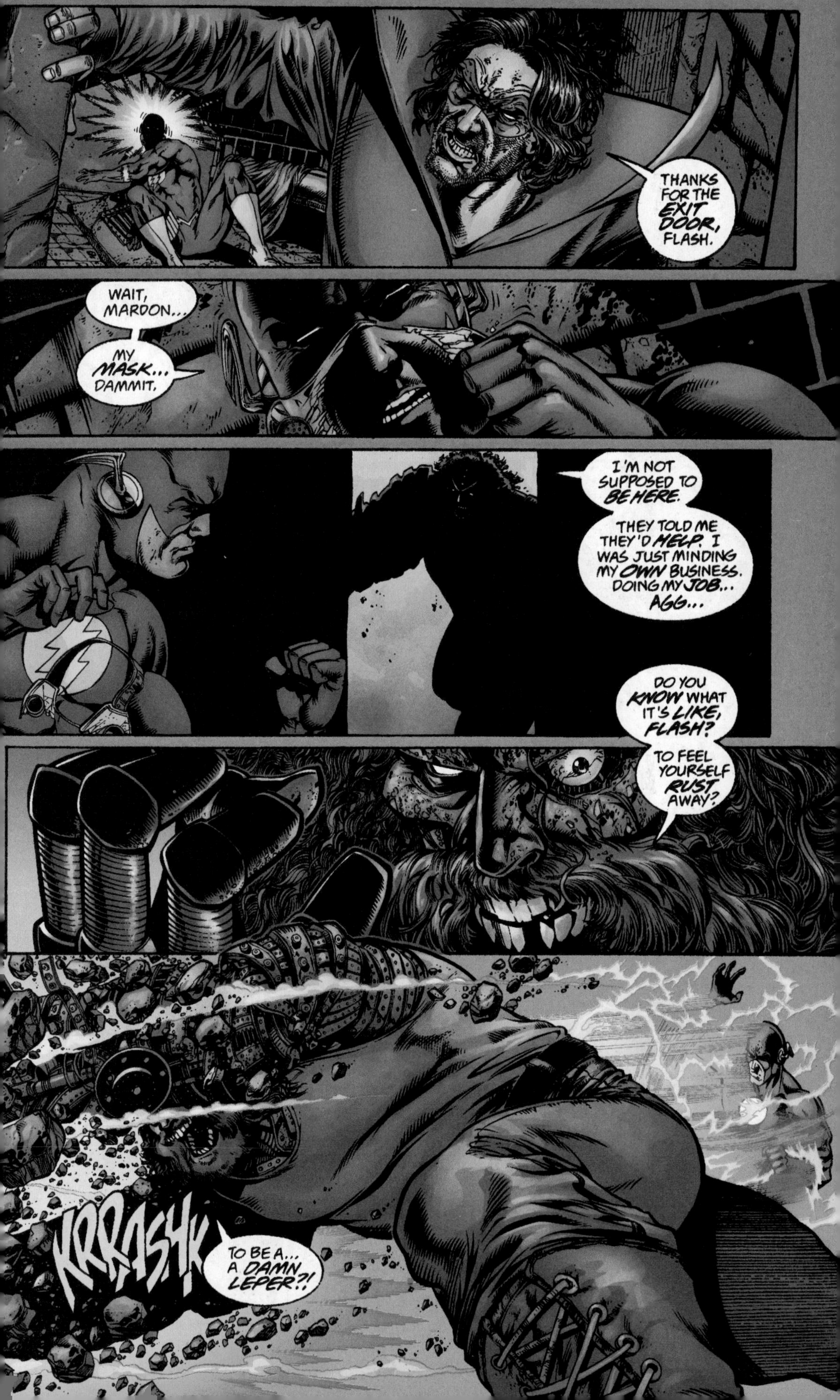
THANKS FOR THE EXIT DOOR, FLASH.
WAIT, MARDON...
MY MASK... DAMMIT.
I'M NOT SUPPOSED TO BE HERE.
THEY TOLD ME THEY'D HELP. I WAS JUST MINDING MY OWN BUSINESS. DOING MY JOB... AGG...
DO YOU KNOW WHAT IT'S LIKE, FLASH?
TO FEEL YOURSELF RUST AWAY?
KRRASHK
TO BE A... A DAMN LEPER?!

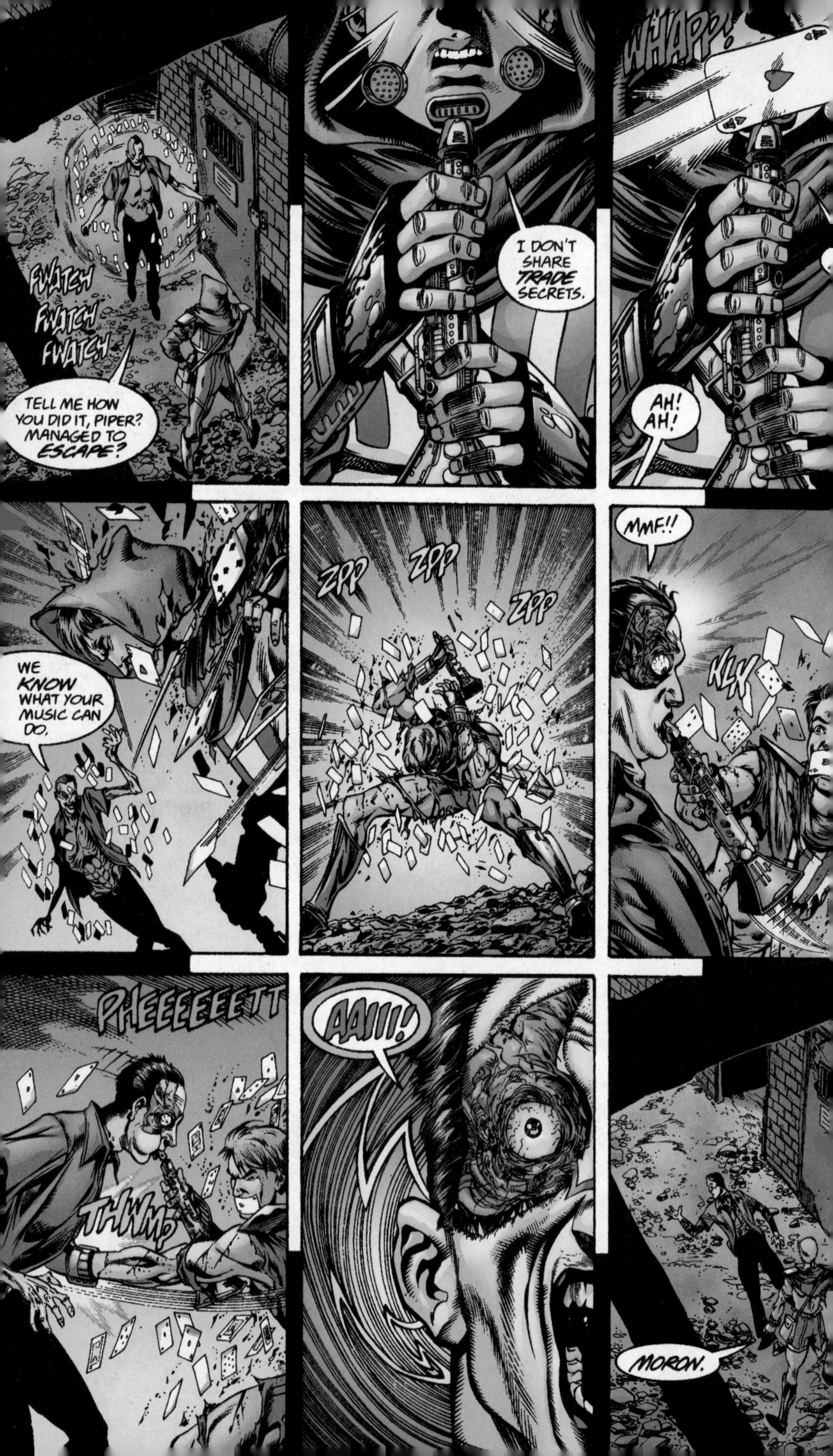
FWATCH
FWATCH
FWATCH
TELL ME HOW YOU DID IT, PIPER? MANAGED TO ESCAPE?
I DON'T SHARE TRADE SECRETS.
WHAPP!
AH! AH!
WE KNOW WHAT YOUR MUSIC CAN DO.
ZPP
ZPP
ZPP
MMF!!
KLK
PHEEEEEEETT
THWMP
AAIII!
MORON.

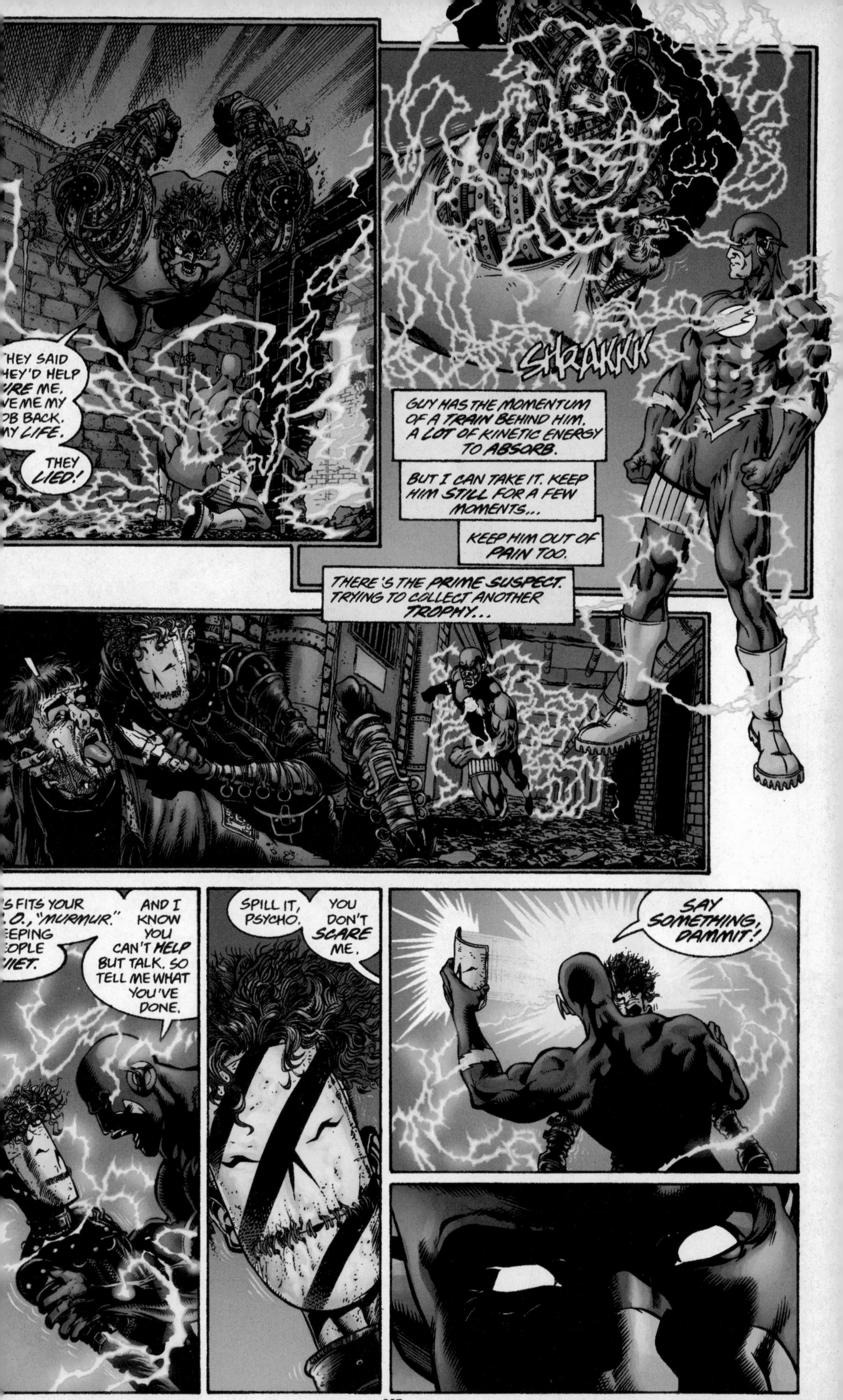
THEY SAID HEY'D HELP URE ME. VE ME MY OB BACK. MY LIFE.
THEY LIED!
SHRAKKK
GUY HAS THE MOMENTUM OF A TRAIN BEHIND HIM. A LOT OF KINETIC ENERGY TO ABSORB.
BUT I CAN TAKE IT. KEEP HIM STILL FOR A FEW MOMENTS...
KEEP HIM OUT OF PAIN TOO.
THERE'S THE PRIME SUSPECT. TRYING TO COLLECT ANOTHER TROPHY...
S FITS YOUR .O., "MURMUR." EEPING EOPLE UIET.
AND I KNOW YOU CAN'T HELP BUT TALK. SO TELL ME WHAT YOU'VE DONE.
SPILL IT, PSYCHO.
YOU DON'T SCARE ME.
SAY SOMETHING, DAMMIT!

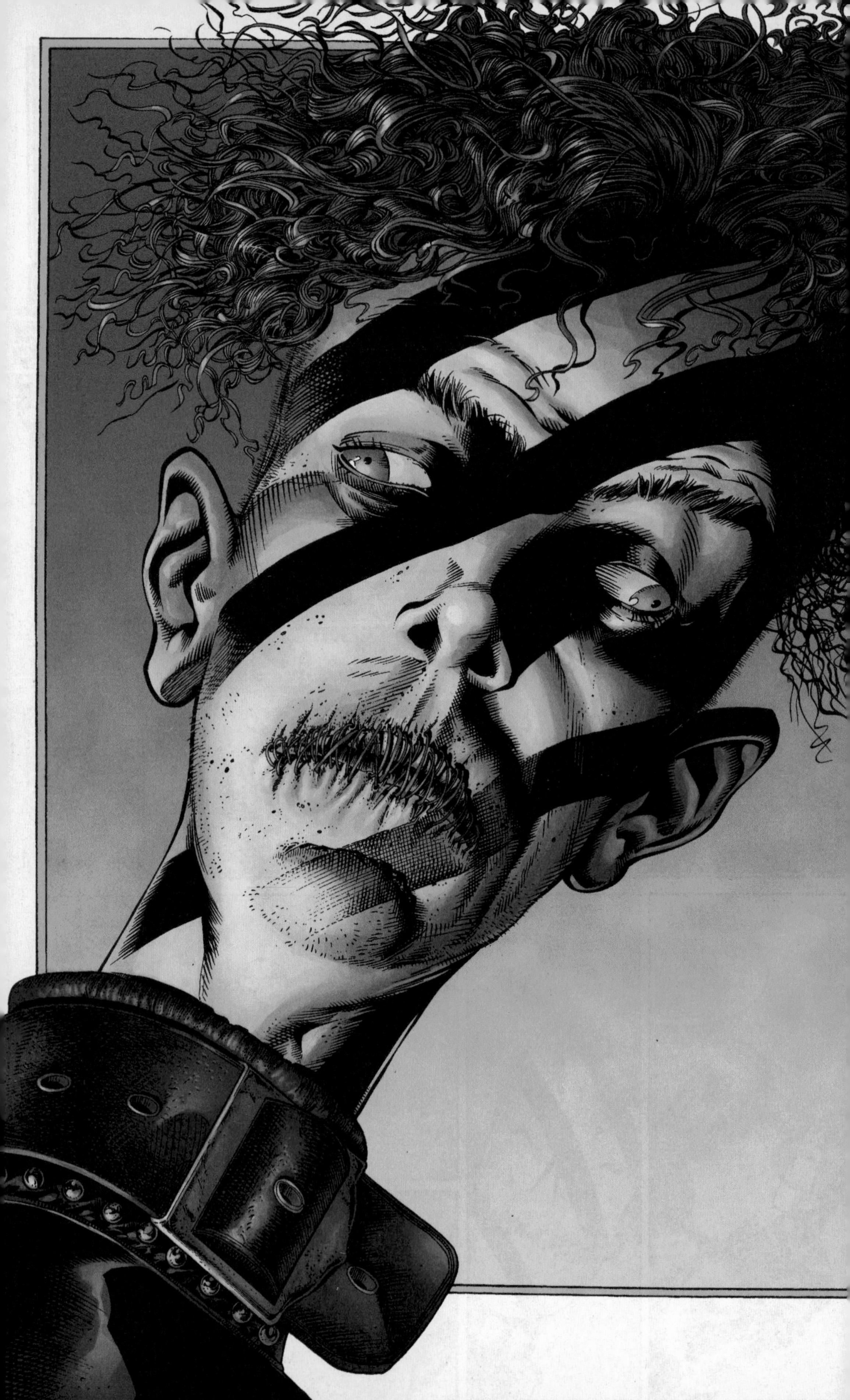

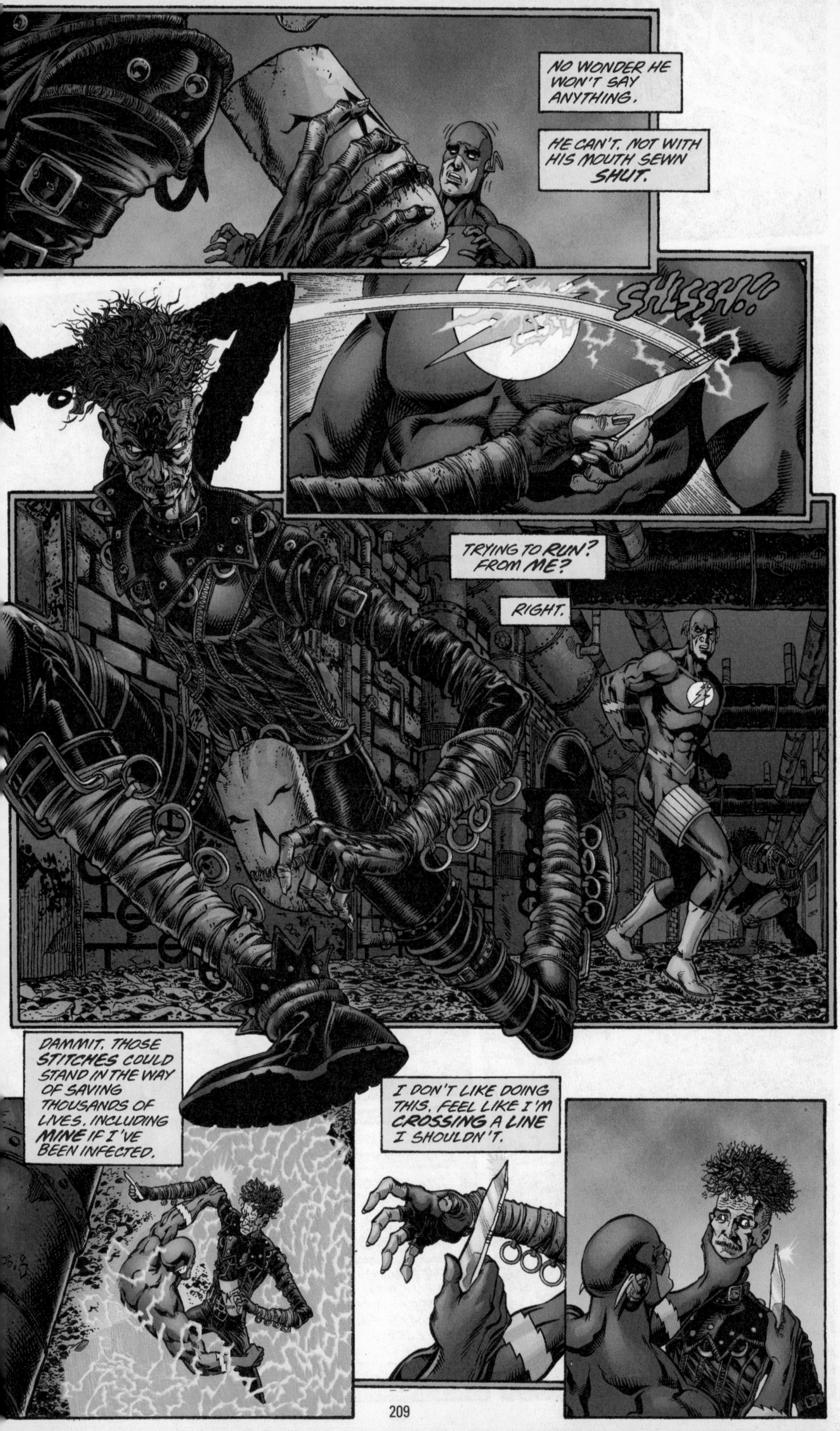

NO WONDER HE WON'T SAY ANYTHING.
HE CAN'T. NOT WITH HIS MOUTH SEWN SHUT.
SHLSSSH!!
TRYING TO RUN? FROM ME?
RIGHT.
DAMMIT. THOSE STITCHES COULD STAND IN THE WAY OF SAVING THOUSANDS OF LIVES. INCLUDING MINE IF I'VE BEEN INFECTED.
I DON'T LIKE DOING THIS. FEEL LIKE I'M CROSSING A LINE I SHOULDN'T.

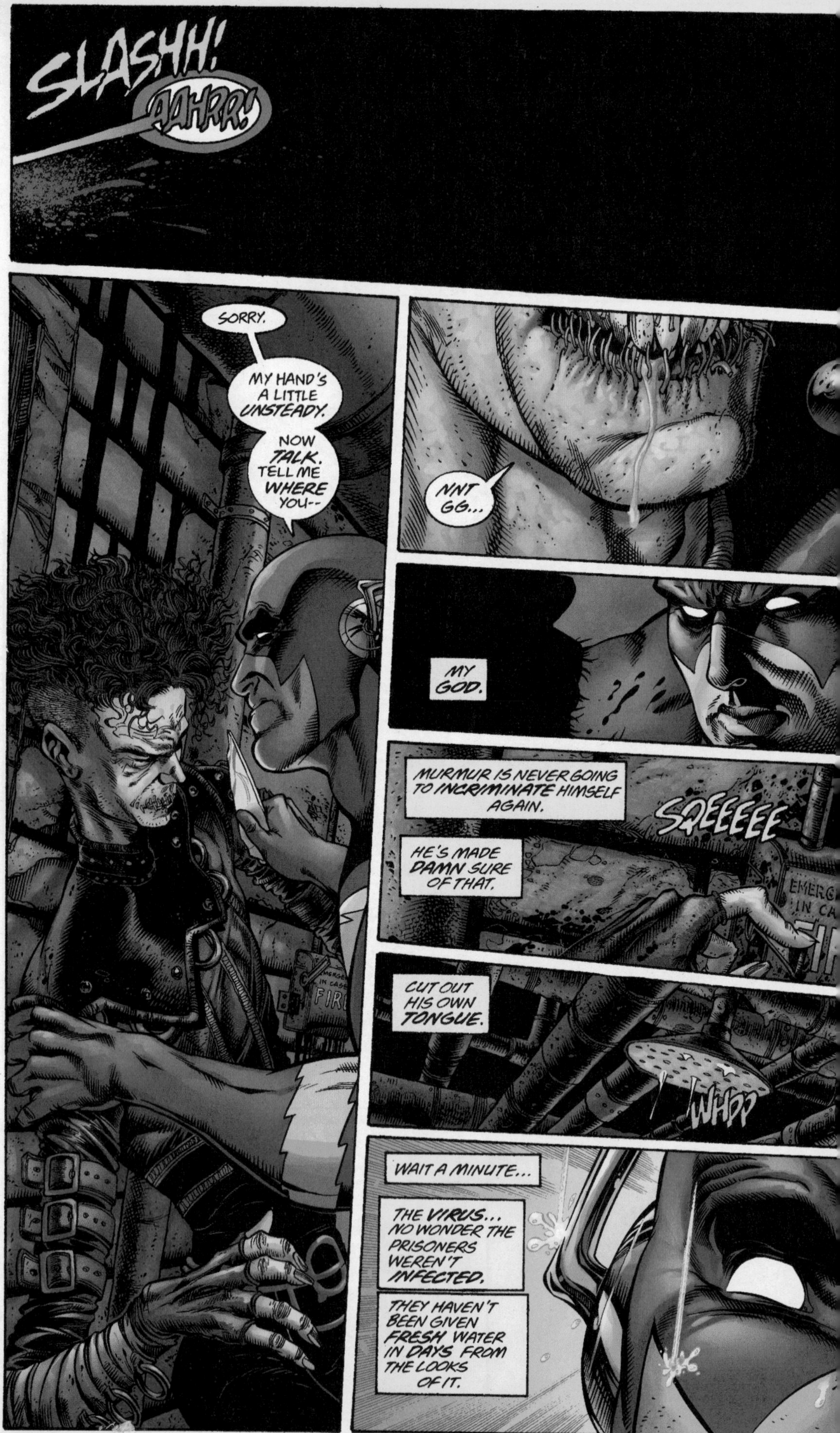

SLASHH!
AAHRR!
SORRY.
MY HAND'S A LITTLE UNSTEADY.
NOW TALK. TELL ME WHERE YOU--
NNT GG...
MY GOD.
MURMUR IS NEVER GOING TO INCRIMINATE HIMSELF AGAIN.
SQEEEEEE
HE'S MADE DAMN SURE OF THAT.
CUT OUT HIS OWN TONGUE.
WHDD
WAIT A MINUTE...
THE VIRUS... NO WONDER THE PRISONERS WEREN'T INFECTED.
THEY HAVEN'T BEEN GIVEN FRESH WATER IN DAYS FROM THE LOOKS OF IT.

IT'S *IN THE WATER SYSTEM!*

FRIIIIISSSH!!

FRIIISSSH!!

EVERYONE IN IRON HEIGHTS IS INFECTED BY NOW. INCLUDING ME.

I HAVE TO FIND THE ORIGINAL VIRUS. NOTHING ON HIM, MAYBE--

--HIS CELL. SOMEONE MUST HAVE SMUGGLED IT IN TO HIM.

IT'S ALL GONE... FLOWING THROUGH THIS PRISON LIKE A POISON.

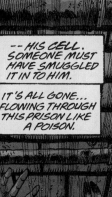

LOOK, *"MURMUR"--*

YOU'RE GOING TO DIE ALONG WITH THE REST OF US.

IS THAT WHAT YOU WANT?

THAT'S IT, PAL. STILL CAN'T *HELP* BUT GIVE ME A CLUE. THERE'S *MORE* TO YOU THAN MEETS THE EYE, ISN'T THERE?

I REMEMBER HOW HARD IT WAS FOR BARRY TO CONNECT THIS GUY TO THE CRIME SCENES, DESPITE THE LARGE AMOUNT OF BLOOD.

BECAUSE AMAR'S BLOOD WAS ABNORMAL.

JAY, WE MAY HAVE ISOLAAAAAA--

TINA? WHAT'S WRONG? WHAT--

SORRY, JAY--

--I TOOK THE LIBERTY OF KICKING YOU INTO *SPEED MODE*.

I THINK I HAVE SOMETHING.

HIS BLOOD'S THE KEY, ALL RIGHT.

THE REASON HE WASN'T *WORRIED* ABOUT *DYING* IS THAT THE DISEASE WON'T TOUCH HIM. MURMUR ALREADY HAS ANTIBODIES DEVELOPED. HIS *BLOOD* IS... I'VE NEVER SEEN ANYTHING LIKE IT. HE *COULD* BE *IMMUNE* TO ANYTHING.

NORMALLY, THERE WOULDN'T BE MUCH WE COULD DO BUT--

--IF YOU CAN *LEND* YOUR SPEED TO THE *VACCINE*, SPEED UP THE ANTIBODIES--

--THEY'LL WIPE OUT THE DISEASE IN *SECONDS*.

JAY?

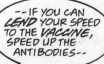

I THINK ⸴ *KAFF* ⸴ --

-- WE BETTER HURRY.

I WAS *INFECTED* IN THERE.

: *KAFF* :

OUR
[MET]ABOLISM
[MU]ST BE
[FE]EDING
[THE]
[VI]RUS.

I NEED **MORE** TIME.

I : *KAFF* : I DON'T THINK WE HAVE ANY MORE TIME, JAY. I : *KAFF* :

WALLY, THIS WILL EITHER *INHIBIT* THE DISEASE OR *ACCELERATE* IT. I DON'T KNOW HOW IT'S GOING TO REACT WITH YOUR BODY CHEMISTRY.

IT COULD **KILL** YOU.

I DON'T CARE WHAT THE MATHEMATICAL CHANCES ARE, JAY.

I **TRUST** YOUR **GUT** MORE THAN : *KAFF* : MORE THAN ANYTHING ELSE.

[WH]AT'S YOUR
[G]UT
[S]AY?

IT'LL WORK.

ROLL UP YOUR **SLEEVE.**

AAHH.

WALLY!?

KRKKKKLLL

YOU'RE THE **MAN,** JAY.

NOW SHOW ME HOW TO MAKE THAT STUFF.

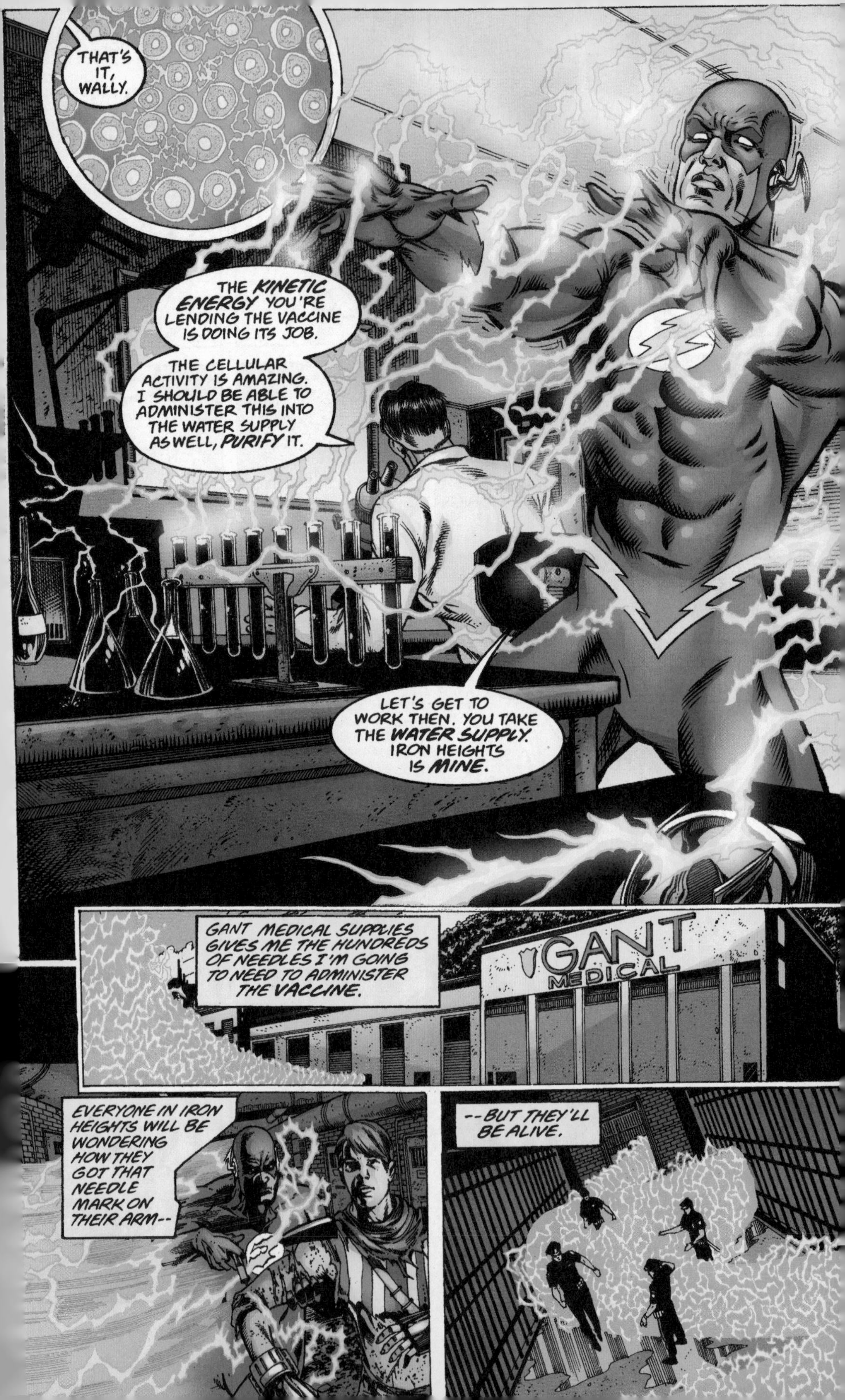
THAT'S IT, WALLY.
THE KINETIC ENERGY YOU'RE LENDING THE VACCINE IS DOING ITS JOB.
THE CELLULAR ACTIVITY IS AMAZING. I SHOULD BE ABLE TO ADMINISTER THIS INTO THE WATER SUPPLY AS WELL, PURIFY IT.
LET'S GET TO WORK THEN. YOU TAKE THE WATER SUPPLY. IRON HEIGHTS IS MINE.
GANT MEDICAL SUPPLIES GIVES ME THE HUNDREDS OF NEEDLES I'M GOING TO NEED TO ADMINISTER THE VACCINE.
GANT MEDICAL
EVERYONE IN IRON HEIGHTS WILL BE WONDERING HOW THEY GOT THAT NEEDLE MARK ON THEIR ARM--
--BUT THEY'LL BE ALIVE.

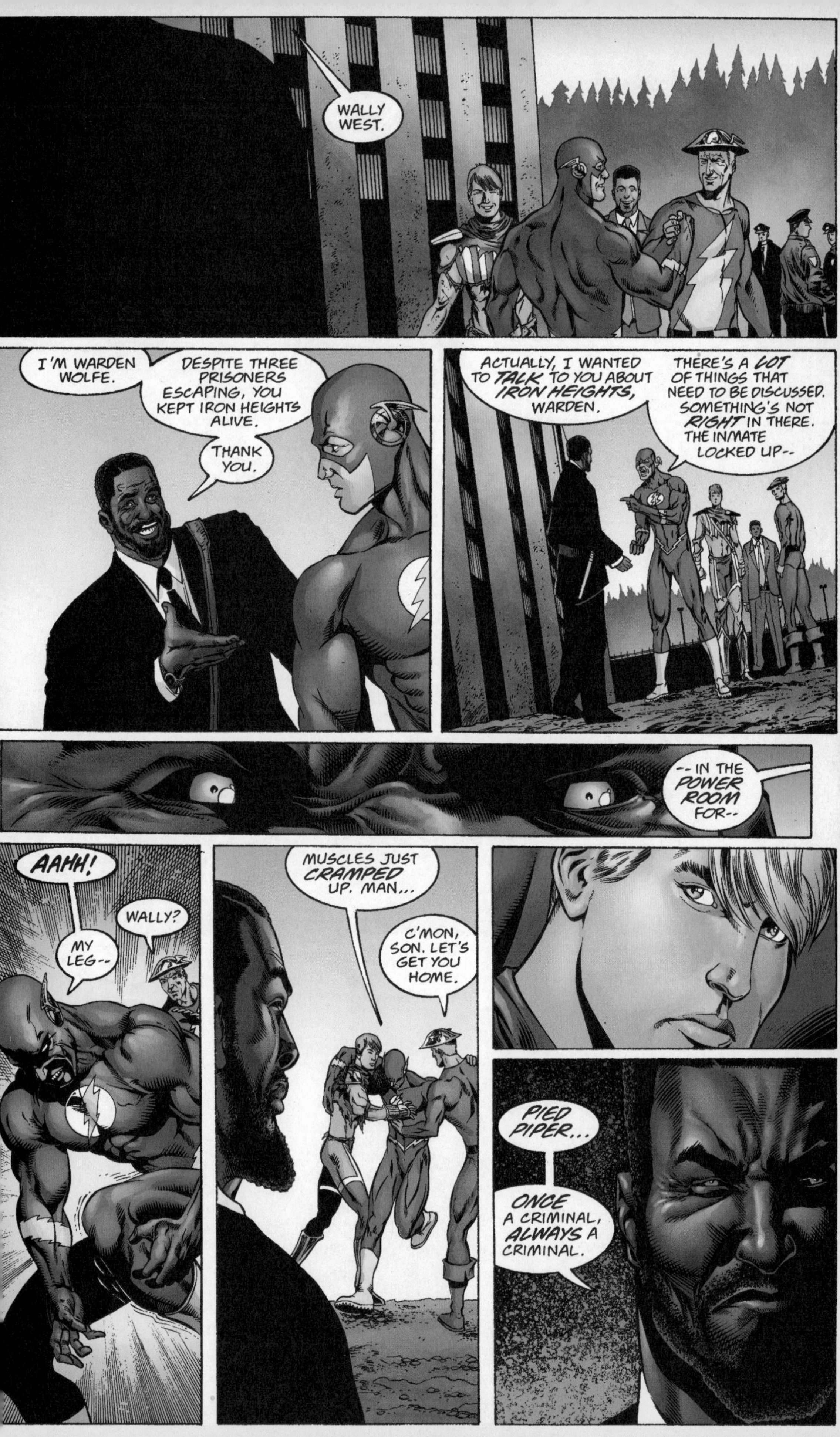

WALLY WEST.
I'M WARDEN WOLFE.
DESPITE THREE PRISONERS ESCAPING, YOU KEPT IRON HEIGHTS ALIVE.
THANK YOU.
ACTUALLY, I WANTED TO TALK TO YOU ABOUT IRON HEIGHTS, WARDEN.
THERE'S A LOT OF THINGS THAT NEED TO BE DISCUSSED. SOMETHING'S NOT RIGHT IN THERE. THE INMATE LOCKED UP--
--IN THE POWER ROOM FOR--
AAHH!
WALLY?
MY LEG--
MUSCLES JUST CRAMPED UP. MAN...
C'MON, SON. LET'S GET YOU HOME.
PIED PIPER...
ONCE A CRIMINAL, ALWAYS A CRIMINAL.

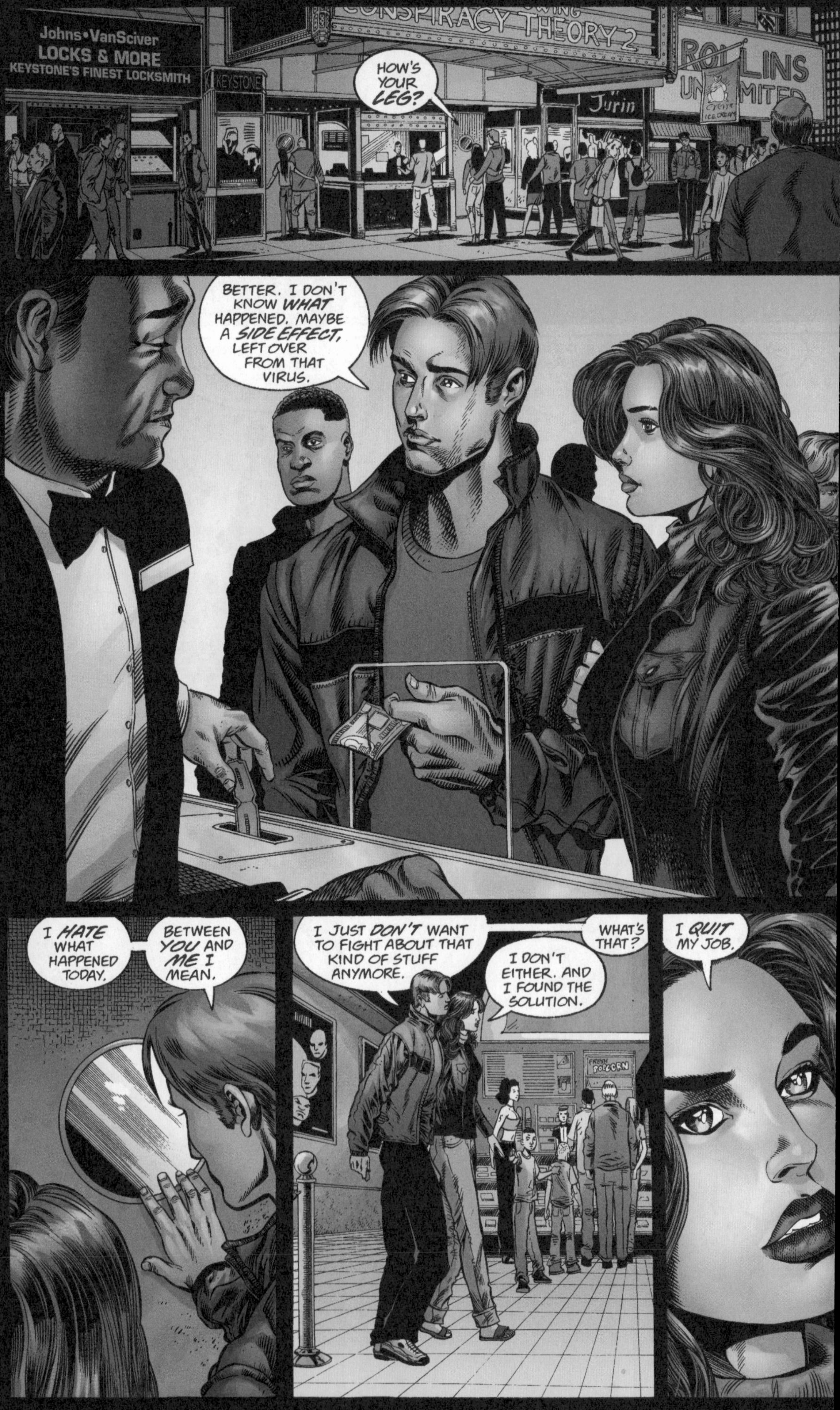

Johns•VanSciver
LOCKS & MORE
KEYSTONE'S FINEST LOCKSMITH
CONSPIRACY THEORY 2
KEYSTONE
HOW'S YOUR LEG?
BETTER. I DON'T KNOW WHAT HAPPENED. MAYBE A SIDE EFFECT, LEFT OVER FROM THAT VIRUS.
I HATE WHAT HAPPENED TODAY.
BETWEEN YOU AND ME I MEAN.
I JUST DON'T WANT TO FIGHT ABOUT THAT KIND OF STUFF ANYMORE.
I DON'T EITHER. AND I FOUND THE SOLUTION.
WHAT'S THAT?
I QUIT MY JOB.

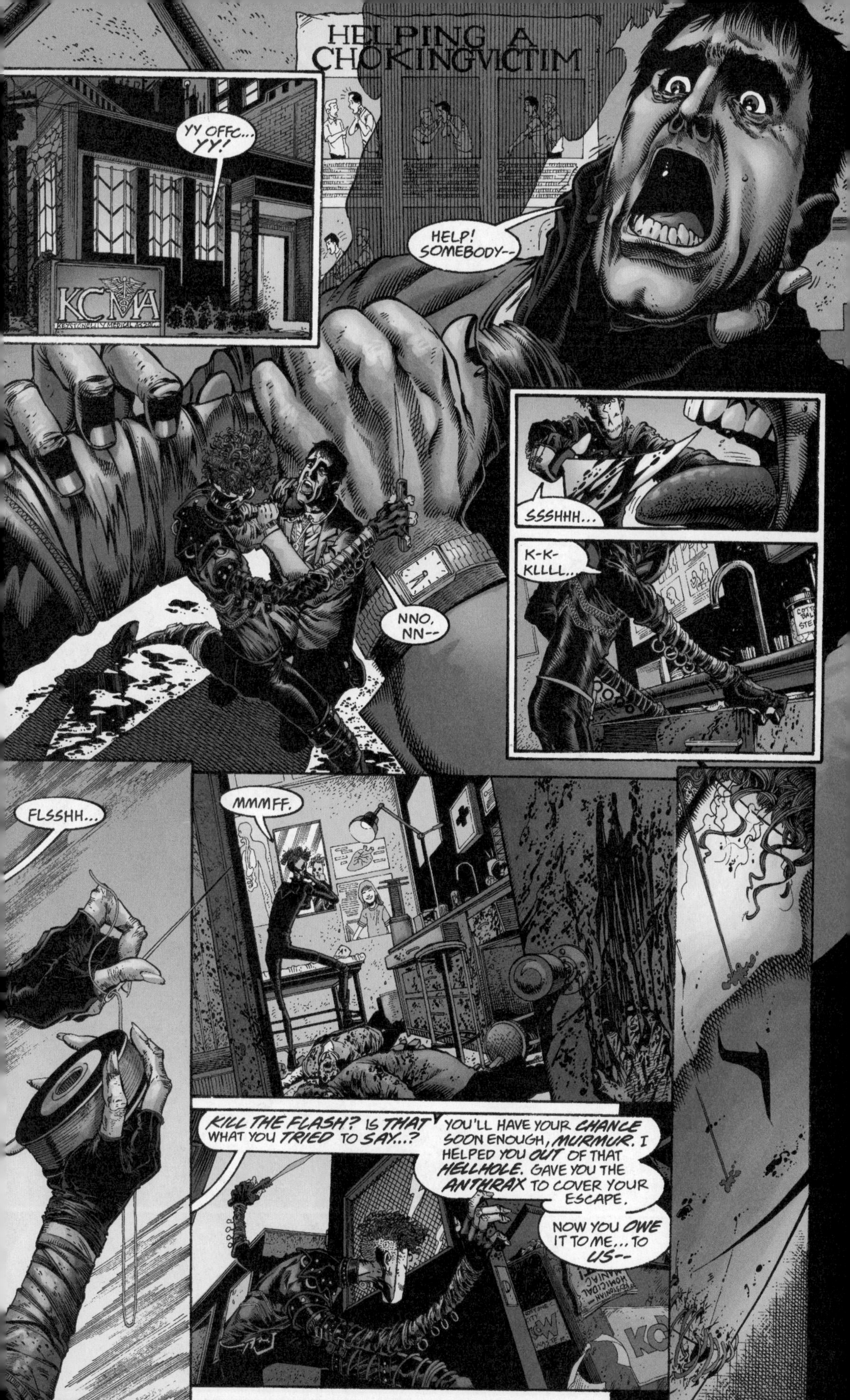
HELPING A CHOKING VICTIM
YY OFFC... YY!
KCMA
KEYSTONE CITY MEDICAL ASSOC.
HELP! SOMEBODY--
NNO, NN--
SSSHHH...
K-K-KLLLL...
FLSSHH...
MMMFF.
KILL THE FLASH? IS THAT WHAT YOU TRIED TO SAY...?
YOU'LL HAVE YOUR CHANCE SOON ENOUGH, MURMUR. I HELPED YOU OUT OF THAT HELLHOLE. GAVE YOU THE ANTHRAX TO COVER YOUR ESCAPE.
NOW YOU OWE IT TO ME... TO US--

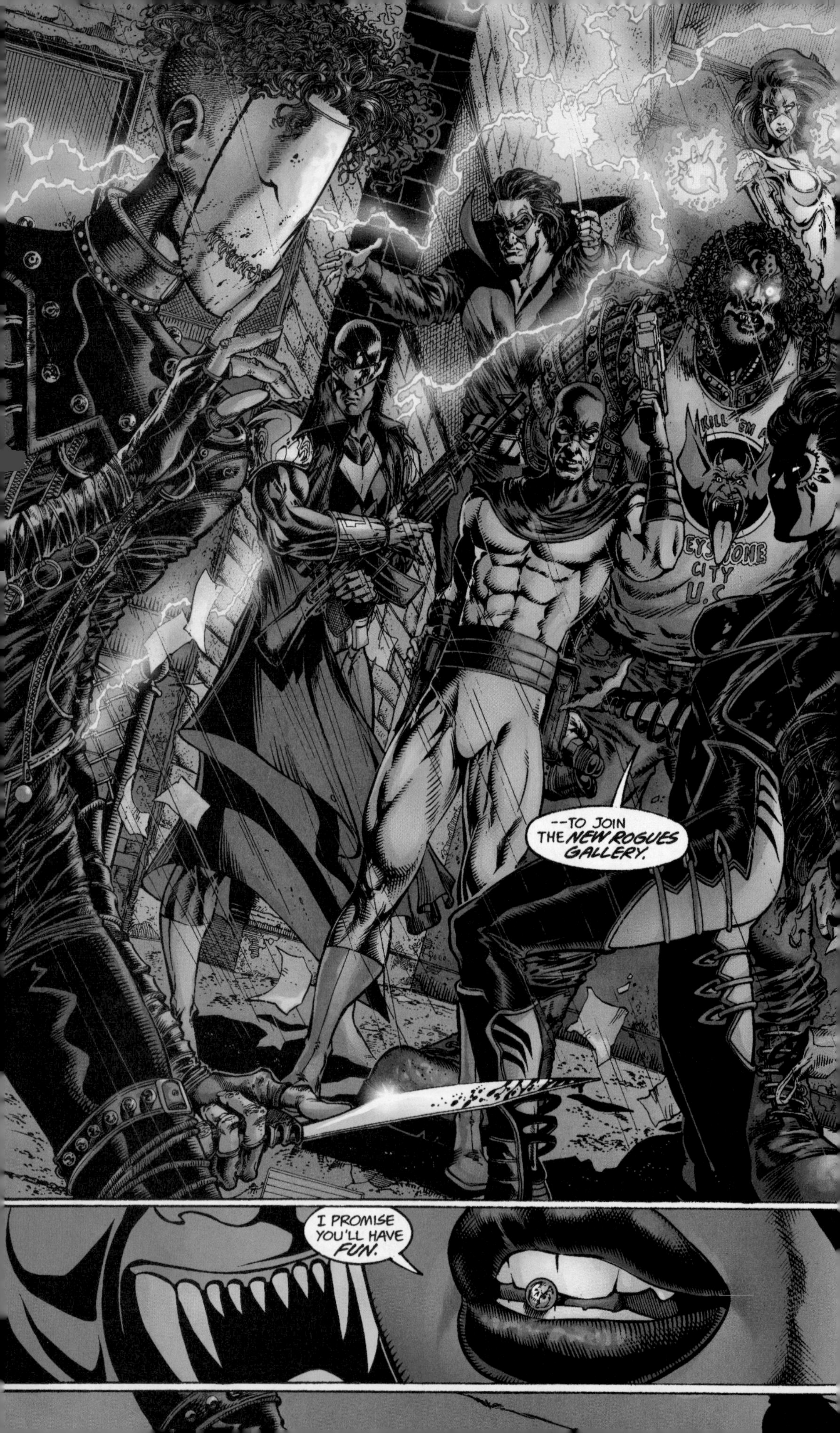
--TO JOIN THE *NEW ROGUES GALLERY.*
I PROMISE YOU'LL HAVE *FUN.*

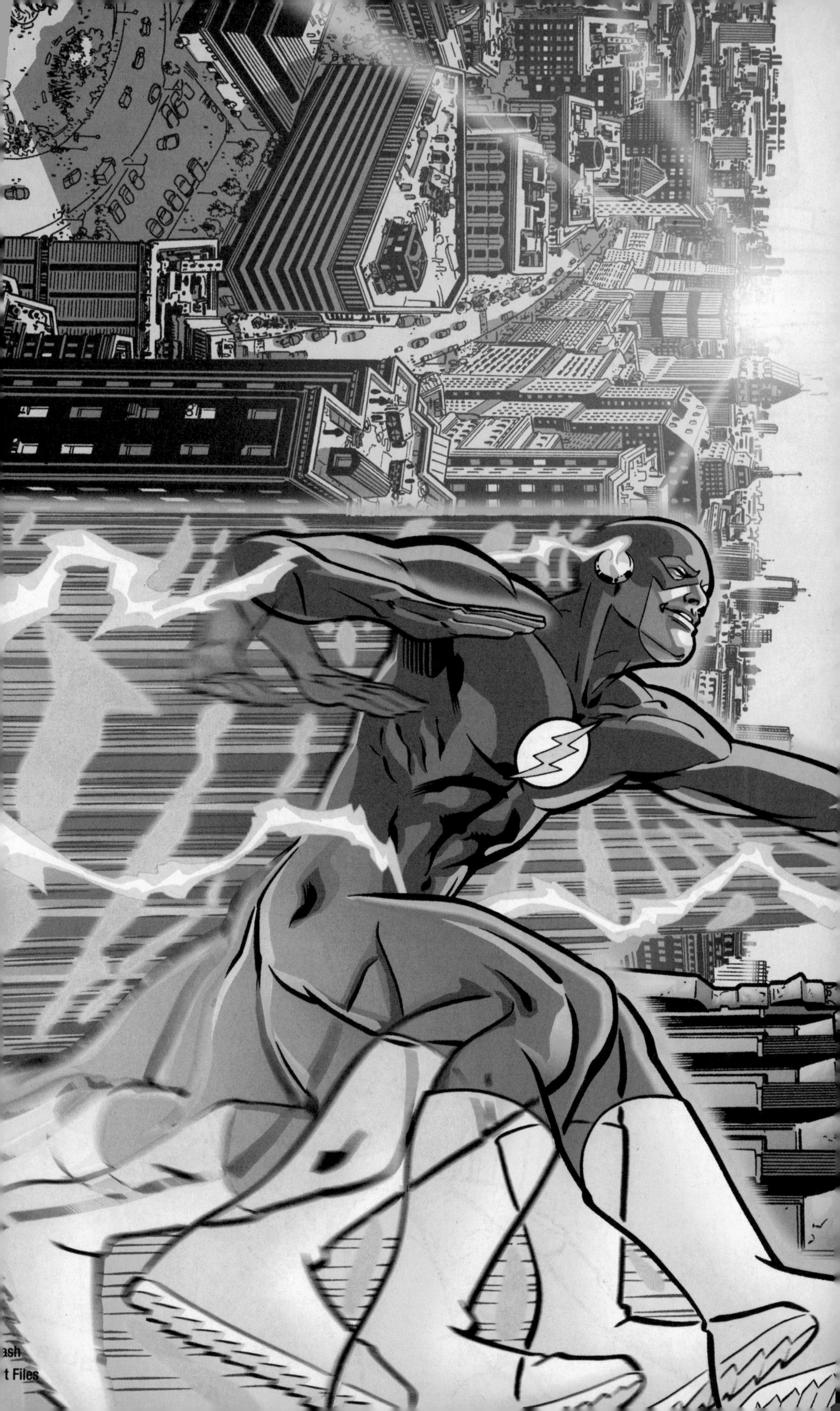

ash
t Files

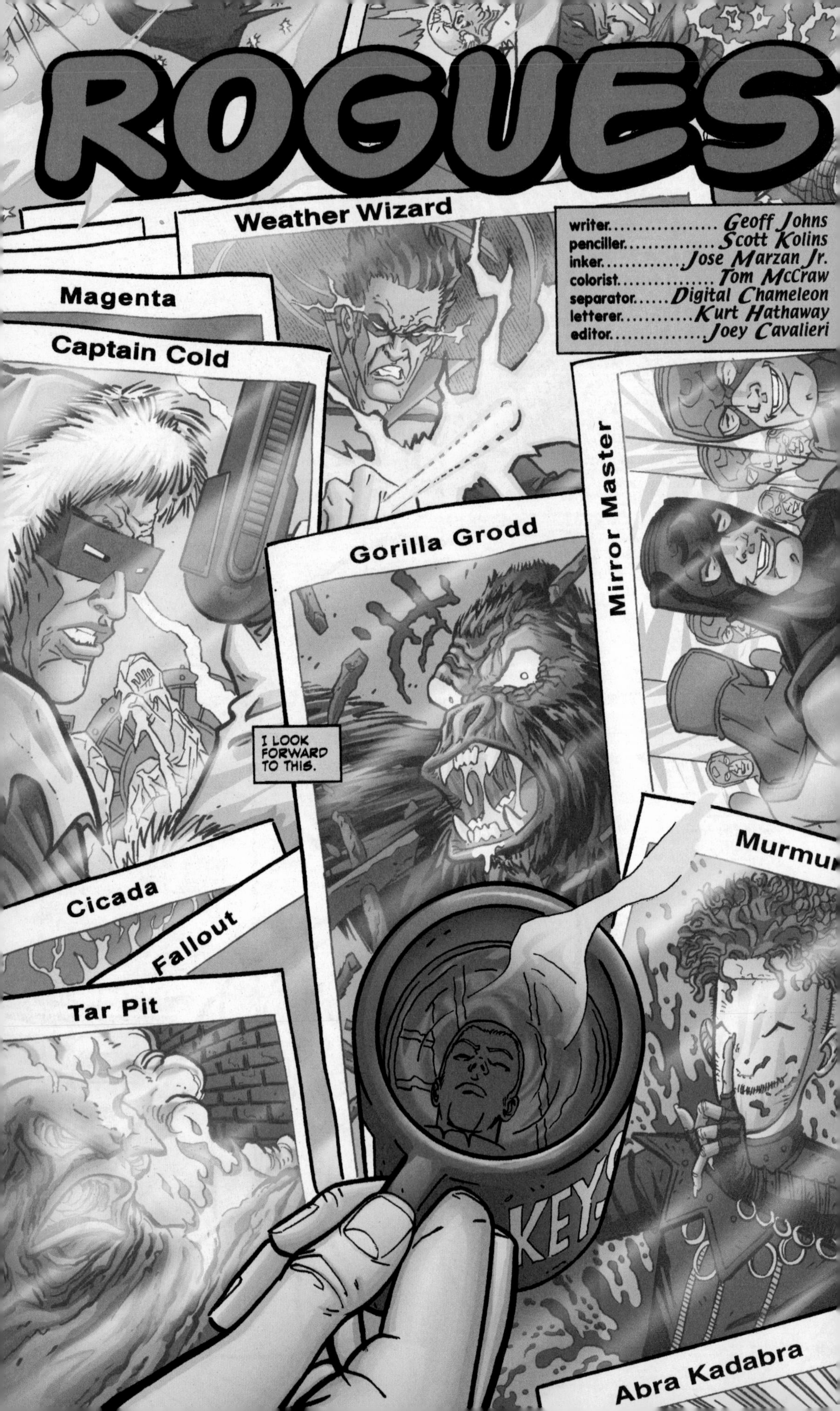

ROGUES
writer................Geoff Johns
penciller...............Scott Kolins
inker............Jose Marzan Jr.
colorist..............Tom McCraw
separator.....Digital Chameleon
letterer...........Kurt Hathaway
editor..............Joey Cavalieri
Weather Wizard
Magenta
Captain Cold
Mirror Master
Gorilla Grodd
I LOOK FORWARD TO THIS.
Cicada
Fallout
Tar Pit
Abra Kadabra

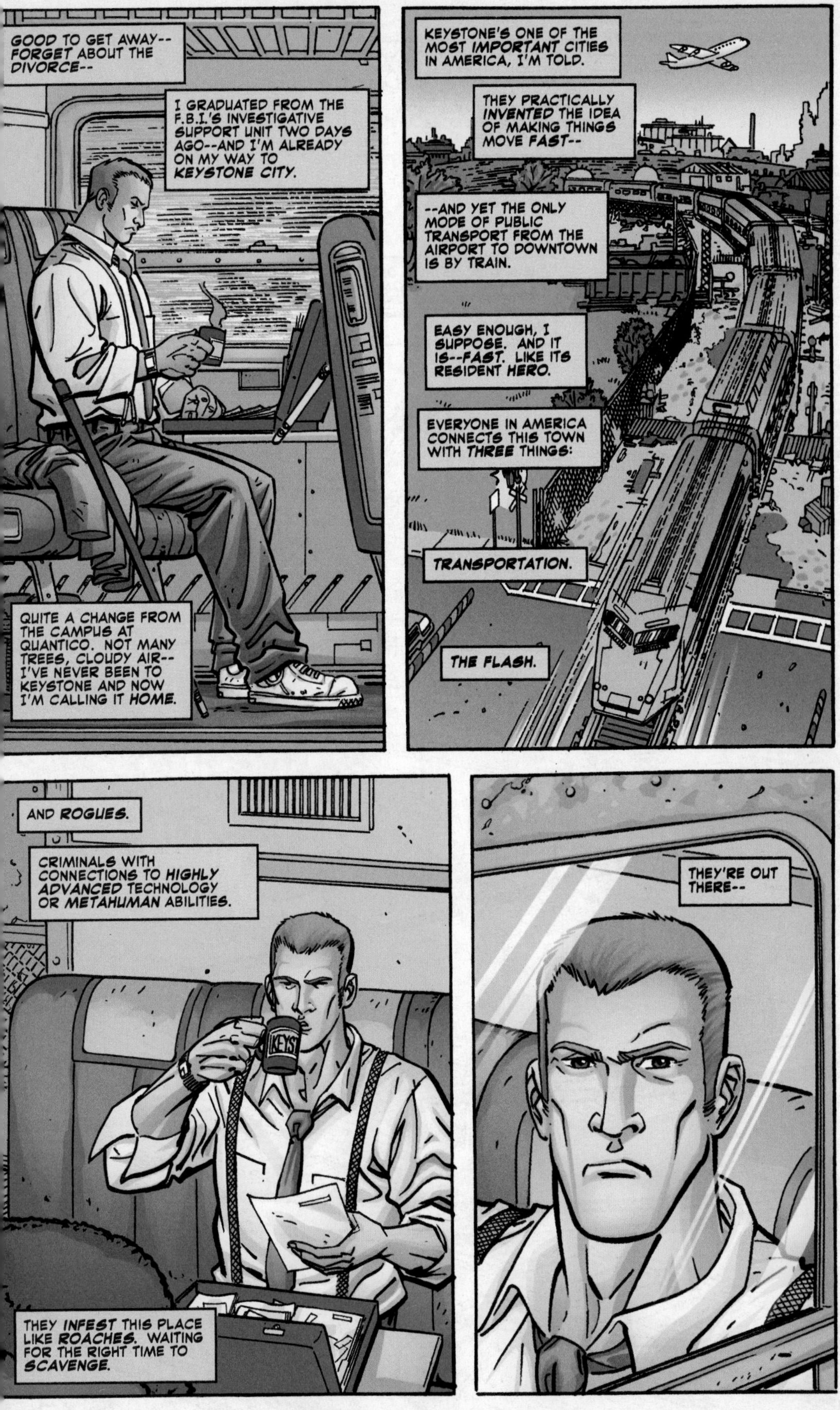
GOOD TO GET AWAY-- FORGET ABOUT THE DIVORCE--
I GRADUATED FROM THE F.B.I.'S INVESTIGATIVE SUPPORT UNIT TWO DAYS AGO--AND I'M ALREADY ON MY WAY TO KEYSTONE CITY.
QUITE A CHANGE FROM THE CAMPUS AT QUANTICO. NOT MANY TREES, CLOUDY AIR-- I'VE NEVER BEEN TO KEYSTONE AND NOW I'M CALLING IT HOME.
KEYSTONE'S ONE OF THE MOST IMPORTANT CITIES IN AMERICA, I'M TOLD.
THEY PRACTICALLY INVENTED THE IDEA OF MAKING THINGS MOVE FAST--
--AND YET THE ONLY MODE OF PUBLIC TRANSPORT FROM THE AIRPORT TO DOWNTOWN IS BY TRAIN.
EASY ENOUGH, I SUPPOSE. AND IT IS--FAST. LIKE ITS RESIDENT HERO.
EVERYONE IN AMERICA CONNECTS THIS TOWN WITH THREE THINGS:
TRANSPORTATION.
THE FLASH.
AND ROGUES.
CRIMINALS WITH CONNECTIONS TO HIGHLY ADVANCED TECHNOLOGY OR METAHUMAN ABILITIES.
THEY INFEST THIS PLACE LIKE ROACHES. WAITING FOR THE RIGHT TIME TO SCAVENGE.
THEY'RE OUT THERE--

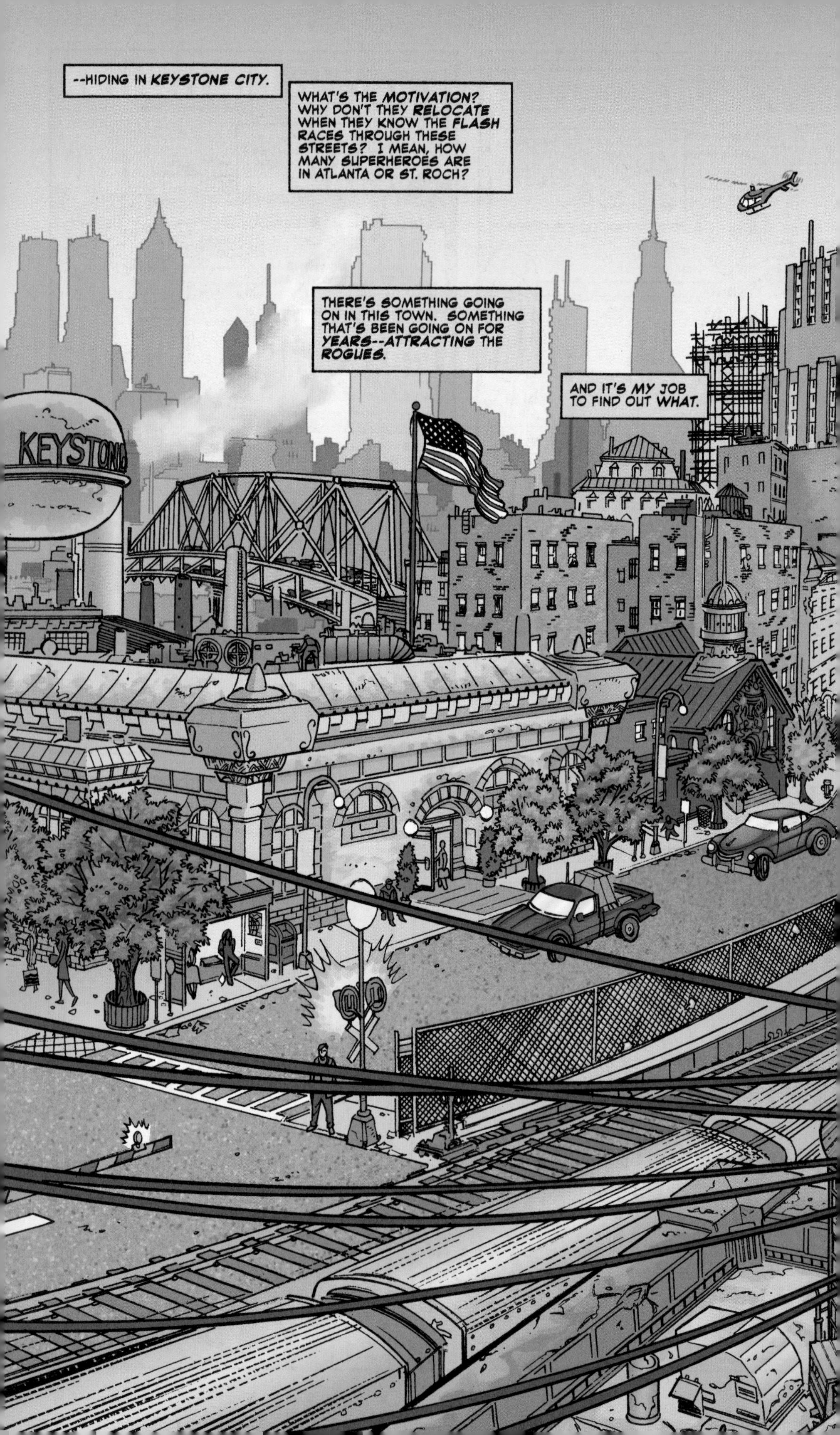
--HIDING IN KEYSTONE CITY.
WHAT'S THE MOTIVATION? WHY DON'T THEY RELOCATE WHEN THEY KNOW THE FLASH RACES THROUGH THESE STREETS? I MEAN, HOW MANY SUPERHEROES ARE IN ATLANTA OR ST. ROCH?
THERE'S SOMETHING GOING ON IN THIS TOWN. SOMETHING THAT'S BEEN GOING ON FOR YEARS--ATTRACTING THE ROGUES.
AND IT'S MY JOB TO FIND OUT WHAT.

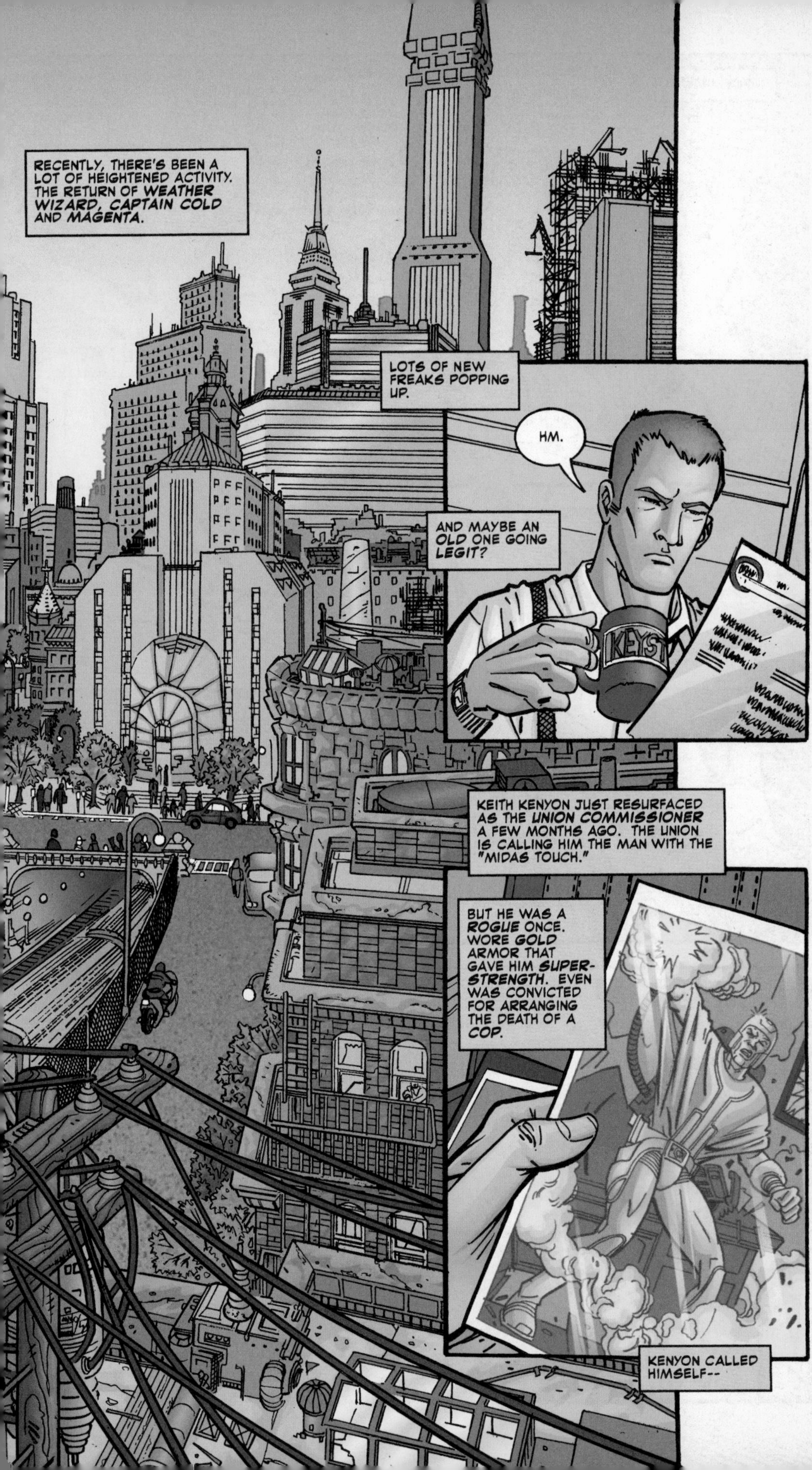
RECENTLY, THERE'S BEEN A LOT OF HEIGHTENED ACTIVITY. THE RETURN OF WEATHER WIZARD, CAPTAIN COLD AND MAGENTA.
LOTS OF NEW FREAKS POPPING UP.
HM.
AND MAYBE AN OLD ONE GOING LEGIT?
KEYST
KEITH KENYON JUST RESURFACED AS THE UNION COMMISSIONER A FEW MONTHS AGO. THE UNION IS CALLING HIM THE MAN WITH THE "MIDAS TOUCH."
BUT HE WAS A ROGUE ONCE. WORE GOLD ARMOR THAT GAVE HIM SUPER-STRENGTH. EVEN WAS CONVICTED FOR ARRANGING THE DEATH OF A COP.
KENYON CALLED HIMSELF--

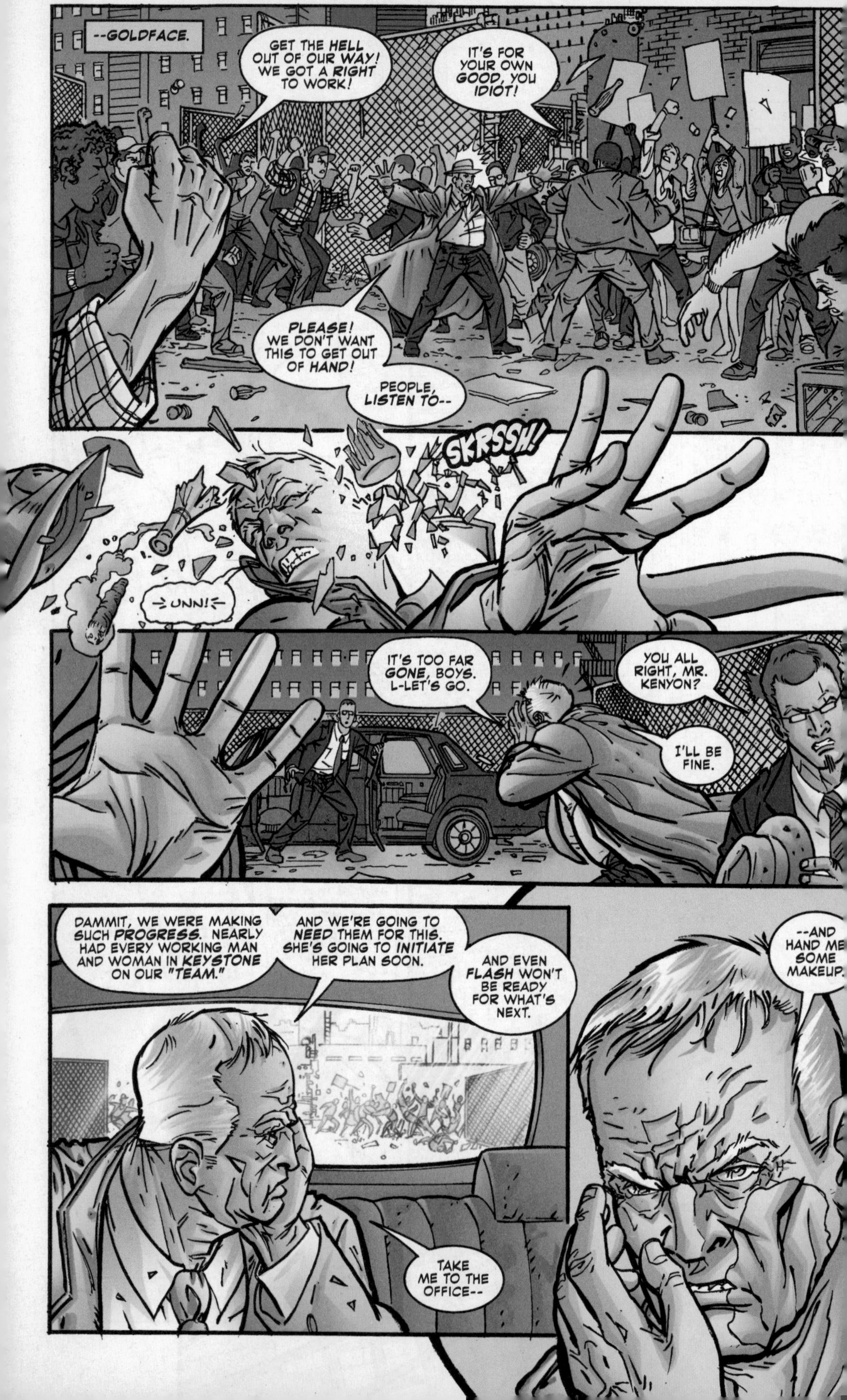
--GOLDFACE.
GET THE HELL OUT OF OUR WAY! WE GOT A RIGHT TO WORK!
IT'S FOR YOUR OWN GOOD, YOU IDIOT!
PLEASE! WE DON'T WANT THIS TO GET OUT OF HAND!
PEOPLE, LISTEN TO--
SKRSSH!
UNN!
IT'S TOO FAR GONE, BOYS. L-LET'S GO.
YOU ALL RIGHT, MR. KENYON?
I'LL BE FINE.
DAMMIT, WE WERE MAKING SUCH PROGRESS. NEARLY HAD EVERY WORKING MAN AND WOMAN IN KEYSTONE ON OUR "TEAM."
AND WE'RE GOING TO NEED THEM FOR THIS. SHE'S GOING TO INITIATE HER PLAN SOON.
AND EVEN FLASH WON'T BE READY FOR WHAT'S NEXT.
TAKE ME TO THE OFFICE--
--AND HAND ME SOME MAKEUP.

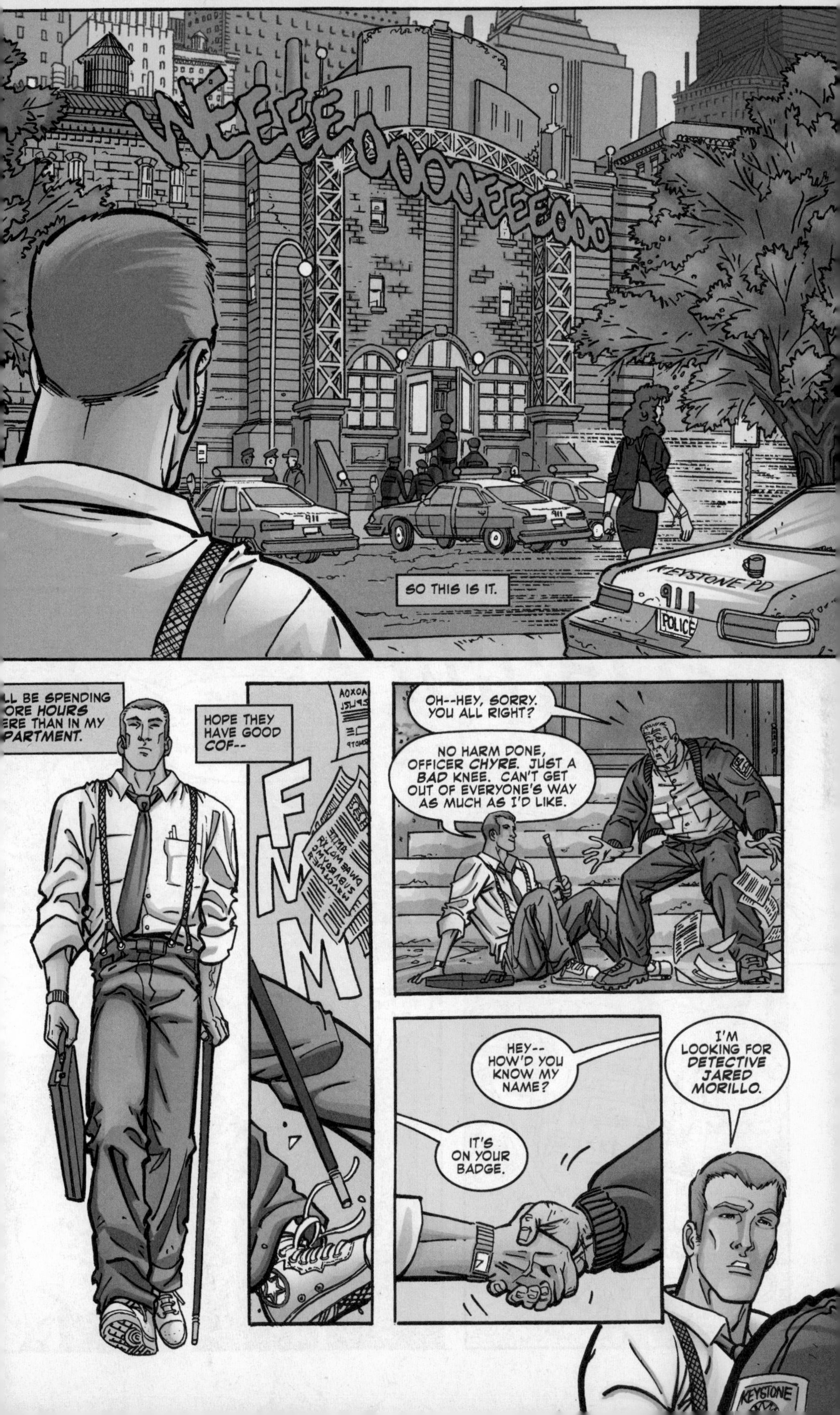
WEEEOOOOEEEOoo
SO THIS IS IT.
KEYSTONE PD
911
POLICE
LL BE SPENDING
ORE HOURS
ERE THAN IN MY
PARTMENT.
HOPE THEY
HAVE GOOD
COF--
FMMM
OH--HEY, SORRY.
YOU ALL RIGHT?
NO HARM DONE,
OFFICER CHYRE. JUST A
BAD KNEE. CAN'T GET
OUT OF EVERYONE'S WAY
AS MUCH AS I'D LIKE.
HEY--
HOW'D YOU
KNOW MY
NAME?
IT'S
ON YOUR
BADGE.
I'M
LOOKING FOR
DETECTIVE
JARED
MORILLO.
KEYSTONE

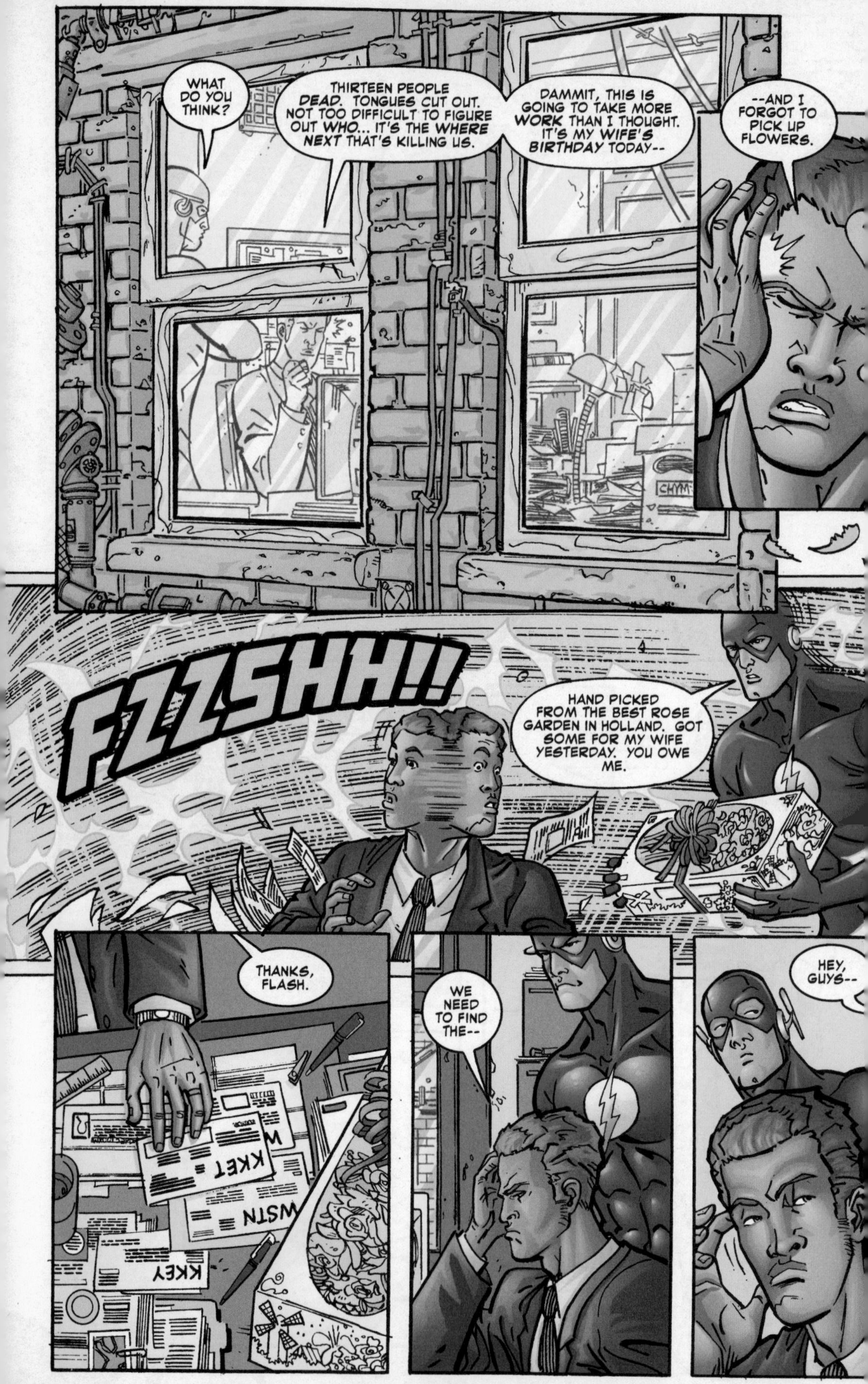

WHAT DO YOU THINK?
THIRTEEN PEOPLE DEAD. TONGUES CUT OUT. NOT TOO DIFFICULT TO FIGURE OUT WHO... IT'S THE WHERE NEXT THAT'S KILLING US.
DAMMIT, THIS IS GOING TO TAKE MORE WORK THAN I THOUGHT. IT'S MY WIFE'S BIRTHDAY TODAY--
--AND I FORGOT TO PICK UP FLOWERS.
FZZSHH!!
HAND PICKED FROM THE BEST ROSE GARDEN IN HOLLAND. GOT SOME FOR MY WIFE YESTERDAY. YOU OWE ME.
THANKS, FLASH.
KKET
WSTN
KKEY
WE NEED TO FIND THE--
HEY, GUYS--

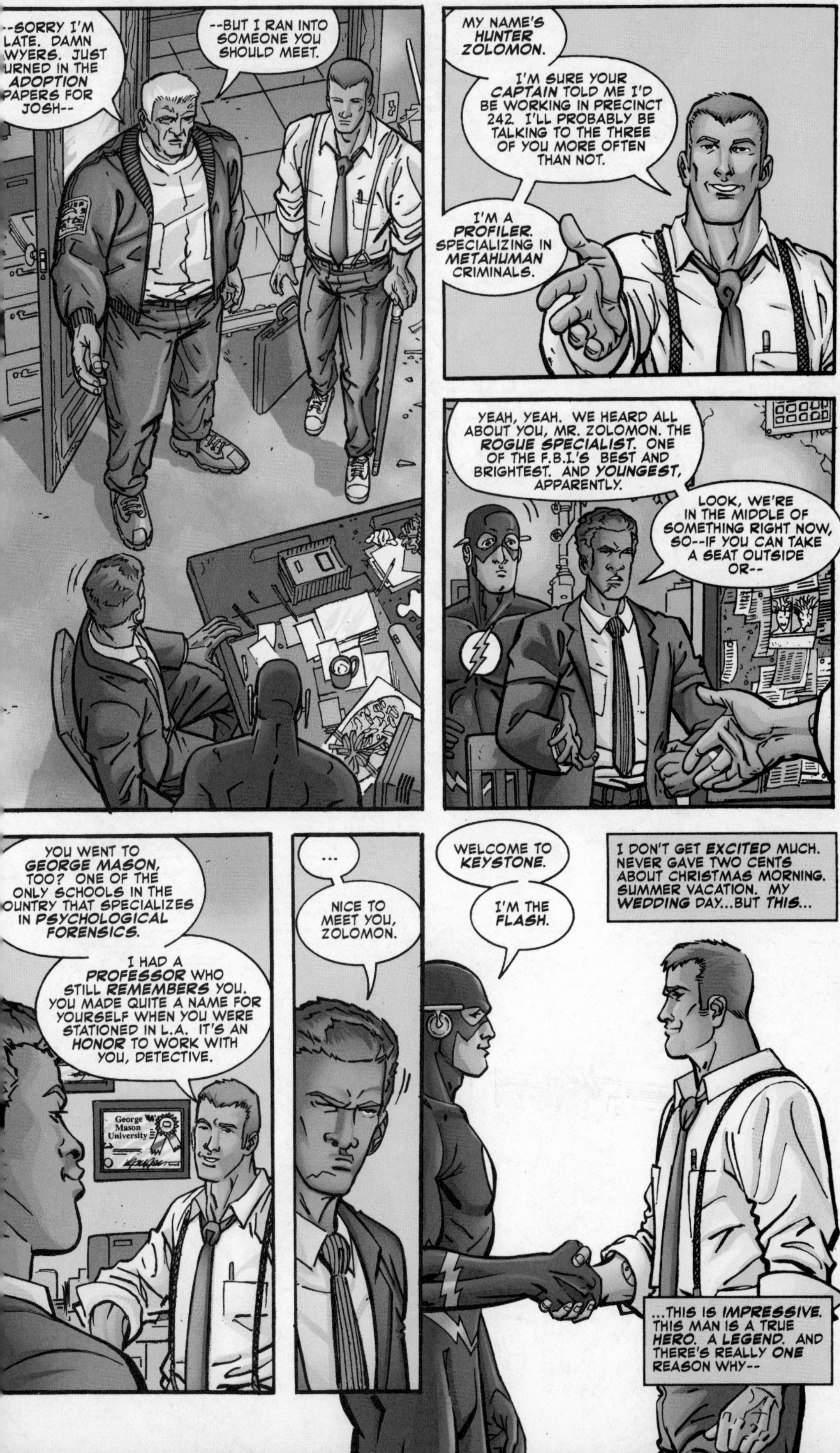
--SORRY I'M LATE. DAMN WYERS. JUST URNED IN THE ADOPTION PAPERS FOR JOSH--
--BUT I RAN INTO SOMEONE YOU SHOULD MEET.
MY NAME'S HUNTER ZOLOMON.
I'M SURE YOUR CAPTAIN TOLD ME I'D BE WORKING IN PRECINCT 242. I'LL PROBABLY BE TALKING TO THE THREE OF YOU MORE OFTEN THAN NOT.
I'M A PROFILER. SPECIALIZING IN METAHUMAN CRIMINALS.
YEAH, YEAH. WE HEARD ALL ABOUT YOU, MR. ZOLOMON. THE ROGUE SPECIALIST. ONE OF THE F.B.I.'S BEST AND BRIGHTEST. AND YOUNGEST, APPARENTLY.
LOOK, WE'RE IN THE MIDDLE OF SOMETHING RIGHT NOW, SO--IF YOU CAN TAKE A SEAT OUTSIDE OR--
YOU WENT TO GEORGE MASON, TOO? ONE OF THE ONLY SCHOOLS IN THE OUNTRY THAT SPECIALIZES IN PSYCHOLOGICAL FORENSICS.
I HAD A PROFESSOR WHO STILL REMEMBERS YOU. YOU MADE QUITE A NAME FOR YOURSELF WHEN YOU WERE STATIONED IN L.A. IT'S AN HONOR TO WORK WITH YOU, DETECTIVE.
George Mason University
...
NICE TO MEET YOU, ZOLOMON.
WELCOME TO KEYSTONE.
I'M THE FLASH.
I DON'T GET EXCITED MUCH. NEVER GAVE TWO CENTS ABOUT CHRISTMAS MORNING. SUMMER VACATION. MY WEDDING DAY...BUT THIS...
...THIS IS IMPRESSIVE. THIS MAN IS A TRUE HERO. A LEGEND. AND THERE'S REALLY ONE REASON WHY--

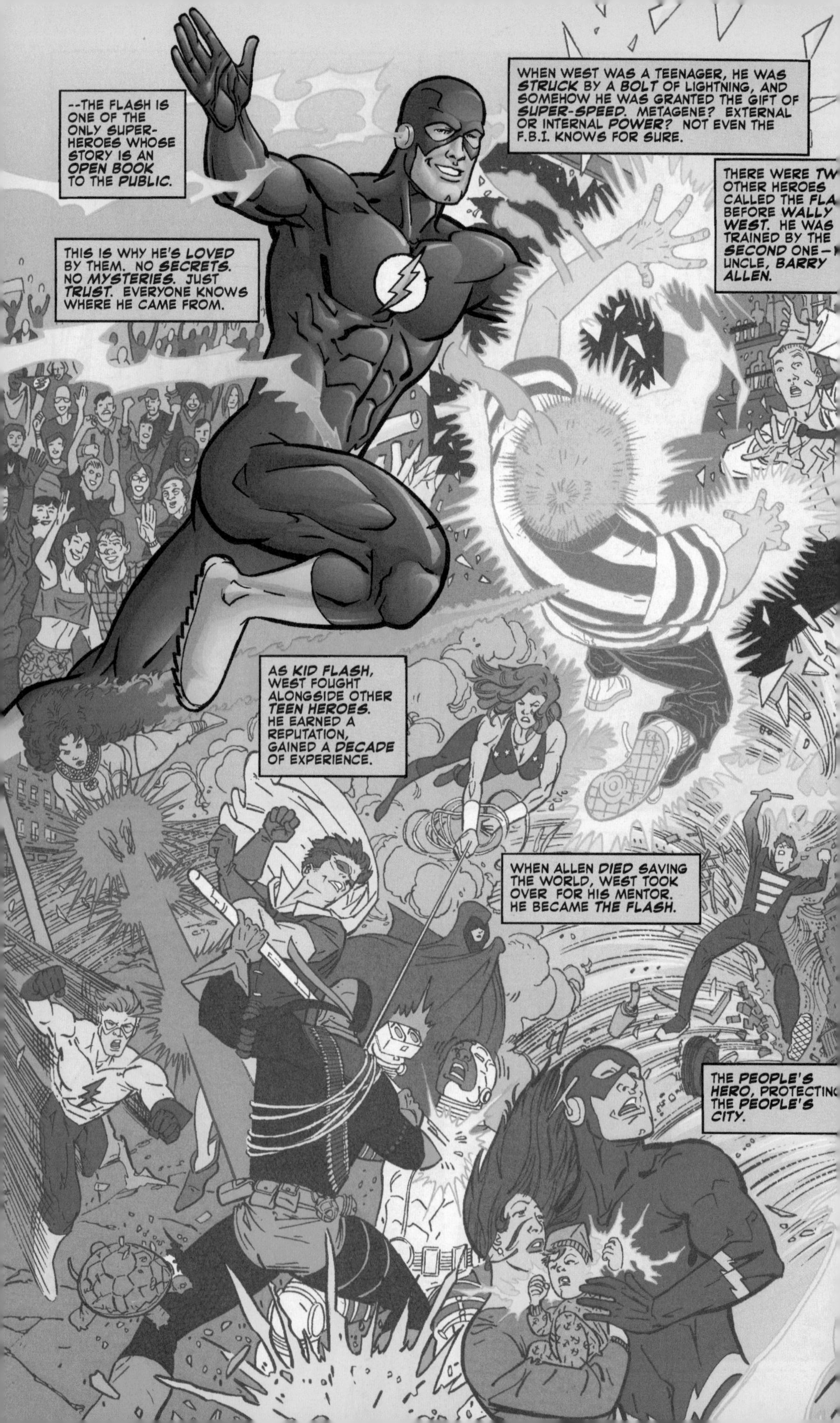
--THE FLASH IS ONE OF THE ONLY SUPER-HEROES WHOSE STORY IS AN OPEN BOOK TO THE PUBLIC.
WHEN WEST WAS A TEENAGER, HE WAS STRUCK BY A BOLT OF LIGHTNING, AND SOMEHOW HE WAS GRANTED THE GIFT OF SUPER-SPEED. METAGENE? EXTERNAL OR INTERNAL POWER? NOT EVEN THE F.B.I. KNOWS FOR SURE.
THIS IS WHY HE'S LOVED BY THEM. NO SECRETS. NO MYSTERIES. JUST TRUST. EVERYONE KNOWS WHERE HE CAME FROM.
THERE WERE TW OTHER HEROES CALLED THE FLA BEFORE WALLY WEST. HE WAS TRAINED BY THE SECOND ONE-- UNCLE, BARRY ALLEN.
AS KID FLASH, WEST FOUGHT ALONGSIDE OTHER TEEN HEROES. HE EARNED A REPUTATION, GAINED A DECADE OF EXPERIENCE.
WHEN ALLEN DIED SAVING THE WORLD, WEST TOOK OVER FOR HIS MENTOR. HE BECAME THE FLASH.
THE PEOPLE'S HERO, PROTECTING THE PEOPLE'S CITY.

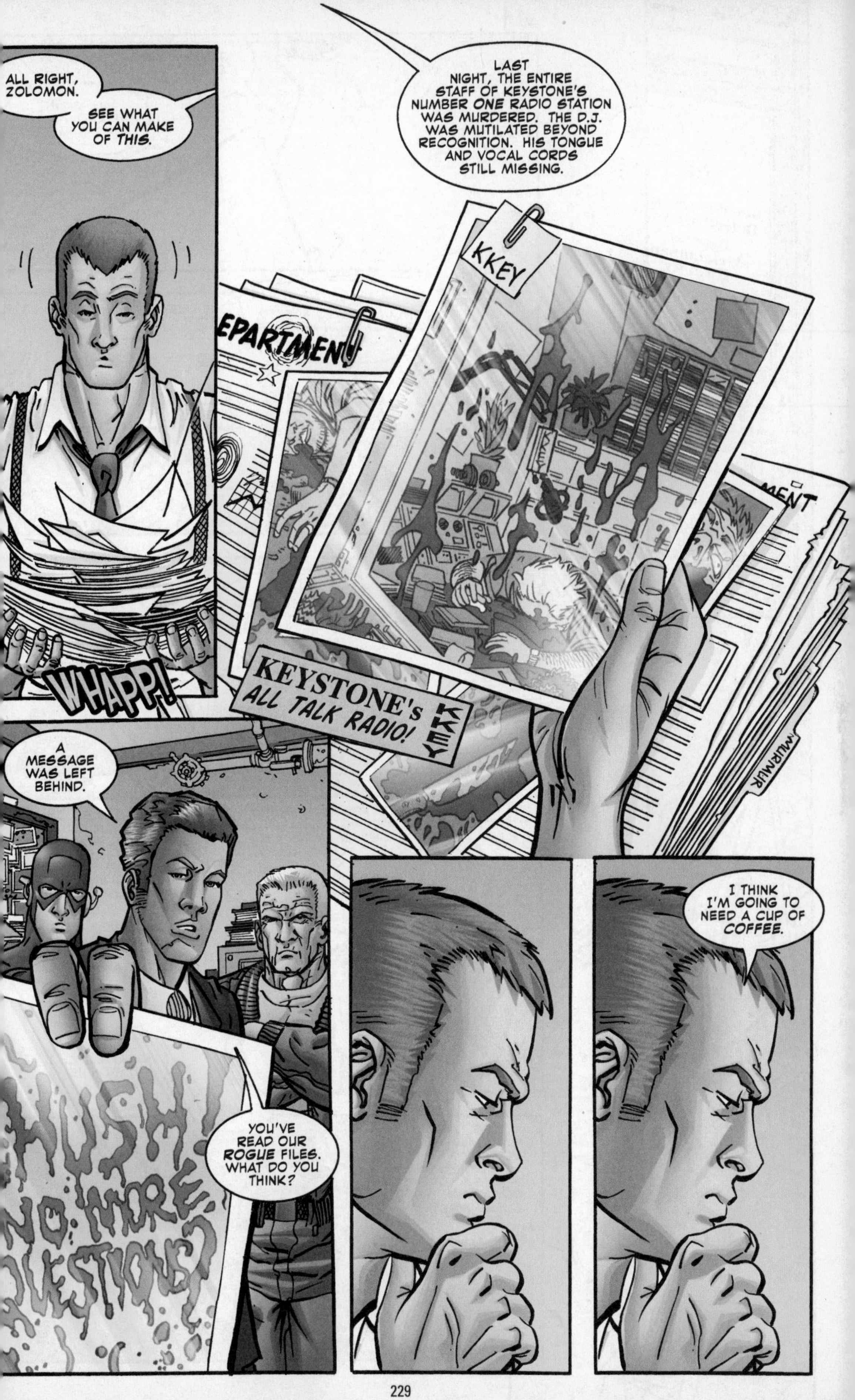

ALL RIGHT, ZOLOMON.
SEE WHAT YOU CAN MAKE OF THIS.
WHAPP!
LAST NIGHT, THE ENTIRE STAFF OF KEYSTONE'S NUMBER ONE RADIO STATION WAS MURDERED. THE D.J. WAS MUTILATED BEYOND RECOGNITION. HIS TONGUE AND VOCAL CORDS STILL MISSING.
KKEY
DEPARTMEN
KEYSTONE's ALL TALK RADIO! KKEY
MURMUR
A MESSAGE WAS LEFT BEHIND.
HUSH! NO MORE QUESTIONS?
YOU'VE READ OUR ROGUE FILES. WHAT DO YOU THINK?
I THINK I'M GOING TO NEED A CUP OF COFFEE.

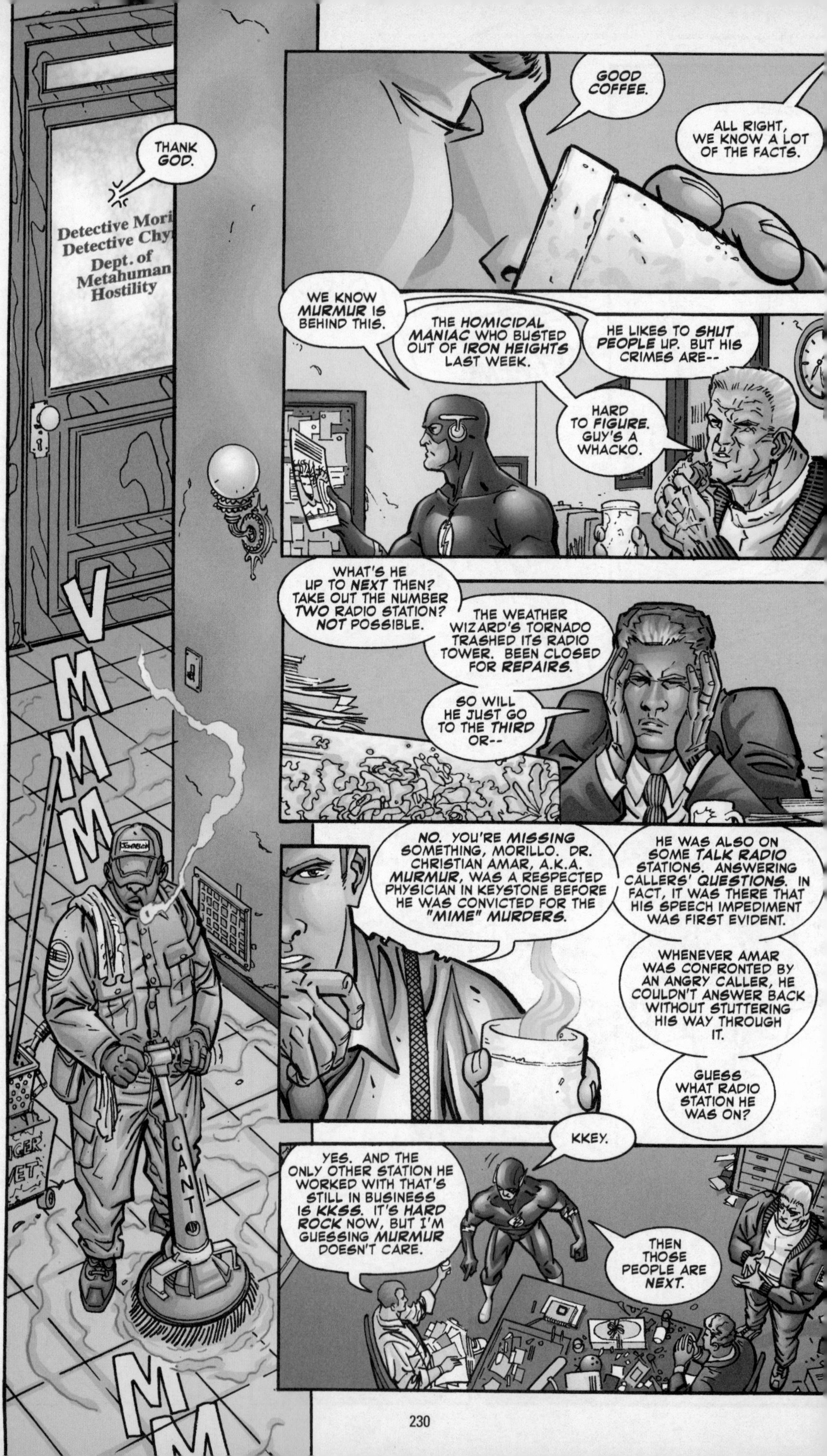
THANK GOD.
Detective Mori
Detective Chy
Dept. of Metahuman Hostility
VMMMM
GOOD COFFEE.
ALL RIGHT, WE KNOW A LOT OF THE FACTS.
WE KNOW MURMUR IS BEHIND THIS.
THE HOMICIDAL MANIAC WHO BUSTED OUT OF IRON HEIGHTS LAST WEEK.
HE LIKES TO SHUT PEOPLE UP. BUT HIS CRIMES ARE--
HARD TO FIGURE. GUY'S A WHACKO.
WHAT'S HE UP TO NEXT THEN? TAKE OUT THE NUMBER TWO RADIO STATION? NOT POSSIBLE.
THE WEATHER WIZARD'S TORNADO TRASHED ITS RADIO TOWER. BEEN CLOSED FOR REPAIRS.
SO WILL HE JUST GO TO THE THIRD OR--
NO. YOU'RE MISSING SOMETHING, MORILLO. DR. CHRISTIAN AMAR, A.K.A. MURMUR, WAS A RESPECTED PHYSICIAN IN KEYSTONE BEFORE HE WAS CONVICTED FOR THE "MIME" MURDERS.
HE WAS ALSO ON SOME TALK RADIO STATIONS. ANSWERING CALLERS' QUESTIONS. IN FACT, IT WAS THERE THAT HIS SPEECH IMPEDIMENT WAS FIRST EVIDENT.
WHENEVER AMAR WAS CONFRONTED BY AN ANGRY CALLER, HE COULDN'T ANSWER BACK WITHOUT STUTTERING HIS WAY THROUGH IT.
GUESS WHAT RADIO STATION HE WAS ON?
KKEY.
YES. AND THE ONLY OTHER STATION HE WORKED WITH THAT'S STILL IN BUSINESS IS KKSS. IT'S HARD ROCK NOW, BUT I'M GUESSING MURMUR DOESN'T CARE.
THEN THOSE PEOPLE ARE NEXT.
GANT
MM

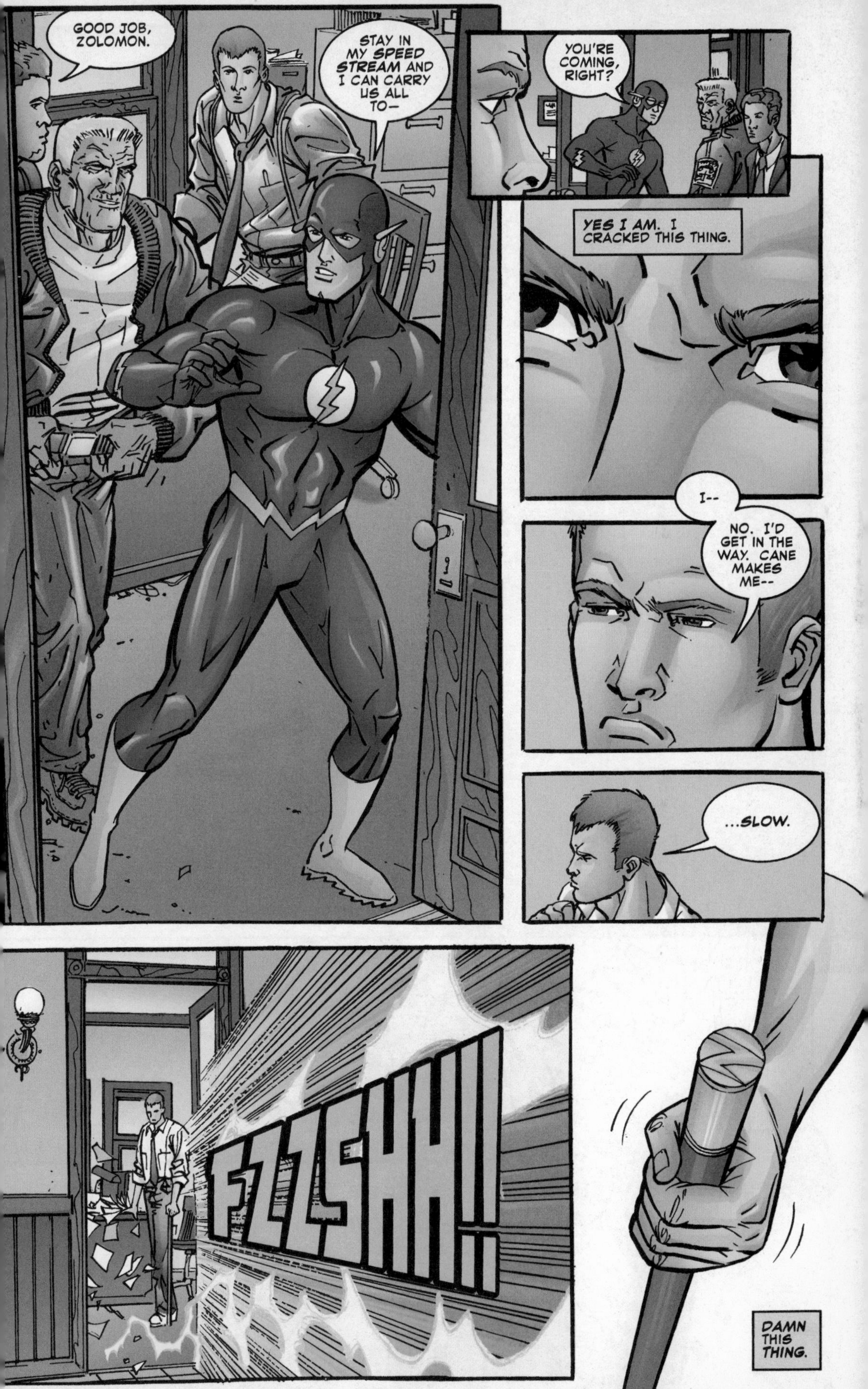
GOOD JOB, ZOLOMON.
STAY IN MY SPEED STREAM AND I CAN CARRY US ALL TO—
YOU'RE COMING, RIGHT?
YES I AM. I CRACKED THIS THING.
I--
NO. I'D GET IN THE WAY. CANE MAKES ME--
...SLOW.
FZZSHH!!
DAMN THIS THING.

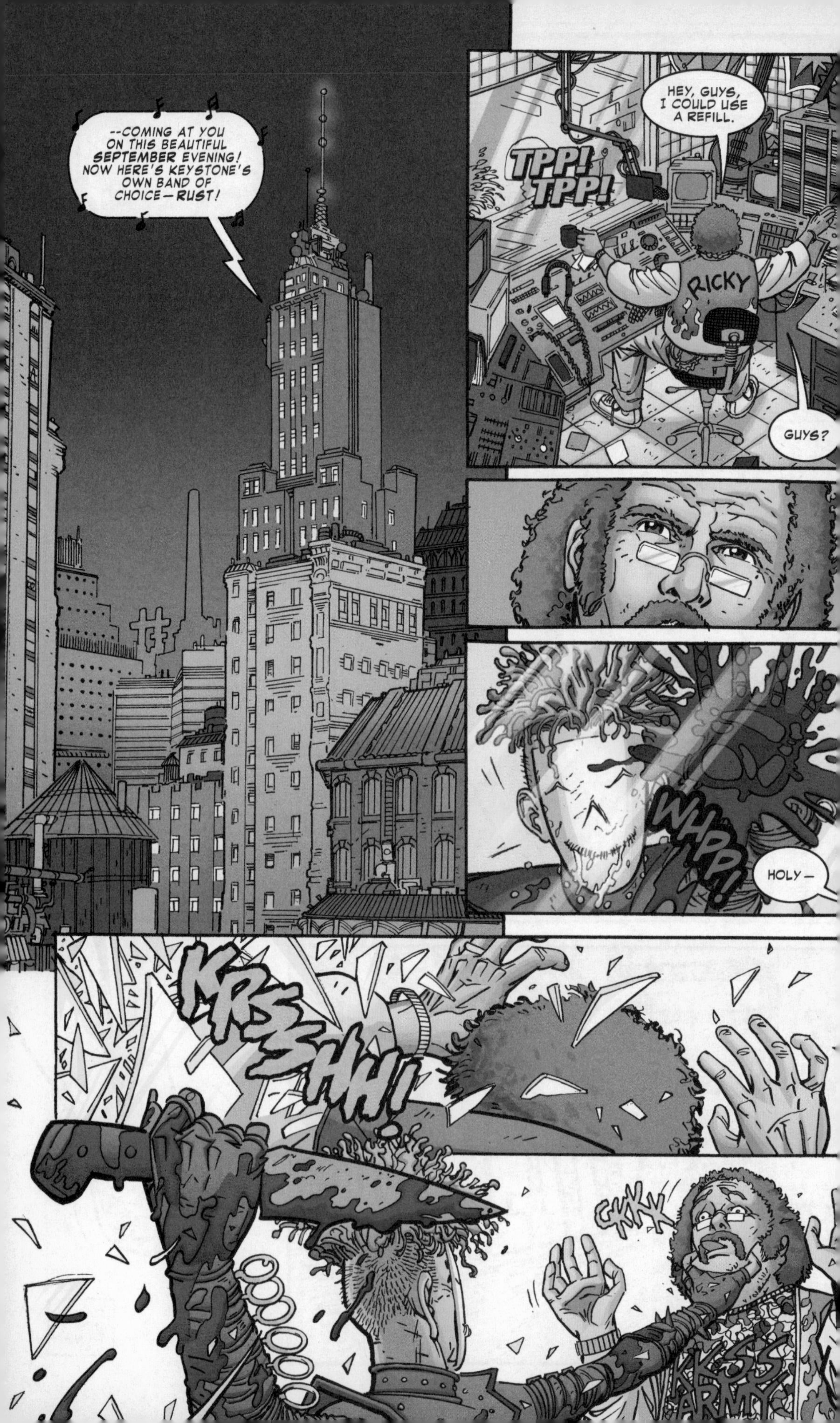
--COMING AT YOU ON THIS BEAUTIFUL SEPTEMBER EVENING! NOW HERE'S KEYSTONE'S OWN BAND OF CHOICE—RUST!
TPP! TPP!
HEY, GUYS, I COULD USE A REFILL.
RICKY
GUYS?
WHPP!
HOLY—
KRSHH!
GKK
KISS ARMY

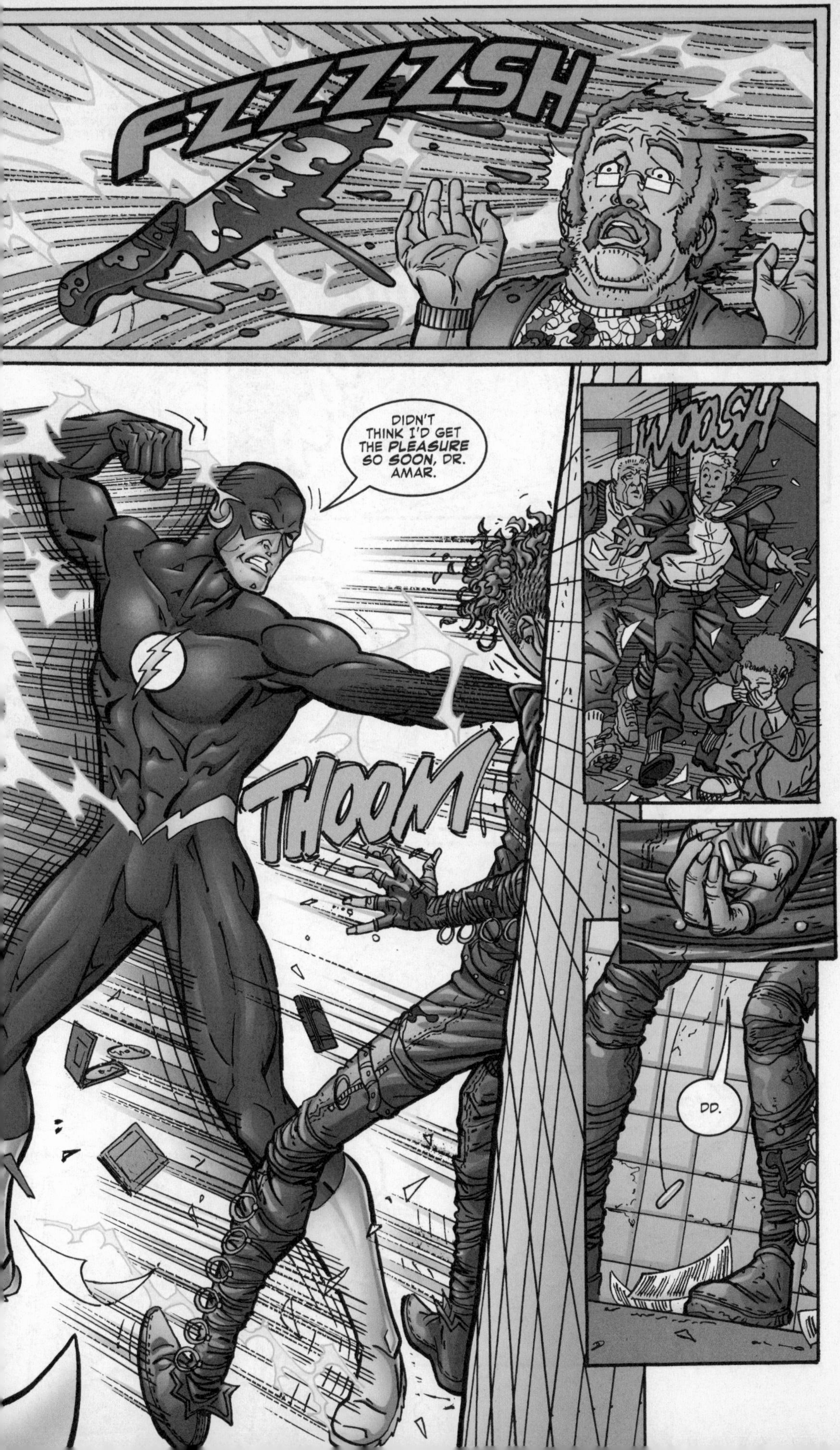
FZZZZSH
DIDN'T THINK I'D GET THE PLEASURE SO SOON, DR. AMAR.
WOOSH
THOOM
DD.

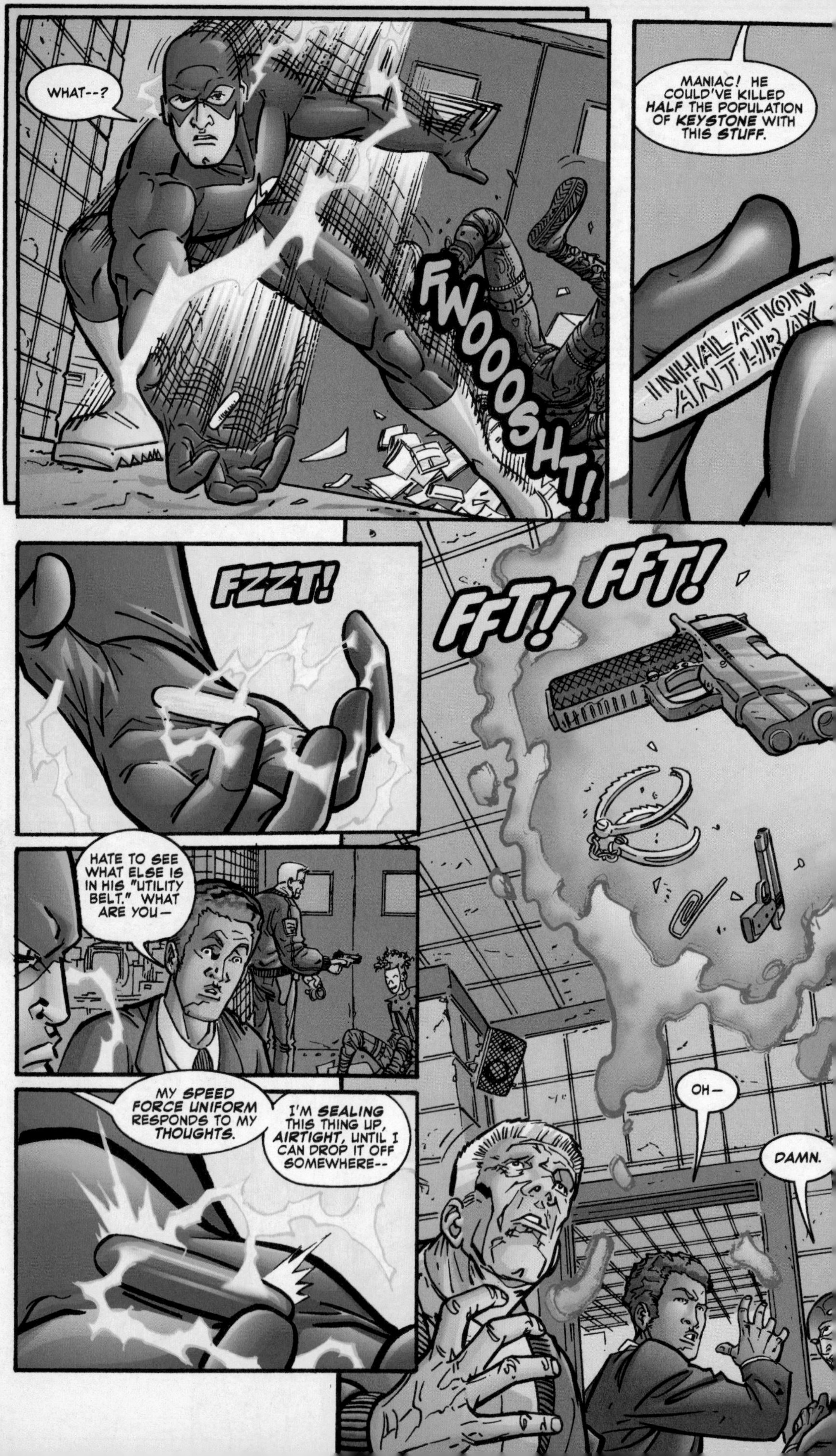
WHAT--?
FWOOOSHT!
MANIAC! HE COULD'VE KILLED HALF THE POPULATION OF KEYSTONE WITH THIS STUFF.
INHALATION ANTHRAX
FZZT!
HATE TO SEE WHAT ELSE IS IN HIS "UTILITY BELT." WHAT ARE YOU—
MY SPEED FORCE UNIFORM RESPONDS TO MY THOUGHTS.
I'M SEALING THIS THING UP, AIRTIGHT, UNTIL I CAN DROP IT OFF SOMEWHERE--
FFT! FFT!
OH—
DAMN.

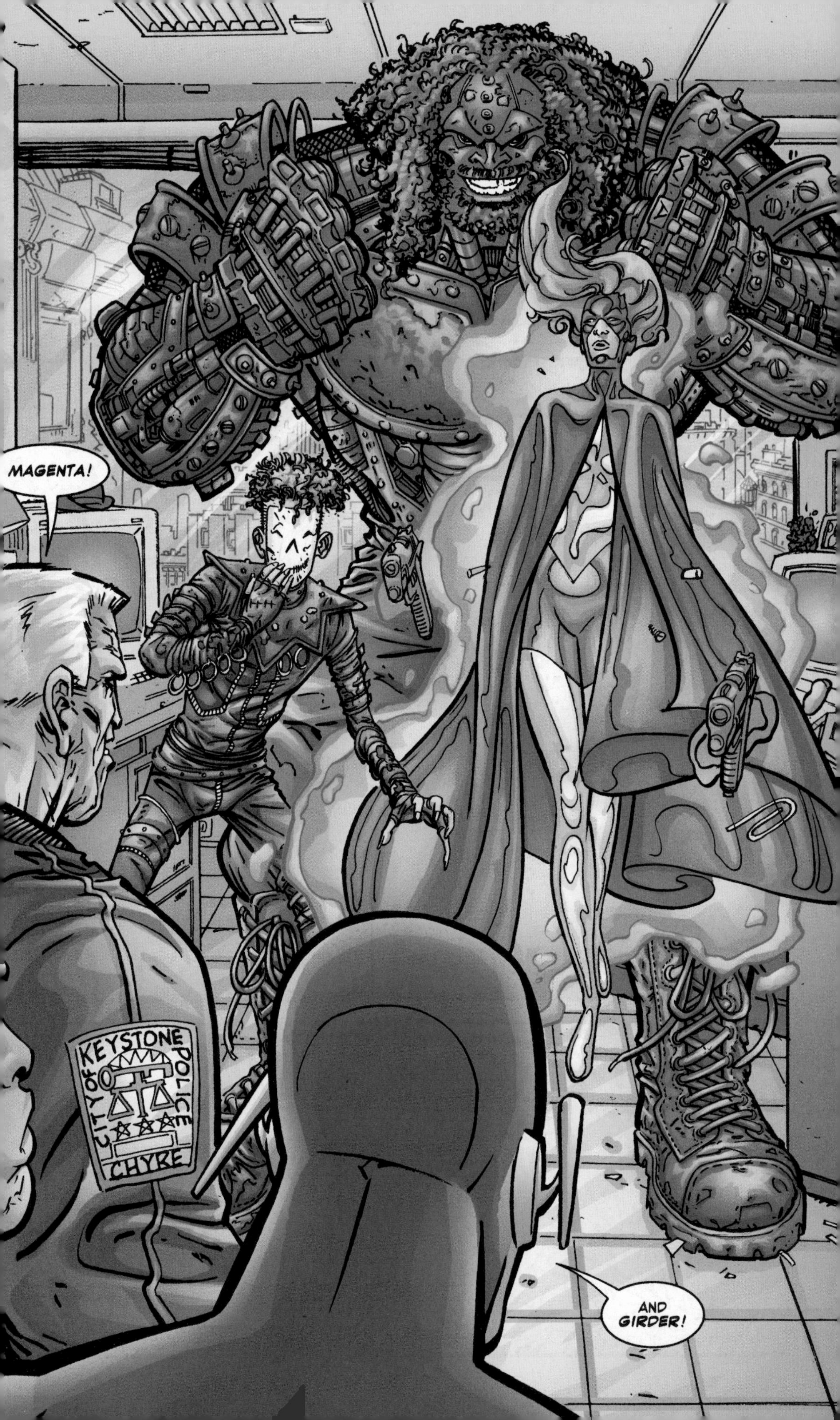
MAGENTA!
AND GIRDER!
KEYSTONE
CITY OF
POLICE
CHYRE

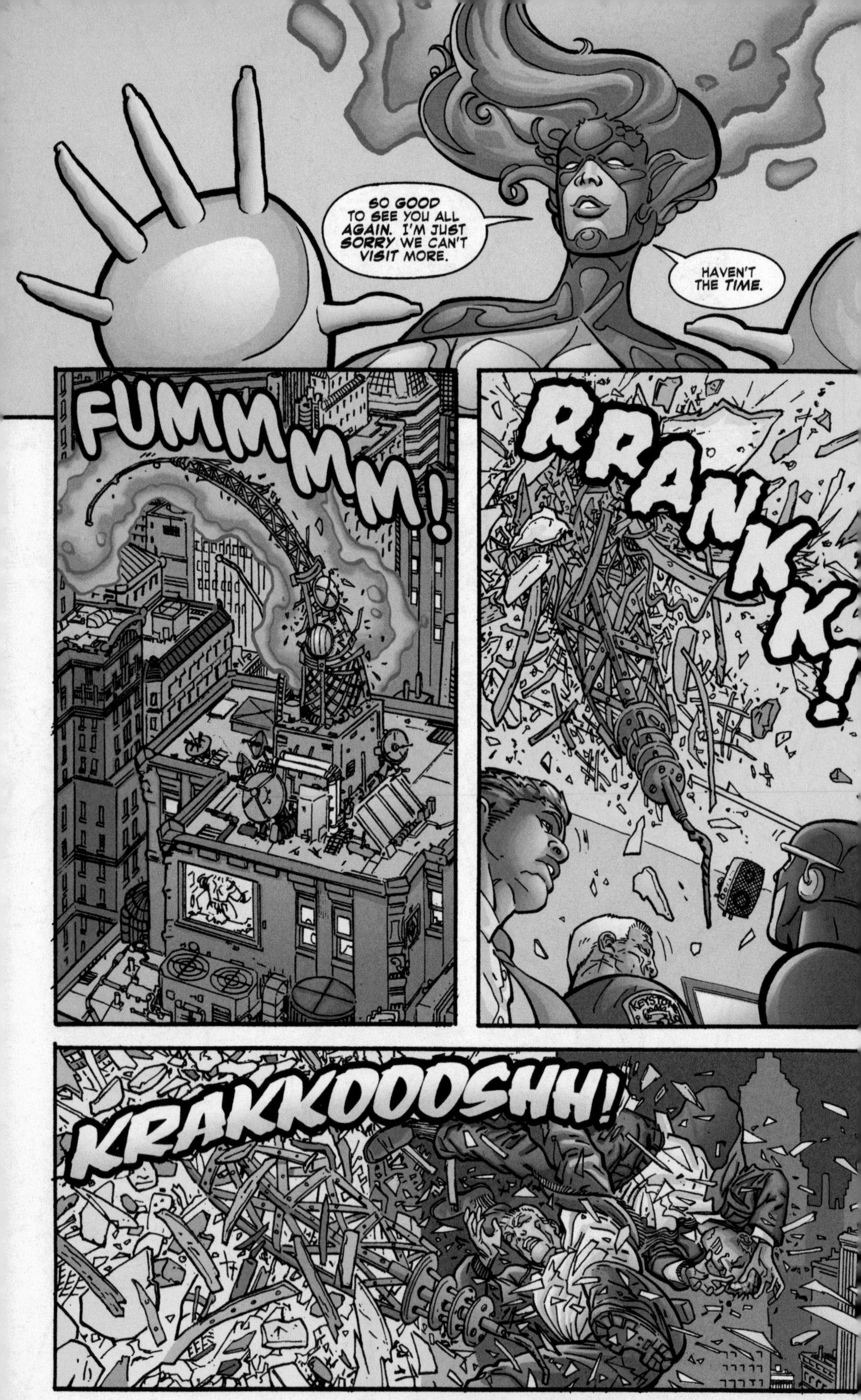
SO GOOD TO SEE YOU ALL AGAIN. I'M JUST SORRY WE CAN'T VISIT MORE.
HAVEN'T THE TIME.
FUMMMMM!
RRANKK!
KEYSTONE
KRAKKOOOSHH!

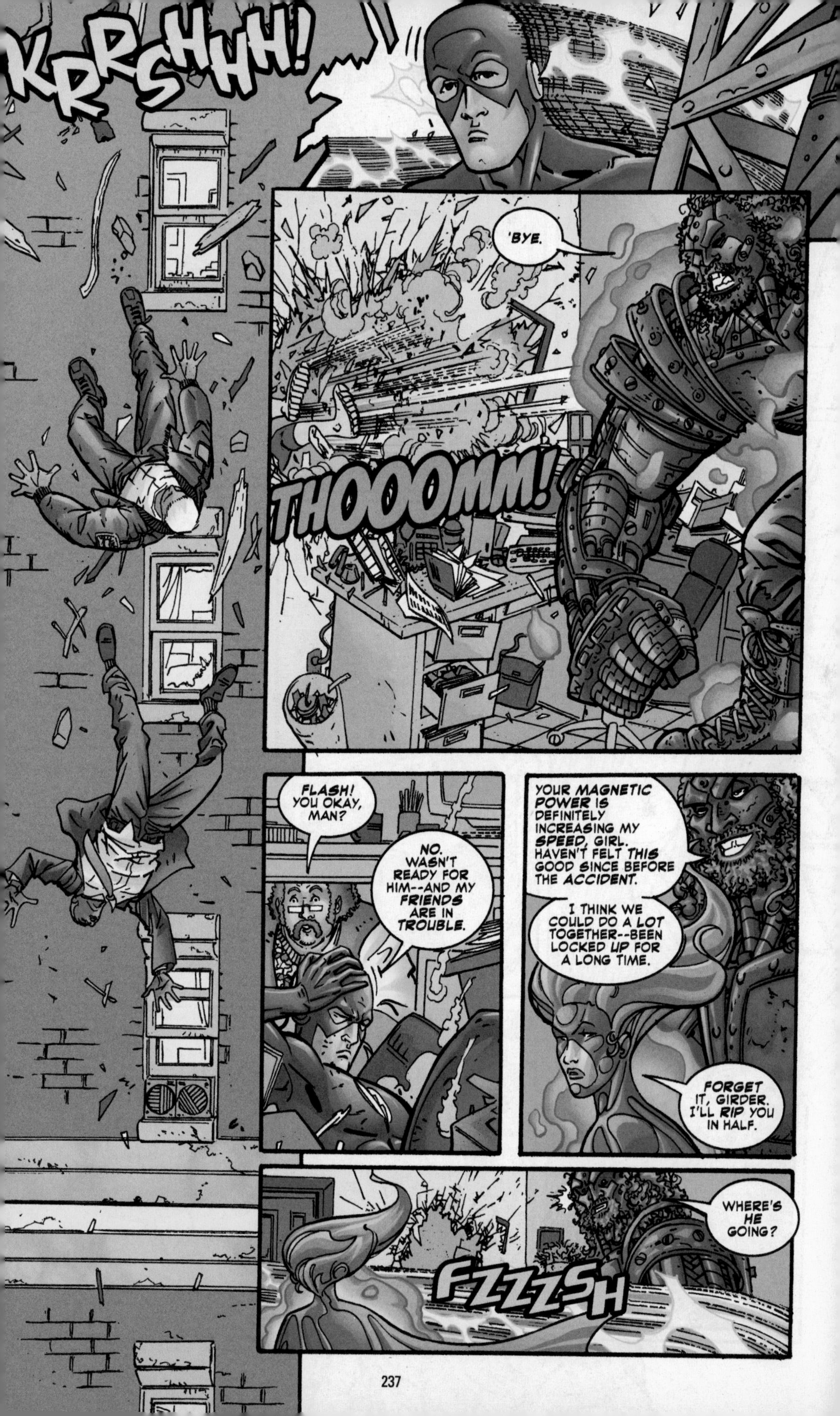
KRRSHHH!
'BYE.
THOOOMM!
FLASH! YOU OKAY, MAN?
NO. WASN'T READY FOR HIM--AND MY FRIENDS ARE IN TROUBLE.
YOUR MAGNETIC POWER IS DEFINITELY INCREASING MY SPEED, GIRL. HAVEN'T FELT THIS GOOD SINCE BEFORE THE ACCIDENT.
I THINK WE COULD DO A LOT TOGETHER--BEEN LOCKED UP FOR A LONG TIME.
FORGET IT, GIRDER. I'LL RIP YOU IN HALF.
WHERE'S HE GOING?
FZZZSH

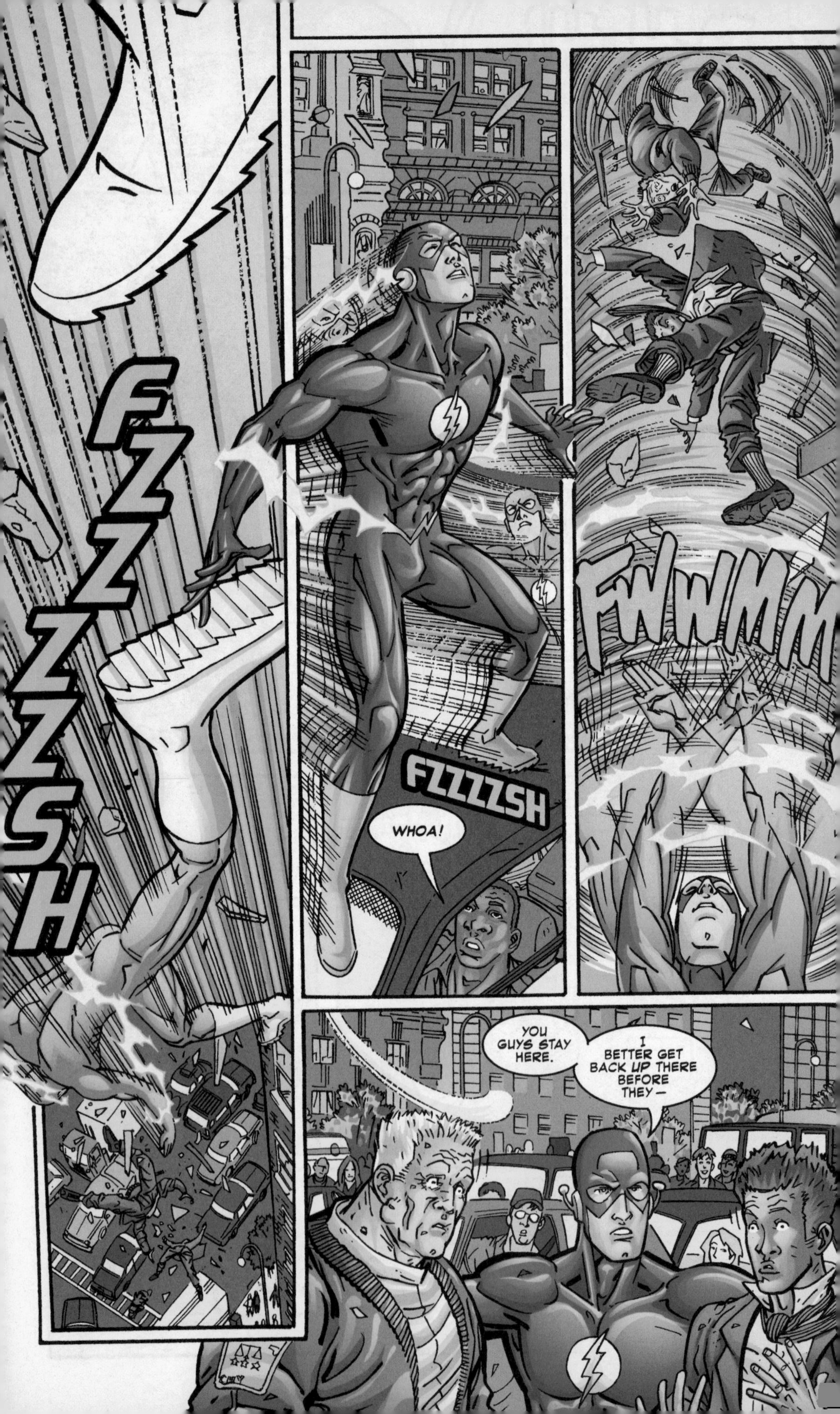
FZZZZSH
FZZZZSH
WHOA!
FWWMM
YOU GUYS STAY HERE.
I BETTER GET BACK UP THERE BEFORE THEY—

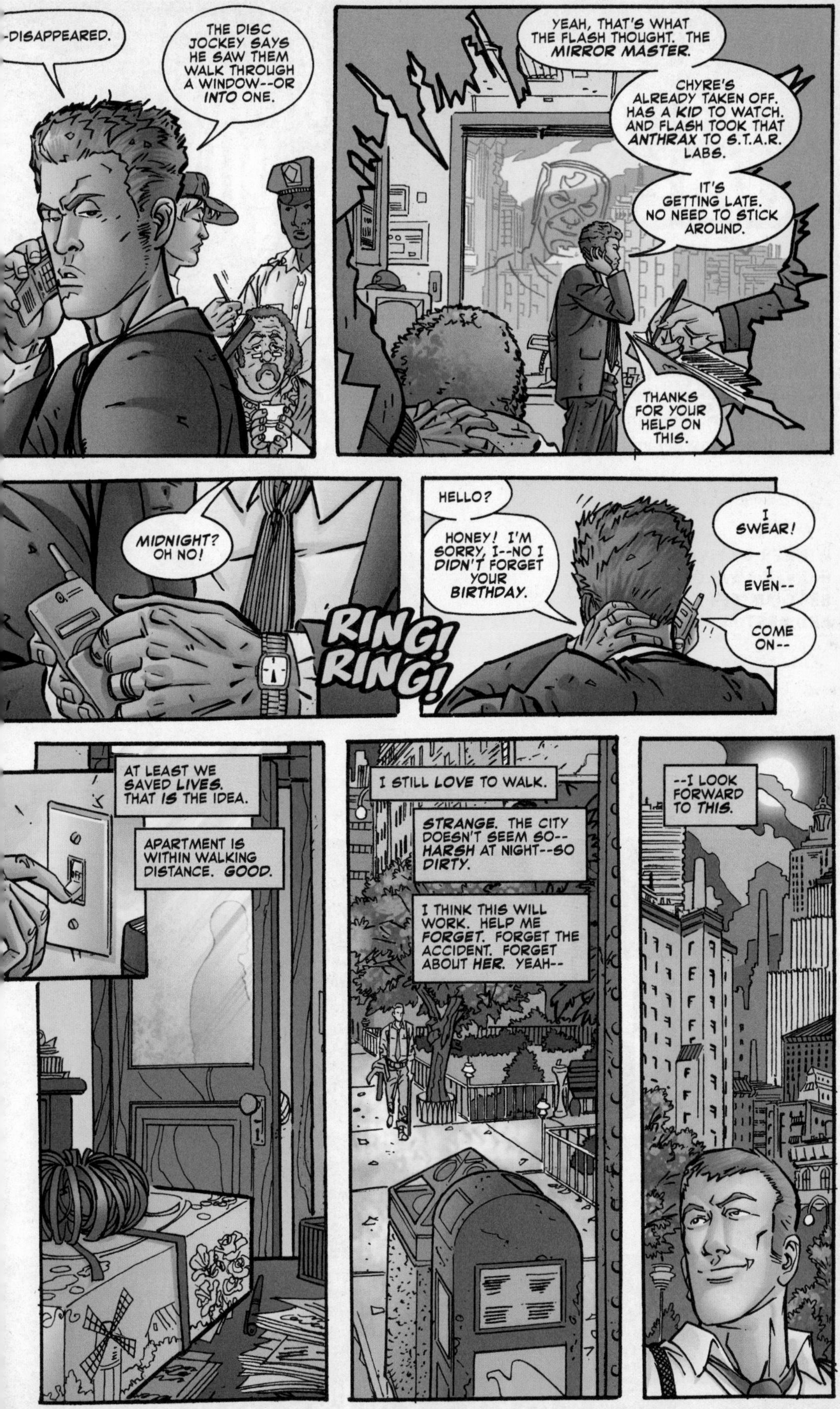
-DISAPPEARED.
THE DISC JOCKEY SAYS HE SAW THEM WALK THROUGH A WINDOW--OR INTO ONE.
YEAH, THAT'S WHAT THE FLASH THOUGHT. THE MIRROR MASTER.
CHYRE'S ALREADY TAKEN OFF. HAS A KID TO WATCH. AND FLASH TOOK THAT ANTHRAX TO S.T.A.R. LABS.
IT'S GETTING LATE. NO NEED TO STICK AROUND.
THANKS FOR YOUR HELP ON THIS.
MIDNIGHT? OH NO!
RING! RING!
HELLO?
HONEY! I'M SORRY, I--NO I DIDN'T FORGET YOUR BIRTHDAY.
I SWEAR!
I EVEN--
COME ON--
AT LEAST WE SAVED LIVES. THAT IS THE IDEA.
APARTMENT IS WITHIN WALKING DISTANCE. GOOD.
I STILL LOVE TO WALK.
STRANGE. THE CITY DOESN'T SEEM SO--HARSH AT NIGHT--SO DIRTY.
I THINK THIS WILL WORK. HELP ME FORGET. FORGET THE ACCIDENT. FORGET ABOUT HER. YEAH--
--I LOOK FORWARD TO THIS.

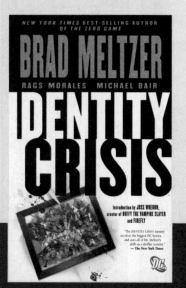